The Human Body and the Law

Second Edition

DAVID W. MEYERS

EDINBURGH UNIVERSITY PRESS

© David W. Meyers 1990

Edinburgh University Press
22 George Square, Edinburgh

Distributed in the U.S.A. and Canada by
Columbia University Press, New York

Set in Linotron Plantin
and printed in Great Britain by
Redwood Press Limited,
Melksham, Wiltshire

British Library Cataloguing
  in Publication Data
  The human body and the law.
  2nd ed.
  1. Medicine. Legal aspects
  I. Title   II. Series
  342

ISBN 0 7486 0213 5

0145181

D239
2056
SFT
(Mey)

5

'006

0748602836

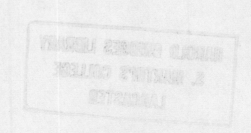

Edinburgh Law and Society Series

Contents

Preface

Two decades have passed since the publication of *The Human Body & the Law*. At the time of the first edition few texts existed in the field, with the notable exceptions of *The Sanctity of Life & the Criminal Law* by Professor Williams, and *Life, Death & the Law* by St. John-Stevas. In the intervening 20 years the literature has become fairly vast. Advancing medical technologies and greater legal recognition of patient autonomy have become topical subjects frequently aired in the press, and on television. Priorities and viewpoints have changed. In 1970 questions remained, for example, over the legality of contraceptive sterilization. Now, the practice has become commonplace and unquestioned. Heart transplants had just begun, were controversial and experimental. Now, while still raising serious issues about resource allocation and the availability of medical care, they are an accepted and successful part of cardiac revitalization and significant life extension for an ever-increasing number of patients.

Twenty years ago issues over the right to die were just beginning to surface. In the interim, improvements in surgery, cardio-pulmonary resuscitation, artificial respiration and feeding, chemotherapy, radiation therapy and pharmacology have allowed life to be extended in many instances far beyond what many expect or want. Much of reproductive technology, and the legal and ethical questions surrounding it, was unheard of in 1970. Today, in vitro fertilization, surrogacy and selective reduction of pregnancy challenge religion, law and ethics. Abortion remains controversial, although the medical and lay majorities both in the U.K. and in the U.S.A. clearly support the mother's right to choose before her fetus becomes viable, or capable of independent existence outside the womb.

In this second edition I have attempted to focus on the issues among these subjects of greatest concern on individuals in general, as well as to doctors and lawyers. The perspectives remain the individual's right to choose, and society's right to dictate, medical treatment. Each subject has been looked at from the Americal legal viewpoint, the English and the Scottish. More often than not strong similarities emerge. At times differences exist. It is hoped the comparative legal look at these highly charged medical-legal issues will help to shed light on the appropriate resolution of each, one that is just, fair and compassionate.

The bulk of the work on the second edition was done in California, although time was spent in London, Edinburgh, Aberdeen and even peaceful Colonsay. While medical commentary is offered, it will be clear my training and experience is in law, not medicine.

As with the first edition, I hope this book will be useful in setting forth the existing legal position on the subjects discussed, in raising those issues that remain unresolved, and in proposing possible solutions where thought appropriate. The book is perhaps not as 'folksy' as was the first edition, for so many more developments have occurred dealing with the human body and the law since 1970. The result is more of a summary of that which has developed, rather that an exploration of what may develop. I hope readers enjoy the book, learn from it, and are stimulated to ponder and discuss the many inter-disciplinary issues these medical procedures raise.

I must reiterate the thanks I gave in 1970 to The St. Andrews Society of the State of New York, to the late Professor Sir Thomas Smith Q.C., who was most responsible for the first edition and whose friendship and encouragement I continued to enjoy and benefit from until his passing, and to David Casey Miller, Senior lecturer in the University of Aberdeen School of Law, whose support, assistance and friendship have been most welcome. Dr. R. A. McCall Smith of the University of Edinburgh School of Law encouraged me first to consider a second edition furing my sabbatical in Edinburgh from the California Bar in 1985. Professor (Emeritus) J. K. Mason of the University of Edinburgh Schools of Medicine and Law provided helpful support and sources. Finally, the Edinburgh University Press was willing to publish me once again. It is always nice to be given a second chance.

DAVID W. MEYERS
July 31, 1990
Napa, California

START OF LIFE

1

Mother and Fetus: Rights in Conflict

A. INTRODUCTION

After fertilization of the female egg (ovum) with male sperm the resulting zygote may implant itself in utero within approximately seven days to become an embryo. While no precise time of transformation is agreed, it is generally accepted that at a gestational age of about eight to twelve weeks the embryo becomes a fetus.[1] Fetal development then continues until birth, normally expected at about 37 weeks gestation.

The fetus generally becomes viable, or capable of independent existence outside the mother's womb with the aid of normal medical science, at about 28 weeks. Eighty percent of infants prematurely born at this stage of development survive. The development of essential internal organs, most notably the heart and lungs, must be sufficient to permit the fetus to survive the trauma of birth and to be able to breathe with the aid of a mechanical ventilator. Such development may be adequate in a minority of premature births as early as 24 weeks, but survival is rare indeed any earlier.[2]

As we will see in Chapter 2, viability plays an important role in determining the legality and morality of abortion. Although intensely controversial and subject to restriction by a currently conservative Supreme Court, at present in the United States a woman enjoys the Constitutional right to elect abortion, with few restrictions, prior to fetal viability. However, after viability abortion may be restricted or even proscribed altogether, unless determined necessary to protect the life or health of the mother.[3] In the United Kingdom, legislation generally permits the mother and two physicians to decide on the need for abortion prior to fetal viability, but imposes criminal proscription to a large degree thereafter.[4] As a practical matter few abortions are performed after fetal viability is reached.

While the woman's abortion decision has long been regulated by the criminal law,[5] until very recently the manner in which she chose to care for or not care for herself during her pregnancy, and thereby the fetus, short of abortion, has not been regulated by the law, civil or criminal. Although certain prenatal conduct of the mother – alcohol, tobacco and drug use, lack of proper medical attention, particularly in high risk pregnancies, poor nutrition – is recognized as putting the fetus at risk, the law has chosen not to intervene. Several reasons explain this.

First of all, until recently, the causative connection between such maternal conduct or habits and fetal abnormality or increased health risk was either largely ignored or not well recognized. Secondly, the law traditionally has held the fetus not to be a 'person' until live birth and, accordingly, not entitled to legal rights or protection prior to live birth.[6] For example, wrongful death statutes have typically excluded the fetus in utero, whether viable or not, from their definition of 'persons' and their protection. Thirdly, the law has been reluctant to interfere in an intensely personal relationship between mother and fetus where rights of the two may well conflict. Fourth, enforcement of fetal rights appears to be a matter arguably largely beyond the reach of society's legal machinery, governed more by the particular morality and socio-economic circumstances of the mother. Finally, society has not wanted to discourage pregnant women from seeking medical attention by the threat of legal intervention in such cases.

More recently, with greater awareness of the impact of the mother's prenatal behavior on the health of the fetus and with advances in prenatal diagnostic and supportive care, have come questions whether the law should not play a more active role in this relationship. Certain legal developments, tentative and controversial, have occurred. More are likely. Some courts have intervened to 'protect' a fetus, against the wishes of the mother. The legal justification for such interventions has been questioned. Strong 'pro-life' and 'pro-choice' sentiments, political and legal pressures, active in the abortion debate, have impacted developments in this field, and are likely to continue to do so.

B.   COMPETING RIGHTS OF MOTHER AND FETUS

The traditional position in England, the United States, and beyond has been that the fetus enjoyed no legal rights of its own until born, thereby commencing an existence separate from its mother.[7] However, modern legal developments have promoted granting the fetus increasing legal protection as it matures to viability and eventual birth. As the legal protection afforded the fetus increases, the restriction on the rights and liberty of the mother inevitably increase. The law's primary role, and its continuing challenge, is to develop a rationale, legally sound and socially acceptable, for dealing with those conflicting rights and resolving them. It may not be fair or proper for the law to decline to protect legitimate rights of the fetus on the basis that to do so would be 'incompatible' with the rights and welfare of the mother.[8] Yet, if it is to intervene, the law must take proper account of these sometimes conflicting rights and resolve them. Developments to date show this resolution has been different in Britain from some American states. No legal consensus has developed among the American courts which have thus far addressed these difficult issues. Most recently the U.S. Supreme Court let stand a Missouri Law which stated, 'the life of each human being begins at conception.' The Court found such a provision not to be unconstitutional because it carried with it no enforceable restrictions on abortion.[9] However, such a declaration clearly portends that abortion restrictions are to follow it.

C. ENGLAND

No English court has, to date, required a pregnant woman to undergo particular medical treatment, or cease particular conduct, in order to protect or promote the health or chances for live birth of her fetus. However, the House of Lords has not decided the issue.

In the recent case of *In Re F (In Utero)*[10] the local child welfare authority sought to make an unborn child a ward of the court. The purpose was to accomplish a safe, medical delivery of the child, expected in several weeks. The mother had suffered from severe mental disturbance, was nomadic, and on welfare assistance, but apparently was not deemed incompetent to decide questions of medical treatment and childbirth.

The Court of Appeal denied the requested care and custody order. It concluded that in such a sensitive area of personal choice and individual liberty, where rights of mother and fetus might well conflict, it was for Parliament, not the judiciary, to extend the law.

The Court concluded that the fetus enjoyed no independent legal rights of its own in English law until it was born. Until then it was not a person, or a 'minor'[11] over whom the courts could assume wardship jurisdiction. It had no legal existence independent of its mother. If the fetus were to be held a person subject to wardship protection, then its welfare under existing law must become the paramount consideration. Ensuring its welfare could greatly impact and restrict the mother's freedom and liberty in many ways. This clearly could have a major social impact on mothering and childbirth. Thus, the Court deferred to Parliament for any changes in the long-established position of the law in this area of human relations.[12] However, after birth, the child in fact was made a ward of court.

Two other English cases suggest, without deciding, that the English courts, absent statutory direction, will not interfere with or interdict a woman's prenatal conduct despite its likely negative impact upon her fetus and its chances for a healthy birth.[13] In one,[14] a husband sought to prevent his wife from undergoing a planned abortion without his consent. The court denied his request, finding that in English law the fetus enjoys no legal rights of its own 'at least until it is born and has an existence separate from its mother.' In other words, it may be argued, if a fetus has no legal rights as a person until born, it has no legal standing in court to restrain maternal conduct thought to be detrimental to its eventual live and healthy birth, or to compel conduct or treatment thought to promote such a result.

It is also misleading to suggest that the fetus does not enjoy legal protection prior to birth. The criminal law, by prohibiting destruction of the fetus except in certain circumstances,[15] does grant protection to the fetus. The criminal law punishes conduct carried out to abort the fetus, unless permitted by law. It does not restrain acts of fetal abuse or neglect by the mother (i.e., failure to seek medical attention) which do not rise to the level of intended fetal destruction. However, the fact an abortion may be authorized where necessary to protect the health of the mother does not necessarily mean that certain care cannot be ordered to protect the health of the fetus where it will not harm the health of the mother.

In the other, more recent English case,[16] a father sought to prevent his girlfriend (and the local health authority) from terminating an 18–21 week pregnancy. The court held that the he did not have legal standing to prevent the abortion, either in his capacity as father of the child, or as next friend of and on behalf of his unborn child. Who then acts for the fetus? At present it has no legal guardian or protector, no *parens patriae*, until born.

The English courts clearly have been concerned that recognizing protectable rights of the fetus would result in efforts to control, restrict, or contradict the conduct or freedom of action of the pregnant mother.[17] Once the courts assume that awesome power, it is difficult to determine where the line might be drawn between maternal and fetal rights. If the court exercises its traditional *parens patriae* powers to act in the best interests of the child,[18] conflicts between maternal liberty and fetal health might well have to be resolved in favor of the fetus. What then of situations where both maternal health and fetal health is implicated? Who decides if a fetus should survive or prosper *in utero* at the expense of the mother's health or freedom? What if only fetus or mother can survive, but not both? Is the fetus, at least if viable, to be preferred because of the potential for longer life?[19] The courts cannot be expected, or be considered competent, to decide such questions.[17]

Certain American decisions have sought to resolve some of these questions. As we shall see, the cases compelling women to undergo caesareans or other prenatal surgery are the most obvious. However, they have reached differing[20] and largely unsatisfactory[21] results. Often surgery ordered has proved unnecessary due to the uncertainties of medical prognosis.[22]

Since both English[23] and American[24] law at present allows abortion of even a viable fetus where necessary to protect the life of the mother, the corollary would seem to clearly be that treatment endangering the life of the mother to protect the fetus cannot be compelled. Yet, as Lord Justice Slaughton theorized in the case of *In Re F (In Utero)*, a court faced with saving the life of fetus or mother, if they are both persons in the eyes of the law, would surely have to act to save that of the fetus.[25] Only by not considering the fetus a person does the law prevent such a confrontation of rights.

There are practical and moral grounds for continuing the legal distinction of recognizing only the live-born child as a person.[26] Until born the fetus has no physicial existence separate from its mother. The fetus owes its existence to its mother, who has carried and cared for it throughout gestation at substantial physical and emotional burden. The relationship is an intensely personal one. American cases for example, have long recognized and sought to foster individual liberty in the procreational process, in matters concerning consentual, adult sexual activity, contraception, pregnancy care and treatment, childbirth and childrearing.[27]

The restrictions on abortion represent, at their core, society's interest in its own preservation, in the preservation of the species as well as recognition of the sanctity of human life. By not pitting the rights of the mother against those of her fetus, the law has encouraged childbirth. It has also avoided restrictions on personal liberty of the mother by not imposing highly selective and in many cases largely unenforceable restrictions on maternal conduct during pregnancy.

On the other hand, once born the infant has established its ability to survive, its identity as an independent being and its right to exist; its rights may be enforced without intruding on the mother's physical integrity, her choices of prenatal care and treatment, or her lifestyle. A realistic alternative – placement in another home – exists once the child is born.

English courts have not hesitated to remove custody of a newborn child in danger of serious neglect or abuse from its mother.[28] Even if that neglect occurred while the child was in utero, it may support a placement for care order immediately upon the child's birth. In one case, where the household had 'an appalling history of sexual abuse of children,' the Court of Appeal found a local authority to have acted properly in removing a newborn from its parents on the day of its birth.[29] In another, the child was born suffering from drug dependency due to drug usage during pregnancy by her mother.[30] Before the child was six weeks old a care order was obtained by the local social services authority. In affirming the order, the House of Lords expressly held it was proper for the juvenile court to consider the mother's conduct during pregnancy and its effect on the then-fetus in determining if the child was 'being' neglected. However, prenatal neglect alone was not sufficient; the neglect or facts showing risk thereof must be continuing after birth. Thus, while prenatal conduct has not permitted custodial transfer or restrictions on that conduct before birth, it has supported a care order and loss of maternal custody immediately following birth where the conduct is thought likely to continue and to be detrimental to the welfare of the child. In the absence of legislative direction from

Parliament, it seems unlikely that the House of Lords will conclude it can regulate a woman's conduct to protect the health of her unborn child.

There may, nonetheless, remain to be defined two exceptions to this general 'hands off' judicial policy. One exists where the mother is incompetent. While one English court refused to grant an order to compel a delusional, nomadic mother to attend hospital for the birth of her soon-to-be-born baby, the same court suggested it might compel hospitalization of a clearly incompetent mother 'to ensure the safe birth of the expected baby.'[31] A Canadian court has done so, relying on the Canadian Mental Health Act, where failure of the mother to seek medical attention was deemed to pose a 'significant risk' to the health of the unborn child.[32]

This Canadian case suggests the second exception: cases where 'significant' risk to the health or safety of the unborn child may be obviated with only 'insignificant' risk of harm or inconvenience to the mother.[33] In such cases, courts will be tempted to find care or treatment refusals by the mother to evidence her incompetence and order treatment on some type of a 'best interests' analysis. American courts have justified a kidney transplant from an incompetent to a sibling on the basis it is in the donor's best interests to feel he has acted to help his brother, not abandoned him.[34] Perhaps similar reasoning will be accepted in certain compelling cases to justify medical care and treatment to foster a live birth where it does not pose significant risk to the 'incompetent' mother.

One American court recently concluded,

> 'It can be argued that the state may not infringe upon the mother's right to bodily integrity to protect the life or health of her unborn child *unless* to do so will not *significantly* affect the health of the mother and unless the child has *significant* chance of being born alive.'[35]

Even if such restrictions on the mother's liberty are determined justified, the task remains to define what is a 'significant' risk to the health of the fetus and an 'insignificant' risk to the health of the mother. English judges have expressed doubt over their ability to make such determinations.[36] One test would be to find a risk to the fetus significant if it posed a material or reasonably possible risk of death, permanent disability or loss of function, or severe pain over an extended period.[37] A risk to the mother's health from treatment could be considered significant if it posed a risk of harm equal or greater than that posed to the mother by her intended course of conduct (i.e., nontreatment, or taking her pregnancy to term without the active intervention proposed.) Under such a standard, compelled caesarean would be a very unlikely alternative to natural birth because of its increased risk to the mother.

If any legal development occurs, it is most likely to come from Parliament, not the courts. However, in extreme cases – such as a full-term or near full-term fetus in serious jeopardy, the availability of life-saving medical care having a high probability of success, and carrying a low risk of only minimal or clearly insignificant harm to the mother – the common law may be used by judges to fashion an innovative solution to positively respond to such dilemmas until some statutory guidance is given. This is probably equally true in England and in Scotland.

D. SCOTLAND

Where a child is not being properly cared for in Scotland, or is in need of medical care to preserve or protect his or her health, statutory procedures authorize that care to be provided by the local authority in lieu of the parents.[38] Parental rights of control must be exercised for the benefit of the child, not the parents.[39] The Scottish courts will exercise their 'inherent protective jurisdiction' over children, or other incompetents, where it is necessary to protect their health and is in their best interests.[40]

However, where the child is unborn, its legal rights have not been articulated. The legal view has been that the child may only exercise legal rights if born alive; if the fetus is never born alive, he or she is deemed legally to have never existed.[41] This does not mean that legal rights are not enjoyed by the fetus, but rather that they cannot be *exercised* until after birth.

An infant once born may sue in Scottish courts to recover for prenatal injuries. There is, however, no obligation in Scottish law for a doctor to attempt resuscitation of a fetus clearly not viable.[42] As in other cases of delict, an infant suing for prenatal injury would have the burden of proving fault (negligence or intentional wrongdoing), injury, and that the fault caused the injury.[43] As yet, while newborn have sued for damages caused to them by loss of their parents, they have not sued to recover for injuries caused to themselves while in utero.[44] Such cases are to be expected. They have been upheld in the United States. If the newborn may sue for the loss of a parent while in utero,[45] or to claim an inheritance received while in utero,[46] then it would seem clear that he or she may, after birth, sue for injuries caused to him or her in utero.

Before suit would be successful, a legal duty to avoid the harm sued for must be established. A third party, such as a physician, other family member, or a stranger, who intentionally or negligently causes injury to the mother must surely be deemed to have foreseen she was or could be pregnant. If this is true, then consequent injury to the fetus is foreseeable and there would normally exist a legal duty to avoid such injury by the exercise of due care.[47]

However, what if the injury is caused by the fault not of a third party, but of the mother herself? Here the question of duty is much less easily resolved. As we have seen, competing rights are involved. The mother is providing the fetus the essential benefit of gestation, without which, at least prior to viability, the fetus could not survive. This benefit is provided at substantial personal burden to the mother. Increasing the burden further by imposing restrictions on the mother's freedom of action may discourage child-bearing or encourage abortion. It may discourage medical care being sought, for fear of adverse consequences if maternal prenatal habits are undesirable or unorthodox. It can also be asserted that such a potential liability detracts from the woman's autonomy, sense of self-worth, and over-emphasizes her role merely as an incubator for another.[48]

On the other hand, imposing a duty of reasonable care on the mother towards her fetus encourages conduct to promote healthy birth, extends normal principles of civil liability to the wrongdoer and of compensation to the person harmed thereby, and grants protection, generally consistent with restrictions on abortion, to the potential for birth and full personhood of the fetus.

In the absence of legislation, indicating a clear social consensus, it seems unlikely that the Scottish courts will intervene to compel particular conduct by a pregnant woman to benefit her fetus, such as medical treatment or confinement. However, the courts might well, in an appropriate case, recognize a claim by a newborn infant for injuries or other detriment suffered while in utero due to maternal neglect.

It is also possible that where maternal neglect is clear and is brought to the attention of the child welfare authorities, that they could seek a court order for the purpose of requiring the mother to submit to particular care or treatment for the benefit of her fetus. Although this has support elsewhere,[49] it seems most unlikely.[50] While no clear Scottish precedent is at hand, it is likely that the Scottish courts would follow the lead of the English courts in finding the mother's rights to autonomy and privacy must be favored when they come into conflict with the 'rights' of the fetus to eventual healthy birth.[51]

One exception might justify court intervention to protect the fetus. If the mother is determined incompetent to understand the consequences of her harmful conduct on the health of her fetus, it may be that a court, if petitioned, would order treatment, hospitalization, or some other less severe custodial care to enhance the likelihood of healthy birth. This might be justified under the authority of a mental health statute,[52] or possibly as an extension of the court's inherent protective jurisdiction over children.[53]

Although very problematic while the fetus remains in utero, unborn, once the fetus is born, the courts are unlikely to hesitate in entering local authority custodial orders to protect the child from serious maternal neglect or abuse. In doing so the courts will be free to consider the prenatal conduct of the mother towards her fetus; if neglectful, and likely to continue, it alone may support a care order being granted and the child being taken from her as has occurred in England.[54] The threat of losing custody after child birth because of prenatal neglect is certainly one way of promoting proper prenatal care. It does so without interfering in the prenatal relationship between mother and unborn child.

E.   THE UNITED STATES

In the United States, a number of cases in recent years have addressed the issue of compelling treatment of a pregnant woman, despite her refusal to consent, in order to protect the perceived health of the fetus.[55] More than 20 cases have sought court orders for treatment – blood transfusion, care and confinement, caesarean delivery – and in more than three-quarters of the cases treatment was ordered. Many involved requests for cesarean section deliveries,[56] although a few requested authorization for other procedures, including hospital detention, blood transfusions[57] and other care deemed 'necessary' to save the fetus.[58]

In few cases was any appeal taken, the issue at hand being moot in most due to the birth of the child. Only two appellate courts have to date addressed the legality of court-ordered caesareans.[59] In both the procedure was upheld. However, in both the fetus was found to be viable and to have virtually no chance of survival without caesarean delivery. In fact, showing the imprecise nature of medical science in this area, in one case a normal delivery occurred, in the other the fetus did not survive birth.

None of the American decisions has compelled treatment in order to assist carrying a non-viable fetus to term. The law would not permit this, since a woman under the present state of the law may abort a non-viable fetus (prior to the third trimester of pregnancy) in the exercise of her constitutional right of privacy,[60] provided she has the funds required to obtain such care.[61] The continued recognition of this right has been cast into serious doubt recently by the U.S. Supreme Court,[9] and it may in large part depend for its continued existence on legislative action by the states, not on judicial protection of such a right based on constitutional interpretation.

There are several troubling aspects to these cases. They rarely offer opportunity for deliberation and reflection. They arise often in wrenching, emotion-charged settings.[62] The women tend to be the underprivileged, being treated in a teaching-hospital or clinic, and of minority racial origin.[63] Often the medical judgments used to justify the treatment interventions prove to be incorrect.[64] The negative impact of such orders in discouraging other pregnant woman from seeking medical attention or hospitalization for fear of forced treatment or detention may result in more lost or damaged fetuses than those few arguably saved by such orders.

Despite these significant drawbacks, a few state courts have attempted to fashion a remedy to protect the fetus, while at the same time not significantly impacting the mother's freedom of action and physical integrity.

They have been criticized on both sides of the Atlantic for meddling in an intensely private area of maternal liberty where they do not belong.[65]

In a recent case from the District of Columbia,[66] the mother was terminally ill. Her fetus was 26 weeks old and potentially viable. She initially consented to a cesarean delivery in the hope it might salvage the fetus, but later changed her mind. The hospital sought emergency authorization for the surgery. The mother only had a few days to live. The evidence was the caesarian would shorten her remaining life, but only by 'a few hours.' The judge, faced with an immediate and very tragic situation, authorized the surgery. The baby did not survive. An opinion was then delivered to support the action taken. The court concluded the state had a compelling interest in protecting the life and health of both children and viable unborn children. It recognized that the latter could significantly impact the rights of the mother and in fact run directly counter to those rights. That apparently was the situation in the case where trying to salvage the child meant violating the mother's express wishes, personal right of privacy, physical inviolability, and health. Nonetheless, the court concluded it could compel cesarean surgery where to do so would 'not significantly affect the health of the mother' and where 'the child has a significant chance of being born alive.'

Undergoing cesarean section delivery will undoubtedly, in many cases, significantly affect health. Where the mother is terminally ill and death is imminent, the intrusion is just as severe, but perhaps the likely impact on health is considerably less. Some courts have been willing to order cesarean surgery in an otherwise healthy woman to salvage an apparently viable fetus.[67] The view is far from universal.[68] Other courts have refused to compel surgery in the hopes of saving a fetus from loss due to miscarriage or stillbirth.[69]

In at least three American cases, brain dead pregnant women have been kept on life supports, one for sixty-four days, to increase the chances of delivering a viable fetus.[70] Some argue this is ethically improper, unless the mother has consented to the use of her body in this way, and unless the fetus is close to viability, so as to avoid prolonged artificial maintenance at the expense of the dignity and peaceful repose to which the woman's body is entitled.[70]

At common law, as in England, the fetus enjoys no legal rights prior to viability. Once viable, the fetus is the beneficiary of the state's compelling interest in protecting that potential life.[71] Some states, to ensure the law's full protection of the viable fetus, have made it a crime to intentionally terminate its existence. In California, for example, murder is defined broadly as the 'unlawful killing of a human being, *or a fetus*, with malice aforethought.'[72] Cases have narrowed this broad statutory definition of feticide to require the fetus to be viable.[73] This restriction is seen as constitutionally mandated by the Supreme Court decision in *Roe v. Wade*, holding a mother entitled to abort her fetus prior to viability, for any reason, in the exercise of her constitutional right to privacy. If the mother may do so, then destruction of a pre-viable fetus may not be criminally proscribed as murder, at least as to her. However, the law is in flux in this sensitive area and more restrictions on the woman's abortion right are likely.[9]

Until recently, state statutes proposing to enact the conclusion that human life begins at conception have been struck down by the Supreme Court. Not so any longer. In 1989 the U.S. Supreme Court upheld the right of the states to impose this scientific conclusion by legislative act.[9] As a result it is now theoretically possible for the states to impose homicide liability for intentional destruction of a fetus at any age; none have done so, but the possibility exists. A newly constituted Supreme Court decidedly unsympathetic to the constitutional underpinnings for a woman's right to abort now is empaneled.

American law clearly establishes that the rights of mother and viable fetus are both worthy of protection. They also represent competing interests where the mother elects a course contrary to the health of the fetus. The solution of American common law to situations where two valid interests collide is often to adopt a 'balancing' test, particularly if the rights are of constitutional dimension, as are abortion and child-rearing. American law has done this to balance the rights of parental control and the best interests of the child in cases involving parental decisions on medical treatment for their children. The right to be protected must be weighed against the harm that will be caused by its exercise. Courts trying to accommodate the mother's right to privacy and bodily integrity on the one hand and the health of the fetus on the other are likely to adopt such a balancing test.

Where the probability of fetal viability is good, the risk posed to the health of the fetus is both clear and substantial, and the risk posed to the mother's health by the treatment sought to be compelled is not significant, the judicial balance will likely be struck in favor of treatment. Where, however, the risks to the mother's health are substantial, compelled treatment is unlikely. If a pregnant mother may abort even a viable fetus where necessary to protect her health, the corollary would seem to be that she cannot be compelled to accept any significant risk to her health to ensure the live birth of a fetus, viable or not. A state court judge, in refusing a petition to require a competent woman to undergo a caesarean, stated the principle as follows:[74]

> 'I would not have the right to require the woman to donate an organ to one of her other children, if that child were dying . . . I cannot require her to undergo that major surgical procedure for this child.'

Where the mother proposes a course of action in regard to a fetus thought to be viable – whether it be to abort or to carry the fetus to term without the treatment proposed – which creates a greater risk to her health than the risk of the treatment proposed to protect the health of the fetus, the courts may well be legally justified in compelling such treatment.[75] However, in light of the significant privacy rights involved and the severe remedy proposed, in any such cases the greater risk to the mother's health from not undertaking the treatment proposed to protect the fetus, over that posed by the treatment itself, should be both a significant, not a trivial, difference in risk to health, as well as one shown by clear and convincing evidence.[76]

In a recent New York case, the husband of a comatose, approximately 18 weeks pregnant woman, sought guardianship status to authorize an abortion for his wife. An automobile accident some eight weeks before had rendered her comatose. The attending physicians believed the woman's chances for survival would be improved by aborting her fetus. Quite amazingly, private third parties intervened in the case, claiming to represent the interest of the unborn child and opposed the husband's petition. The guardianship authority was granted the husband by the trial court and affirmed on appeal, the third parties being held to be without legal standing to intervene. Nonetheless, they unsuccessfully appealed to the U.S. Supreme Court for a stay. The case points out the lengths to which members of the 'pro-life,' anti-abortion lobby will go in the charged atmosphere surrounding the abortion issue in the United States today. It also reaffirms that American courts will not exacerbate existing or threatened health problems of a pregnant mother in the interests of protecting a clearly non-viable fetus.

Cases of fetal abuse or neglect often are not as clearly drawn as those requiring immediate surgical intervention. It has become more clear and accepted in recent times that certain pre-natal habits of the mother have an important impact on the health and chances for complication-free birth of the fetus. These include general nutrition, smoking, drinking, and other drug use. A recent California poll found 53 per cent of woman respondents favored holding the mother legally liable for harm done to the fetus by smoking or drinking (43 per cent of the men responding agreed).[77] No American cases have, as yet, imposed such legal liability.

A fetus, once born, has been held entitled to sue his or her mother for prenatal injury negligently caused in an auto accident.[78] The fetus, once born, may also sue third parties for negligently caused personal injury,[79] just as a person recklessly attacking a full-term pregnant mother may be convicted of murder for the consequent death of her viable fetus.[80] Given this precedent, an action imposing legal liability on the mother for prenatal injury proved to have resulted from poor maternal habits, or drug use, may only depend on clear proof of causation after birth. For example, in Michigan, a child was allowed to sue his mother for tooth damage allegedly caused by the mother's use of tetracycline during pregnancy.[81]

The New York courts have issued protective orders for the benefit of a fetus. This has occurred where a husband had a pattern of assaulting the mother, thereby endangering the fetus,[82] and where the mother's neglect (alcohol abuse and failure to obtain prenatal medical care) endangered the health of the fetus.[83]

American courts do not like to intervene between mother and fetus. However, they are being called upon with increasing frequency to do so. Several reasons account for this. These include the politicizing of the abortion debate; the ability of medical technology to keep younger and younger fetuses alive once born; the lack of effective, accessible prenatal care for the poor; the prevalence of certain harmful drugs and infectious diseases, such as syphilus and AIDS among inner-city women of child-bearing age; the increased knowledge of causation between the woman's behavior or health status and negative prognosis of normal birth of the fetus; and a tendency of some to look to the courts to resolve difficult social issues left unsettled by legislative inaction.

Different courts, depending on the viewpoint of the judge or judges, will strike the balance between maternal and fetal rights at different points. Few will intervene unless faced with convincing evidence that, (1) the fetus is viable (24–28 weeks old), (2) prompt action is needed to protect the health and the potentiality for live birth of the fetus, and (3) to do so will not pose the risk of significant harm to the health of the mother, or require any significant restraint on her liberty, such as forced hospitalization, for more than a brief period of time.

F.   CONCLUSIONS

The traditional position of the law has been that a fetus is not a 'person' within the eyes of the law until born alive. The consequence of this has been that the law, with few exceptions, has not attempted to compel the mother to act in a particular way, or to undergo certain treatment, for the benefit or protection of the fetus.

For example, since most wrongful death statutes do not consider the fetus as a person, the negligence of a physician causing the prebirth death, or stillbirth, of a fetus will not make the physician legally liable for wrongful death. However, the physician may well be held liable to the parents for their emotional distress damages resulting from such an occurrence.[84]

Upon attaining viability, an ability to survive outside the womb, albeit with the aid of medical technology and treatment, the fetus enjoys protection from destruction, except where clearly necessary to protect the life or health of the mother.[85] Even though capable of independent existence, the well-being of the fetus is subordinate to that of its mother. Several reasons account for this.

Most significantly, the liberty of the mother and her right to bodily inviolability are strong, deeply-rooted principles in Scottish, English, and American law. In addition, even in modern times it is frequently unclear what course of treatment is necessary to benefit the fetus, which materially attenuates the justification for compelling unwanted treatment upon the mother.[86] From a practical point of view, society does not want to discourage the voluntary seeking of medical care by the vast majority of pregnant mothers for fear of censure, legal supervision of pregnancy, or forced treatment.

Where third party misconduct threatens a fetus, it can be enjoined without intruding on the rights of liberty of the mother. Restrictions on abortion serve to protect the fetus, but at the expense of the mother's liberty. British law requires a showing that an abortion is necessary for maternal health, although this is liberally construed and may include social considerations,[87] whereas American law, at least for the present, only imposes this requirement after fetal viability.[71] Once the fetus is viable, under English law an abortion is only proper where necessary to save the life of the mother.[88] The position in Scotland is less clear.[89] Both British and American viewpoints represent a balancing of interests, valuing maternal health over the live birth of the fetus.

Where destruction of the fetus (abortion) is not involved, but the issue is compelling particular medical treatment or other care for the fetus which is considered to be 'proper' or 'desirable,' the legal solutions are still evolving. The key question for resolution is probably whether active intervention is proper in certain of such cases, or whether permitting only post-birth sanctions against the mother is preferable. Those post-birth sanctions could be loss of custody of the child,[90] liability for damages for harm proven by the child,[91] or even criminal penalty.[92]

The appeal of restricting legal involvement to post-birth sanctions rather than pre-birth interference is that it may be as effective a deterrent to maternal neglect. It may be imposed without physical interference with the mother's bodily sanctity, or her pre-partum relationship with her fetus.

The English courts have, to date, elected to authorize loss of custody after birth for neglect before birth, but not to permit any physical interference with the mother or her behavior during pregnancy.[93] This may offer the best accommodation of obviously competing rights of mother and fetus.

The American courts, as we have seen, have been more willing to impose treatment over the wishes of the mother. This has resulted not in small part from a strong preference of the physicians involved in many such cases to impose treatment, the traditional deference paid to medical views by the courts, and the fact most such cases arise in a highly charged environment calling for immediate action where the views of the mother may often be unrepresented. Faced with saving the life of an apparently salvagable fetus, the pressures on the judges involved to order treatment are great, particularly, where medical evidence suggests no *material* harm to the mother.[66]

Still, there has not developed a consensus in American law, the majority of scholarly comment does not support state intervention in the mother–fetus relationship, and most courts have not as yet confronted the issue. Depending on the specific facts of a given case, the firm recognition of the 'balancing of interests' test in American constitutional law can, however, be expected to support compelled medical treatment where there is a showing of clear medical benefit to a fetus with a significant chance of being born alive and where the treatment is convincingly shown not to pose a risk of significant harm to the health of the mother.[94]

It is not clear how the law will continue to evolve in this sensitive area of maternal and fetal rights. While its general outlines can be seen, it is still very much an evolutionary process, not in small part dependent on medical advances in the detection and treatment of suspected fetal distress. In the interim, the law should strive to maximize the liberty and physical integrity of the pregnant mother, while at the same time seeking to accommodate these goals with protecting the developing fetus and its eventual live birth to the greatest extent reasonably possible.

The circumstances of certain cases may be so clear as to call out for state intervention, but these cases are likely to be few and far between and only those that present the most compelling need to protect a fetus approaching term by means without significant detriment to the mother's health. What must be remembered is that where pregnancy is consensual, women have chosen to perpetuate the species at considerable physical difficulty and at some considerable sacrifice to individual freedom. It is not for society to further intrude on the pregnant woman, unless upon clearly defined, socially accepted and morally compelling grounds.

Parliament or the legislature is the body best able to decide these questions because it is far more representative of society than the courts. The courts readily acknowledge this, on both sides of the Atlantic.[66,93] However, legislative consensus is slow to develop in areas of sensitive personal rights such as this, and quite rightly so. Until such a societal consensus develops, the courts will have to deal with these kinds of cases brought to them for resolution for lack of any alternative forum. They should act cautiously and only in the clearest, most compelling of circumstances. In other cases, their traditionally-recognized lack of jurisdiction over the unborn child may well be sufficient reason to decline involvement.

One knowledgeable British practitioner has suggested the rights of the fetus will support no intrusion against the competent mother's refusal to accept care or treatment. She has stated,[95]

> 'In Britain, fortunately, medical decision-making where the patient is competent is still a matter for the individual concerned and nobody else.'

However, this simple rationale does not seem adequate. The picture is not so simple where competing interests and, at least after fetal viability, competing lives are involved. The fact the fetus only enjoys the potential for independent life does not eliminate the obligation of the law to evaluate that interest in the decisional process.

Another distinguished commentator has asserted, for instance, that the rights of the fetus evolve from 'minimal' at implantation to 'near equivalence' with those of the mother when it is capable of being born alive, and that this 'progression of fetal rights' is increasingly being legally accepted.[96] While this seems to be quite accurate, it is also true that British judges have to date not been inclined to intervene. Nonetheless, the full weight of the criminal law in Britain prohibits killing a fetus capable of being born alive;[97] a viable fetus may only be aborted to protect the life of the mother.[98]

It is obvious the law is at pains in all jurisdictions considered – Scotland, England and the United States – to resolve the dilemma posed by often conflicting rights of fetus and mother. The effect of American common law development[24] and of statute in England and Scotland,[99] has been to recognize fetal viability as a legal landmark, compelling greater protection for the fetus and greater encroachment on the mother's liberty. Some American courts have also considered such gestational development to be sufficient basis for physical intrusions on the mother's bodily inviolability in certain instances. Other courts have disagreed, both in America and in England.

The law is still evolving. Medical advances, changing social attitudes, and much greater public awareness of the issues are contributing to it. Whether current legal developments we have surveyed outline the eventual position of the law remains to be seen. The issues are much too dynamic, controversial, and new for anyone to say at this time.[100] An example of this changing attitude is reflected by yet a further development in the unfortunate case of A.C. referred to earlier in the chapter.[20,35,58,66,94] The trial judge, presented with an emergency request to possibly save a viable fetus being carried by a terminally ill woman whose death was imminent, ordered a caesarian delivery intended to salvage the fetus, despite its likely negative impact on the mother's ability to survive and despite an apparent refusal to consent by her. An order for stay was denied by a rapidly assembled appeal panel, the caesarian was performed, but both mother and child died. Thereafter, a formal appeal was taken and the full District of Columbia Appeals Court vacated the order authorizing surgery. In *Re A.C.* (1990) 573 A 2d 1235. The court held that where the mother is competent, treatment can only be undertaken to save a viable fetus, except in the truly exceptional case, where the mother consents to it. If she is not competent to decide, then the decision must be made based on what the available evidence shows she would have wanted done (the so-called 'substituted judgment' rule). The case is significant because it was extensively briefed by numerous interested parties and organizations and carefully considered by a well-respected, although perhaps more liberal than average, court. It may well signal a shift in American judicial thinking to a position more analogous to that in Britain. There seems to be an increasing realization that only mothers, not courts, can decide what treatment they will undergo to save a threatened fetus.

NOTES

1 *Webster's New Collegiate Dictionary* (9th ed., 1985) defines embryo as the developing human individual from implantation to the end of the *eighth week* after conception (p.406), yet defines a fetus as the developing human being from *three months* after conception until birth (p.458).
2 Yu, et al., 'Prognosis for infants born at 23 to 28 weeks' gestation,' 293 *Brit. Med. J.* 1200 (1986).
3 *Roe v. Wade*, (1973), 410 U.S. 113, at 165
4 Abortion Act, 1967, s.5(1); Infant Life (Preservation) Act 1929, s.1(1); Offenses Against the Person Act 1861, s.58, 59.
5 Gordon, *The Criminal Law of Scotland*, Edinburgh: W. Green and Sons (2d ed.) 1978; *Rex v. Bourne* (1939) 1 K.B. 687; Offenses Against the Person Act 1861, s.58, 59.
6 *In Re F (in Utero)*, (1988) 2 W.L.R. 1288; Fortin 'Legal Protection for the Unborn Child,' 51 *Mod. L.R.* 54 (1988); Yorke, 'The Legal Personality of the Unborn Child,' 1979 *S.L.T.* 158; *Giardina v. Bennett* (1988, N.J.) 545 A.2d 139.
7 *Paton v. Trustees of the British Pregnancy Advisory Service* (1978) 2 All E.R. 987; See Mason, 'Abortion and the Law' in McLean (Ed.) *Legal Issues in Human Reproduction*. Aldershot: Gower, 1989, p.57.
8 May, L.J., in *In Re F (in utero)*, (1988) 2 W.L.R. 1288.
9 *Webster v. Reproductive Health Services, Inc.* (July 3, 1989) U.S., 109 S.Ct. 3040.
10 (1988) 2 W.L.R. 1288 (C.A.).
11 Family Law Reform Act, s. 1.
12 Brahams, 'Fetus as Ward of Court?' 1988 *The Lancet* 369.
13 *Paton v. B.P.A.S.* (1979) 1 Q.B. 276; *C. v. S.* (1987) 2 W.L.R. 1101
14 *Paton v. B.P.A.S.*, *supra*
15 Offenses Against the Person Act 1861, s.58, 59; Infant Life Preservation Act 1929, s.1(1) (discussed in Chap 2, Abortion).
16 *C. v. S.* (1987) 2 W.L.R. 1101.
17 *In re F (In Utero)*, (1988) 2 W.L.R. 1288, Balcombe, L.J.
18 *Re B* (1987) 2 W.L.R. 1213 (H.L.), (Sterilization); *Re B (A Minor)* (1981) 1 W.L.R. 1421 (C.A.), (surgery for Downsian newborn).
19 Kluge concludes that when the fetus' right to life conflicts with the mother's right to a certain quality of life, the right of the fetus is predominant. 1988 *J. Med. Ethics* 206, 209.
20 Compare *In Re A.C.* (1988, D.C. App.) 533 A 2d 611 (caesarean ordered), with *Taft v. Taft* (1983, Mass) 446 NE 2d 395 ('purse string' operation to prevent miscarriage denied.)
21 See Kolder, et. al., 'Court-Ordered Obstetrical Interventions,' 316 *N. Eng. J. Med.* 1192 (1987); Brahams, *supra*, 1988 *The Lancet* 1006.
22 Annas, 'Protecting the Liberty of Pregnant Patients,' 316 *N. Eng. J. Med.* 1213 (1987).
23 Abortion Act 1967, s.1(1); Infant Life Preservation Act 1929, s.1(1).
24 *Roe v. Wade* (1973) 410 US 113; cf., *Webster v. Reproductive Health Services, Inc.* (July 3, 1989) U.S., 109 S.Ct. 3040.

25 (1988) 2 W.L.R. 1288, at 1293; see Kluge, *supra*, 1988 *J. Med. Ethics* 206.
26 Fletcher, Joseph, 'Abortion, Euthanasia and Care of Defective Newborns,' in Shannon (ed.) *Bioethics* (3d. ed.), p.99, 102–3.
27 Criminal proscriptions on abortion are a notable exception; see *Griswold v. Connecticut* (1965) 381 U.S. 479; *Pierce v. Society of Sisters* (1925) 268 U.S. 510.
28 See cases in note 54, *infra*.
29 *In re P (a Minor) (Wardship)*, (1987) All E.R. (C.A.)
30 *D. v. Berkshire C.C.* (1987) 1 All E.R. 20 (per Lord Goff, concurring, with Lords Griffiths and Mackay in agreement.)
31 *In re F (In Utero)*, (1988) 2 W.L.R. 1288, at 1293.
32 The Ontario Provincial Court is reported to have compelled hospitalization for a 38 weeks pregnant itinerant, homeless mother who refused medical attention for severe abdominal pains.Brahams, 1988 *The Lancet* 369.
33 For probably the farthest extension of this principal to date on either side of the Atlantic, see *In re A.C.* (1988, D.C. App) 533 A.2d 611. There a cesarian was ordered for a terminaly ill, non)consenting mother in the hope (futile) of saving her fetus, despite evidence the surgery would shorten the mother's remaining 24–48 hour life expectancy. For critical comment, see Brahams, *supra*, 1988 *The Lancet* 1006.
34 *Strunk v. Strunk* (1969 Ky. App.) 445 S.W. 2d 145; accord, *Little v. Little* (1979, Tex. App.) 576 S.W. 2d 493; *Guardianship of Pescinski* (1975, Wis.) 226 N.W. 2d 180
35 *In Re A. C.*, *supra*, 533 A. 2d at 617 (emphasis supplied.)
36 *In re F (In Utero)*, (1988) 2 W.L.R. 1288, at 1293 (Staughton, LJ).
37 Perhaps over a period of 1 week or longer and not amenable to control without resort to narcotic (morphia) analgesics. (This arbitrary standard is offered to stimulate thought rather than suggest a solution.)
38 Social Work (Scotland) Act 1968, s.16; Law Reform (Parent and Child) (Scotland) Act 1986, s.3(1)
39 *Docherty v. McGlynn*, 1983 *S.L.T.* 645,651; see also the speech of Lord Fraser in the English decision, *Gillick v. West Norfolk & Wisbech Area Health Authority* (1986) A.C. 112, (1985) 3 All E.R. 402, (HL), (not as yet determined whether applicable in Scotland.)
40 *Docherty v. McGlynn* 1983 *S.L.T.* 645 (Lord Pres. Emslie, SC), at 651 (Lord Grieve), (blood test); *Porchetta v. Porchetta*, 1986 *S.L.T.* 105 (visitation); *Dick v. Douglas* 1924 *S.L.T.* 578(SC), (tutor dative for senile mother); A.D. Ward, 1987 *S.L.T.* (News) 69; Thomson, 'Prima Facie Parental Rights,' 54 *Scot. Law Gaz.* 71 (1986).
41 See Yorke, 'The Legal Personality of the Unborn Child,' 1979 *S.L.T.* 158
42 Brahams, 'No Obligation to Resuscitate a Non-Viable Infant,' 1988 *The Lancet*, 1176.
43 McLean, *Legal Issues in Medicine*. Aldershot: Gower, 1981, p.152; *Connachan v. S.M.T.* 1946 *S.L.T.* 346; *Leadbetter v. N.C.B.* 1952 *S.L.T.* 179.
44 Yorke, 1979 *S.L.T.* 160; Loss of a fetus *in utero* caused by the negligence of another may well, in Scots law, be an element of the mother's damages. See *Bourhill v. Young*, 1941 S.C. 395, 431.
45 *Leadbetter v. N.C.B.* 1952 *S.L.T.* 179.
46 *Elliot v. Joicey* 1935 S.C. 57 (H.L.).
47 *Hunter v. Hanley* 1955 S.C. 200; *Donoghue v. Stevenson* 1932 *S.L.T.* 317.
48 See Shannon, 'Keeping Dead Mothers Alive During Pregnancy: Ethical Issues,' in Shannon (ed.) *Bioethics* (3d Ed), p.230.
49 Ontario Provincial Court (Kirkland, J.), (April, 1987), reported in 1987 *New Law J.* 443, and 1988 *The Lancet* 369; *Hoener v Bertinato* (1961, N.J.J. and D.R. Ct.) 171 A. 2d 140.
50 *In Re F (In Utero)*(1988) 2 W.L.R. 1288; Brahams, 'A Baby's Life or a Mother's Liberty: a United States Case,' 1988 *The Lancet* 1006; *Medhurst v. Medhurst* (1984) Ont. Rpt. (2d) 263.

51 *In re F (In Utero), supra.*
52 Such as the Mental Health (Scotland) Act 1984. See *In re F (In Utero)* (1988) 2
    W.L.R. 1288, at 1293; the Canadian Mental Health Act was relied upon to
    admit to hospital a homeless, nearly full term mother who refused care for severe
    abdominal pains in the Ontario Provincial Court decision, *Medhurst v. Medhurst,
    supra* note 21. See also, Yorke, 1979 *S.L.T.* 158, at 161.
53 *Docherty v. McGlynn, supra,* note 40; Smith, T.B., *A Short Commentary on the
    Law of Scotland.* Edinburgh: W. Green & Son, 1962; pp.370–372; see also, *Re B
    (A Minor).* (1981) 1 W.L.R. 1421.
54 *Re D (a minor) Times Law* Rpt., December 5, 1986, (1986) All E.R. (H.L.); *D.
    v. Berkshire C.C.* (1987) 1 All E.R. 20 (H.L.); *In re P (a Minor) (Wardship) Times*
    Law Rpt., March 24, 1987 (C.A.); Fortin, 'Legal Protection for the Unborn
    Child,' 51 *Mod. L.R.* 54 (1988).
55 See Kolder, et. al, *supra* 316 *N. Eng. J. Med.* 1192 (1987)
56 See *Jefferson v. Griffin Spalding County Hospital* (1981, Ga) 274 S.E. 2d 457; *In re
    Maydeen* (1986, D.C. Super.Ct.) 114 Daily Wash. L.Rptr. 2233 (noted in 533
    A. 2d 611, 613).
57 *Raleigh Fitkin – Paul Morgan Mem. Hosp. v. Anderson* (1964, NJ) 201 A. 2d 537
    (cert. den., 377 U.S. 985); *Crouse Irving Mem. Hosp. Inc. v. Paddock* (1985,
    N.Y. Sup. Ct.) 485 NYS 2d 443.
58 *In re Jamaica Hosp.* (1985, N.Y. Sup. Ct.) 491 N.Y.S. 2d 898; cf., *Taft v. Taft*
    (1983, Mass) 446 NE 2d 395 (order for 4 most pregnant woman to undergo
    'purse string' surgery to prevent miscarriage reversed; record not so compelling
    as to justify competent refusal to consent by woman based on religious
    convictions).
59 *Jefferson v. Griffin Spalding County Hosp.,* (1981, Ga.) 274 S.E. 2d 457; *In Re
    A.C.* (1987, D.C. App) 533 A. 2d 611.
60 *Roe v. Wade* (1973) 410 U.S. 113; *Thornburgh v. American College of Obste-
    tricians and Gynecologists* (1986) 476 US 747. It should be noted, however, that
    90 per cent of the approximately 1,400,000 abortions performed in the U.S. each
    year are carried out during the *first* trimester of pregnancy.
61 *Webster v. Reproductive Health Services, Inc.* (1989) U.S., 109 S.Ct. 3040.
62 *In Re A.C., supra* 533 A.2d 611; Annas, *supra* 316 *N. Eng. J. Med.* 1213 (1987)
63 Kolder, et. al, 316 *N. Eng. J. Med.* 1192 (1987).
64 Berg, 'Georgia Supreme Court orders cesarean section – mother nature reverses
    on appeal.' 70 *J. Med. Assoc. Ga.* 451 (1981), (medical testimony concluded 99
    per cent chance child not survive natural childbirth; in error); Annas, *supra.*
65 Rhoden, 'The Judge in the Delivery Room: The Emergence of Cour)Ordered
    Cesareans,' 74 *Calif. L. Rev.* 1951 (1986); 37 *Hastings L.J.* 729 (1986); Bra-
    hams, 'A Baby's Life or a Mother's Liberty: A United States Case,' 1988 *The
    Lancet,* 1006; Annas, *supra,* note 62.
66 *In Re A.C.* (1987, D.C. App) 533 A. 2d 611 (aff'd 539 A 2d 203).
67 *Jefferson v. Griffin – Spalding County Hospital Authority* (1981, Ga.) 274 S.E. 2d
    457; *Re Jamaica Hosp.* (1985, N.Y. App.) 491 N.Y.S. 2d 898.
68 Nelson and Milliken, 'Compelled Medical Treatment of Pregnant Women:
    Life, Liberty and Law in Conflict,' 259 *J.Am.Med.Assn.* 1060, 1066 (1988).
69 *Taft v. Taft* (1983, Mass.) 446 N.E. 2d 395.
70 Shannon, 'Keeping Dead Mothers Alive During Pregnancy: Ethical Issues,' in
    Shannon (ed.) *Bioethics.* New Jersey: Paulist Press, 1987 (3d. ed.), pp. 223,231
71 *Roe v. Wade* (1973) 410 U.S. 113, 160)65.
72 Cal. Penal Code Section 187(a), (1970), (emphasis supplied.)
73 *People v. Smith* (1987) 188 Cal. App. 3d 1495, 1514; *People v. Bunyard* (1988) 45
    Cal. 3d 1189, 1214.
74 See reference in Kolder, et. al, *supra* 316 *N. Eng. J. Med.* at 1194.
75 See Meyers, *Medico)Legal Implications of Death and Dying.* New York: Lawyers
    Cooperative Pub Co., 1981, Dec., 1988 Cum. Supp, Section 14:23, p.283;

Kluge, *supra* 1988 *J. Med. Ethics* 206, 208; Mason, *Human Life & Medical Practice* Edinburgh: The University Press, 1988, p.77

76 The clear and convincing evidence standard is a standard of proof higher than that normally required in civil cases that has been adopted by some American courts dealing with such sensitive issues as sterilization of an incompetent (*In re Valerie N.* (1985) 40 Cal. 3d 143), and termination of life-sustaining treatment for an incompetent (*Re Gardner* (1987, Me.) 534 A. 2d 947). It is a higher standard than mere preponderance of the evidence (evidence more convincing than not), but not as stringent as the general criminal standard requiring proof beyond any reasonalbe doubt, proof to a moral certanty.

77 *San Francisco Chronicle*, July 3, 1988 'This World,' p.9.

78 *Stallman v. Youngquist* (1987, N.Y. App.) 459 N.Y.S. 2d 814.

79 See *Hughson v. St. Francis Hospital* (1983, N.Y. App.) 459 N.Y.S. 2d 814.

80 *Peo. v. Bunyard* (1988) 45 Cal. 3d 1189

81 *Grodin v. Grodin* (1980, Mich. App.) 301 N.W. 2d 869.

82 *Gloria C. v. William C* (1984, N.Y. App.) 476 N.Y.S. 2d 991

83 *Re Smith* (1985, NY App) 492 N.Y.S. 2d 331; Cf., *In Re Steven S.* (1981) 126 Cal. App. 3d 23.

84 *Giardina v. Bennett* (1988, N.J.)545 A. 2d 139.

85 Infant Life (Preservation) Act, 1929, s.1(1) Abortion Act 1967, s 5(1); *Roe v. Wade* (1973) 410 U.S. 113.

86 For example, in 3 of the first 5 cases imposing court-ordered cesareans for pregnant women on the grounds such was essential to save the fetus, the women in fact delivered normally. Annas, 'Protecting the Liberty of Pregnant Patients,' 316 *N.Eng.J.Med.* 1213 (1987)

87 Abortion Act 1967 s.1(1)

88 Infant Life (Preservation) Act 1929, s 1(1), and Abortion Act s.5(1). However, this by case law has become synonomous with the health of the mother. See discussion in Chapter 2.

89 Norrie, 'Abortion in Great Britain: One Act, Two Laws,' 1985 *Crim L. R.* 474.

90 *D. v. Berkshire C.C.* (1987) 1 All E. R. 20 (H.L.)

91 *Hughson v. St. Francis Hosp.* (1983, N.Y. App.) 459 N.Y.S. 2d 814.

92 A California woman was charged with criminal responsibility and jailed for the birth of her fetus brain dead allegedly because of drug usage during pregnancy and wilfull disregard of doctor's orders.The charges were dismissed as without legal basis, but statutory efforts have been taken to impose criminal liability in such cases.Kolder, et. al., *supra*, 316 *N. Eng. J. Med.* 1192, 1195)6. Prosecutors threaten prosecution for child abuse where fetuses are born drug dependent. A drug addicted mother was recently convicted in a Southern state of
child abuse for drug-induced harm after birth and before severance of the umbilical to her newborn child.

93 *In re F. (In Utero)*, (1988) 2 W.L.R. 1288 (H.L.) see notes 29, 30, *supra*.

94 *In Re A.C.*, *supra*, 533 A. 2d 611, 617; *Taft v. Taft* (1983, Mass.) 446 N.E. 2d 395, 397 ('We do not decide whether, in some situations, there would be justification for ordering a wife to submit to medical treatment in order to assist in carrying a child to term. Perhaps the State's interest, in some circumstances, might be sufficiently compelling . . . to justify such a restriction on a person's constitutional right of privacy.')

95 Brahams, *supra*, 1988 *The Lancet*, 1006

96 Mason, *supra*, *Legal Issues in Human Reproduction*, p. 57; see also, Mason and McCall Smith, *Law and Medical Ethics* (2d ed), *supra*, p. 76; Kluge, EW 'When cesarian section operations imposed by a court are justified' 14 *J Med. Ethics* 206 (1988), (suggesting that at 17–22 weeks, when the fetus has developed a 'functionally integrated and structurally developed central nervous system or brain,' it is a person with equal rights to the mother).

97 Infant Life (Preservation) Act 1929, s.1(1).

98 *Ibid*; Abortion Act 1967, s.5(1).

99 The Infant Life (Preservation) Act 1929 does not extend to Scotland, but the
    Abortion Act 1967 does. The result is a more permissive legal climate for
    abortion in Scotland, since the Abortion Act 1967 is enabling in nature and the
    Infant Life (Preservation) Act 1929 is restrictive in nature, making it criminal
    to destroy the life of a child capable of being born alive unless excused by the
    need to save the life of the mother.

100 For example, most informed comment predicts a more conservative U.S.
    Supreme Court may overrule, or at least significantly restrict, the holding in
    Roe v. Wade, supra, by returning most control over the regulation of abortion
    to the 50 individual states. In *Webster v. Reproductive Health Services, Inc.* (July
    3, 1989) U.S., 109 S. Ct. 3040, the Supreme Court found it proper for the state
    to prohibit all abortions with the use of public facilities or tax monies except
    where necessary to save the life of the mother, to require expensive testing for
    viability on all post-20 week abortions and to legislate that life begins at
    conception. Four members of the 9 member Court appeared ready to overrule
    Roe v. Wade if presented the opportunity to do so.

2

Abortion

A. INTRODUCTION

Abortion, the forced removal of a fetus from the womb to end pregnancy, has been practiced throughout modern history. Most societies are said to have permitted the practice, to varying degree, based upon a belief that the right of pregnant women to abort is above the rights of the fetus to continued uterine development.[1] The *Talmud*, for example, permits child destruction to save the life of the mother at any time prior to birth of the head of the fetus.

Medieval scholars, including St. Thomas Aquinas, believed the fetus did not have a soul at the time of conception. It was widely believed for many centuries that a fetus without a soul could be sacrificed, where necessary, for the welfare of the mother.[2] In the United States, for example, abortion remained legal up to the time of 'quickening' – that time when the fetus could be felt to move within the womb – until the middle of the 19th century.[3]

After that time, better understanding of the process of conception prompted legislation outlawing abortion, except where necessary to protect the life or health of the mother (or because of rape or incest). Some state statutes were more restrictive than others, but almost all permitted the procedure where necessary to save the mother.

The vast majority of abortions are carried out in the first stages of pregnancy. In the United States, of the approximately 1,500,000 abortions carried out per year, at least 90 percent are performed in the first trimester, the first three months of pregnancy. Approximately 90 percent of the remaining 10 percent are carried out between 13 and 20 weeks gestation during the second trimester.[4] Only a handful are performed in the third trimester of pregnancy, normally for reasons felt necessary to protect the life or health of the woman, or because of late-discovered serious fetal abnormality.

Similarly, in Britain, the vast majority of abortions are carried out early in pregnancy. In 1986, of 172,286 reported abortions in England and Wales, only 5 percent were performed after 18 weeks.[5] In 1985, of some 141,000 abortions performed, only 31 were performed after the 25th week of gestation.[1]

Conception occurs upon successful fertilization of the ovum to form a zygote. Within approximately 7 days this zygote implants itself on the uterine wall of the mother. Mason believes that the implanted embryo has acquired 'humanity' by attaching itself anatomically to the mother and thereby acquiring a physical and 'spiritual' association with her.[6] However, this is far from a settled viewpoint.

After 8 to 12 weeks the developing embryo becomes a fetus, with recognizable human features. As the fetus matures, its identity as a human becomes more defined and its organ systems begin to become distinguishable and eventually self-supporting. At some point, normally between 24 and 28 weeks gestation, at the start of the third trimester of pregnancy, the fetus becomes viable. To be viable, the fetus must be capable not simply of being born alive, but must also have the ability to survive outside the womb. This will at times require ventilatory and other 'high tech' medical support.

At 24 weeks the fetus weighs an average of only 740 grams and if born has a very low one year survival probability, perhaps 10 percent, whereas at 28 weeks the fetus has grown to 1120 grams and has a 75 percent probability of survival to at least one year.[7]

The fetus, to be viable, must have sufficient organ maturity, particularly of the lungs, so that they are capable of inflating to oxygenate the fetus' tissues after placental connection is severed.[8] 'Air sac development sufficient for gas exchange [in the lungs] does not occur until at least 23 weeks after gestation and often later.'[9]

We will see that the current law, both in Britain and the United States, has established fetal viability as a critical point in a woman's pregnancy. While a woman and her doctor may be able to decide on abortion with few restrictions prior to viability, significant restrictions are imposed from that time forward. In the United States, abortion may be prohibited by the state after fetal viability unless necessary to protect the life or health of the mother.[10] In England, prohibition is imposed after viability unless abortion is necessary to preserve the life of the mother.[11] Some confusion has been created here because the English statute of 1929 prohibits destruction of a child capable of being 'born alive,' while the later Abortion Act of 1967 refers to the early enactment as one protecting the 'viable foetus.' Since a fetus can be born alive, but have no chance of survival because it is not viable, it is logical that the law look at viability as the critical criterion. In Scotland, the position is less restrictive than in England and more consistent with the present U.S. position. It permits abortion at any stage of pregnancy if necessary to prevent injury to the health of the mother.[12]

Since so few abortions are carried out after apparent viability of the fetus, differences in the legal rights of the woman to abort in such circumstances are of quite limited practical application. American public opinion polls show the clear majority of people support a woman's right to abort. However, that support is tied to the age of the fetus. A recent poll found two out of three Californians supported abortion on demand during the first three months of pregnancy, but that number fell to only 15 percent in the final three months of pregnancy, after the fetus is viable.[13]

There exists a wide divergence of views on abortion, dependent in large part on the point at which life is viewed as beginning. Some view life as beginning at conception,[14] while others believe it does not begin until live birth and survival of the fetus. Others point to implantation,[15] to quickening,[16] to the development of an integrated central nervous system,[17] to the ability to be born alive,[18] or to viability[19] as the proper stages in fetal development where personhood should be acknowledged. These are value judgments. In a brief recently filed with the U.S. Supreme Court by a large number of scientists and medical experts, they concluded 'there is no scientific consensus' on when human life begins, but rather it 'will depend on each individual's social, religious, philosophical, ethical and moral beliefs.'[20]

The law has attempted to reconcile competing interests of mother, of fetus, and of physician. It has done so by means of a compromise solution which seeks to strike a balance at the proper place between the developing life and personhood of the fetus on the one hand, and the liberty, bodily integrity, and freedom of choice of the mother on the other. The laws have been adopted by Parliament, or fashioned by judges. The current state of that law is quite similar in all three jurisdictions: England, Scotland, and the United States. However, as we shall see, efforts to significantly change the current state of the law, as well as ongoing efforts to clarify and refine its application, are also underway. We turn our attention first to England.

B.   ENGLAND

1.   *Abortion once strictly prohibited*

More abortions per capita are carried out in England than in Scotland. Despite that, the legal position is more restrictive, and more complicated, than in Scotland. An understanding of the law must start with the Offences Against the Person Act 1861. The act punishes any attempt to procure an abortion, whether by a pregnant woman, or by anyone else who administers a drug or uses an instrument with intent to procure a miscarriage, whether or not the woman is actually pregnant. The Act punishes the act done with intent to abort, regardless of whether it is successful or even can be. The act was passed at a time when therapeutic abortions were unheard of, due essentially to the unavailability of anaesthesia and frequency of mortal infections.[21] There were no exceptions in the Act, such as treatment made necessary to protect the life or health of the mother.

Given the restraints imposed by the law and the state of medical science, elective abortion was not available. However, this left open the risk of killing the fetus during the normal delivery process before (or at the time) it was born alive, as by not invigorating the fetus upon delivery. The Infant Life (Preservation) Act 1929 was enacted to prevent this practice. It prohibited the destruction of a fetus 'capable of being born alive.' It imposed the presumption that any fetus of 28 weeks gestation was capable of being born alive. It did, however, excuse any such destruction of the child before it had 'an existence independent if its mother' where it was necessary to do so in order to save the life of the mother. No such excuse was available to justify procuring a miscarriage.

2. *Rex v. Bourne creates a therapeutic privilege*

In 1939 an English physician invited prosecution by carrying out an abortion on a young girl who had been raped by a gang of soldiers, in order to prevent her from becoming a 'physical or mental wreck.'[22] Doctors in England, as in Scotland, had long carried out therapeutic abortions in compelling cases, but there was no sanction in English law for them.[23] Dr. Bourne prompted the now-famous case that bears his name by stating publicly,

'I have done this [therapeutic abortion] before and have not the slightest hesitation in doing it again. I have said that the next time I have such an opportunity I will write to the Attorney-General and invite him to take action.'[24]

Judge Macnaughten, in his oft-quoted direction to the jury after the presentation of evidence, concluded that the proviso in the 1929 Act excusing the destruction of the child where 'done in good faith for the purpose only of preserving the life of the mother'[25] should also be applied to the 1861 Act prohibiting abortion. The judge instructed that not all abortions, but only unlawful abortions, were criminal. Finally, the judge directed that 'preserving the life of the mother' could properly include preventing her from becoming a 'physical or mental wreck.'[26] The jury had little trouble finding Dr. Bourne not guilty.

3. *The Abortion Act 1967*

For nearly 30 years the jury instruction of the learned judge in the *Bourne* case was recognized as the law of England. It was strengthened further by a later decision holding that the 'life' of the pregnant woman should include the preservation of her 'health.'[27] Then, in 1967, the Abortion Act was enacted. It made lawful any abortion carried out after a good faith decision arrived at by two registered medical practitioners that the procedure was (1) of less risk to the life or health of the woman, or the health of her existing children, than continuation of the pregnancy; or, (2) there existed a substantial risk the fetus would be born suffering from serious physical or mental abnormalities.

The Act puts abortion in the hands of the medical profession to decide. Two doctors in effect decide the legality of an abortion; not the woman, or, with rare exception,[28] the courts. 'Thus, a great social responsibility is firmly placed by the law upon the shoulders of the medical profession.'[29] There is no entitlement to elect abortion given to the woman. Rather, she is given the right to consent, but must convince her physicians that one ground or the other to justify the procedure applies. Some physicians interpret the Act as allowing abortion on demand, at least early in pregnancy, on the ground that termination carries fewer risks than continuation of the pregnancy; others refuse to take part in performing almost all abortions on moral or religious grounds.[30]

4. *Viable or capable of being born alive*

The Abortion Act is expressly subject to the Infant Life (Preservation) Act 1929, so abortions are limited to non-viable fetuses unless necessary to save the life of the mother. This seems clear, since the Abortion Act references the earlier statute as 'protecting the life of the viable foetus.'[31] However, the earlier statute does not talk in terms of viability, but rather of a 'child capable of being born alive.' This is a more legally restrictive term, since more premature fetuses not viable – not capable of surviving independent of their mother after birth – may well be fully capable of being born alive. Certain commentators feel the two Acts are best reconciled as prohibiting abortion of a child capable of being born alive, even if medically approved in good faith, unless necessary to save the life of the mother.[32] As mentioned, a reading of the Abortion Act as only restricting medically-approved abortions after viability seems more sound for several reasons.[33] First, the Abortion Act does not amend the earlier statute, but only limits its application to an abortion carried out in accordance with the protections of the Abortion Act. Second, the concept of fetal viability is a more compelling one than capable of being born alive, since it denotes a fetus capable of independent survival and more entitled to restrictions on both the woman's and the physician's freedom of choice. Third, given the fact that English courts have in the past equated the 'life of the mother' referenced in the 1929 Act to simply the mental or physical 'health' of the mother,[34] there is as a practical matter little additional protection afforded the fetus by insisting on the more restrictive application of the two statutes. Fourth, recent parliamentary attempts to amend the Act seem to acknowledge this broader interpretation of its reach. Finally, to an American lawyer, there is more legal sense, when balancing maternal and fetal rights, to reliance upon fetal viability as the touchstone for significant restriction on the mother's and the doctor's freedom of choice.[35]

Whichever interpretation of the current statutory scheme in England is accepted, it is clear that after fetal viability a pregnancy may only be terminated to save the life of the mother. Since a very small number of terminations occur after fetal viability – only 31 of 141,000 abortions performed in 1985[36] – few are affected by this restriction. Given that the Abortion Act did not disapprove earlier common law cases equating the mother's life with the mother's health,[34] the position in practice seems nearly the same in England, Scotland and the United States: If the fetus is believed to be viable, abortion is only proper where necessary to preserve the life or the health of the mother. See note on p. 53.

5. *The doctor controls the abortion decision*

Most of the efforts at reform seek to lower the permissible gestational age for abortion, or the permissible abortion indications, after 12 or 18 weeks. For the present, however, it is clear that 'the legality of an abortion [in England] depends upon the opinion of the doctor.'[37] If two physicians concur, in good faith, that pregnancy termination is in the best interest of the woman, and she knowingly consents, there is very little likelihood their decision will be challenged. In the more than 20 years since adoption of the Abortion Act, only one doctor has been prosecuted for the performance of an abortion in England. He was convicted for not performing the operation in accordance with the requirements of the Act that the continuance of the pregnancy be determined, in good faith, to pose more risks to the woman than its early termination. The good faith of the doctor was held a question properly for the jury to decide.[37]

6. *Minors and abortion*

As to abortion requests by minors, the recent decision of the House of Lords in the *Gillick* case[38] dealt with consent by girls under 16. Where the girl is a minor, but over age 16, she is given the power of consent by statute in England. The Family Law Reform Act 1969 gives a minor aged 16 the right to consent (and presumably the corollary right to refuse consent) to any medical treatment.[39] Where the girl is under 16 the legal position was unclear prior to *Gillick*; it is now much more clear, but still not free from doubt. *Gillick* did not directly involve abortion, but rather the giving of contraceptive advice or treatment. The majority concluded a minor under 16 could give consent to the treatment if possessed of sufficient understanding and intelligence to comprehend the treatment proposed and to be able to make up her own mind.

However, in trying to properly balance the rights of parents and child on a very sensitive issue, the Law Lords went beyond requiring only that the minor understand the nature and purpose of the treatment or medical advice. An additional qualitative or moralistic component was added to the consent requirement. Lord Scarman concluded,

> When applying these conclusions to contraceptive advice and treatment it has to be borne in mind that there is much that has to be understood by a girl under the age of 16 if she is to have legal capacity to consent to such treatment. It is not enough that she should understand the nature of the advice which is being given: she must also have a sufficient maturity to understand what is involved. There are moral and family questions, especially her relationship with her parents, long-term problems associated with the emotional impact of pregnancy and its termination and there are the risks to health of sexual intercourse at her age, risks which contraception may diminish but cannot eliminate. It follows that a doctor will have to satisfy himself that she is able to appraise these factors before he can safely proceed on the basis that she has at law capacity to consent to contraceptive treatment . . .'

Professor Williams has criticized this reasoning as unfairly placing the doctor at risk by imposing not a standard simply of consent, but rather one of wise consent.[40] The preferable rule would seem to be the apparent rule in Scotland, in Canada[41] and in the United States:[42] if the minor is mature enough to understand fully the nature and consequences of the treatment, whether abortion or otherwise, she may give a legally valid consent.

An English court has addressed the issue of permitting an abortion for a girl under 16 in the face of parental opposition.[43] In the case the 16 year old girl wanted to terminate the pregnancy and understood the implications of her decision. The court authorized the surgery, and the fitting of an intrauterine contraceptive device. The fact the girl was already the mother of an 11 month old child and in the care of the local authority undoubtedly influenced the decision.[44] Likely the issue of the minor's 'best interest' played a clear role in the outcome.

7. *The incompetent pregnant woman*

Where the pregnant woman is incompetent to decide for or against abortion, someone else must decide for her. If she is a minor, the English courts have wardship jurisdiction, based on the doctrine of *parens patriae*, to act in her best interest, so as to ensure that her welfare is protected. In a recent case, applying this 'best interests' standard, the House of Lords authorized compulsory sterilization for a 17 year old girl with a mental age of 6 who was wholly incapable of understanding and coping with the processes and responsibilities of pregnancy, childbirth, and child care.[45] Childbirth was deemed to very likely involve caesarean delivery and attendant health risk to the girl. In another recent case, involving abortion,[46] an adult, but incompetent, woman of 19 with a mental age of only 3 became pregnant. On application to the court for authorization to abort and sterilize the young woman, it was determined that there was no one able to authorize the surgery, even though it was deemed to be in her best interests. The removal of *parens patriae* jurisdiction over incompetents as a result of the Mental Health Act of 1959 was felt to be a serious bar.[47] The court, however, concluded that medical practice 'demanded' that the surgery proceed, a species of the doctrine of legal necessity.

In yet another case abortion was authorized for an adult incompetent who was 20 weeks pregnant. The reasoning, though unstated, may well have been that the courts retain a 'residual' *parens patriae* jurisdiction to act in compelling circumstances to protect the welfare and best interests of adult incompetents no longer eligible for wardship due to age.[48] However, it now seems clear that courts can and will act to protect adult incompetents not based on any perceived *parens patriae* theory, but rather based on what is clearly in their best interests.[49]

In a December, 1988, case, a High Court judge authorized a sterilization for a 35 year old incompetent woman. She had a mental age of 4 or 5, a verbal capacity of 2, and it would have been catastrophic for her to become pregnant because of her inability to comprehend and deal rationally with pregnancy, birth and child rearing.[47] Judges continue to feel compelled to act in such cases, where the medical evidence supports it, despite the lack of express authority to do so. The express authority to do so should be restored. If a court may act for any incompetent minor, to protect his or her welfare, there is no reason to withhold this same power (and responsibility) in the case of incompetent adults. Protection is needed by the incompetent, regardless of age.

The courts act hesitantly in such situations. The procreative freedom and the bodily integrity of the incompetent are just as important as those of the competent.

In an earlier decision,[50] a judge refused to order an 11 year old girl sterilized. She suffered from only mild mental disability, was expected to improve as she matured, and the procedure would irreversibly deprive her of her basic human right to reproduce. In a Canadian decision,[51] the court concluded that 'non-therapeutic' sterilization could not be ordered for an incompetent. Presumably the court was equating therapeutic with best interests. That is to say, if a sterilization is determined to be in the best interests of the incompetent, it is hard to imagine it would not be considered therapeutic.

In England, then, it appears that abortion or sterilization will be ordered for an incompetent – adult or minor – where the medical evidence clearly shows it to be in the woman's best interests and where no less intrusive solution, such as non-surgical contraception is feasible.[49] However, since the right to reproduce is viewed as an important human right, the courts have and will continue to intervene only in compelling cases where the mental and physical health of the woman is threatened. Despite a judicial suggestion to the contrary,[52] court involvement does not seem necessary in all such cases, but rather only in those where uncertainty, disagreement, or the absence of clear and compelling medical indications for protection of the woman's health mandate court resolution. However, a wise precaution in such cases would be to require the concurrence, in good faith, of a qualified second physician and a clear notation in the patient's medical chart of the rationale for the decision, medical concurrence, and concurrence of the available family, or guardian, if one has been appointed.

8. *Rights of the foetus*

The Abortion Act has been criticized for its apparent failure to recognize the rights of the fetus. Nothing in the Act expressly requires the doctor to consider the interests of the fetus. However, by limiting abortions in most instances to the pre-viable fetus, the Act does in fact recognize that the rights of the fetus do increase in significance as it matures. The effect of the Infant Life (Preservation) Act 1929 and the Abortion Act 1967, read together is to recognize that the rights of the viable fetus are superior to any effects on the health of other children, or the right of the mother to abort a fetus due to its physical or mental handicaps. Only where the life of the mother is at risk are the rights of the viable fetus clearly subordinated to those of its mother. Judge Macnaughten stated it this way 50 years ago in the case involving Dr. Bourne,

> '. . . The unborn child in the womb must not be destroyed unless the destruction of that child is for the purpose of preserving the yet more precious life of the mother.'[53]

This value judgment has, however, been judicially questioned very recently. In the case of *In Re F. (In Utero)*,[54] the justices wondered whether, once a fetus was recognized as a person in the eyes of the law, the life of the fetus must be saved if in conflict with the life of the mother. Surely the fetus is more vulnerable, more in need of the protection of the state, and faces the prospect of a longer life to be preserved than the mother. On the other hand, the mother has allowed the fetus to exist, nurtured and carried it at considerable physical and emotional expense and must not have her rights so relegated to those of the fetus as to discourage others from procreation, pregnancy and childbirth.

Few would argue that where thought viable, the fetus should be aborted in such a manner as not to destroy it, if this is possible without further jeopardizing the health of the mother in any material way.[55] The current law does not, however, encourage this. It encourages still birth to avoid risk of prosecution under the Infant Life (Preservation) Act 1929 for child destruction.

If an effort is made to save the viable aborted fetus, then abortion need not be viewed as condoning neonaticide. Abortion may be permitted due to fetal abnormality, but effort still made to save the fetus if viable. Such a procedure is not justification for neonaticide because a newborn infant is severely deformed. It is likely most parents see a difference between abortion due to handicapped fetal status on the one hand, and failure to treat a newborn child due to similar handicaps.[56] This may be because, as Fletcher has suggested,[57] the newborn has a separate, independent, physical existence apart from the mother, parental acceptance of a newborn is much more developed than that of a fetus, and the newborn's defects are more readily amenable to medical treatment. Despite such differences, there seems no moral or legal reason not to try and save a viable aborted fetus, absent serious harm to the mother from doing so.[58]

9.   *The working of the Abortion Act*

The Abortion Act has been in place for more than 20 years in Britain. It appears to be accepted and in little risk of serious changes. Those who conscientiously object to abortion are exempted from participating in any abortion treatment.[59] The Act places the social responsibility for abortion upon the medical profession.[28] However, the profession appears to have accepted that responsibility, and with the exception of one criminal conviction, doctors have not been reported to have disregarded its requirements of good faith, a concurring second opinion and satisfaction of the admittedly broad abortion criteria.

The Act remains a broad, enabling piece of legislation, offering few limits on the pre-viability indications for abortion[60] before the fetus has matured to the point of being able to breathe on it own.[8] Clarification whether it is viability or capability of live birth that limits the right to abortion would be helpful. Does an abortion necessary to 'preserving the life of the mother' mean one necessary to preserve her physical (or mental) health? Does the duty of physician, and mother, to act to save a viable fetus need clarification? Without it, it may be safer for the physician to ensure that the abortion method selected causes a still birth, to avoid the risk of liability for child destruction. This ambiguity in the law is unfortunate for it almost surely encourages a still born abortus rather than efforts to save the viable aborted fetus. While the effort to salvage the possibly viable fetus should not prejudice the mother's health,[61] the law should encourage an accommodation of the health interests of the mother and fetus wherever reasonably possible to do so.[62] The freedom of the attending physician to exercise his or her clinical judgment must however, at the same time, be respected.[63]

It is undeniably true that these questions might be answered if legislation were adopted making clearly consistent the three statutes that now apply to abortion in England.[64] Refinements are likely, but just as likely is the fact that abortions in both England and Scotland will continue in very large degree to be a matter felt best left to the professional judgment of the physician. Naturally, patient consent is a prerequisite. Where, due to incompetence, it is lacking, the courts are available to approve or refuse such procedures as mandated by the welfare and well-being of the woman.

Finally, where fetal viability is likely, careful consideration will be given to the fetus by physicians and the courts, if involved, before authorizing abortion. Both the common law and statute requires this. Fortunately, this dilemma is infrequently confronted given the few late term abortions performed in Britain.[1]

10.   *The rights of the father*

Although the father contributes half of the genetic makeup of the fetus, he has no direct physical involvement in the birth of the fetus beyond the procreative act. The woman carries the embryo after implantation throughout its development to fetus and eventual live birth. The physical and emotional changes the woman undergoes, the physical effort required, and the restraints on her freedom of action, are substantial in both degree and duration. For these reasons, the law has concluded that the abortion decision is one that the woman may make, with the necessary concurrence of her physicians. The father may not require an abortion by the mother, nor may he interfere with or overrule her decision to abort.[65] The English courts have held that the unborn child has no legal standing to restrain the woman's abortion decision, nor does the father. In the most recent case, *C. v. S.*, the court held that a fetus is not capable of being born alive, so as to gain the statutory protection against child destruction, unless the fetus is able to breath because of a sufficiently developed lung capacity. If the lungs are not mature enough to oxygenate fetal tissue, with or without the help of a respirator, after the placental connection is severed, then the fetus cannot be capable of being born alive. This cannot occur before a gestational age of 23 weeks.[66]

The position of the English courts on the absence of the father's standing to restrain an abortion is the same as the American position. While we will see many similarities between English and American legal developments, the development of the law in Scotland has been quite independent.

C. SCOTLAND

1. *Abortion as a crime*

Abortion is the only specific medical procedure that was considered illegal in and of itself by the common law, unless excused by the necessity of saving the mother's life or health.[67] Professor Smith has opined that in Scots law the additional element of criminal intent is necessary for abortion to be a crime.[68] This seems to be correct since in Scotland no criminal prosecution would be maintained, nor has one ever occurred, where a physician has carried out an abortion 'in good faith, for therapeutic reasons, according to reputable medical practice.'[69]

The well-known English case against Dr. Bourne discussed earlier,[22] which created in England a therapeutic justification for abortion where necessary to protect the health, as well as the life, of the mother,[70] would not have been brought in Scotland. Scots law would not prosecute a licensed physician, acting in good faith to protect the health of the mother.[71] Scots common law in effect recognizes a therapeutic privilege for the physician to abort a fetus, provided it is performed by a registered practitioner and in accordance with sound medical practice.[72]

2. *The therapeutic exception*

When a practitioner acts in good faith and in accordance with sound medical practice, no criminal intent can be inferred.[73] Criminal intent in Scots law requires the presence of wicked or felonious intent, plan or design.[74] Thus, it has been relatively easy for abortions to be carried out by medical practitioners in Scotland for therapeutic reasons. Several other factors, in addition to the wicked intent requirement of the criminal law, account for this practice. One is that the medical profession has traditionally enjoyed a high degree of respect from the populace and from the Scottish courts.[75] Another is that the Crown Office enjoys broad discretion in the exercise of its powers of prosecution and would not be about to charge a physician, nor obtain his conviction from a Scottish court, except upon a clear showing of evil intent or manifest abuse.[76]

3. *The Abortion Act 1967 and Scots Law*

The result of the Abortion Act 1967[77] has been to permit pregnancies to be terminated on rather broad grounds prior to fetal viability.[78] Where two registered medical practitioners concur in good faith, abortion is apparently authorized by the act prior to fetal viability where risk to life, or injury to the physical or mental health of the pregnant woman (the health clause), or of any of her existing children (the social clause) is greater from continuance than from termination of her pregnancy, or where there is substantial risk the child if born would suffer from 'such physical or mental abnormalities as to be seriously handicapped' (the eugenic clause).[79] The health clause is very broad indeed, since modern methods of abortion, at least during the early stages of a pregnancy, carry risks of harm to the mother that are far, far less than those associated with full term delivery of the fetus.

The Abortion Act 1967 applies to Scotland.[80] However, the earlier Infant Life (Preservation) Act 1929 to which it refers, which prohibits destruction of a fetus capable of being born alive, does not extend to Scotland.[81] As a result, fetal viability does not prevent application of the entitlements to abortion under the Abortion Act 1967 in Scotland. Thus, in Scotland, even though the fetus is capable of being born alive, or is viable – that is, capable of surviving after being born – a woman may still abort upon obtaining the concurrence of two practitioners that one of the entitlements to abortion under the Act applies. Norrie has stated it this way,[12]

'. . . while the 1967 defences [the health, social, and eugenic clauses mentioned above] are available in England only from conception until the foetus becomes capable of being born alive, the more 'liberal' position in Scotland holds that the 1967 defences are available from conception of the foetus until its birth at term.'

For any crime to be committed under Scots law, the abortion must be one procured with criminal or wicked intent and it must also be shown that the woman was pregnant at the time.[82] This seems too obvious to dwell upon. The victim of the crime of abortion in Scotland is the fetus, since it causes the destruction of 'potential human life.'[83] If there is no pregnancy, it seems there can be no crime of abortion or attempted abortion. A critical element is missing – the fetus to be aborted. Nonetheless, English criminal law punishes attempts to procure abortion without regard to whether the woman is pregnant,[84] a rather odd state of affairs.[85] It is possible the Abortion Act 1967 extended this crime to Scotland,[86] but this is not considered likely and it has not been so applied.[12]

4. *Consent a necessary element*

Of course, the woman must consent to the abortion, for otherwise it, like any other unauthorized bodily invasion, is an assault. The perpetrator of an assault, whether physician or ruffian, incurs both civil[87] and criminal[88] liability. Consent will absolve the actor of civil liability, but consent does not normally provide a defense to criminal liability.[89] However, where the *prima facie* assault is a surgical procedure carried out for therapeutic purposes, consistent with accepted medical practice, the common law has come to accept consent as a defense. It operates in conjunction with the doctrine of necessity to justify the physical intrusion.[90]

5. *The minor and consent*

In Scotland, a woman or girl of any age may consent to an abortion if she is able to understand the general nature, risks, and consequences of the procedure.[91] In Scots law, once a girl reaches puberty and is therefore able to conceive, she becomes a 'minor' rather than a 'pupil' child. Once having become a minor, the rights of the parents to decide for her are substantially diminished. The parents' rights of control generally apply only to the minor's property, not to her person. Thus, if the minor understands the abortion procedure, its risks and consequences, she can consent to it.[92] As stated in an early Scottish case, 'the wishes and feelings of the child himself are entitled to a degree of weight corresponding to the amount of intelligence and right feeling which he may exhibit.'[93]

In other words, if the minor child is able to understand the medical procedure proposed, which necessarily includes an understanding of its material risks and consequences, then the child may consent (or refuse consent) to it. It may well be that with such a morally and legally sensitive operation as abortion, the understanding that courts will require may include the minor's comprehension of her obligations to her parents, their feelings, and the emotional impact of abortion upon her, as well as simply the nature and purpose of the medical treatment involved. This is, not without doubt, apparently now the law in England,[94] but it has not been extended to Scotland.

6. *Efforts to amend the law*

Some moves are afoot in England to modify or restrict the reach of the Abortion Act 1967, which could affect Scots law. One proposal would allow termination of pregnancy after 24 weeks gestation only if necessary to protect the health of the mother, not for the social reason of preventing harm to existing children, or for the eugenic reason of avoiding birth of a seriously abnormal child.[95] The Abortion (Amendment) Bill considered, by the House of Commons in 1988 would have lowered the maximum limit for terminating pregnancy to 18 weeks, unless necessary to save the life or prevent grave injury to the health of the mother. Finally, it has been proposed the presumption found in the current English law[96] that a child is capable of being born alive at 28 weeks gestation be lowered to 24 weeks gestation (but see note on p. 53).[30]

None of these proposed changes, if adopted, would be likely to have significant impact on abortion practice in Scotland. The Abortion Act 1967 is an enabling act, not really needed in Scotland because of the common law position there and because the existing restrictive legislation which prohibits abortion does not apply to Scotland.[97] Neither the Offences Against the Person Act 1861, which was enacted to prohibit procuring abortion, and the

Infant Life (Preservation) Act 1929, which was enacted to prohibit destruction of a live born fetus, apply to Scotland.

McLean suggests[98] that abortion need not be synonymous with child destruction. This perception may well have arisen more from surgeons' desires to avoid the risk of prosecution for child destruction by ensuring that the abortus does not survive the abortion than from any intent by women that their aborted fetus die. Efforts to reduce the age of fetal viability are undoubtedly aimed at reducing child destruction, but they also reduce women's freedom of abortion choice. Perhaps the better emphasis is to promote a legal climate which encourages survival of the fetus, rather than unrealistic efforts to reach ever lower levels of fetal viability in order to restrict abortion.

7.   *The need for some late abortions*

While there is continuing debate, there is little support to significantly amend the Abortion Act 1967. There is a recognized need to permit some late abortions, given late discovery of pregnancy, reluctance of some – particularly the disadvantaged – to seek early medical supervision of their pregnancy, the differing views of the medical profession[30] on the scope of the woman's right to abort and the often time-consuming and difficult process of intra-uterine diagnosis of significant fetal abnormality.[99] Even though techniques such as chorionic villus biopsy, ultrasound imaging, and magnetic resonance imaging have greatly enhanced the diagnosis of congenital abnormality, it still remains a process that may well require considerable fetal maturity before diagnosis can be confident. Some have suggested that rather than trying to prohibit the relatively few late term abortions that occur in Britain,[100] perhaps the woman should be given an unimpeded right to choose abortion during the first trimester of pregnancy and greater emphasis should be placed on contraception education and efforts at fetal survival.[30,98]

As can be clearly seen, both legal development and the abortion debate in general has been more active in England than Scotland. The medical profession in England is more polarized on the issues, perhaps in part because of demand from non-residents for abortion, including late term abortion,[30] and due to higher demand than in Scotland.[101] However, the most controversy, debate and legal development has occurred in the United States, to which we now turn our attention.

D.   UNITED STATES

1.   *Abortion before Roe v. Wade*

Before 1973 when the United States Supreme Court in *Roe v. Wade*[10] recognized a woman's right to choose abortion in the exercise of her constitutional right of privacy, abortion was controlled by each of the 50 states. All states restricted the abortion decision. Some held it was criminal, except where necessary to protect the life of the mother.[102] Other, more liberal state statutes permitted abortion where necessary to protect the health of the mother, or in cases of serious fetal abnormalities.[103] Despite these restraints, the clear majority of American public opinion favored freedom of choice for a woman to select abortion, at least early in her pregnancy. The variations in restrictiveness of the numerous state statutes caused unequal access to care, provided the motivation for residence in another jurisdiction to accomplish an abortion, and encouraged a substantial number of unlawful abortions, often under conditions placing the woman's health at great risk. The U.S. mortality rate in 1970 per 100,000 abortions, before *Roe v. Wade* was decided, was about 18 (.018 per cent).[104] By 1983 it had dropped to about 1 per 200,000 abortions (.0005 per cent). By contrast, the mortality rate per 100,000 live births in 1970 was approximately 16, and had dropped to 7.5 by 1983. The legalization of abortion in the U.S., as well as improvements in the technique, have made it 10 to 20 times more likely a woman will die during childbirth than as the result of abortion surgery.[105] Abortion normally carries a far lower risk than continuing the pregnancy to term. More than 1.5 million abortions are performed annually in the U.S., a rate estimated to be approximately 30 per every 1,000 American women of child-bearing ages 15–44 years.[106]

2. *Roe v. Wade, and the Right to Privacy*

In 1965 the U.S. Supreme Court for the first time recognized an implied constitutional right of individual privacy.[107] The right was unwritten in the Constitution, but to be inferred from the individual rights and freedoms expressly guaranteed by the Bill of Rights, the first ten Amendments to the Constitution, and by the 14th Amendment guarantee of 'due process' of law.

This right of privacy had, in effect, been applied earlier by the Supreme Court in order to protect certain individual rights felt to be 'fundamental' in nature. Although not referred to as such, the Court had upheld the right of individuals to procreate,[108] to marry,[109] to receive contraceptives,[110] to raise and educate one's children as one saw fit,[111] and to refuse surgery or other invasive physical treatment, even if proposed to obtain evidence of criminal wrongdoing.[112] As early as 1891, the Supreme Court had refused to permit a forced medical examination of a litigant alleging personal injury, reasoning that it would violate the deeply rooted right of bodily integrity and 'to be let alone.'[113]

In *Roe v. Wade*, the Court extended this emerging right of privacy to the woman's decision to abort her fetus. The Court adopted what has proven to be a controversial three-tiered or trimester approach in its decision. During the first trimester, the first three months of pregnancy, the woman was free to choose abortion without any interference or regulation by the state, other than requiring it to be performed by a licensed physician. The Court relied in part for this portion of its decision on the fact that mortality from abortion during the first trimester is considerably less than mortality from childbirth.[114]

At the end of the first trimester, the court reasoned, the interests of the state in regulating the abortion procedure to protect the health of the mother becomes 'compelling.' As a result, the state could regulate the procedure in any reasonable way to accomplish that objective, such as by requiring that the abortion be carried out in approved medical institutions by the use of approved medical techniques and staff.

At the end of the second trimester, when the fetus becomes 'viable,' the state's interest in the 'potentiality of human life' represented by the fetus becomes compelling. The fetus is considered viable when 'potentially able to live outside the mother's womb, albeit with artificial aid.' The court felt viability was 'usually' placed at about 28 weeks, but may occur even at 24 weeks. That has proved to be quite accurate. Despite significant advances in neonatal medicine, 80 percent of premature infants survive birth at 28 weeks, 40 percent at 26–28 weeks, 20 percent at 24 weeks, and only 7 percent at 23 weeks.[115] Prior to that age, the lungs are insufficiently developed to allow even respirator-assisted breathing. As recently concluded by a prestigious body of scientific and medical opinion,

> 'Although advances in technology have improved the chances of sur-vival for premature births within the range of 24 to 28 weeks, the outer limit of viability at 24 weeks has not significantly changed . . . More-over, there is no reason to believe that a change in this outer limit is either imminent or inevitable.'

The court in *Roe* held that when the fetus had reached the presumed age of viability, at or about the start of the third trimester, the state could regulate or even proscribe abortion altogether, save where necessary to preserve the 'life or health' of the mother. Thus, the Supreme Court accomplished by judicial interpretation (some would say judicial legislat-ing) what the British Parliament had essentially done by statute some six years before when passing the Abortion Act 1967.[116]

Roe has been a controversial decision. Although a clear majority of the American public supports the decision, a vocal and significant minority, politically active, have consistently opposed it.[117] Presidents Reagan and Bush have opposed it, the former selecting conservative justices for the Supreme Court in the hopes of causing reconsideration and limitation, if not reversal, of *Roe*. The Supreme Court has consistently upheld *Roe*, but the voting margin has slipped from 7–2 to 5–4.[118] The Supreme Court through its 1989 *Webster* decision,[9] has now invited the state legislatures to enact restrictions on the application of *Roe*. *Roe* will be narrowed and abortion will become more difficult to obtain in some states. Restrictions on state funding, the use of public facilities, abortions for minors without parental notice, abortions without warnings and a waiting period and abortions in less expensive clinics rather than hospitals are likely to be upheld. The current Court has set the stage by suggesting that the right to privacy should be narrowly interpreted, stating that courts are,

> 'most vulnerable and [come] nearest to illegitimacy when . . . [dealing] with judge-made constitutional law having little or no cognizable roots in the language or design of the Constitution'[119]

The current Supreme Court has stated that the right of privacy should only be extended to protect personal decisions which are 'implicit in the concept of ordered liberty,' or those which are 'deeply rooted in this Nation's history and tradition.'[119] That the Court has elected not to bring private homosexual conduct within the ambit of the right to privacy suggests that the Court may seek to distinguish abortion from privacy rights to procreation, contraception, marriage and child-rearing on moral grounds. Since the right of privacy is not absolute, but must be balanced against state interests, the Court could conclude that the state may restrict abortion at any stage in the interest of protecting the developing embryo or fetus.

3.   *Rights of the fetus*

The right of privacy is to be balanced against any competing interests of the state. The state can compel restrictions on liberty or bodily intrusions in the interests of public health or safety, as by requiring vaccination to avoid spread of disease,[120] or even sterilization where felt necessary to avoid transmission of mental illness.[121] *Roe v. Wade* recognized that the state's interest in the 'potential' life represented by the viable fetus is compelling. The state's interest could regulate the grounds for abortion or even proscribe it altogether, except where necessary to protect the mother's life or health. Thus, *Roe v. Wade* reached a similar result to that arrived at more than 30 years earlier in *R. v. Bourne*: the fetus is valued, is to be preserved where possible, but even where viable the health of the mother is deemed paramount to the health or life of the fetus.

States have sought to increase their control over abortion by adopting legislation that human life begins at conception, thereby justifying restrictions on any abortions to preserve that life. However, while the Supreme Court previously held that the state may not adopt one theory of when life begins to justify its regulation of abortion,[122] it has now concluded states may decide life begins at conception if such a declaration is not the basis for impermissible restrictions on abortion.[14] This does not seem appropriate when there is no medical or scientific consensus on the point.[15-20]

Roe is subject to challenge for its conclusion that viability is the point at which the rights of the fetus are first considered. Nothing in the law would have prevented the court from finding the interests of the state compelling at an earlier stage in embryo or fetal development. Pennsylvania, for example, is expected to pass legislation restricting abortion by prohibiting it after the 24th week of pregnancy except where necessary to save the life of the mother.[123]

Viability is defensible, for the law has never recognized the unborn child as a person until live born. Once viable, the fetus has that potential of live birth and legal personhood. However, that is not to say that by statute an earlier stage of fetal development could not become the criterion for imposing various legal entitlements.

It appears, however, to be the moral view of most in western society that the mother's health comes first when in conflict with that of the fetus. A choice must be made. By giving preference to the health of the mother, procreation, pregnancy and childbirth are encouraged, for the mother knows she is protected. Also, since the mother has carried the burden of pregnancy, protecting her health seems proper in the event of conflict.

Where it is possible to save both mother and child, it seems moral to do so. However, the obligation to save the child cannot interfere with the discretion and breadth of judgment the physician needs to determine what in his clinical judgment is best for the mother.[124] For this reason the Supreme Court has rejected state statutes which specify how a physician must undertake to ascertain viability of the fetus,[124] which require hospitalization without determination of the need for it,[125] require two attending physicians regardless of the circumstances,[126] or require that late-pregnancy abortions utilize the technique providing the least risk to survival of the viable fetus.[126] However, the *Webster*[14] decision and a newly constituted Supreme Court may no longer find these restrictions impermissible if they are deemed not to 'unduly burden' the woman's abortion decision.

The procedure most likely to allow fetal survival may not be the safest for the mother. Thus far the American courts have not compelled preference for fetal over maternal health. Some argue they should; that third trimester abortions be limited to those inducing early labor with the intent of producing a live newborn.[127] Given the reluctance of both mother and physician to undergo a post-viability abortion, as evidenced by the few that are performed, it seems best to leave it to physician and patient to decide, the former in the exercise of good faith and professional judgment, to do what is necessary to protect the life or health of the mother. If live birth can be accomplished with no material risk to the mother's health, then the state's interest in that live birth clearly can require all reasonable medical efforts be undertaken to accomplish it.[128] The law should encourage fetal survival after abortion, but not at the expense of the mother's health. The physician should be free in the exercise of his or her sound professional judgment to decide the most appropriate clinical means to employ. An abortion decision by the woman and her physician should not imply that either does not wish the fetus to survive where feasible.[98]

4. *Abortion and the pregnant minor*

In the absence of a specific statute, whether or not a minor can give a valid consent to medical treatment depends on whether or not he or she is mature enough to give an informed consent to it.[129] She must be capable of understanding the nature and purpose of the procedure, its material risks and the available alternatives to undergoing it.[130] This is called the 'mature minor' rule and it has been equally applied to abortion as to other medical treatments.[131] The minor has the burden of satisfying the physician that she 'has the requisite understanding and maturity' to give an informed consent. Absent such a showing treatment may only be given if supported by medical necessity, parental consent, court order, or statutory authorization.[132]

Many states authorize a pregnant minor to consent to any medical treatment related to her pregnancy.[133] However, this does not rule out resort to one of the other alternatives mentioned if in fact the minor is unable to give an informed consent. As a practical matter of course, age of fertility (puberty) provides the minimum age limit to consent to abortion. A pre-pubertal girl cannot require an abortion, so ability to consent is irrelevant.

If the minor is competent to decide, her parents cannot overrule her decision to abort.[134] However, where there is no parental consent, prompt judicial review to determine if the abortion is in the minor's best interests, or if she is mature enough to consent to it herself, is validly imposed.[135]

5. *The incompetent pregnant woman*

The modern American cases all state than an incompetent patient should enjoy the same rights and privileges as the competent patient.[136] The same right extends to a pregnant woman who is incompetent.[137] The difficulty is how to exercise those rights, since the patient cannot.

In an attempt to protect the procreative rights of the incompetent, certain states have legislated that no one may authorize sterilization or abortion for an incompetent.[138] However, some courts have struck down those statutes as interfering with the right of the incompetent, by surrogate, to exercise her procreative freedom by electing such a procedure.[139]

Where possible, the choice the incompetent would have made if competent should be ascertained and honored. This 'substituted judgment' should not be limited to only one outcome in the event of pregnancy, or no real choice for the incompetent is preserved. If the wishes of the incompetent are unknown, then what is determined to be in her best interests should control the decision. This will normally mean the abortion is necessary to protect her physical or mental health.[140]

The views of the incompetent should be considered. If they are consistently stated, they may be the best evidence of what the patient really wants (and would also want if competent to decide.)[141] If the incompetent wishes the child, and pregnancy does not pose a significant health risk, the court is likely to deny an abortion sought by a surrogate on grounds of inability to care for the child.[142] Adoption remains a less-intrusive option.

6. *Webster – the attack on Roe v. Wade*

A new conservative majority now controls the U.S. Supreme Court.[143] In *Webster v. Reproductive Health Services, Inc.*,[144] it was presented its first clear opportunity to set forth its views on abortion. The new majority, on a 5–4 vote, upheld the abortion restrictive provisions of a Missouri law that the courts below had stricken down as an unconstitutional interference with a woman's right to choose abortion in the exercise of her right to privacy. The Court upheld this and other state laws banning the use of tax money for 'encouraging or counseling' abortion, banning the performance of abortion by any public employee (doctor, nurse or other health care provider), and banning the use of any public hospital or other taxpayer-supported facility to perform an abortion, unless such abortion services were necessary to save the life of the mother. It also upheld a legislative declaration that 'the life of each human being begins at conception,' finding it carried with it no impermissible restrictions of any kind on abortion. Finally, the Court upheld the requirement of expensive testing to determine fetal viability in abortions past 20 weeks, given a reasonable medical basis to suspect viability.

If, however, the law is that life begins at conception, then the potential exists to radically alter the long-established common law principle that a fetus is not a person in the eyes of the law and, at least prior to viability, enjoys no established legal rights.

Four of the five justices in the majority strongly suggested they are prepared to overrule *Roe v. Wade* outright. A fifth vote cannot be far away, with three of the four dissenters not far from retirement and President Bush inclined to appoint more conservative justices when given the chance. The feeling of these justices is that rights not *expressly* set forth in the Constitution should, with rare exception, not be judicially engrafted onto it. The right to abortion is nowhere in the Constitution, nor is the controversial trimester approach to delineation of a woman's abortion right laid down by Justice Blackman in *Roe*.

While this approach has a certain initial appeal, one wonders what the Constitution's guarantee of 'life, liberty and the pursuit of happiness' means to most if not judicial recognition and protection of the right to marry,[109] to procreate,[108] to raise children[11]1 and to decide upon medical treatment for one's physical and emotional health.[145] The current Court, it is clear, intends to leave the control of abortion to state legislatures, where differing attitudes prevail. Some states can be expected to restrict abortions to cases of rape, incest or threat to the mother's life; other states with express rights of privacy set forth in their constitutions can be expected to leave the woman's abortion choice largely uncontrolled short of fetal viability.[146]

Overturning *Roe v. Wade* will have limited impact. Women may need to cross state lines to have an abortion. This will cost more and poor women will be disadvantaged. Doctors will still be able to conclude the procedure is necessary to protect the life of the woman and this may come to mean, as it did in Britain, the health of the woman. Legislatures are likely to be more sympathetic to early abortions and this is where by far the most occur. In the U.S. 50 percent of all abortions occur in the first 8 weeks, 90 percent in the first 12 weeks, and less than 1 percent occur after 20 weeks.[147] Thus, almost no abortions occur when the fetus may be viable, as is also the case in Britain.

Politically, legislation in many states is likely to be a compromise, allowing early term abortions much more freely than late term abortions, but requiring such things as counseling, an explanation of the alternatives to abortion, parental consent and a waiting period for reflection. The majority of Americans appear to support first trimester abortions, oppose near-viability abortions, support *Roe* and disagree with *Webster*, but favor pre-abortion viability tests, counseling, explanation of abortion alternatives, parental notification and consent, and limits on the use of public funds for abortion.[146,134'117]

A recent editorial in the *Wall Street Journal* seemed to sum up the U.S. sentiment in the aftermath of *Roe* and *Webster*, harkening back to much earlier days in the law, when it stated:[147]

> 'We agree that early abortion decisions are best left to women themselves, but at some point in the pregnancy the state has a right to protect the unborn.
>
> ...In the Common Law, abortions before 'quickening' were not viewed as murder. This is more-or-less good enough for us, and our sense is that despite the militants on each side, society generally agrees.'

While *Roe v. Wade* might represent good social policy, protecting early abortions and prohibiting most at fetal viability, its basis in the Constitution is murky. The Supreme Court has had difficulty defining the parameters of the implied right of privacy. The current Court will not expand it and, as with abortion, may contract it and leave the rights to be granted or denied to the state legislatures as the architects of social policy.

The U.S. is probably moving toward an unfortunate patchwork of laws on abortion. The likely result, overall, will be a legal climate similar to Britain after the *Bourne*[34] case, but before the Abortion Act 1967. Only time, and some rather tumultuous political decisions, will tell.

E. CONCLUSION

Abortion is practiced in Scotland, England and the United States to differing degree. England and the United States both rely on statutes, as interpreted by the common law, to define the lawful parameters of abortion. Doctors and women in Scotland enjoy the protection of the Abortion Act 1967, but the statute has added little to the position at common law. The right of privacy places the abortion decision on the woman's shoulder in the U.S., whereas the medical profession is given greater control over exercise of the right in England.

In all three jurisdictions the law has to date been able to very largely avoid acceptance of any particular moral or religious position on when life begins. The traditional legal view in all three jurisdictions that a fetus is not a 'person' in the eyes of the law until born alive, thereby exhibiting an existence of its own, has allowed the courts to uniformly side with the mother when her health has been endangered by continued pregnancy.

English and American law clearly and explicitly gives increased deference to the fetus upon its attaining viability. Scots law in practice does the same. At this time the fetus has the potential to survive on its own. It seems proper to limit the mother's right to abort in deference to this potentiality. Nonetheless, the few that elect to abort at this late stage, after enduring pregnancy, should be permitted to do so where necessary to protect their health. A choice must be made. While not made lightly, it should be made for the mother.

The law does so. The U.S. Supreme Court has invalidated a state statute requiring the use of the abortion procedure which provides the 'best opportunity for the fetus to be aborted alive,' because the statute did not 'clearly specify . . . that the woman's health must always prevail over the fetus' life and health when they conflict.'[148]

This legal preference for the mother's health, however, does not mean that efforts should not be made to accomplish a live birth where possible without material risk to maternal health. The law needs clarification in this area. Room for the exercise of professional judgment must be afforded the physician, but the law should encourage and protect efforts to accomplish live birth of an aborted viable fetus, not discourage them due to fear of legal liability for child destruction.

While adoption remains an option to abortion, it is not a panacea. Women cannot be compelled to carry fetuses against their will in significant numbers without doing violence to the societal interest in encouraging childbirth. The experience prior to liberalization of the abortion laws in England in 1939 and again in 1967, and in the United States in 1973, shows the undesirable social effects of unsafe and illicit pregnancy terminations. It is also troubling for society to impose restrictions on the woman's individual decision to carry on a pregnancy, yet fail to provide assistance to her in caring for children born into a fatherless and/or impoverished household, one perhaps already over-taxed by the demands and needs of existing children.

The law as it now exists, very similar in application in England, Scotland, and the United States, seems to reflect a reasonable accommodation between rights of mother and fetus. No perfect solution exists. No one can claim to know the only proper or moral answer.

As with most other personal rights – free expression, individual liberty, rights to medical, educational, and other social services – the right to abortion is not absolute, nor can its prohibition be absolute. A reasonable balance of competing rights must and has occurred. Other than reasonable refinements, the basic legality of the procedure, at least where health is implicated, should remain. A strong case can also be made that, given the fact the woman carries the fetus at considerable physical and emotional burden, that she normally has the ability to conceive and give birth again, and that she has the burden to raise and nurture the child (or society will have to assume it), that few situations prior to viability of the fetus should prevent exercise of her informed decision to abort.

It should perhaps be stated that the new French abortion pill RU-486, or discoveries similar to it, have the potential to radically change the practice of abortion. In use in France for about a year, where it is being used for one-third or more of all abortions, it apparently is more than 90 percent effective during the first seven weeks of pregnancy. It halts pregnancy by inhibiting delivery of progesterone essential to the embryo. Its importation and use in Britain or the United States, legally or illegally, could become a significant counter and to some extent moot abortion restrictions during the first trimester, if adopted by the courts or the legislatures.

Finally, there should be certain limited circumstances of serious fetal abnormality that justify post-viable abortion of the fetus. This seems to be consistent with the social consensus.[149] As we shall see, courts on both sides of the Atlantic have sanctioned a certain amount of parental and physician discretion in this area in the face of severe, heart-wrenching abnormality, even following live birth.[150] We will consider this exceedingly difficult topic in Chapter 4.

NOTES

1 Bromwich, 'Late Abortions,' 294 *Brit. Med. J*. 527 (1987).
2 See Dunstan (1984) 10 *J. Med. Ethics* 38; Lattin, 'The Ethical Aspects of Abortion,' *San Francisco Chronicle*, Feb. 6, 1989, p.B3.
3 *Ibid.*
4 Reidinger, 'Will *Roe v. Wade* Be Overruled?' *Am. Bar Assn. J*., July 1, 1988, pp.66, 69.
5 296 *Brit. Med. J*. 446 (1988).
6 Mason, *Human Life and Medical Practice*, Edinburgh: The University Press, 1988, p.77; Mason, 'Abortion and the Law,' in McLean, *Legal Issues in Human Reproduction*. Aldershot: Gower, 1989, p.57.
7 Yu, et. al., 'Prognosis for Infants Born at 23 to 28 Weeks' Gestation,' 293 *Brit. Med. J*. 1200 (1986), (7 per cent survival at 23 weeks gestation).
8 *C. v. S.* (1987) 1 All E.R. 1230, 2 W.L.R. 1101 (C.A.)
9 *Los Angeles Times*, April 1, 1989, p.20 (quoting Nobel laureates' brief in support of upholding *Roe v. Wade* (1973) 410 U.S. 113, filed in *Webster v. Reproductive Health Services*, U.S.S. Ct. No. 88–605), (1989) U.S., 109 S.Ct. 3040.
10 *Roe v. Wade* (1973) 410 U.S. 113.
11 Abortion Act 1967 1(1), 5(1); Infant Life (Preservation) Act 1929 1(1).
12 Abortion Act 1967, §1(1); Norrie, 'Abortion in Great Britain: One Act, Two Laws' 1985 *Crim. L. R*. 475, 483. See also, *R. v. Woolnough* (1977) 2 N.Z.L.R. 508.
13 *San Francisco Chronicle*, Feb. 21, 1989, p.1. A national poll found 58 per cent opposed restricting a woman's right to abortion prior to the third trimester of pregnancy, a right established by *Roe v. Wade*, *supra*, whereas 37 per cent favored overturning the decision. *San Francisco Chronicle*, Jan. 23, 1989, p.A4.
14 *Webster v. Reproductive Health Services, Inc.* (1989) U.S., 109 S.Ct. 3040.
15 At approximately 7 days after conception. Mason, *Legal Issues in Human Reproduction*: p.57; Havard, 75 *J. Roy. Soc. Med*. 351 (1982).
16 Blackstone, *Commentaries*, I, 129.
17 At approximately 17 to 22 weeks. Kluge, E. W., 'When casarean section operations imposed by a court are justified,' 14 *J. Med. Ethics* 206 (1988); see also, Kushner, 'Having a life versus being alive' 10 *J. Med. Ethics* 5 (1984), (abortion permissable prior to development of fetal brain capable of consciousness).
18 Infant Life (Preseration) Act 1929, §1(1).
19 *C. v. S.* (1987) 1 All E.R. 1230, 2 W.L.R. 1101; *Roe v. Wade, supra*.
20 *Los Angeles Times*, April 1, 1989, p.20.
21 Havard, 'Legal Regulation of Medical Practice Decisions of Life and Death: A Discussion Paper,' 75 *J. Roy. Soc. Med*. 351 (1982).
22 *R. v. Bourne* (1939) 1 K.B. 687, reported earlier, before revisions, in (1938) 3 All E.R. 615.
23 Williams, *The Sanctity of Life and the Criminal Law*, p. 151.
24 Williams, *supra*, pp 151–52.
25 Infant Life (Preservation) Act 1929, §1(1).
26 (1939) 1 K.B. at 693–4.

27 *R v. Newton & Stungo* (1958) *Crim. L.R.* 467, 600.
28 *R. v. Smith (John)* 1973 1 W.L.R. 1510, 1512.
29 *R. v. Smith (John), supra.*
30 Smith, 'Late Abortions and the Law,' 296 *Brit. Med. J.* 446, 447 (1988).
31 Abortion Act 1967, §5(1); see Tunkel, 'Late Abortion and the Crime of Child Destruction,' 1985 *Crim. L.R.* 133, 134–5.
32 Norrie, *supra*, 1985 *Crim. L.R.* 475; Mason, *Legal Issues in Human Reproduction*, p. 49.
33 See also, Skegg, *Law, Ethics & Medicine*. Oxford, Clarendon Press, 1985, p.10; Tunkel, *loc. cit.*
34 *R. v. Bourne* (1939) 1 K.B. 687; *R. v. Newton & Stungo* (1958) Crim L.R. 467, 600.
35 *Roe v. Wade*, (1973) 410 U.S. 113.
36 Bromwich, 294 *Brit. Med. J.* 527 (1987) (after 25 weeks gestation; the fetus may be viable at 23 weeks, which seems the lower end of the scale at the present time, with only about 7 percent of such infants able to survive for a year or more. See Yu, et. al., 293 *Brit. Med. J.* 1200 (1986).)
37 *R. v. Smith (John)* (1973) 1 W.L.R. 1510, 1512.
38 *Gillick v. West Norfolk and Wisbech Area Health Authority* (1985) 3 All E.R. 402 (H.L.), is the subject of numerous scholary comments; see, for example, Norrie, 1985 *S.L.T.* (News) 157; Parkinson, 1986 *Family Law* 11; Williams, 135 *New Law J.* 1156 and 1179 (1985); De Cruz, 1988 *Family Law* 306; Meyers, *Paediatric Forensic Medicine and Pathology*, Chap. 28.
39 §8(1).
40 Williams, 'The Gillick Saga II,' 135 *New Law J.* 1179, 1180 (1985).
41 *Johnston v. Wellesley Hosp.* (1970) 17 D.L.R.(3d) 139; see also, 1986 *Family Law* 11, 12; *J.S.C. and C.H.C. v. Wren* (1987) W.W. reps. 669 (C.A., Alberta).
42 *In the Matter of Anonymous (A Minor)*, (1987, Ala.App.) 515 So. 2d 1254; *Ballard v. Anderson* (1970) 4 Cal. 3d 873.
43 *Re P (A Minor)*, (1982) 80 L.G.R. 301
44 De Cruz, *Loc. Cit.*
45 *Re B. (A Minor)*, (1987) 2 W.L.R. 1213 (H.L.)
46 *T. v. T.* (1988) 2 W.L.R. 189 (Wood, J.)
47 See Brahams, 'Sterilization and Mental Handicap,' 1988 *The Lancet* 1377, 1378; Mental Health Act 1983, §57.
48 Mason, *Legal Issues in Human Reproduction*, p. 54; but cf. *Re B., supra*, 2 W.L.R. 1213.
49 *In Re F.* (1989) 2 W.L.R. 1025 (Lord Brandon).
50 *Re B* (1976) 1 All E.R. 326 (Heilbron, J.). Procreative freedom can, of course, be as much served by sterilization as not, depending on the wishes of the incompetent. See, *Conservatorship of Valerie N.* (1985) 40 Cal. 3d 143.
51 *Re Eve* (1986) 31 D.L.R. (4th) 1
52 Lord Templeman in *Re B.* (1987) 2 W.L.R. 1213 (H.L.); see also, Thomson, 'Sterilization of Mentally Handicapped Children,' 1988 *S.L.T.* (News) 1.

53 *R. v. Bourne* (1938) 3 All E.R. 615, 620 (this language was omitted from the later Law Reports version of the case, (1939) 1 K.B. 687).

54 (1988) 2 All E.R. 193, 2 W.L.R. 1288, 1293 (Slaughton, L.J.); *In Re F.* (1989) 2 W.L.R. 1025.

55 Bok, Sissela, 'Ethical Problems of Abortion,' in Shannon (ed), *Bioethics* (3d ed., 1987), p. 41.

56 Shepperdson, 'Abortion and Euthanasia of Down's Syndrome Children – The Parents' View' 9 *J. Med. Ethics* 152 (1983)

57 Fletcher, John 'Abortion, Euthanasia and Care of Defective Newborns,' in Shannon (ed.) *Bioethics, supra,* pp. 102–103.

58 Mason, *Legal Issues in Human Reproduction, supra,* p.67; cf., *Colautti v. Franklin* (1979) 439 U.S. 379 (state could not compel surgeon to abort by means most likely to permit fetal survival).

59 Abortion Act 1967, §4(1); see Brahams, 1988 *The Lancet* 893.

60 See, for example, Morgan, 'Foetal Sex Identification, Abortion and the Law,' 18 *Family Law* 355, 357 (1988)

61 *R. v. Bourne* (1939) 1 K.B. 687; *Paton v. British Pregnancy Advisory Service Trustees* (1978) 2 All E.R. 987.

62 Mason and McCall Smith, *Law and Medical Ethics,* (2d.ed.), p.80.

63 See the American legal position, as expressed in *Colautti v. Franklin* (1979) 439 U.S. 379; *American College of Obstetricians and Gynecologists* (1986) U.S., 106 S. Ct. 2169 (statutory obligation to use abortion method most likely to result in live birth of viable fetus, overturned as unreasonable interference with exercise of physician's clinical judgment.)

64 Tunkel, *supra,* 1985 *Crim. L.R.* 133, 140; Mason *Legal Issues in Human Reproduction, supra,* p.74.

65 *C. v. S.* (1987) 1 All E.R. 1230, (1988) Q.B. 135; *Paton v. British Pregnancy Advisory Service Trustees* (1979) Q.B. 276, (1978) 2 All E.R. 987.

66 *Los Angeles Times,* April 1, 1989, p.20.

67 Gordon, G.H., *The Criminal Law of Scotland.* Edinburgh: W. Green & Son, 1978 (2d. ed), p.812.

68 Smith, Professor Sir Thomas B., *A Short Commentary on the Law of Scotland.* Edinburgh: W. Green & Son, 1962, p.141.

69 Davis, 'The legalization of therapeutic abortion,' 1968 *S.L.T.* (News) 205; see, *H.M. Advocate v. Graham* (1897) 2 Adam 412.

70 In England The Offenses Against the Person Act 1861 §58, 59, provided no therapeutic privilege for abortion. The Infant Life (Preservation) Act 1929 provided that only saving the life of the mother justified destruction of a fetus capable of being born alive.

71 Norrie, 1985 *Crim. L. R.* p.482.

72 Smith, Professor Sir Thomas B., 'Law and the Human Body: the Relevance of Consent,' Address to the Royal Medical Society, Edinburgh, 17 Nov. 1967.

73 Anderson, *The Criminal Law of Scotland* (1892), p.76; note 72, *supra*.

74 *H.M. Advocate v. Graham, supra,* 2 Adam 412, at 415; Macdonald, *Criminal Law of Scotland* (5th ed.), p.114.

75 Witness the remarks of Lord Pres. Clyde in *Hunter v. Hanley* 1955 S.C. 200, 'It is a tribute to the high standard in general of the medical profession in Scotland that there are practically no decisions on this

question [the standard for medical malpractice liability] in the reported cases.' *Id.* at 205.

76 Davis, *supra*, 1968 *S.L.T.* (News) 205.

77 1967 c.87 (effective 27 April 1968).

78 §5(1) indicates the Abortion Act 1967 does not restrict the provisions of the Infant Life (Preservation) Act 1929, which prohibited destruction of a fetus capable of being born alive, unless necessary to save the life of the mother. However §5(1) expressly references the 1929 Act as one 'protecting the life of the viable foetus.' It seems logical to assume that Parliament by this reference indicated its belief that the provisions of the Abortion Act apply up to the stage of fetal viability, the provisions of the Infant Life (Preservation) Act 1929 starting with fetal viability and thereafter during pregnancy. Norrie, *supra*, note 13, disagrees; Mason & McCall Smith, *Law and Medical Ethics*. London: Butterworths, 1987 (2d. ed.), p.78, do not take a position on this issue.

79 This is a liberal construction of the Act in conjunction with the Infant Life (Preservation) Act 1929. It may be argued that the grounds stated for abortion apply in England only until the fetus is capable of being born alive, presumably at about 23–24 weeks in many instances, perhaps even earlier, although survival would not follow from such a live birth. (See text at notes 8 and 17, *supra*). However, this narrow construction seems unlikely. See Abortion Act 1967, s.5(1), and Infant Life (Preservation) Act 1929, §1(2). Parliament seems to agree. See Tunkel, 1985 *Crim. L.R.* 133, 134–5.

80 §7(3), 'This Act does not extend to Northern Ireland.'

81 §3(2).

82 *H.M. Advocate v. Anderson* 1928 J.C. 1,3; *H.M. Advocate v. Semple* 1937 J.C. 41, 45.

83 1928 J.C. 1, at 4 (Lord Anderson).

84 Offenses Against the Person Act 1861, §58, 59.

85 One can assert, however, that the purpose of the 1861 Statute was to protect the woman whether or not she was pregnant.

86 §5(2), 'For the pruposes of the law relating to abortion, anything done with intent to procure the miscarriage of a woman is unlawfully done unless authoried by Section 1 of this act.

87 Walker, *The Law of Delict in Scotland*. Edinburgh: W. Green & Son, 1981 (2d. ed.), p.493.

88 Gordon, *The Criminal Law of Scotland*, p.429.

89 *H.M. Advocate v. Rutherford*, 1947 J.C. 1.

90 Williams, Glanville, *The Sanctity of Life and the Criminal Law*. London: Faber & Faber, 1958, p. 152, Gordon, *supra*, p.812.

91 Norrie, 1985 *Crim. L. R.* 487; Norrie, 'The Gillick Case and Parental Rights in Scots Law,' 1985 *S.L.T.* (News) 157.

92 Meyers, 'Parental Rights and Consent to Medical Treatment of Minors,' in Mason (ed.) *Paediatric Forensic Medicine & Pathology*. London, Chapman & Hall, 1989; *Murray v. Fraser* 1916 S.C. 623; Norrie, 'The Gillick Case and Parental Rights in Scots Law,' 1985 *S.L.T. (News) 157, 159.*

93 *Harvey v. Harvey* (1860) 22 D. 1198, 1209 (Lord Justice, Clerk Inglis).

94 See *Gillick v. West Norfolk and Wisbech Area Health Authority* (1985) 3 All E.R. 402 (H.L.), *supra* (Lord Scarman); *JSC v. CHC Wren*, (1987)

W.W. Reps. 669 (C.A., Alberta), (discussed in De Cruz, 'Gillick in Canada,' 1988 *Family Law* 3060.

95 Institute of Med Ethics (1988) Bull. No. 36, p.15 (Select Committee, House of Lords).

96 Infant Life (Preservation) Act 1929, s.1(2).

97 McLean, *Medicine, Morals and the Law*, Aldershot: Gower, 1981, p.35.

98 McLean, S.A.M., 'Women, Rights & Reproduction,' in McLean (ed.), *Legal Issues in Human Reproduction*. Aldershot; Gower, 1989, pp 220–21.

99 Mason, *Human Life & Medical Practice*, p. 83.

100 In 1986, of 172,286 reported abortions in England and Wales, 144,857 (84 per cent) were carried out in the first 12 weeks. Only 8276 (5 per cent) were performed after 18 weeks, and of these, nearly 50 per cent (3688) were on non)resident women. That leaves only $2\frac{1}{2}$ per cent performed after 18 weeks on English and Welsh women. 296 *Brit. Med. J.* 446 (1988).

101 Mason, *Legal Issues in Human Reproduction*, pp.61–64. Scotland appears to have one of the lowest rates of abortion among British Commonwealth countries, reporting 8.8 per 1,000 women of childbearing age, or less than 1 in 100. England reported (for 1985) 12.97, the U.S.A. about 30, and New Zealand, 9.3. *Ibid.*

102 Calif.Penal Code §274 (1872).

103 Approximately 3 per cent of pregnancies result in a seriously malformed infant, but only about 1 per cent may be detected early by means of procedures such as amniocentesis. See Laurence, 'Prenatal Diagnosis, Selective Abortion and the Abortion Act (Amendment) Bill,' 1980 *The Lancet* 249.

104 *San Francisco Chronicle*, Feb. 6, 1989, pp. B3–B4.

105 Petit, 'Abortion Now a Safe Procedure,' *San Fran.Chron.*, Feb 6, 1989, p. B3.

106 Mason, *Issues in Human Reproduction, supra*, p.62.

107 *Griswold v. Connecticut* (1965) 381 U.S. 479 (contraceptive use by married couple could not be proscribed), (Douglas, J.).

108 *Skinner v. Oklahoma* (1942) 316 U.S. 535.

109 *Loving v. Virginia* (1967) 388 U.S. 1.

110 *Eisenstadt v. Baird* (1972) 405 U.S. 438.

111 *Pierce v. Society of Sisters* (1925) 268 U.S. 510; *Prince v. Massachusetts* (1944) 321 U.S. 158.

112 *Rochin v. California* (1952) 342 U.S. 165 (forced stomach pumping of accused improper as 'offensive to human dignity').

113 *Union Pac. Ry. Co. v. Botsford* (1891) 141 U.S. 250, 251.

114 410 U.S. 113, 163.

115 Yu, 1986 *Brit. Med. J.* 1200; 25 *Clin. Pediatrics* 391 (1986).

116 The Abortion Act 1967, when read in cnjunction with its effect on the Infant Life (Preservation) Act 1929, and the cases interpreting it (*R. v. Bourne* (1939) 1 K.B. 687; *R. v. Newton and Stungo* (1958) *Crim. L.R.* 467, 600).

117 See polls in *N.Y. Times*, Jan. 22, 1988, (25 per cent favored overturning *Roe*); *San Fran. Chron.*, Jan. 23, 1989, p. A4 (58 per cent opposed overturning *Roe*; 37 per cent supported overturning *Roe*); *San Fran.*

Chron., Feb. 21, 1989, p.1 (66 per cent support woman's right to first trimester abortion; 31 per cent second trimester; 15 per cent third trimester); and San Francisco Chronicle, July 26, 1989, p.1 (67 per cent approve of first trimester abortion; 74 per cent disapprove Constitutional Amendment outlawing abortion).

118 See Reidinger, 'Will *Roe v. Wade* Be Overruled?' *Amer. Bar Assn. J.*, July 1, 1988, p.69; compare *Roe* (7-2), with *Thornburgh, supra* (1986) U.S. 106 S. Ct. 2169 (5-4)

119 *Bowers v. Hardwick* (1986) 478 U.S. 186, 194 (right of privacy held not to encompass homosexual conduct in private between consenting adults.)

120 *Jacobson v. Massachusetts* (1985) 197 U.S. 11.

121 *Buck v. Bell* (1927) 274 U.S. 200. It is questionable that the compulsory sterilizations once upheld for so-called eugenic reasons would be upheld today, absent clear and convincing evidence of their necessity to protect the best interests of the individual concerned. See, *Conservatorship of Valerie N.* (1985) 40 Cal. 3d 143; *Re M* (1981, Alas.) 627 Pac. 2d 607.

122 *City of Akron v. Akron Center for Reproductive Health* (1983) 462 U.S. 416, 444.

123 *San Francisco Chronicle*, Oct. 4, 1989, p.A8.

124 *Doe v. Bolton* (1973) 410 U.S. 179, 192; *Colautti v. Franklin, supra,* 439 U.S. 379, 388–9.

125 *Planned Parenthood Assn. v. Ashcroft* (1983) 462 U.S. 476, 482.

126 *Thornburgh v. American College of Obstetricians and Gynecologists* (1986) U.S., 106 S. Ct. 2169.

127 Paul, 'Self-ownership, Abortion and Infanticide,' 5 *J. Med. Ethics* 133, 135 (1979).

128 *Roe v. Wade, supra*, 410 U.S. 113, 163–65; *In Re A.C.* (1987, D.C.App.) 533 A. 2d. 611; *Jefferson v. Griffin-Spalding Co. Hosp. Auth.* (1981, Ga.) 274 S.E. 2d. 457; cf. *Taft v. Taft* (1983), Mass) 446 N.E. 2d 395.

129 *Baird v. Atty Gen.* (1977, Mass.) 360 N.E. 2d. 288; *Cardwell v. Bechtol* (1987, Tenn.) 724 S.W. 2d 739.

130 *Ballard v. Anderson* (1970) 4 Cal 3d 873; *Cobbs v. Grant* (1973) 8 Cal 3d 229; *City of Akron v. Akron Ctr. for Reproductive Health* (1983) 462 U.S. 416, 439–40.

131 *Matter of Anonymous* (1987, Ala. App.) 515 So. 2d. 1254; *Ballard v. Anderson* (1970) 4 Cal. 3d. 873.

132 *Planned Parenthood Assn. v. Ashcroft* (1983) 462 U.S. 476, 492.

133 Cal. Civ. Code §34.5 (amendment to require parental consent or court order pending).

134 *Planned Parenthood Assn. v. Ashcroft* (1983) 462 U.S. 476. *Akron v. Akron Ctr. for Repro. Health* (1983) 462 U.S. 416; appellate courts in both Florida and California have recently found laws requiring parental consent before mature minors can consent to abort appear to violate minors' privacy rights quaranteed expressly by state constitutions. Calif. Assn. of Hosps., *News*, Oct 13, 1989, pp. 1–2; *Napa Register*, Oct. 13 ,1989, p.12.

135 *In Re Moe* (1987, Mass.) 517 N.E. 2d 170; *Bellotti v. Baird* (1976) 428 U.S. 132.

136 *Rasmussen v. Fleming* (1987, Ariz.) 741 Pac.2d. 674, 686; *John F. Kennedy Mem. Hosp. v. Bludworth* (1984, Fla.) 452 So. 2d 921.

137 *Foy v. Greenblott* (1983) 141 Cal. App. 3d 1.

138 Cal. Probate Code §2356(d).

139 *Conservatorship of Valerie N.* (1985) 40 Cal.3d 143, 168.

140 *Guardianship of Hayes* (1980, Wash.) 608 Pac. 2d 635; *Wentzel v. Montgomery Gen. Hosp. Inc.* (1982), Md.) 447 A. 2d. 1244.

141 *Re Hier* (1984, Mass.App.) 464 N.E. 2d 959.

142 *Conservatorship of Hargis* (1984) Napa Co. (Cal.) Super. Ct. No. 21248 (no appeal).

143 *Wall St. J.* 5 July 1989, p. B1.

144 *Webster v. Reproductive Health Services, Inc.*, (July 3, 1989) U.S., 109 S.Ct. 3040 (For: Rehnquist, White, O'Connor, Scalia, Kennedy, J.J. Against: Marshall, Brennan, Blackmun, and Stevens, J.J.)

145 *Roe v. Wade* (1973) 410 U.S. 113; *Doe v. Bolton* (1973) 410 U.S. 179 ('the freedom to care for one's health and person' per Mr. Justice William O. Douglas, concurring). See also discussion in Chapters 10 and 11, *infra* on constitutional right to refuse medical treatment, even if life-saving.

146 *Time*, 17 July 1989, pp. 62)4; *Newsweek* 17 July, 1989, pp. 14)20.

147 *Wall St. J.* 5 July 1989, p. A12.

148 *Colautti v. Franklin* (1979) 439 U.S. 379; accord, *Thornburgh v. American College of Obstetricians and Gynecologists* (1986) 106 S. Ct. 2169 (state's interest in viable fetus preservation 'cannot justify any regulation that imposes a quantifiable medical risk upon the pregnant woman' per White, J., dissenting in reference to effect of majority opinion in his view.)

149 For example, a poll of Americans conducted by *Hippocrates* magazine and the Gallup organization in 1988 found 56 per cent supported abortion in the face of diagnosed Down's syndrome or other major birth defects, 34 per cent were opposed and 10 per cent undecided. The same poll found 78 per cent supported abortion where necessary to protect the mother from serious health risks, 17 per cent were opposed and 5 per cent undecided. *San Francisco Chronicle*, 'This World,' p.9 (July 3, 1988).

150 See *In Re B (A Minor)*, (1981) 1 W.L.R. 1421; *U.S. v. University Hosp.* (1984, 2d cir.) 729 Fed. 2d 144; *In Re L.H.R.* (1984, Ga.) 321 S.E. 2d 716; see also Mason and Meyers, 'Parental Choice and Selective Non-treatment of Deformed Newborns: A View from Mid-Atlantic,' 1986 *J. Med. Ethics* 67.

Note In 1990, a Bill is going through Parliament which will lower the legal presumption that a child is capable of being born alive from 28 weeks, as originally noted in the Infant Life (Preservation) Act 1929, to 24 weeks. This comports with current medical and legal thought as to the time of commencement of fetal viability. However, it will also make it clear that there are no time limits as to any abortion deemed medically necessary in order to avoid 'grave permanent injury to the physical and mental health of the pregnant woman' or because of the risk of serious fetal handicap in the mental or physical health of the child. Most believe the net effect of these changes will be to liberalize the protective application of the Abortion Act 1967.

The change from 28 to 24 weeks as to presumed age for live birth is of little practical significance. In 1988, of 183,798 abortions reported in Britain only 23 occurred after 24 weeks gestation.

3

Promises and Pitfalls of the New Reproductive Technology

A. INTRODUCTION

Nowhere have biomedical technological advances been greater than in reproductive medicine. Procedures unheard of just a few years ago are now assisting couples, unable to conceive and bear children as the result of sexual intercourse, to have children. These advances are seen by some as a precious gift to those who cannot bear children normally. To others, they raise the moral and legal spectre of abortion, child destruction, treating children and wombs as commodities to be bought or rented, and disintegration of the traditional physical and emotional bonds between parents and child.

The new reproductive technology includes many procedures. Artificial insemination is a process by which the male seminal fluid is collected and artificially injected into the womb in the hopes of fertilizing the female egg. The sperm can come from a donor where the husband is infertile ('artificial insemination donor' or AID), may be a combination of donor and husband sperm ('artificial insemination husband and donor' or AIHD), or may be the husband's sperm where there may be technical reproductive problems other than male sterility ('artificial insemination husband' or AIH).

The female egg, or ovum, may be collected, stored, fertilized outside the womb, and implanted in the womb. This is known as *in vitro* fertilization (IVF). At present, neither Britain nor Australia permits the use of stored ova for IVF. The ova may come from the wife, or may come from a donor. The sperm used to fertilize the egg may be the husband's, if he is fertile, or that of a donor.

If the wife is unable to implant or carry the fertilized egg (the zygote), the resulting embryo, or the later developing fetus, the couple may commission another woman, a surrogate, to carry the baby for them. Fertilization may occur, *in utero*, by sexual intercourse or by artificial insemination,[2] or *in vitro* as a result of laboratory fertilization of donated ovum and sperm.

Infertility drugs, designed to stimulate female ovulation, or surgical implantation of multiple embryos in the uterus to enhance one 'taking' may

54

result in multiple pregnancies and the need – to protect the health of the mother and to improve the chances of a healthy birth – to practice 'selective reduction of pregnancy.'[3]

The embryos resulting from *in vitro* fertilization may be frozen for future use, as may sperm and ova. The woman bearing a child may not have contributed any genetic material to its makeup. Women may produce children outside the traditional family model, without any sexual relationship to the father, or because of an agreement to bear the child for another in return for money.

Few laws exist to regulate this technology. Both the law and medical practice are developing in this area. As we will see in the chapters to follow, the law almost always lags behind developments in medical practice. The law is often cumbersome and slow to react. The law normally does not develop before a fairly clear moral consensus has developed. While our common legal systems seek to adopt laws which are moral, so that what is unlawful is also immoral, the law does not proscribe all that is immoral. It may be immoral for a passerby not to try and save a drowning man, but it is not unlawful. Hopefully, all that is unlawful is immoral, but not all that is immoral is unlawful. Nowhere is this more clear than in the laws regulating the new reproductive technologies.

What tends to occur is that technological advances prompt opportunities for changes and improvements in medical practice. Existing laws, unless given a tortured interpretation, often do not contemplate such changes and neither condone nor condemn them. The result is a permissive, or at least uncertain, legal climate which encourages those practitioners anxious to apply the new practices for the aid of their patients to do so. The resulting medical practice is reported in the scholarly journals, discussed in the media to an increasingly 'hi-tech'-oriented society of medical care consumers, and debated by doctors, lawyers, more recently bioethicists, and laypeople. From this interaction evolves a consensus, at which point the law is normally prepared to intervene. That intervention may often start as one or more relatively isolated court decisions, which may be a precursor of others to follow,[4] or it may take the form of a broad[5] or very narrow[6] legislative enactment.

In either case, the law has traditionally tended to follow good medical practice; that is, with few exceptions,[7] the law has accepted prevailing medical practice, once a clear consensus exists, as setting the proper legal and moral limits of acceptable conduct.[8] Since consensus does not develop overnight, the law has usually been content to await the development of that consensus without too much meddling in the process.

In recent times this process has broken down. The development of a clear medical consensus concerning many of these controversial practices has been slow to develop or to be articulated. Not infrequently the public, as well as the doctors themselves, have been unwilling to have the legality of such new and morally difficult practices decided by the medical profession alone. When doctors in England recently asked a judge for permission to discontinue further life-sustaining treatment for a four month old severely and hopelessly brain damaged infant, with which decision the parents agreed, the response of the British Medical Association was, somewhat surprisingly,

> 'It is quite proper that the decision of whether Baby C. should be allowed to live or die should not be taken by doctors alone.'[9]

Thus, the traditional formation of medical consensus, and the reliance of the law thereon, has not occurred in the field of new reproductive technology. Changes have been too rapid and manifold. Moral feelings are more pronounced and disparate than in other areas of medical practice. Doctors have not felt confident to articulate clear practice standards and guidelines. Consensus has not been evident. The result is considerable uncertainty, limited new laws to regulate these practices, sometimes unproductive attempts to rely upon pre-existing legal precedents or rules that have little clear application, and an unsettled and unsatisfactory legal and medical practice environment.

Against this backdrop we will look at selected medical and legal developments in Britain, in the United States and, in passing, elsewhere. From such a review may come at least the outline of certain legal standards for fairly dealing with these new procedures – exciting and promising on the one hand, yet highly controversial, subject to abuse and potentially harmful on the other. We turn first to the United Kingdom.

B.   ENGLAND AND SCOTLAND

1.   *Artificial insemination*

The practice of artificial insemination, both AIH and AID, has been carried out for many years with few legal restraints. It is not unlawful. There is no law requiring husband and wife to conceive a child solely by means of sexual intercourse.

However, several legal issues have been raised concerning AIH. For example, may a prisoner use AIH to father a child while incarcerated?[10] If conjugal rights are not given, AIH may provide the only realistic avenue for conception. On 'wholly exceptional grounds' this has been permitted by the Home Office, but on rare occasion only. It has been suggested such a denial violates the rights of the prisoner, as well as his wife, 'to marry and to found a family according to the national laws governing the exercise of this right,' as provided by Article 12 of the European Human Rights Convention. The question is whether prisoners sacrifice this right as a result of conviction and incarceration. If the period of incarceration is substantial, both husband

and wife request the privilege, and it may be accomplished without any significant interference with prison administration goals, then it seems a right that should be honored. An interesting question is raised where the wife is not able to economically support the proposed child. Here the state's interest in avoiding fatherless family environments and additional children on welfare, when added to the punitive purpose of imprisonment, may well be adequate to outweigh the individual prisoner's right to procreate.

Sperm may be stored by freezing for a considerable length of time without affecting its potency. As a result, women have been inseminated well after their husband's donation and subsequent death. This raises several issues. Is the child to be considered illegitimate and born out of wedlock? Is the child entitled under British law to share in the father's estate?[11] This is particularly problematic if use of the sperm, conception, and birth occur long after the father's estate is settled. The Warnock Committee, which studied the problem in 1984, recommended that a child conceived by AIH must be *in utero* at the time of the father's death in order to share in his estate.[12] This seems sensible, to make the position comparable to normally conceived children.

A child born by AIH is, of course, the child of husband and wife. Where AID is used, due to male infertility, the resulting child is generally considered to be the legitimate child of the husband if he consented to the procedure.[13] This is law in England, but suprisingly it has not been expressly extended to Scotland.[14] With or without the husband's consent, a Scottish court has opined the artificially inseminated wife cannot be guilty of adultery.[15] This seems sound, since the element of extra-marital intercourse is absent. It would nonetheless seem to be a breach of one of the basic tenets of marriage – that the child rearing decision be consensual between spouses (or at least volitional where conception is the unintended but foreseeable consequence of intercourse). Mason and McCall Smith suggest, quite rightly so, that AID without the husband's consent may well constitute intolerable conduct for the purpose of divorce.[16]

AID also raises the issue of the unmarried woman's right to conceive a child. The Human Rights Convention, for example, extends the right to bear children to married couples, not to a single woman. Catholic morality points to the 'reciprocal commitment of spouses'[17] to conception and would find such a practice, as well as other third party donors in the conception process,[18] to be a violation of the marriage covenant and of basic human values concerning marriage, persons, and the family.[19] In practical social terms, what must be balanced here is the desire and freedom of the unmarried woman to have a child against the disadvantages to the child of being born into a home with only one parent. Since the best interests of the child must be given priority,[20] it is clear that legislation could prohibit such a practice if felt necessary to limit the number of (already substantial) fatherless families.

It is well established that the donor of sperm should remain anonymous,[21] that sound practice standards should limit the number of children any one donor may father by AID,[22] that the donor should have no support or other parental obligations to the resulting child,[23] and, less clear, that the child, upon reaching majority, should be entitled to learn limited genetic information about his or her donor father.[24] There are those who disagree that this latter 'right to know' is wise,[25] and find it quite different from such rights in the context of adoption. Even the Government, while presently supportive of such disclosure if desired by the child, is not at all sure of its position.[26]

Approximately 1,500 to 2,000 children are born each year in the United Kingdom as a result of AID. This is not insignificant, but its notoriety and controversy has been eclipsed more recently by IVF and surrogacy.

2.   *In Vitro Fertilization (IVF)*

Female eggs (ova) may be collected from a woman, whether or not the wife of the sperm donor, and mixed with sperm in a laboratory dish to accomplish fertilization and the creation of a zygote. Thereafter, the fertilized egg may be placed in the womb, or fallopian tubes, in the hopes of accomplishing implantation.[27] It is even possible for both ova and sperm to be donated where both husband and wife are infertile.[28]

It has been estimated that more than 1,000 children have been born in Britain as a result of IVF. However, despite suggestions for its legal regulation,[29] the practice is not presently controlled by legislation. For example, the embryo *in vitro* is not protected from destruction, whereas the embryo *in utero* is by laws against procuring miscarriage, child destruction, and abortion.

To date, embryos have not been kept alive *in vitro* for more than 10 days.[30] Both the Warnock Committee, which studied the issue in 1984, as well as more recent Government proposals for legislation, suggest that embryo research be limited to the first 14 days after fertilization.[31] By this time 'twinning' occurs if it is going to and the so-called 'primitive streak' appears, a heaping up of cells at one end of the embryonic tissue. Most medical and ethical bodies to consider the issue have agreed with this limitation.[32] However, there is no neural or brain development and no identifiable human characteristics at this early stage. Some argue that different stages from 14 days up to 10 weeks is a more appropriate limit, based on development of first nervous tissue and then the brain, for prohibiting embryo research and use.[33] Any cutoff point is undoubtedly an arbitrary stage of embryo development. We are talking about a continuous process. Short of foetal viability, one cannot say with any certainty that at a particular stage an embryo definitely has the potential to develop into a person.[34] That certainly seems true at only 14 days old.[35] On the other hand there are those who would say creation of the embryo is the start of life and no use of it aside from implantation in the womb should be permitted.

The ability to freeze an embryo resulting from IVF raises many legal issues. For example, there is the question of who owns the frozen embryo and whether, after legal separation or divorce, the wife still has a right to its 'custody' and implantation even if the father objects. One U.S. trial court judge recently ruled the wife does enjoy this right, holding 'it is in the manifest best interest of the child or children, *in vitro*, that they be made available for implantation.[36] Child support, visitation and final custody was deferred pending a live birth from the implantation.

In an Australian case, AID was used because of the husband's infertility. The wife provided eggs for *in vitro* fertilization (IVF). One of the resulting embryos was implanted in the woman, but two other embryos were frozen for future use.[37] The mother miscarried and she and her husband thereafter died 'intestate,' or without a will. This meant their estate would be shared by their legal heirs. The issue was raised as to whether the frozen embryos had a 'right' to be implanted into a surrogate mother and to inherit as heirs the sizable estate. A special committee appointed by the government concluded the embryos had neither a right to be implanted, carried by a surrogate and born, nor to claim any inheritance as heirs,[38] and should be destroyed. However, special legislation was passed by the state of Victoria providing that the embryos should if possible be implanted in a willing surrogate mother, to be placed for adoption, presumably without inheritance rights, after birth. Doctors have been reluctant to implant them in any volunteer mothers because of concerns the genetic material used to create the embryos had not been tested for AIDS and because the freezing technique used for them in 1981 is unlikely to permit survival.[39] While their fate is unclear, the case points out that storage of sperm, ova, or the resulting embryo by freezing does raise legal issues, among others, of paternity, legitimacy, preservation of a living embryo and inheritance.

It is estimated there are at present as many as 10,000 frozen embryos awaiting implantation in Australia and perhaps 20,000 in Europe. Some countries, like Britain, disallow such storage.

In 1990, Parliament voted (364–193) to permit embryo research up to 14 days of embryonic existence, as recommended by the Warnock Committee. The research will be regulated for legal and ethical propriety by a new statutory body, the Human Fertilisation and Embryology Authority.[40] Since no definite scientific answer can be given to what is basically a matter of personal philosophy,[41] it seems the issue of continued embryo research will be decided on a practical and ethical basis: may the *in vitro* embryo be sacrificed at times, with the consent of its donors, in order to promote medical research? It seems probable the answer will be yes.[42] The research and fertility benefits for many would seem to promise a greater good than the implantation of all *in vitro* embryo *in utero*. We will discuss the related topic of using embryonic and fetal tissue for transplantation to others in Chapter 7.

Legislation, when adopted, will probably formally establish a licensing agency which will be required to approve many of the new reproductive techniques. A voluntary agency, the Interim Licensing Authority, now exists. Permits will probably be required for programs involved with AID, IVF, embryo research, storage, and transfer, and with surrogacy.[32] Limits will be set on the type, duration and purpose of embryo research and storage, on standards of practice and, where applicable, confidentiality for AID, IVF and surrogacy, and sanctions will be set for violation.

The state of Victoria, a pioneer in this field, provides by its Infertility (Medical Procedures) Act that IVF clinics keep confidential information on the biological origins of gamete donors so the resulting child may some day learn of his biological origins, genetic material donated must be tested to avoid disease transmission, embryo storage beyond five years is to be discouraged, that couples undergo 12 months of fertility counseling before being accepted as candidates for IVF, that donor couples specify uses of their eggs, sperm and resulting embryos, releases the donors from any rights to or responsibilities for the resulting child, and bans the creation or storage of embryos for the purpose of experimentation.[39]

For those otherwise childless, IVF may hold the only hope of bearing a child. Reasonable standards for access to the practice are likely. In a recent case, for example, a hospital refused to place a woman on its IVF waiting list after learning she had been rejected by the local agency as a foster or adoptive parent due to criminal convictions for offenses related to prostitution. The rejection was upheld, the hospital being entitled to establish reasonable access standards.[43] Parents are not normally subject to eligibility standards, but where scarce and state of the art resources are needed to facilitate a pregnancy, such standards seem sensible and inevitable and, so long as not based on social standing or wealth, not unfair.[44]

3. *Selective reduction of pregnancy*

Where certain female fertility problems exist, it is generally true that the introduction of several embryos into the womb or fallopian tubes for possible uterine wall implantation increases the odds of a pregnancy successfully 'taking.' However, if more than two embryos attach themselves to the uterine wall, then the risk to the mother's health as pregnancy progresses is increased. Also, the likelihood of one or more healthy, live births, decreases. Superovulatory (fertility) drugs are given or multiple embryos are implanted by the physician in the hopes of maximizing the chances of creating pregnancy. However, this may cause the physician and mother to have to face the prospect of eliminating one or more implanted embryos to enhance the chances of a successful conclusion to that pregnancy once it is created.

The procedure used to accomplish this is called selective reduction of pregnancy. In effect it is abortion, without expelling the embryo or fetus. A needle penetrates the embryo's heart, guided through the mother's abdomen by ultrasound, resulting in death and absorption of the embryonic tissue. In theory it can be said to be the opposite of abortion, whose aim is to end a pregnancy. The aim of selective reduction is to save a pregnancy.

Only 200 or so of these procedures have been done to date in the United States.[45] Probably less in Britain. Many are preventable by limiting the number of embryos transferred to the womb. The Voluntary Licensing Authority, a professional body presently without statutory powers, but imposing professional standards by voluntary compliance, only licenses implanting of up to three embryos at any one time.[46] There are still reports, in a few instances, of doctors transferring up to 12 to 15 embryos in the case of very difficult patient pregnancy problems.[47] This seems irresponsible. While reasonable efforts to effect pregnancy are warranted for the childless, such excessive implantations seem unreasonable, with little thought of the embryo reduction implications. It seems likely such practices will be prohibited.

However, with limitations, the practice of selective reduction will very likely continue. It has been undertaken since about 1980 and is apparently supported by the majority of physicians. It may be used at times because of fetal abnormality or other medical indications, as well as to reduce the risk of pregnancy complications.[48]

Aside from its technical difficulty and the moral issues it raises concerning embryo destruction, selective reduction poses another dilemma. It must be performed early in pregnancy, often before fetal abnormality can be detected with reasonable accuracy.[49] The result is that a healthy embryo may be destroyed leaving what may be an abnormal one to develop. The normal practice is to leave twins, but to remove the third or additional implanted embryos because of the increased risks they pose.[50]

If reasonable restraint is placed on the number of embryos transferred to the womb, assuming proper consent,[51] and a reasonable medical consensus that reduction is necessary to protect the health of the mother or of the other developing embryos, the practice seems both lawful and ethical.[52] Abortion is expressly authorized to protect the health of the mother or of existing children under the Abortion Act 1967.[53] Thus, it seems appropriate that selective reduction of pregnancy, performed to protect the physical health of the mother or of the remaining embryos, to remove an abnormal embryo, or to protect the mother's emotional health by acting to protect her pregnancy should come within the protection of the Act.[54] However, this has yet to be resolved.

4. *the surrogate mother*

A surrogacy contract is an agreement by which a surrogate or substitute mother agrees to bear a child for another woman who either cannot, or does not wish to, carry a child to term. These situations have arisen where the wife is either infertile or cannot carry a pregnancy. In the former situation the husband donates his sperm, either by artificial insemination or sexual intercourse, to the woman who has agreed to act as surrogate. In the latter situation husband and wife donate sperm and ova for IVF and subsequent embryo transfer to the surrogate.

Thereafter, the surrogate carries the child to term, and if she honors her agreement, delivers up custody of the child to the 'commissioning' parents. The child is at least biologically related to the husband of the infertile wife. Consent is normally solicited from the husband of the surrogate if she is married.

The surrogate and her husband agree, in advance, to not only turn over custody of the child, but also to give up all parental rights to the child. Payment is normally made to the mother, at least to reimburse her for pregnancy expenses and loss of earnings. There is not any established payment amount, although about £5,000 to £10,000 seems to have been agreed in several reported cases. This is considerably less than the probable expenses for a successful IVF-based pregnancy.[85]

The 'Baby Cotton' case brought surrogacy arrangements into the limelight in Britain in 1985. The father in America contracted with an agency to locate a surrogate mother to conceive with his donated sperm and to carry the resulting baby for him and his infertile wife.[55] A willing mother was located in England, through the use of another agency, she conceived, bore the child and delivered it to the father and his wife without ever having met them. The local agency applied for a temporary place of safety order from the court, which was granted, it then completed its investigation as to the welfare of the child, supported the application of the commissioning 'parents,' and the Judge awarded them custody.[56] They were permitted to remove the child to the United States. The mother did not object.

The case aroused considerable controversy. The result was legislation, the Surrogacy Arrangements Act 1985.[57] The Act prohibits commercial surrogacy arrangements: advertising, promoting, negotiating or contracting surrogacy services for another. It does not, however, prohibit private arrangements. A woman is free to become a surrogate as the result of a direct arrangement. A father is free to make a direct arrangement with a surrogate mother and to pay her for her services. The effect of the Act has been to eliminate surrogacy agencies or the advertising of or for surrogacy services. This doubtless has reduced the opportunities for and the incidence of such arrangements.

English courts have denied transfer of custody from a surrogate mother to the commissioning father, where the natural mother was unwilling to voluntarily give up custody.[58] The courts see their fundamental role as acting to promote the welfare of the child. The bond between mother and child may well make it best for the child that custody remain with the mother. Parties to a surrogacy arrangement may not by such a contract detract from the inherent and legislatively granted wardship jurisdiction of the courts to act in the best interests of a child – that is true whether the issue is medical treatment, adoption, legal custody, or otherwise.[59] Thus, the provisions of a surrogacy contract will not be enforced, unless they happen to coincide with the best interests of the child. Even in that event the contract is not really being enforced, but rather the best interests of the infant are being promoted.

A further reason to find a surrogacy agreement uninforceable is the Children Act 1975, which applies in England and Wales, but not to Scotland.[60] It provides that a person may not surrender or transfer parental rights or duties to another person. A surrogacy agreement seeks to do just that. In addition, the Adoption Act 1958 prohibits anyone from offering a reward to another in return for adoption of a child.

Whether a payment was made for adoption will depend on the facts of any given case.[61] In a 1987 case a surrogate mother became pregnant after sexual intercourse with the father, delivered a healthy baby and gave possession to the commissioning parents after accepting only £5,000 of an agreed £10,000 payment. When the baby was two adoption was sought and an order granting it made, on evidence it was in the child's best interests. The payment to the surrogate was by a private party and upheld as simply reimbursement for services rendered or expenses incurred.[62] The Surrogacy Arrangements Act 1985 does not prohibit such payments between private parties. Adoption had not been thought of until afterwards opined the court. That seems rather unlikely, but the Court seems to have rightly been looking for a way to fulfill the expectations of the parties which clearly appeared to be in the best interests of the young child.

Even where payment was involved, an English court has upheld adoption by the commissioning parents, with the consent of the surrogate mother.[61] However, the court pointed out the reasons people should give pause before entering such arrangements:

'Other than those outlawed by the Surrogacy Arrangements Act 1985, surrogacy arrangements are not against the law as it stands. But those contemplating taking this path should have their eyes open to the kind of pitfalls, obstacles and anxiety they are likely to meet... These people have had three years of unremitting anxiety and many moments of distress, though I know that it has all been worthwhile for them in the end.

... in other cases it might well not end up happily. In the nature of things those who undertake the role of surrogate mother are those with very strong maternal instincts. The likelihood must be there that when the baby arrives the mother cannot bear to part with it. The trauma and turmoil then for all needs no describing.

One cannot sit in these courts and hear all the multitude of professionals and others without knowing well the depth of longing in couples, devoted to each other, who cannot have a child through no fault of their own. But before they go down the path of surrogacy they should know and know fully what it may entail. It is not a primrose path.'[62]

To illustrate the problems that can result, in another 1987 case a surrogate mother gave birth to twins following AID. She, however, refused to part with the children. The local authority sided with the mother. The court declared that, as in any other wardship proceeding, the best interests of the child must control.[63] The court left custody with the mother, citing the factors that she had borne the twins, cared for them for 5 months since birth, her care was satisfactory, and the infants had bonded with their mother.[64]

These cases suggest several conclusions: (1) while private surrogacy arrangements are not unlawful, they will not be enforced by the courts; (2) the best interests of the child will control where disputes over child custody arise between parties to the arrangement; (3) normally this will mean that custody will remain with the natural mother,[58,60,63] unless the baby has been given up and has had a good chance to bond with the commissioning parents because of the passage of substantial time in their custody;[65] (4) the natural mother is free to change her mind, it is not surprising she will often want to keep the child, and without her free consent transfer of custody will be most unlikely.[66]

The Government is proposing legislation which will make it clear that surrogacy agreements are unenforceable in all respects.[67] However, surrogacy is not proposed to become criminal beyond the Surrogacy Arrangements Act 1985. Thus, individuals will be free to pursue surrogacy arrangements privately, but either may dishonor whatever bargain is made without legal recourse. The idea here is not to encourage the practice, to have no legal rights interfere with the welfare of the child, and to leave further regulation to the time when a clearer consensus exists as to the advisability of the practice.

While no clear social consensus may have formed on surrogacy, most comment seems to be critical. The Warnock Committee felt surrogacy was an attack on the value of the marital relationship, distorted the normal relationship between mother and child and could damage the child. The British medical Association is opposed to the practice because of the risks to the well-being of the child.[68]

Others have seen the practice as exploitative of the woman, in effect 'womb leasing' for pay, compromising of the child's self-identity, moving subtly toward the practice of eugenics and a distortion of 'basic human values on life, marriage and the family.'[22]

A West German appellate court, in refusing to enforce a surrogacy agreement, found that its 'manifest treatment of the child as merchandise offended the basic legal and moral order.'[69] French law is similar, holding that since human beings cannot be traded, any surrogacy agreement is unenforceable.[70]

The potential exploitation of the woman comes not just from her use as an incubator for another, but also from the financial pressures on the disadvantaged to act as surrogate for pay. As evidence of this concern, it has been reported that some 40 percent of surrogate mothers in the United States are unemployed or on welfare.[71]

On the other hand, strong argument can be made that where surrogacy is the only reasonable treatment alternative open to an infertile couple and the wife cannot safely carry a child, it should be permitted between fully informed, consenting adults. Such an approach, however, seems to look only at the desires of the parents, not at the impact of the practice on the children that result from it and the surrogate who accomplishes the birth for the parents-to-be. One issue is whether the would-be mother can even give a truly free and knowing consent before pregnancy – with its strong physical and emotional impact upon her – and birth have occurred.[72]

If permitted, then a good case can be made that commercial agents be outlawed, that payment be limited to actual medical expenses and loss of earnings, that the mother have a reasonable time after birth to rescind the agreement, that the father have no paternity or support obligations if the mother does so, and that once custody is transferred from mother to commissioning couple, they be eligible for full adoption rights and have all normal parental obligations of care and support for the child.

It may be wise to be satisfied with individual court decisions, relying on the welfare of the child, to decide these issues until a clearer social consensus on surrogacy is reached. At that time a legislative solution seems appropriate.

We turn now to the United States to see how its courts and legislators have dealt with these issues.

C.   THE UNITED STATES

1.   *Artificial Insemination*

Artificial insemination, both AIH and AID, exists through the United States. While these practices are generally accepted, they are not promoted. A few states in fact prohibit AID and treat it as the legal equivalent of adultery.[73] Beyond recognizing the status of the child, few laws regulate the practice, which is largely left to be dealt with by existing legal principles of consent, contract and good medical practice.

Since there are at any one time 10 to 15 percent of married couples who are infertile for one reason or another, the demand for both AIH and AID seems clear. AIH does not appear to present any problems legally or morally. As Father McCormick has pointed out, while a child should be the fruit of the parents' love, to conclude 'a child must always be born of an act of sexual lovemaking is to imply that the only act of love in marriage is an act of sexual lovemaking . . . A child can be born of technological intervention and still be the result, the product, of an act of love.'[74]

On the other hand, the Catholic Holy See has condemned AID as allowing a third party to intrude into the intimacy and unity of the marriage. It is seen as a violation of the 'reciprocal commitment of spouses and a grave lack of regard of that essential property of marriage, which is its unity.'[75] This viewpoint has not, with few exceptions, been adopted by American legislatures and AID by and large remains a lawful procedure. However, husbands, following divorce, have legally challenged their obligation to support an AID child. Arguments have been raised of no paternity or of adultery. This is a difficult position to assert when the husband's consent to the AID was obtained at the time (and this is, of course, standard practice). Most of the states, in such circumstances, consider the child to be the legitimate offspring of the husband and wife.[76] Many states presume the consent of the husband where the child is born during wedlock, requiring the husband to rebut this with clear evidence to the contrary.[77]

2.   *In vitro fertilization*

IVF enjoys a much less settled legal status than AIH or AID. It not only may raise the issue of involving a third party in the reproductive decision of husband and wife as does AID, but it also raises concerns about embryo research and use of embryonic tissue. The practice is as yet too recent and the development of a social and moral consensus is as yet unclear. As a result, the law and public policy is still largely in the discussion and formulation stages.

Issues between husband and wife have yet to be clearly resolved. Divorce may interfere with plans for the use of ova, sperm or embryos. In a recent Tennessee case a couple donated sperm and ova for IVF after the wife suffered five tubal pregnancies. Seven laboratory embryos resulted. Before they were implanted the husband filed for divorce. Despite that, the wife sought to pursue implantation of the embryos. The husband objected, asserting the embryos were joint property and without his consent could not be implanted in his estranged wife because it would be a violation of his right to become a father.[78] The trial court sided with the wife, finding the embryos were entitled to be implanted in order to protect their 'manifest best interest' in living.[36] The Judge stated, 'Life begins at conception.' Issues of child support, permanent custody and visitation were deferred by the court until it was ascertained whether any of the embryos would survive implantation and mature to a live birth. Use of the embryos has been enjoined pending an appeal by the husband.

It can be argued that both husband and wife should consent to an embryo implantation, given their presumed joint obligation to financially support and nurture the child. However, the rights of the embryo are clearly implicated. Some argue the issue is one for the parents, the frozen embryo being too 'rudimentary' in human development to enjoy legal rights.[79] The issue may well be decided by legislation. Although a father may not be able to force an abortion,[80] he may be granted the right to prevent embryo implantation.[81] It seems either party should retain this right. However, once implantation goes forward, the matter should then be one to be decided by the woman carrying the embryo and her physician.

Some states prohibit any research on an embryo that would threaten its life or health.[82] While a large number of states prohibit or restrict research on fetuses, this is normally not applicable to *in vitro* fertilization. The fertilized egg passes from zygote, to blastocyst, to embryo, and then to fetus at 8 or more weeks gestation. Since the fertilized egg has, to date, remained *in vitro* for only the beginning few days of embryonic life, the concerns about research or other use of fetal tissue do not arise. As in Britain, the U.S. Ethics Advisory Board also concluded that the *in vitro* embryo should only be the subject of research before implantation and not beyond its fourteenth day of development.[83]

IVF centers have been established in various states, including California, New York, Texas, Virginia and Tennessee. There are now 20 or more centers in operation. They each service up to 400 patients per year, who may pay $5,000 to $10,000 for initial screening, egg recovery, *in vitro* fertilization and subsequent embryo transfer.[84] Since each procedure only carries with it about a 10 percent chance of successful implantation and pregnancy, many such procedures may be required, suggesting total costs of $50,000 may not be unexpected for the persistent couple.[85] This may restrict the practice to one largely available only to the rich, since insurance policies are likely to decline coverage for IVF on the grounds that either it is 'experimental' treatment or not 'medically necessary' for the patient.[86]

Despite the growth of IVF in the United States, because of its potential to assist infertile women bear children,[87] and the controversy surrounding the practice, it remains essentially unregulated. Louisiana in 1986 became the first state to legislate in this area, prohibiting the sale or destruction of embryos and declaring they enjoy 'certain' unspecified rights under the law. In 1975 the Federal Department of Health and Human Services issued regulations requiring health providers receiving federal aid to submit any IVF research proposal to the newly-established Ethics Advisory Board for approval.[88] The Board was appointed, studied the issues raised by IVF, and published its conclusions in 1979.[83] Soon thereafter the Board was dissolved, the Reagan administration thereby taking the federal health establishment out of the field (presumably to discourage IVF and its funding, at least at the federal level).

The conclusions of the Ethics Advisory Board represent one of the few clearly articulated public policy statements on IVF in the United States to date. The Board concluded, among other things, that,

1. the human embryo was entitled to 'profound respect,' although, at least by implication, not to the same degree of legal and moral recognition and protection as a 'person';

2. IVF research is acceptable, subject to compliance with appropriate regulations to avoid abuse, most particularly that the research be for the primary purpose of improving the safety and effectiveness of IVF;

3. embryos not remain *in vitro* beyond implantation stages;[89]

4. embryos should come from married couples;

5. research projects for other than relief of infertility should be referred for specific consideration by the Ethics Advisory Board;

6. a model law on the legal status of IVF children and related issues was needed.

Although these recommendations do not have the force of law, they do appear to form the general basis for current medical practice standards in the U.S. While the National Institutes of Health has appointed an advisory committee to set recommended standards for the use of fetal tissue, including for research and transplantation purposes,[90] the 10 year old conclusions of the since-disbanded Ethics Advisory Board remain intact.[91] Other countries, including Australia[92] and Great Britain,[93] as well as certain states,[94] have extended IVF to include ovum donors other than the woman to receive the embryo. This is the female equivalent of *in vitro* AID.

Clearly IVF offers great promise to childless couples. Like AIH, if the embryo is derived from a married couple it seems to pose few legal or moral issues.[76] It does, however, raise issues of scarce medical resources[84-5,87] and the demands that individuals may properly make on a finite system, which we will consider more fully in Chapter 12.

Many issues remain to be resolved before IVF will be on a clear moral and legal footing. They include: the permissible research on a zygote or embryo; the length of time that research or other *in vitro* use may continue;[95] the length and purposes of embryo storage and disposition, particularly in the light of death or divorce; acceptable donors of sperm, ova and the resulting embryo; the selection, regulation and identity of donors; the transfer process – limits on number of embryos; and the use of embryonic tissue for other than inducing pregnancy.

Most of these issues are unresolved. Since they raise broad-based questions of ethics, morality, medical practice and law, ethics committees with substantial lay representation should be charged to consider the competing interests involved: those of childless adults, embryos, researchers, and others who stand to gain. As has been recently said of the whole field of genetic engineering, the decisions are so important and wide-ranging that, 'We can't leave these decisions to a small elite of scientists and public officials.'[96] From such a committee may come recognition of practice guidelines, or perhaps the bases for legislative regulation. However, even with legislation, many specific applications of the practice standards by a licensing or ethics committee authority will still be necessary.[97] The Ethics Advisory Board, presently disbanded, or an advisory panel such as that currently advising the National Institues of Health on the permissible uses of fetal tissue could fulfill such a role. Requests for the use of IVF technology could be referred to it for scrutiny and approval, just as the Government has proposed a Statutory Licensing Authority to do so in the United Kingdom.[88]

3. *Selective reduction of pregnancy*

The surgical transfer of multiple embryos to the woman following IVF, or the use of superovulatory drugs is carried out in the United States to aid infertile women to bear a child. Only about 100 women had undergone the procedure of selectively reducing the resulting multiple pregnancies as of 1988.[98] Only a handful of hospitals perform the procedure, normally done prior to the twelfth week of pregnancy during the first trimester of pregnancy.

At this early stage of development the diagnosis of fetal abnormality is difficult. Amniocentesis, the testing of amniotic fluid to determine Down's syndrome or other congenital anomaly, is usually not performed until 16 to 18 weeks gestation. Ultrasound, or sonography, is a developing diagnostic tool, as yet unrefined, but offering great promise in skilled hands. Chorionic villi sampling uses a catheter to take cells from pre-placental tissue to diagnose fetal abnormality. It offers the opportunity of diagnosis during the first trimester of pregnancy, but remains largely experimental at present.[99] The result is decisions must be made to destroy one or more 'excess' embryos or fetuses before the healthy can conclusively be separated from the unhealthy.

Several practice standards have been espoused to deal with the difficulties posed by selective reduction. Multiple transfers can be limited to three or four embryos at most. Rather than multiple transfers during one of the woman's cycles, one or two embryos may be transferred during each of several successive cycles. Any consent to selective reduction (as well as to the earlier IVF consent) can include discussion with the institution's ethics committee to ensure an informed consent and that all questions have been addressed.

Legally, the practice of selective reduction appears to be protected by the Supreme Court's decision in *Roe v. Wade*,[100] the landmark 1973 case recognizing the woman's Constitutional right to abortion in the exercise of her right to privacy. *Roe* holds that during the first trimester of pregnancy, when selective reduction normally occurs, the woman has an absolute legal right to choose abortion. Selective reduction appears to come within the definition of abortion, even though it involves absorption of the dead fetus rather than expulsion.[101] However, whereas traditionally abortion has meant a medical procedure to end pregnancy, selective reduction has as its goal the opposite: the preservation of (the remaining) pregnancy.

Under the *Roe* case, the state can regulate or even proscribe abortion after the start of the third trimester. That is the approximate time of fetal viability, when the fetus is able to survive outside the womb. However, abortion remains the right of the woman if necessary to protect her life or her health. Since selective reduction is intended to protect the mother's health, or that of the remaining embryos and to improve their chances for healthy live birth, it would not seem difficult to bring it under the scope of protection presently offered by *Roe v. Wade*, even if performed at times much later in the pregnancy. However, with the uncertain future of the *Roe* case, given a newly-composed Supreme Court, it may be dangerous to opine on the protections offered by that decision, whether relating to traditional abortion by choice or to selective reduction.[102]

Destroying certain embryos to encourage the healthy growth of others raises questions about the physician's potential liability for unintentionally salvaging an unhealthy or birth defective child. At birth, the parents may claim damages for 'wrongful birth,' that is, negligently allowing a handicapped child to be born without determining and warning the parents of the embryonic or fetal abnormality in time for abortion. Some states refuse to allow such a claim, either on statutory, public policy or legal causation grounds.[103] These courts generally reason that a child, even if handicapped, cannot be considered a legal injury either to himself or to his parents.[104] Other courts hold damages may be recovered if negligent failure to diagnose is proved, but they must be offset by the natural joy provided by a child.[105] Other decisions conclude that only the extraordinary costs of caring for the handicaps are recoverable, not normal child-rearing expenses.[106]

While the U.S. courts have split on the wrongful birth claim of the parents, only several cases out of many have allowed a 'wrongful life' claim by the handicapped child.[107] To do so, they reason, would be to say the child were better off dead, to try and equate the value of handicapped existence to non-existence, and to require lines to be arbitrarily drawn on a continuum from healthy to impaired to severely handicapped existence. Those courts allowing the claim have said where negligence causes injury, damages (i.e., extraordinary medical, educational or custodial care) are proper.[108] This to some at least begs the question, since it assumes injury when none may exist.

Is impaired existence an injury when the alternative is non-existence of the child due to termination of the pregnancy of the child's mother? If so, does the child, upon later learning of the suit when the damages recovered are assigned to him, conclude his parents feel he would have been better off never having been born? What potential damage does this create to the child's psyche and self-esteem? Also, at what level of abnormality does a child qualify to recover these damages? These problems suggest that the goal of ensuring compensation to all for negligently-caused harm may create more problems that it solves. Nonetheless, the plight of the handicapped child and the extraordinary medical, educational and other care expenses for him will likely remain. The goal of the law should be to compensate fairly for negligently-caused harm,[109] but to do so in such a way as not to deprecate life or the rights and role of the handicapped to it and without doing violence to their sense of dignity, worth and self.

The courts, although reaching differing results in different states, have probed the legal and ethical issues involved, raised the social consciousness and suggested various ways of dealing with these problems. This is healthy and a bridge towards consensus. Most have, however, indicated a preference for legislative guidance in this area, which has occurred in many states.[103,106]

No cases have as yet directly raised the legality of selective reduction. Legislative guidelines may be helpful, although it is better to allow a medical consensus the opportunity to develop an appropriate standard of practice first. This is more flexible than legislation as a rule, easier to change, update or adjust to meet continually evolving technology and practice standards. However, the physicians have no corner on ethical imperatives in this area and may welcome help from others.[9] Legislative standards may provide this if they are not merely restrictive, but also enable continued practice developments to occur.

4. *Surrogacy*

A minority of states have expressly declared surrogacy contracts unenforceable. However, only one, Michigan, has declared surrogacy a crime and prohibited any financial compensation for surrogate mothers.[110] In the majority of states it remains for the common law to uphold or reject the practice, in whole or in part.

Several cases have reached the appellate courts dealing with surrogacy. The most notorious, the *Baby M*[111] case involved the surrogate mother Mary Beth Whitehead. In it, the New Jersey Supreme Court invalidated a surrogacy contract whereby the mother, for a fee of $10,000, agreed to be artificially inseminated with the semen of the father, another woman's husband; she was to conceive a child, carry it to term, surrender it after birth to the commissioning couple, and give up her parental rights so that adoption may occur.

The parties in *Baby M* were brought together by a commercial surrogacy agency, which was paid $7,500 for their services by the father. The deal was struck, Ms. Whitehead conceived by AID, delivered and, reluctantly, turned the baby over to the Sterns three days after birth. However, she returned the next day for the baby, saying she could not live without her. She refused to return the baby, the father obtained a court order requiring enforcement of the contract and return of the child and upon learning of it the Whiteheads fled to Florida with the child. There she was apprehended, the child forcibly removed and returned to the Sterns. A trial was then held and the surrogacy contract held valid.

The New Jersey Supreme Court decision holds the surrogacy contract is in conflict with laws prohibiting the payment of money for an adoption ('baby selling'). It also holds it is contrary to the normal finding that parental rights are only lost if unfitness is shown and the child's best interests are served thereby. As the English Courts have held, best interests, not contract provisions, decide child custody. The court put it this way,[112]

'Worst of all, however, is the contract's total disregard of the best interests of the child. There is not the slightest suggestion that any inquiry will be made at any time to determine the fitness of the Sterns as custodial parents, of Mrs. Stern as an adoptive parent, their superiority to Mrs. Whitehead, or the effect on the child of not living with her natural mother.

This is the sale, of a child, or, at the very least, the sale of a mother's right to her child, the only mitigating factor being that one of the purchasers is the father. Almost every evil that prompted the prohibition on the payment of money in connection with adoptions exists here.'

The court found little of redeeming value promised by the surrogacy arrangement. It felt it was detrimental to all concerned. The court found the contractual agreement to pay money for a child to be degrading to women, illegal and perhaps even criminal. The court, however, did not outlaw private arrangements, but it did conclude that,[113]

'The long-term effects of surrogacy contracts are not known, but feared – the impact on the child who learns her life was bought, that she is the offspring of someone who gave birth to her only to obtain money; the impact on the natural mother as the full weight of her isolation is felt along with the full reality of the sale of her body and her child; the impact on the natural father and adoptive mother once they realize the consequences of their conduct.

The surrogacy contract is based on, principles that are directly contrary to the objectives of our laws. It guarantees the separation of a child from its mother; it looks to adoption regardless of suitability; it totally ignores the child; it takes the child from the mother regardless of her wishes and her maternal fitness; and it does all of this, it accomplishes all of its goals, through the use of money.'

Not all U.S. courts have taken such a dim view of surrogacy. In one case[114] the Kentucky Supreme Court found significant differences between a surrogacy arrangement and the buying and selling of children. In the latter case unfair financial pressure may be put on an expectant mother or on new parents to part with the child. In the former situation the decision is made before conception. The court referenced the state statute authorizing IVF with a donor egg (other than the wife into whom the fertilized egg would be placed) and from it concluded,

'All we can derive from this language is that the legislature has expressed itself about one procedure for medically assisted conception while remaining silent on others. To this extent the legislature puts its stamp of approval on tampering with nature in the interest of assisting a childless couple to conceive. The 'in vitro' fertilization procedure sanctioned by the statute and the surrogate parenting procedure as described in the Stipulation of Facts are similar in that both enable a childless couple to have a baby biologically related to one of them when they could not do so otherwise. The fact that the statute now expressly sanctions one way of doing this does not rule out other ways by implication. In an area so fundamental as medically assisting a childless couple to have a child, such a prohibition should not be implied.'

The Kentucky court made it clear that the mother could, however, change her mind after birth; the contract was voidable. This was necessitated by a law requiring a child to be at least 5 days old before a mother could consent to terminate her parental rights.[115] If she recanted, she lost her right to receive payment. The father could, presumably, have paternity obligations,[116] although it can be argued these should attach only if the mother honors the agreement.[117]

A similar result has been reached by a New York court.[118] The court first explained the pressure for surrogate parenting arrangements,[119]

> 'With legalization of abortion and the development and widespread use of contraceptives, there has been an appreciable reduction in the number of available children for adoption by loving and wanting prospective adopting parents. Couples unable to have children who seek a child through the traditional methods of adoption, namely adoption agencies and private placement adoptions, have been discouraged by the considerable wait for a child (usually 3 to 7 years) together with the uncertainty and, in many instances, the painful anxiety connected with the process. Through the use of sperm donors, surrogate mothers, and in vitro fertilization, science has sought to satisfy the childless couple's demand for children. In an attempt to ease the process, scientific methods now provide a means for couples unable to have children whereby the child conceived and ultimately adopted may be genetically related to one or both of the adopting parents.'

The court had reservations about the practice, particularly the payment to the mother, but like the Kentucky court before it the New York court felt this was a social policy issue for the legislature to decide. It encouraged the legislature to review the issues involved. It found the contractual agreements voidable, depending on the best interests of the child, which always must take priority.

The U.S. Supreme Court has recognized a Constitutional right to bear or beget a child.[120] However, competing interests of the state or other parties may act to restrict such a constitutional right.[121] For example, while there is a recognized right to marry protected by the Constitution, it does not extend to polygamy, even if religiously inspired. Religious beliefs are unfettered, but practices are not. Whether the right to bear a child implies the right to bear the child with the aid of a third party remains to be seen. At least one court has suggested this may be the case,[123] and another that it may not be.[124] It seems unlikely. If the legislature can outlaw polygamy in the event of an infertile wife, it would seem that it can also do the same with surrogacy or IVF.

As long as private payment is not outlawed, the pressures for surrogacy to continue are likely to prevail. However, the stresses and strains it imposes on all parties, added to by the voidability of any such agreements, make it unlikely to emerge as a common practice. Financial pressures may be difficult for some, particularly the poor, to resist when large payments are offered by the childless rich. Prohibition on payment for other than expenses, as well as perhaps a pre-established modest stipend, would seem appropriate if the practice is to be legally condoned. To whatever extent practiced, it must at all times be legally subordinate to the best interests of the child, absent the enactment of a legislative scheme to define the rights of the involved parties in some other way.[125]

D. CONCLUSIONS

The new reproductive technology has required society to face many ethical dilemmas it is ill-prepared to resolve. There are strong competing considerations. On the one hand is the strong and quite legitimate desire of many childless couples to experience the joy of child-rearing which technology now makes possible for many heretofore without hope of having children. On the other hand, laboratory and commercial involvement in the fertility process raises legitimate concerns of tampering with the natural process of creation, whether for financial gain or personal gratification. Also implicated is the use of extensive and limited technology to benefit a few, presumably at the expense of directing those resources toward other more broad-based medical and social needs. Finally, the issue of when life begins and whether certain reproductive treatments – particularly IVF and selective reduction of pregnancy – offend against human life is yet to be resolved morally and legally.

Several conclusions seem reasonable to draw from a comparison of practices and legal developments to date in the United Kingdom and the United States. Some must necessarily be tentative for consensus and practice are as yet unsettled in certain areas. Also, the extent of further technological advance and practice changes remains unclear and presently in flux.

Artificial insemination has presented few problems. Several standards seem wise: the anonymity of the donor if other than husband, the prohibition of other than a nominal payment, the restriction on number of donations, the donor's submission to certain qualifying tests and procedures to ensure a healthy specimen free of AIDS or other communicable disease or genetic defect. While AID may offend certain moral or religious viewpoint,[22,42] it seems to facilitate parenthood for many, allows conception and pregnancy to occur in the mother's womb and should be a matter of personal choice, not of legislative prohibition. The child should be recognized as having all rights of a naturally conceived child, the consent of the husband should be required for AID, and there should perhaps exist a central registry of records where the child can learn at majority if he or she is the product of AID and if so some general, non-identifying, information about the ethnic background of the father. However, this is a troublesome area. A little information can be more troubling than none, and it may well be preferable to provide only information, *if requested by the child after age 18*, as to whether or not the mother accepted AID within 10 months of the child's birth. There will still remain the question whether the donor, or the husband's supposedly infertile semen was responsible for conception.

Of course, the AID donor should have no rights to learn the identity of the (presumably) resulting child and have no parental rights, whether of support or otherwise.

Married couples only, with the written consent of both, should be eligible for AID. If a third party is to be legally involved in the process of conception, it should be to foster – bringing a child into the world within the matrix of a loving family who can provide emotional support and guidance of both sexes and financial support, thus increasing the odds for a stable upbringing.[126]

In vitro fertilization is in many ways the logical extension philosophically and biologically of AIH and AID. It too should be available to married couples, with reasonable controls in place. Efforts should be made to use the couples' own sperm and ova, although resort may be necessary to donation from a third party in the event of one party's infertility. Where both parties are infertile the process should not be available. Parenthood is not a guarantee to everyone and where the embryo does not include any genetic material contributed by husband or wife, implantation and pregnancy seems inappropriate. In such instances adoption remains an alternative. Genetic contribution by either husband or wife should remain a legal requirement for IVF pregnancy, as it is with AID. However, where husband and wife knowingly consent, it should be possible to bear a child from a pregnancy which results from either the husband's sperm or the wife's ova, as well as from both. Donor selection would remain anonymous, unless disclosure was agreed by all parties in writing. Licensed labs should ensure healthy sperm or ova from ethnically compatible donors.

Implantation of IVF embryos should be limited to three or less. Twins do not put pregnancy at risk. Triplets may, but the evidence is not conclusive one way or the other.[99] Implantation should be required by day 17, the time at which the first stages of neural development begins,[127] or sooner at day 14.[128,83]. Since most transfers occur prior to 10 days, this seems a sensible cutoff point, before development proceeds further. Any use of zygotes, blastocysts or embryos during this laboratory period should be limited to preparation for transfer to the prospective mother, unless some other research use is expressly approved by an appropriately constituted ethics committee or authority. It should have lay representation as broadly based as possible, bioethicists, child's rights advocates, scientists and physicians in the concerned discipline, social workers, and government planners to express concerns over economics and resource allocation as well as addressing the ethical or medical practice improvement issues of the proposal

If the decision is to store ova, sperm or embryos for future use, there should be a clear agreement between the donors and custodian as to their disposition upon death, divorce or disagreement between the donors. Fertilization and implantation should only occur with express consent of both donors. Unless otherwise agreed, the sperm, ova or embryos should be allowed to perish upon death, divorce or withdrawal of consent of or by either donor. If the material is to be used for other than fertilization and implantation, it should only be for such use as expressly consented to by both donors and approved by the ethics or licensing committee authority established to regulate such practices.

In general, research should be limited to improvement of fertility, but may extend to other therapeutic purposes such as treatment and avoidance of genetically transmitted disease. Certain research should be prohibited, such as tampering with cell genes in order to genetically preordain characteristics of offspring,[129] embryo transfer to other species (or vice versa),[130] or the creation of hybrids by fertilization of a human egg with the sperm of another species (or vice versa).[131]

With surrogacy, legal developments have largely defined the parameters of acceptable practice. Commercial encouragement or involvement is outlawed by statute in Britain and by the most prominent of the judicial pronouncements in the U.S.[132] Private arrangements remain legal. Payment should be restricted to actual medical expenses and loss of earnings during pregnancy. A small stipend would seem acceptable, not to exceed say $5,000, so as to largely avoid economic pressure for the poor to act as surrogates for the rich.

A reasonable 'clinical trial' between the wife and her physician in an effort to induce pregnancy should be a pre-condition to the legality of surrogacy, to avoid making the practice one of convenience rather than medical necessity. The surrogate should be given the right, for a certain period of time after birth, to elect to keep the child. Thirty days seems a reasonable time for her to revoke her consent, even if custody has been transferred to the infertile wife and her husband.[133] Thereafter the commissioning couple would retain custody, subject only to a court order changing it if necessary to protect the welfare and best interests of the child. That power must always transcend all contractual provisions. The commissioning couple should be eligible to formally adopt. Once they have custody, they should have full parental responsibilities and the child have all the rights of support, legitimacy and inheritance. Visitation by the surrogate mother would be up to the parties' agreement, but always subject to court modification. However, in general, the bias should be against visitation, so as not to create emotional or identity conflicts for the child. A strong showing should be required to order visitation by the non-custodial parent.

If the surrogate keeps the child, she and her husband if she is married would have full parental responsibilities. On relinquishment they should have none. The consent of the surrogate's husband must be required before conception.

What is needed is a careful, compassionate approach to the reproductive technology. While it offers promise to many, it also has the potential for abuse. We must not pervert or depreciate our reverence for life in an overly-zealous quest to bring children into every relationship or to manipulate the genetic composition of embryos to further some particular formula or concept of mankind. As one commentator pointed out some time ago, but whose remarks are even more relevant today,

> '. . . the time has come to question just how far we can safely go in the process of bending the nature of Man for the sake of social comfort and convenience. We need the natural product – warts and all.'[134]

NOTES

1 *In Re-Adoption Application* (1987), 2 All E.R. 827, 3 W.L.R. 31, 2 F.L.R. 291 (Latey, J.)
2 *Matter of Baby M.* (1988, N.J.) 537 A. 2d 1227.
3 Craft, 'When a code catches out the childless,' *The Times*, 24 Sept. 1987, p. 16.
4 *Matter of Quinlan* (1976, N.J.) 355 A. 2d 647.
5 Abortion Act 1967.
6 Surrogacy Arrangements Act 1985.
7 *Helling v. Carey* (1974, Wash.) 519 Pac. 2d 981 (superceded by statute, 550 Pac. 2d 1158), (failure to test for glaucoma in patients under 40 by simple means not reasonable and proper, even though established practice of responsible physicians was not to do so).
8 See, for example, *Hunter v. Hanley*, 1955 S.C. 200; *Bolam v. Friern Hosp.Mgt.Committee* (1957) 2 All E.R. 118.
9 *The Times*, 17 April 1989, p.9.
10 *The Sunday Times*, 5 March 1989, p.A9.
11 Law Reform (Parent and Child) (Scotland) Act 1986; Family Law Reform Act 1987.
12 Report of the Committee of Enquiry into Human Fertilization and Embryology ('Warnock Report') Cmmd. 9314. London, HMSO 1984, 10.09, *et. seq.*
13 Dept. of Health and Social Security, Human Fertilization and Embryology: A Framework for Legislation CM 259, London, HMSO, Nov., 1987, s.89. (hereafter, 'White Paper, 1987').
14 Family Law Reform Act 1987, s.27.
15 *MacLennan v. MacLennan* 1958 S.C. 105.
16 Mason and McCall Smith, *Law and Medical Ethics*, (2d 3d.) p.40.
17 Vatican, *Instruction on Respect for Life in its Origin and on the Dignity of Procreation* (Holy See, 1987).
18 AID, egg or embryo donation, or surrogacy.
19 McCormick, 'The Ethics of High-Tech Reproductive Methods,' *Networking*, Calif. Ass'n. Cath. Hosps., Vol. 15,p.8 (1987).
20 *Re B (A Minor)*, (1981) 1 W.L.R. 1421.
21 White Paper, 1987, ss.79–84
22 *Ibid.*, s.87

23 *Ibid.*, s.88.
24 *Ibid.*, s.83
25 Mason and McCall Smith, *Law and Medical Ethics*, pp.44–5.
26 White Paper, 1987, s.84.
27 Also called placentation. The point, usually within about 7 days of fertilization, when the embryo affixes itself to the uterine wall. The success rate of IVF is about 20 per cent. 292 *Brit. Med. J.* 1740 (1986).
28 Craft and Yovich, 2 The Lancet 642 (1979); O'Rourke, 'Family Law in a Brave New World,' 1 *Berkeley Wom. L. J.* 140 (1985). Robertson, 'Procreative Liberty and the Control of Conception, Pregnancy, and Childbirth,' 69 *Va. L. Rev.* 405 (1983).
29 Warnock Report, *supra*; White Paper, 1987, ss.1–91.
30 White Paper, 1987, s.31.
31 *Ibid.*, s.34.
32 Cusine, *Legal Issues in Human Reproduction*, MacLean (ed.), p.24.
33 'Legal Protection for the Unborn Child,' 51 *Mod. L. R.* 62 (1988), (referencing Lockwood's position.)
34 White Paper, 1987, s.31.
35 Mason lists the emergence of identifiable embryonic structures, the start of specialized fetal growth and maturity beyond the normal implantation period as sound physiological reasons for the 14 day cutoff standard. Mason, *Human Life and Medical Practice*. Edinburgh: The University Press, 1988, p.94.
36 *Davis v. Davis* (Maryville, Tenn. Circuit Court, Sept. 21, 1989), reported in *Internatl. Herald Tribune*, Sept. 22, 1989, p.2 and *The Sunday Times*, Sept. 24, 1989, p.A20.
37 Smith, 'Australia's Frozen 'Orphan' Embryos: A Medical, Legal and Ethical Problem,' 24 *J. Fam. Law* 27 (1985–86).
38 Waller Committee Report, On the Disposition of Embryos Produced by In Vitro Fertilization, Victoria, 1984.
39 Kay, *The Boalt Hall Transcript*, Vol. 20, No. 2, pp. 3,5 (1987). Pirrie, 'Reinventing the Law of Human Life', *The Wall Street Journal*, Sept. 26, 1989, p.6.
40 16 *J. Med. Ethics* June, 1990, p. 101; see generally, Austin, C. R., *Human Embryos: The Debate on Assisted Reproduction*. Oxford: Oxford University Press, 1989.
41 Dawson, 'Fertilization and Moral Status: A Scientific Perspective,' 13 *J. Med. Ethics* 173, 176 (1987).
42 Compare Dunstan, 'The Moral Status of the Human Embryo: a Tradition Recalled,' 1984 *J. Med. Ethics* 38, with, Iglesias, 'In Vitro Fertilization: The Major Issues,' 1984 *J.Med.Ethics* 32.
43 *R. v. Ethical Committee of St. Mary's Hosp. (Manchester) ex parte Harriott* (1988) 1 F.L.R. 512.
44 See Singh, 'Infertility Treatment and the Courts,' 18 *Fam. Law* 299, 302 (1988).
45 *Time*, 2 May 1988, p.63.
46 Second Annual Report of the Voluntary Licensing Authority, 1987, s.3, p.8.
47 295 *Brit.Med. J.* 1134 (1987).
48 Craft, 'When a Code Catches Out the Childless,' *The Times*, 24 Sept. 1987, p. 16.
49 Horowitz, *Los Angeles Times Mag.* 23 April 1989, pp.12, 44.

50 *Ibid.*, p.44.
51 See discussion in Chap.5, *infra.*
52 Price, 'Selective Reduction and Feticide: The parameters of Abortion' 1988 *Crim.L.R.* 199.
53 See discussion in Chap.3, *infra*; *Rex v. Bourne* (1939) 1 K.B. 687.
54 Price, *op. cit.*, p.204. See also, Keown (1987) 137 *New Law J.* 1165.
55 Kay, *Boalt Hall Transcript, supra*, p.3.
56 *Re C (A Minor)(wardship: surrogacy)* (1985) F.L.R. 846 (Latey,J.)
57 11 Elizabeth, 1985 Chapter 49.
58 See *A. v. C.* (1978) 8 Fam. Law 170; *A. v. C.* (1985) F.L.R.
59 See Staines, 'Who To Be or Not To Be: The Surrogacy Story,' 49 *Mod. L. R.* 358 (1986).
60 White Paper, 1987, s. 65; see also, *A. v. C.* (1978) 8 *Fam. Law* 170 (surrogacy contract not enforceable as pernicious and against public policy).
61 *Re An Adoption Application (surrogacy)* (1987) 2 All E.R. 826 (Latey, J.).
62 *Ibid.*
63 *Re P.* (1987) 2 F.L.R. 421 (Sir John Arnold, J.)
64 See De Cruz, 'Surrogacy, Adoption and Custody: A Case-Study,' 1988 *Fam.Law* 100, 103.
65 See, to similar effect in the U.S., the celebrated American case of *Matter of Baby M.* (1988, N.J.) 537 A. 2d 1227 (commissioning parents given custody where lower court order gave them custody *pendente lite*, during which time bonding would occur); *In Re Baby Girl M.* (1987) 191 Cal.App. 3d 786 (custody given adoptive parents because of long custody and bonding despite fact father not unfit.).
66 De Cruz, *supra*, p.105.
67 White Paper, 1987, s.73.
68 De Cruz, *supra*, p.107 (*The Times*, 8 May 1987).
69 Frank, 25 *J. Fam. Law* 103, 108 (1986–87).
70 Rubellin-Devichi, 25 *J. Fam. Law* 127, 132 (1986–87).
71 Winslade, 'Surrogate Mothers: Private Right or Public Wrong?' 1981 *J.Med.Ethics* 153.
72 See discussion on Consent in Chapter 5, *infra.*
73 Kass, '"Making Babies" Revisited,' in Shannon (ed.) (*Bioethics* (3d ed., 1987), pp. 453, 479.
74 McCormick, 'The Ethics of High-Tech Reproductive Methods,' *Networking*, Vol.15, Fall, 1987, p.8.
75 Holy See, Instruction on Respect for Life in its Origin and on the Dignity of Procreation, (Vatican, Feb. 22, 1987).
76 See, for example, Calif.Civil Code §7005 (1982).
77 Shaman, 'Legal Aspects of Artificial Insemination,' (1979) 18 *J. Fam. Law* 331; see also Warnock Report, *supra*, para. 4. 24.
78 'Judge to Decide Embryo Custody,' *USA Today*, 17 May 1989, p.2A.
79 Curriden, 'Frozen Embryos, The New Frontier,' *Amer. Bar Assn. Journal*, August, 1989, p.68.
80 *C v. S.* (1987) 1 All E.R. 1230.
81 The Government's pending proposal for legislative regulation of IVF

in Britain concludes storage of embryos should be limited to a maximum of 5 years, may only be used with their donor's permission and only for the purposes for which consent may have been given. In addition, donors are given the right to withdraw consent before use (implantation). White Paper, *supra*, §54–57. See also, *Wall Street Journal* Sept. 26, 1989, note 39, *supra*.

82 See Quigley and Andrews, 'Human in vitro fertilization and the law,' 42 *Fertility and Sterility* 348 (1984).

83 Ethics Advisory Board, *Report and Conclusions: HEW Support of Research Involving Human In Vitro FErtilization and Embryo Transfer* (Gov't. Printing Office, Wash. D.C., 1979), (hereafter Ethics Advisory Board 'Report'); see also, Mason, *Human Life and Medical Practice*, p.94.

84 See Grobstein, Flower and Mendeloff, 'External Human Fertilization: An Evaluation of Policy,' *Bioethics* (3d. ed., 1987), pp. 481, 488, 490.

85 *Ibid.*, p. 489.

86 *Kinzie v. Physician's Liability Ins.Co.* (1987, Okla. App.) 750 Pac.2d 1140.

87 Estimated at 35,000 annual female patients with dysfunctional fallopian tubes alone, of childbearing age, wishing to use IVF to become pregnant. Grobstein, et.al., *supra*, p. 489.

88 Similar to the Voluntary Licensing Authority in Britain, which the Gov't proposes to make mandatory. White Paper, §9–11.

89 Fertilization typically takes approximately 24 hours and is followed by implantation in the uterine wall by approximately 7 days gestation. No embryo is reported to have been kept alive *in vitro* beyond 9 days. White Paper, §31.

90 Thorne, 'End Fetal-Tissue Work? Only More of It will Guide,' *Wall Street J.*, 7 November 1988, p.3.

91 The President's Commission for the Study of Ethical Problems in Medicine and Biomedical and Behavioral Research issued several reports during its existence, but did not do so on IVF (see, *Making Health Care Decisions*, 1982; *Deciding to Forego Life-Sustaining Treatment*, 1983; *Splicing Life*, 1982).

92 See, for example, The Status of Children (Amendment) Act 1984 (Victoria) s.5.

93 White Paper, s.30.

94 See, for example, Kty. Rev. Stat 199.590 (1984), *Surrogate Parenting Associates, Inc. v. Armstrong* (1986, Kty.) 704 S.W.2d 209.

95 Various times have been suggested from fertilization to the 10 week stage of the embryo or fetus, including 14, 17 and 30 days development. See Cusine, *Legal Issues In Human Reproduction*, p.24.

96 Genetic-engineering experiments are subject, as a result of court agreement, to a similar public review and approval process.Sperling, 'Genetic research: Public wins a voice,' *USA Today*, 17 May 1989, p.1A

97 Cripps, 'A legal perspective on the control of the technology of genetic engineering,' 44 *Modern L.R.* 369 (1981).

98 *Time*, 2 May 1988, p.63.

99 *Los Angeles Times Mag.*, 23 April 1989, p.p. 12,44.

100 (1973) 410 U.S. 113.

101 Price, 1988 *Crim. L.R.* 199.

102 Reidinger, *ABA Journal*, 1 July 1988, p. 66; see discussion in Chapter 2, *supra*; see also, *Time*, 1 May 1989, p.20, *Los Angeles Times*, 19 May 1989, p.4.

103 *Rolf v. Youngblood* (1988, Mo.App.) 753 S.W. 2d 24; *Di Natale v. Lieberman* (1982, Fla.) 409 So.2d 512.

104 *Azzolino v. Dingfelder* (1985, No.Car.) 337 S.E. 2d 528; cf. *Harbeson v. Parke)Davis, Inc.* (1983, Wash.) 656 Pac. 2d 483.

105 Compare *Gallagher v. Duke University* (1988, 4th cir.) 852 Fed. 2d 773 (no offset even though child healthy, if *conception*, not *birth* result of negligence).

106 *James G. v. Caserta* (1985, W.Va.) 332 S.E. 2d 872.

107 Meyers, *Medico-Legal Implications of Death and Dying, supra* (Dec., 1988, Cum.Supp., §14:20.2); Dickens, *Legal Issues In Human Reproduction*, Chap.4.

108 *Turpin v. Sortini* (1982) 31 Cal. 3d 220.

109 Dickens, *Legal Issues in Human Reproduction*, pp.80,107)8.

110 *Time*, 11 July 1988, p.21.

111 *Matter of Baby M* (1988, N.J.) 537 A.2d 1227.

112 537 A.2d at 1248.

113 537 A.2d at 1250.

114 *Surrogate Parenting Associates, Inc. v. Armstrong* (1986, Kty.) 704 S.W. 2d 209, 212.

115 KRS 199.601(2).

116 see *Syrkowski v. Appleyard* (1985, Mich.) 362 N.W. 2d 211 (father could establish filiation, even if surrogate contact contrary to public policy; *Doe v. Atty. Gen.* (1981, Mich. App.) 307 N.W. 2d 438).

117 Eisenberg, 'Surrogate-Mother Contracts' *The Boalt Transcript*, Vol. 20, No. 2, Fall, 1987 , p.10.

118 *Matter of Adoption of Baby Girl L.J.* (1986, Surr.Ct.) 505 N.Y.S. 2d 813.

119 505 N.Y.S. 2d at 815.

120 *Maher v. Roe* 1977) 432 U.S. 464; *Carey v. Population Services* (1977) 431 U.S. 678.

121 *Whalen v. Roe* (1977) 429 U.S. 589; *Buck v. Bell* (1927) 274 U.S. 200.

122 *Reynolds v. United States* (1878) 98 U.S. 145.

123 *Doe v. Kelley* (1981, Mich.App.) 307 N.W. 2d 438,441.

124 *Matter of Baby M* (1988, N.J.) 537 A.2d at 1254.

125 Federal Legislation to outlaw surrogacy agreements and to penalize agencies who arrange them is pending in Congress.

126 Mason & McCall Smith, *Law and Medical Ethics*, p.41.

127 Supported by the Royal College of Obstetricians and Gynaecologists in its 1983 *Report of Committee on In Vitro Fertilization and Embryo Replacement or Transfer*, s.13.8.

128 Warnock Report, *supra*, s.11.22; White Paper, *supra* s.34.

129 White Paper, s.37–38; *USA Today*, 17 May 1989, p.1A.

130 White Paper, s.39

131 White Paper, s.42.

132 *Matter of Baby M* (1988, N.J.) 537 A.2d 1227.

133 Zimring, 'Beyond Solomon: The 'Tragic Choice' Cases' *The Boalt Hall Transcript*, Fall, 1987, p.11.

134 Gould, 'Castrating into conformity,' *New Statesman*, 27 October 1967, p.540.

4

Selective Nontreatment of Seriously Handicapped Newborns

A. INTRODUCTION

1. Medical advances

Modern medicine is a technological marvel. Procedures unheard and unthought of 30 years ago – dialysis, magnetic resonance imaging in place of X-ray, chemotherapy, coronary bypass surgery, and neonatal intensive care – are common today. Neonatal[1] intensive care procedures include resuscitation, mechanical ventilation, artificial tube feeding and other technologically sophisticated means of maintaining seriously handicapped, seriously ill, or premature very low birth weight neonates. These advances have not always proved to be a blessing. While they have resulted in saving many eventually healthy babies, they have also allowed seriously handicapped newborns to survive, sometimes in the most tortured circumstances.[2]

2. The premature newborn

Not long ago infants weighing less than 1350 grams were not considered salvageable. The threshold was then lowered to 900 grams, normally achieved at 26 or 27 weeks gestation.

Neonatal medicine now makes it possible for infants as premature as 23 weeks, weighing less than 700 grams, to survive, although only approximately 7 percent survive to one year, while the others die.[3] By the time the fetus has matured to 28 weeks, its average weight has increased to more than 1100 grams and its chances of one year survival to 75 percent.[4] Nonetheless, nearly a fourth of these premature infants will suffer some form of significant handicap, either physical or mental, such as cerebral palsy, heart defect, brain hemorrhaging, deafness, blindness or intellectual deficiency.[5] Fortunately, premature births at 27 weeks or earlier are a very small portion of live births, accounting for well below 1 percent of the total.[6]

Doctors, with the full assistance of modern technology have been unable to save fetuses younger than 24 weeks because critical organs, most particularly the lungs and kidneys, are not mature enough to support independent existence. The air sacs in the lungs are not sufficiently developed to permit necessary gas exchange in respiration until at least 23 weeks gestation, often later.[7] The result is the fetus cannot be born alive,[8] despite the help of medical science.

3.   *Other handicaps at birth*

Extreme prematurity is only one cause of serious birth defects. Congenital anamolies and abnormal prenatal development result in significant newborn handicaps. Approximately 7 percent of newborns in the United States are born with physical or mental handicaps.[9] The most troubling of those handicaps normally concern abnormalities in the central nervous system, including the brain.[10] They include: anencephaly, an absence of the brain, either partial or total; hydrocephaly, the presence of free fluid in the cranial cavity, often affecting mental and physical development such as head enlargement, posture, and spasticity; spina bifida, an abnormality in development of the osseous spine occurring at different levels which may be accompanied by a failure of the spinal canal to close and the protrusion of an external sac containing brain or spinal tissue;[11] and Down's syndrome, a chromosomal disorder resulting in mental retardation of differing degrees and reduced life expectancy.[12]

4.   *Infants with myelomeningocele*

Those infants with myelomeningocele, the most severe form of spina bifida, present perhaps, as a group, the most challenging neonatal treatment dilemmas. Much depends on the severity of the spinal defect and upon the level of the spine at which it occurs. Generally, the lower the defect, the better the chances for normal or near-normal mental development and limited or no paralysis.[13]

Professor Lorber was the first to suggest the need for publicly-recognized medical criteria for selective treatment of those newborn afflicted with myelomeningocele.[14] Of some 848 such infants treated over a ten year period from 1959–1968, he found 50 percent died within one year. Of those who survived, 81 percent had severe handicap,[15] 17 percent moderate handicap,[16] and only 1 percent had no handicap.[17]

From this extensive experience, Dr. Lorber developed criteria for active treatment and passive treatment in such cases. The latter contemplated only comfort care for the infant – nursing care, symptomatic relief of pain or fits, normal feeding – but not antibiotics for infection, oxygen, or IV feeding.[18] This was only proposed in very severe cases.[19]

At about the same time as Lorber was openly discussing these difficult issues, Doctors Duff and Campbell risked prosecution in the United States by disclosing their experience at Yale – New Haven Hospital in withholding active treatment from severely handicapped newborn whose parents concurred.[20] They recognized in doing so that they were breaching a longstanding 'public and professional silence on a major social taboo.'[21]

5. *The parental role in decisionmaking*

While these commentators acknowledged the obvious need to involve the parents in treatment decisions, it was also recognized that the parents were extremely agitated and beset with conflicting emotions seriously impacting their abilities to make an independent, reasoned decision. They are likely to experience feelings of 'shock, fear, guilt, horror, and shame.'[22] As a consequence, the recommendation and prognosis of the doctor becomes all the more important, since the parents are very likely to leave it up to the doctor to do what he thinks best.[23] Traditionally, doctors in large degree made decisions against active treatment in severe cases with little or no parental involvement.[24] The feeling was the parents were at the time ill-equipped to deal with the choices to be made, given their emotional strain and the fundamental role played by clinical prognosis. There was a desire not to place an 'impossible onus' on the parents; their views should be solicited, but they should not be left to decide.[25]

With the advent of a greater recognition on both sides of the Atlantic of the importance of patient autonomy in medical treatment decisionmaking[26] has come a greater legal realization that parents should be actively involved in treatment decisions for their severely handicapped newborns.[27] Joint consultation and discussion between physicians and parents is now considered the norm. Parents, although in grief and shock, can participate in the choices that need to be made, provided they are provided frank and full information on diagnosis and prognosis, and their questions are answered, including the quality of life it is believed the infant has the potential to enjoy.[28]

6. *Elements in decisionmaking*

The parents must be told the treatment options open to them, what benefits each can reasonably be expected to produce for the child, at what physical and emotional burden to the child and to them, at what cost, with what likelihood of success, and what alternatives are realistically available. Duff and Campbell have stated that there should be 'reasonable disclosure of material facts relevant to the decision' which the parents are asked to reach with the doctor.[29] It may be wise to involve other trained professionals in this process. In the UK there is strong feeling that the nurses should be involved in the process, since it is they who must carry the burden of any clinical treatment or nontreatment decisions. Other professionals should include at least one specialist consultant,[30] as well as perhaps a social worker, psychologist, or other appropriate consultation and support where indicated.

Dr. Lorber has stated that in deciding what treatment is appropriate, the physician needs to look beyond the immediate tactical problem posed by the neonate's condition to what life lies ahead for him or her. 'If he [the doctor] would not like a child of his own to survive, he should take the logical long-term strategic view and resist the temptation to operate.'[32]

While the welfare and best interests of the neonate must be the touchstone for decisionmaking, other elements are said to enter the process of deciding on the appropriate course of treatment. Of foremost importance is the 'qualitative' element: what level of living, of consciousness and cognition, of existence without intolerable pain, does the treatment promise. Also present is the 'hardship' element: what burdens – physical, emotional, social and financial – will the treatment impose on the parents and the rest of the family. Thirdly, there is a 'societal' element: what strains and dislocations will the treatment regime place on finite medical resources,[33] which may perhaps be more cost-effective, for example, in pre-natal preventive care, than in post-natal critical care.[34] The interplay between these elements and the weight to be assigned to them makes decision-making in this sensitive area of medical care exceedingly difficult. The vagaries of individual responses to treatment and the difficulties of accurate diagnosis, particularly of mental deficit, of the neonate only add to the moral and ethical challenges imposed on parents and physicians seeking to do what is right and what is best, under very trying circumstances.

7. *Futile care not required*

Where the hopeless prognosis is clear and cannot be improved with treatment, there is neither moral nor legal obligation to impose that treatment.[35] 'The doctor has no ethical obligation to treat cases in which the likely benefits are very dubious.'[36] Robertson[37] has stated the general rule this way,

> '. . . a physician's duty to undertake a medical procedure is determined by what can reasonably be expected in light of customary medical practice, the likelihood of success, and the available alternatives. Of course, physicians may often employ extraordinary means in particular cases, but they are not legally obligated to do so.'

The difficulty in applying this general rule lies in ascertaining customary medical practice standards for particular congenital anamolies. Given the many variables in the decisionmaking process, this is no easy task. While it seems clear that a medical consensus supports selective nontreatment of severely handicapped neonates at times, such as in cases of anencephaly and severe spina bifida, it is much less clear if there is agreement what standard medical practice should be in many other cases of serious infant abnormalities.[38]

8. *Treatment guidelines needed*

Because the law generally defers to established standards of medical practice,[39] the development of consensus on indicated medical treatment for handicapped newborn would do much to resolve the legal uncertainties which pervade this area of medical care.[40] While the law need not accept a medical practice as proper merely because adhered to by responsible doctors,[41] it is a rare case indeed when a responsible body of practitioners is deemed to have adopted a legally unacceptable standard of care.[42]

Such guidelines and practice standards have not been forthcoming from the medical profession. Several reasons explain this. These decisions (not to actively treat) have traditionally been taken privately. There has been little public discussion of the appropriate treatment standards to apply, with the notable exceptions of certain pioneering and influential articles and recommendations, most particularly those of Lorber and Duff and Campbell.

The uncertain legal picture and the distinct risk of prosecution[43] has discouraged public revelation of practice standards for fear of consequent legal liability. Conflicting decisions by the courts have added to this uncertainty.

The role of parental discretion in nontreatment decisions for their newborn has not been clearly articulated and the views of physicians on the subject have varied considerably. The inevitable, subjective evaluations of quality of life for the infant are often clinically difficult, undoubtedly involve personal beliefs and philosophy of life as well as solely medical prognosis, and have not engendered clear, easily definable treatment standards or legal rules of conduct.

Finally, physicians and family alike are often distraught by these difficult decisions and are disinclined afterwards toward the kind of detached, open discussion among colleagues and other disciplines to promote accepted standards of conduct. This is a necessary prerequisite to resulting legal norms.

9. *Reasonable clinical trial proper*

Most agree that where neonatal defect is present the most important task is to make a careful clinical assessment of the infant. Treatment should be given until the clinical picture is clear.[44] This reasonable clinical trial will serve several purposes. It permits the treating team to have the necessary information for the most informed prognosis possible. It permits the parents an opportunity to come to grips with the shocking revelation of their newborn's significant handicap. It permits the infant an opportunity to respond to aggressive treatment, if imposed initially.

To encourage careful clinical assessment there should be no legal difference between withholding treatment in the first instances and withdrawing treatment after it is tried without success.[45] The law should encourage careful evaluation and the use of all available treatment which may offer reasonable hope of benefit.

At the same time, the decision whether to continue, or commence, active treatment of a severely handicapped newborn must not be made by default, or as a result of the inertia of the medical procedures imposed routinely without analysis of benefit. Mason and McCall Smith at one time suggested a 72 hour period for decisionmaking,[46] but have since removed that limitation from their proposed model statute, which states,[47]

> 'In the event of positive treatment being necessary for a neonate's survival, it will not be an offence to withhold such treatment if two doctors, one of whom is a consultant paediatrician, acting in good faith and with the consent of both parents if available, decide against treatment in the light of a reasonably clear medical prognosis which indicates that the infant's further life would be intolerable by virtue of pain or suffering or because of severe cerebral incompetence.

No arbitrary time limit should be imposed on decisionmaking. The medical treatment picture will vary from infant to infant, as will his or her response to that treatment. Where, however, it is clear that further treatment is futile, or the clinical picture clearly presents a prognosis falling within acceptable nontreatment criteria, the decision of parents and physicians should be prompt, public (that is, documented in the written medical record),[48] and compassionate. While no one wants to unduly delay these difficult decisions, the most important consideration is that the decisionmakers – parents, physicians, other members of the treatment team – have the information necessary to make a fully informed decision.

Against this general backdrop of rather unclear medical practice standards, we will now look at the legality of selected nontreatment of handicapped newborns in England, Scotland, and the United States. What we will find are few legal precedents, which at times seem in conflict. However, from them it may be possible to discern certain basic and guiding principles for parents and physicians seeking to deal with these very challenging treatment decisions.

B. ENGLAND

In England several judicial decisions have shed light on the right of parents to elect nontreatment as an option in the treatment of their severely handicapped newborn child. While these decisions do not provide clear legal guidance for parents or physicians, they do suggest the outlines of the legal terrain in England. The most significant of these cases will be discussed first.

1. *The case of Re B.*[49]

In 1981 a child was born suffering from Down's syndrome and a surgically correctable intestinal blockage. With surgery it was probable the child would live to be 20 to 30 years old. Without surgery the infant would die of starvation in a matter of days. The parents refused consent to the surgery, having concluded it would be kinder to allow her to die rather than to live with physical and mental handicaps. The local authority was contacted by the physicians involved and made the child a ward of the court. The surgeon at a second hospital to which the child was transferred elected, however, to honor the wishes of the parents.[50] An application was made to the local trial judge for authority to operate, but the judge ruled the wishes of the parents should be respected and refused to order the corrective surgery.

On review, the Court of Appeal held that while great weight should be given to the wishes of the parents, they do not necessarily control in such matters. The guiding principle must be the best interests of the child, not the powers or rights to decide of the parents. The motives of the parents were unquestioned; they were acting in what they felt to be the best interests of their child.

As with the typical Down's syndrome child, it was not possible to predict the extent of the child's mental or physical abnormality. While the evidence was that she would not be a 'cabbage,' it was clear that she would be 'severely mentally and physically handicapped.'[51]

The court concluded that it could only condone the parents' decision not to treat the child and to allow her to die if 'the life of this child is demonstrably going to be so awful that in effect the child must be condemned to die.'[52] Lord Justice Templeman suggested in cases of 'severe proved damage where the future is so certain and where the life of the child is so bound to be full of pain and suffering' that the parents' decision not to treat might be upheld.

Since such severe circumstances were not existent in the case before them, the Appeal Court Judges overruled the trial judge and authorized the local authority with custody of the infant to direct that the surgery be carried out. It was clear to them that the infant's best interest required that the surgery be performed. An accurate prognosis as to the degree of handicap could not be made until the child was two. The quality of life she would enjoy could not be determined, but there was no evidence it would be 'intolerable.' Since most would concur that the infant's quality of life is the key determinant in any nontreatment decision[53] the court had really no choice but to order treatment as it did.

Re B remains the law of England. It indicates that parental decisions will be given substantial deference, as the medical profession has traditionally done. However, if treatment will allow a handicapped infant to survive without 'intolerable' pain or suffering, and without an existence that is 'demonstrably awful,' it will be ordered.

As a practical matter, only cases where the doctors feel that treatment can benefit the child, or there are conflicting medical opinions on the subject, will involve decisions to treat over the wishes of the parents. In other cases, where parents and physicians concur treatment is not beneficial to the infant, the decision not to treat will be taken privately without local authority or court involvement, unless a nurse or other affected person involves the authorities. This is most unlikely, as shown by the dearth of such cases that are reported.

2.   *The case of McKay v. The Essex Area Health Authority*[54]

In 1982 a child was born severely handicapped. During pregnancy the infant's mother was not informed of exposure to the rubella virus and thus was not given the opportunity to abort in the face of suspected fetal abnormality, as permitted by the Abortion Act.[55] An action on behalf of the infant for 'wrongful life' was brought, it being contended the physician's negligence resulted in the infant being born into a life of misery and suffering, which proper disclosure and abortion could have avoided. The Court of Appeal concluded such a claim was against public policy and would constitute a further inroad upon the sanctity of all human life, beyond that already permitted by the Abortion Act.[56]

The court in *McKay* also concluded, as have most American courts to address the issue,[57] that the law would not recognize a claim based on he premise it was worse to have been allowed to be born handicapped rather than not to have been born at all. How possibly, the court theorized, could impaired existence be compared to non-existence and the difference quantified in legally cognizable damages?

While the holding suggests, at least inferentially, that handicapped existence of a newborn provides no legal justification for nontreatment, the court was not asked to address this issue. It is interesting to note, however, that at least one of the appeal court judges was of the view that there may occur births involving such extreme mental and physical handicaps as to justify the conclusion that non-life was preferable to such severely impaired life.[58] This suggests decisions not to treat in such severe cases could legally be taken. It is very similar in tone to the limited exception to the life-sustaining treatment obligation sought to be carved out by the Court in the case of *Re B.*.

3. The case of R. v. Arthur[59]

Both the cases of *Re B*. and *McKay* were civil cases. One sought authority to operate on a Downsian infant to allow her to take nourishment. The offer involved a claim for damages because of the birth of a seriously handicapped child. The *Arthur* case was a criminal prosecution against a physician for allegedly attempting to murder a Downsian newborn infant. While it has received by far the most notoriety of these cases, it is only a trial court decision, never appealed, lays down no clear principles and was undoubtedly decided on the particular facts presented to the jury. Thus, while its importance should not be overstated, it does represent perhaps the only modern illustration of the attitude of English jurors and the judiciary toward nontreatment of newborns in selected cases, based on their congenital abnormalities. For that reason it deserves careful consideration.

In 1980 a boy was born with Down's syndrome. Following discussion with the parents, the paediatrician, Dr. Arthur, entered in the child's medical record, 'Parents do not wish the baby to survive. Nursing care only.'[60] Dyhydrocodeine was prescribed to alleviate the baby's distress from not eating. Sixty-nine hours after birth the infant died. Cause of death was stated by the pathologist to be 'bronchopneumonia due to dyhydrocodeine poisoning in an infant with Down's syndrome.' The matter was reported to the authorities, a police investigation ensued, and Dr. Arthur was charged with murder.

The prosecution contended the baby had died as the result of drug poisoning, which had been intentionally administered to kill the baby. More than a year after the baby's death Dr. Arthur came to trial. However, post-mortem histological tissue slides evidenced vital organ abnormalities of the brain and lungs. Since these could have caused death, the judge ordered the charges reduced from murder to attempted murder and the case proceeded.

The evidence in the case did not support a claim the child was allowed to starve to death. Although the dyhydrocodeine does suppress appetite, the child was fed fluids, did not lose weight from birth until death, and in any event at 7 pounds, 4 ounces, could go without milk for 3 days without harm.[61]

A number of prominent paediatricians were called to testify for the defense. They concluded that Dr. Arthur's deference to the wishes of the parents and course of treatment under the circumstances was appropriate and consistent with good medical practice. Dr. Arthur did not testify.

In summing up the case and directing the jury on the law it was to apply in the case, the judge emphasized it was the intention of the doctor that counted, not his motive. If, his intention was to cause the infant's death, it did not matter that his motive was to relieve suffering. However, in addition to intending that the infant die, there must also be proved acts or conduct that actually amounted to an attempt to kill.[62]

The jury were told that there was a distinction in the law between an act intended to bring about death and 'simply allowing the child to die.' This classic distinction between act and omission, between commission and omission, has long been recognized by the criminal law. It has not seen fit to punish nonfeasance or omission as criminal, except in rare circumstances. However, those rare circumstances – the existence of a legal duty to affirmatively act to protect another – are present in the case of physician who has agreed to care for a patient. Once that duty to act has arisen, it may be manslaughter rather than murder to do nothing, knowing it will bring about the death of the patient or other dependent and vulnerable person.[63] Thus, whether the failure to feed the patient is an act, or merely an omission as suggested during the trial,[64] it will be criminal if the doctor was under a *duty* to furnish it to the patient.

The doctors who testified stated there was no duty to feed the child. Yet they reached this result by the rather artificial means of characterizing the withholding of food as an omission, 'a negative, not a positive act,'[64] saying '[n]o paediatrician takes life; but we accept that allowing babies to die – and I know the distinction is narrow, but we all feel it tremendously profoundly – is in the baby's interest at times.'[65]

As discussed elsewhere, the distinction the law offers to acts or omissions is artificial at best. At least in the medical treatment context, any failure to treat can be characterized as an act or an omission. Withholding food is a good example. If no further food is given, how is it different from leaving the patient on the operating table? both patients have had care commenced, both need that care continued to survive and both patients will die from its withholding. The fact one may die from septis, shock or loss of blood, the other from starvation seems not a significant distinction.

This is not to say, however, that there is not an important legal and ethical difference between a deliberate act to kill (injecting a patient with poison) and allowing the patient to die (not providing antibiotics for pneumonia). If there is no legal duty to act, because for example, the condition is hopeless and the treatment futile, then allowing a patient to die without active intervention is not a breach of duty to that patient. On the other hand, any deliberate act intended to kill is murder, regardless of motive, patient consent, prognosis, or life expectancy.

Legal duty is the standard of care the law places on a person due to his or her status. In the case of a doctor, it normally is what responsible doctors of ordinary skill and prudence would do in the circumstances.[66] However, neither doctors nor any other profession has the sole authority to decide the legality of their own conduct. The courts are the final arbiters of what is reasonable, what is proper, what is legal.[67] The judge in the *Arthur* case made this clear to the jury, although the great deference paid to the self-imposed standards of the medical profession was very clear from his charge,

'Certainly, in this country no individual is given sole power of life or death over another . . . All must be alive to the danger of giving too much power to anyone, in the medical or other professions, to exert influence over the life and health of the public at large.

Whatever ethics a profession might evolve they could not stand on their own or survive if they were in conflict with the law . . . *I imagine you will think long and hard before concluding that doctors of the eminence we have heard here have evolved standards that amount to committing a crime.*' (emphasis supplied)[65]

It is not surprising that it took the jury only two hours to return a unanimous verdict of acquittal after a lengthy trial. First and foremost the case likely stands for the proposition that an English jury can probably not be persuaded to convict a respected physician of murder unless presented with undeniable evidence of an intent to kill and deliberate acts to carry out that intent. Second, the case stands for the proposition that an English jury will not convict a respected physician of a criminal offense for honoring the express wishes of the parents to allow their handicapped infant to die.[68] Third, it is a clear example of the great deference that the law, in the form of judge and jury, will normally give to the treatment (and nontreatment) standards developed by the medical profession. While theoretically possible,. it is exceedingly unlikely that a judge or jury will choose to disregard testimony of physicians as to good medical practice, unless a dispute exists among them.

If the result would have been any different had a lesser offense been charged is, of course, speculation. Manslaughter could have been charged, or the offense of child endangerment, carrying a 2 year penalty rather than life imprisonment.[69] English juries, although given three opportunities to convict physicians of murder for allegedly acting to accelerate the deaths of their patients, have refused to do so.[70] Although it is common knowledge that doctors, with parental concurrence, elect not to treat seriously handicapped newborns in England,[71] no other criminal prosecutions apart from *Arthur* have been brought. This stems also in large part from few reported instances of abuse.

4.   *The case of Baby C*[72]

Baby C. was born in Yorkshire on December 23, 1988. She suffered from a more serious than usual form of hydrocephalus, an abnormal accumulation of brain fluid causing swelling of the head and pressure on the brain. The condition caused brain damage, with resulting blindness, deafness, lack of normal growth and an inability to take nourishment normally. The infant was made a ward of court by the local authority approximately two weeks after her premature birth, apparently for reasons unrelated to her medical condition, since it was felt her unmarried parents would have difficulty caring for her. She had been born about five weeks premature, weighing 5.5 pounds, but following birth the brain damage suppressed normal development, preventing growth of limbs, hair and nails. She had to be fed by means of a syringe every four hours. Despite six to eight hours of feeding each day, the infant would only take twelve teaspoons of milk and gained no weight.

After she was made a ward, the local authority requested court approval to place a shunt in her head to drain off extra cerebro-spinal fluid to relieve pressure on the brain. The surgery was approved, ordered and performed. However, it became apparent the infant was terminally ill and her severe brain damage was irreversible. The issue then arose as to whether active medical intervention in the form of naso-gastric feeding or administration of antibiotics should be undertaken if necessary to keep the infant alive.

The physicians caring for this most unfortunate infant requested the High Court in Leeds for a ruling as to whether or not life-sustaining treatment need be continued, or whether the infant, then aged nearly four months, should be allowed to die. The parents did not object to allowing the child to die. It was conceded her prognosis was such that she had no prospects of being able to lead a happy life. There was no hope of any improvement in her condition. Mr. Justice Ward considered the evidence in private to protect the privacy of parents and child, and ruled that the child should be allowed to die. He ruled that no further active medical treatment to keep the child alive need be taken. The syringe feeding, clearly a life-sustaining medical procedure, could presumably be withdrawn, as well as other medical support such as artificial respiration and drugs to combat the infant's multiple dysfunctions. The order first provided that the hospital treat the child 'to die.' However, this raised an outcry and was promptly modified to state that the infant should be treated 'in such a way that she may end her life and die peacefully with the greatest dignity and in the least pain, suffering and distress.'

The trial judge determined that the baby was so severely ill that she came within the exception to treatment established by the case of *Re B.*, which we discussed earlier. The judge concluded that no treatment not felt to be appropriate by the doctors should be ordered because,

> 'any quality to live has already been denied to this child because it cannot flow from a brain incapable of even limited intellectual function. In as much as one judges, as I do, intellectual function to be a hallmark of our humanity, her functioning on that level is negligible if it exists at all. Coupled with her total physical handicap, *the quality of her life will be demonstrably awful and intolerable within the B test.*

Asking myself what capacity she has to interact meaningfully with her surroundings, mentally, socially and physically, I answer none. This is her permanent condition.' (emphasis supplied.)

The judge placed primary reliance on the infant's inability to interact with her surroundings, or those around her. This quality of life test is essentially the same test applied to a similar case by one of the most prominent U.S. decisions in this difficult area, which we will discuss shortly. The judge did, however, also rely on the fact that her physical handicap and pain was 'demonstrably awful' and 'intolerable,' in concluding no active treatment was required except that necessary to ease her obvious pain and distress.

Because the Official Solicitor was not happy with the way in which the order was worded, an appeal was taken from the decision of the Leeds High Court. The Court of Appeal modified the trial judge's order to provide that the child be given only that treatment deemed 'appropriate' to the child's condition, in accordance with the general recommendations of a report by a consulting paediatrician. The court emphasized the child was terminally ill and would not survive. All available life-sustaining treatment need not be given, but only 'appropriate' medical care need be given. That appropriate care was to be defined by the physicians in attendance. The court, in announcing its decision, read extensively from and relied upon the report of a consulting paediatrician. He had indicated that neither antibiotics in the event of infection nor nasogastric feeding were indicated in light of the infant's hopeless prognosis, unless the medical staff felt it was appropriate to provide one or the other for the comfort of the infant. Any course of treatment that would cause the infant to suffer less was appropriate. The proper balance between short-term gain (as by giving antibiotics to forestall death from pneumonia) and needless prolongation of life needed to be kept in mind by the doctors. The emphasis of treatment should be to ease the baby's suffering during the remainder of her life, rather than to accomplish a short prolongation of her life without regard to her pain and suffering.

The case seems to stand for the proposition that where parents elect to refuse consent to life-sustaining treatment for a terminally and incurably ill infant in reliance on reasonable medical judgment, the parties act properly in not providing that treatment. The court's use of the term 'appropriate' care is intended to mean reasonable care; that is, care that ordinarily skilled practitioners in the exercise of reasonable judgment would provide under the particular circumstances, taking into account the particular condition of the infant.

It seems quite clear that in such hopeless cases, if medically reasonable, antibiotics and artificial (nasogastric) feedings may properly be withheld. The court will not second guess the physicians where they and parents concur. The court makes no distinction between the naso-gastric feeding and antibiotics; both are apparently accepted as medical treatment subject to the same standard of reasonableness.

The case, consistent with *dicta* in earlier cases,[73] recognizes that life need not be preserved at all costs, but that at times it is in the best interests of the incompetent patient that treatment should ease pain and suffering, rather than achieve a difficult and short prolongation of life. The sanctity of life is to be revered and respected, but it is not an absolute. Where death cannot be avoided and where mental and physical defects are severe, the Baby C. decision makes it clear that even where the child is a ward of the court, the court will not disturb the efforts of medicine to ease suffering even though it may hasten inevitable death. In that sense, the case is merely a current reaffirmation of the now-famous words of Lord Justice Devlin in the 1957 murder prosecution and acquittal of Dr. Adams, that,

> 'If the first purpose of medicine, the restoration of health, can no longer be achieved there is still much for a doctor to do, and he is entitled to do all that is proper and necessary to relieve pain and suffering, even if the measures he takes may incidentally shorten human life.'[74]

The appeals court deleted the portion of the order not requiring specific treatment.[75] It left intact that portion authorizing treatment to continue in accordance with the specialist's advice as to what was appropriate. The court emphasized the importance of 'wide consultation' before taking critical decisions in such a difficult case.

The Baby C. case does not address the situation of a severely handicapped newborn who is *not* terminally ill. The case is limited to the facts and particular condition of the infant presented to the court. However, the reasoning of the court suggests a basic judicial approach applicable in similar cases of severe newborn handicap. If the impact is very severe, if reasonable medical judgment is that certain care is not appropriate given the condition of the child, if reasonable expert consultation is obtained and followed, and if the parents concur, there is no obligation to provide that treatment. In the normal case no court involvement is necessary. As Brahams has stated, in reviewing the case,[72]

> Wardship proceedings apart, therefore, it seems that doctors will and should continue to bear their traditional responsibility for deciding, with the patient and family, when treatment should be withdrawn and for implementing such decisions. It would be undesirable for the courts to usurp the doctors' role and to become routinely involved in a medical decision which is the prerogative of the patient (if capable), family, and doctors in privacy.'

However, where the child is a ward of court, court approval or guidance is necessary, since 'once a child was a ward of court, no important step in the life of the child can be taken without the consent of the court.'[76] Where the condition is terminal and irreversible, and treatment is consistent with prevailing medical practice, there seems no need to involve the courts absent some disagreement.

This reading of the case makes it consistent with *Re B*. The judges in *Re B*. would, presumably, have concluded that the infant's life was 'demonstrably awful' or 'intolerable' and only palliative care was necessary. What remains unresolved is how severe the infant's handicaps must be. Baby C. was severely mentally and physically handicapped and *terminally* ill. What of other infants with handicaps of similar severity who are *not* terminally ill? The standards remain to be articulated.

The decision seems correct for a number of reasons. First of all, it is a clear example of the basic principle that a newborn must have the prospect of some minimal quality of life before continued active medical intervention will be mandated over the wishes of parents or physicians.[72-3] Futile treatment is not required. If treatment offers no hope of improving the patient's condition, and that condition involves either intolerable pain, or precludes the capability for some minimal level of interaction with others and with the environment, then it should not be legally compelled.[77] As one distinguished commentator has concluded, 'the propriety of non-treatment may be considered established, at least in those cases where there is no hope of any reasonable life for the infant.'[78]

This opinion is challenged by some who believe quality of life evaluations are inherently subjective and cannot be made by a healthy adult, who has never experienced handicapped life, for the infant. As one author has stated, 'opinions regarding the value of life are so disparate, and ability to calculate an infant's capacity to enjoy life so feeble, that withholding treatment on the basis of the 'quality of life' rests life and death decisions on pure speculation.'[79] Perhaps it would be most appropriate to say that quality of life for the infant is a factor to weigh in deciding what is in the best interests of the infant. This does assume, however, that there will be – on rare occasion – circumstances of living which support the conclusion that allowing the infant to die is in his or her best interests.

Second, the physicians undertook a reasonable clinical trial to determine if treatment might improve the newborn's prognosis. The decision to seek authority for withdrawal of further active treatment was not taken before deliberation and careful consideration of the prognosis for the child. Third, parents and physicians supported the decision to withdraw treatment. Fourth, there being no clear treatment guidelines,[78,5] the parties sought judicial approval before acting to withdraw treatment. On this latter point, the British Medical Association was quoted by *The Times* as concluding that, 'It is quite proper that the decision on whether Baby C. should be allowed to live or die should not be taken by doctors alone.'[72] This points up, once again, the need for professionally workable, legally acceptable and ethically proper non-treatment guidelines and standards. Such guidelines would provide protection to newborns, reassurance to parents and physicians, encourage consistency of application, reduce the need for court involvement and provide a framework for judicial guidance and decision-making where court involvement could not be avoided. Courts are no better qualified than doctors and parents to decide these questions. Clear guidelines should ensure acceptable and reasonable criteria for nontreatment and the due process (reasonable clinical trial, expert consultation, clear written record of prognosis, informed consent of parents, no disputes, etc.) necessary to keep the need for courts out of these intensely personal and heart-wrenching decisions.

5. *Some observations*

Despite proposals for the adoption of nontreatment guidelines and standards, or for the enactment of enabling but at the same time restrictive legislation to legitimize practice standards for newborn nontreatment,[80] it appears neither parliament nor the medical profession are anxious to intervene in this exceedingly personal, private, and perplexing area of medical care and parental responsibility. Given the lack of reported abuse, there is not great impetus for reform, but concern about subjective and ill-founded treatment decisions remains.

The lack of criminal prosecution of any doctors in England for electing not to actively treat a newborn child, before or since the *Arthur* case, defies simple explanation, since the practice is known to occur[71] and the law is clear that the best interests of the child must come before the wishes of the parents.[49] Several reasons explain this. First, a social consensus seems to exist that parents, in consultation with their physicians, should be able to decide against active medical intervention to save a severely handicapped newborn infant. The Abortion Act 1967, by expressly authorizing abortion in the face of substantial evidence that the fetus, if carried to term, will 'suffer from such physical or mental abnormalities as to be seriously handicapped,' represents perhaps the clearest social recognition that parental rights of decision and choice increase when the expected child is seriously handicapped.

Once birth occurs, a very significant legal event occurs: an independent legal person now exists who was not recognized as such while in utero. Nonetheless, the law in practice reflects social consensus. Just as juries have been unwilling to convict doctors caring for their patients of criminal wrongdoing,[70,74] so too have prosecutors and judges been unwilling to file and entertain criminal charges against doctors for electing to forego aggressive intervention with the seriously handicapped newborn.[81] For example, only one physician other than Dr. Arthur is reported to have been charged with attempted murder for failing to provide proper, active treatment for a premature fetus after birth. However, in that case, the Magistrates' Court concluded the case was not legally sufficient to bring to trial and the matter was dismissed.[82]

While parents must act in the best interests of their children, whether they are normal or handicapped,[86] a social and medical consensus seems to exist that parents may at times decide that no treatment is in the best interest of their severely handicapped child. The courts will construe this very narrowly if given the opportunity to act for the child,[49] but will normally not see such cases. The decisions are private, except in rare instances of physician or other staff disagreement with parental views.

The lack of clear legal standards doubtless contributes to the substantial latitude afforded private decisionmaking in such cases. As stated by the editors of the *British Medical Journal*,[83]

> We believe that in the absence of a clear code to which society adheres there is no justification for usurping parents'rights, or for believing that the courts are any more likely to reach a more humane solution.'

What seems to emerge from these few precedents is that a gap exists between the doctors' perceived legal duty to treat a severely handicapped newborn and what may be considered to be in the best interests of that infant. Where Down's syndrome is the only handicap, duty to treat and best interests are in accord; the child should be treated. Where some additional, life-threatening defect exists, the child's best interests may well support treatment, but there does not appear to be a clear legal duty to treat if the parents refuse consent.[84] There may be no treatment required; the parents may simply not want the infant to live in light of his or her handicaps.[59] Where more severe abnormalities of the central nervous system and brain are present, such that treatment is futile and death inevitable,[72] or that the infants pain and suffering is intolerable by any reasonable definition of humanity and cannot be alleviated,[49] or unconsciousness is permanent, or cerebral dysfunction is so great the infant will be unable to relate to others and the environment around him, there is without doubt no duty to treat in the face of parental refusal.[85] Physicians need only do what is reasonable to do; they need not undertake, by legal compulsion, the unreasonable, the extraordinary, or the hopeless.[66]

This being said, it is hard to assert that allowing a child to die is in his best interests. How can one alive say that being dead is better than being alive, but severely handicapped? The *McKay*[54] case refused to recognize a damage claim based on such a value judgment.[86] It may be more honest to say that the burden of caring and sorrow may be so great to the parents of a severely handicapped child, *if they* decide against treatment, that the law will abide by that choice in very limited circumstances, than to say allowing the infant to die is ever in his best interests.[87] Those 'normal' and healthy cannot judge, nor do they have the experience from which to make such a judgment on behalf of the abnormal infant. Nonetheless, a social consensus does exist, it is submitted, that it is in the best interests of a newborn to be allowed to die where treatment can only prolong inevitable death, or an existence of intolerable pain or hopelessly severe mental incompetence preventing any social interaction.

There are many safeguards against nontreatment decisions being taken lightly. They undoubtedly explain why, despite an ambiguous and ill-defined legal climate, there are only rare occasions of any reported abuse. These safeguards include, first and foremost, the threat of the criminal law. If the doctor's decision not to treat is seen as a breach of his legal duty to the child, the death that may result will expose him to murder, manslaughter or child endangerment liability. While Dr. Arthur was acquitted, the jury could have convicted. The doctor's duty to the patient is decided by the courts, not by professional practice alone.[88] The latter may strongly influence the former, but it is not conclusive.[89]

It is also true that parental attachment, biologically in the case of the mother and emotionally in the case of both parents, grows as the fetus nears term and is then born. Lorber and others have observed the vast majority of parents wish their child , even in the face of handicaps, treated. If the decision is made not to treat, it is presumptively and practically made out of love, a valuable safeguard.

Finally, while doctors tend to respect parental wishes in clear or border-line cases of severe defect[2,14,17,23,31] their ingrained professional bias is to treat.

With these safeguards in place, the traditional decision-making process of physician(s) and parents seems to have worked well. There has been little need for the law to intervene and in England, as in Scotland, it has rarely chosen to do so. To the extent it has, it has arguably produced conflicting legal standards, suggesting in *Arthur* the doctor may abide by the wishes of the parents in the face of newborn handicaps, but countering in *Re B* that the child's best interests compel treatment, at least in cases of uncertain or 'tolerable' handicap. Only action by parliament or clear definitive articulation of treatment and nontreatment criteria by the profession will remedy this legal uncertainty in Britain. Insight in this regard may be gained from the American experience, which has by statute authorized creation of such treatment and nontreatment criteria. However, before we consider the legal position in the United States we look at the limited developments in Scots law in this field.

B. SCOTLAND

There is no reported court decision in Scotland on the legality of parents or physicians deciding not to actively treat a handicapped newborn child. No statutory enactment exists to control or delineate parental or physician discretion in making such decisions.

The developed law of both Scotland and England does, however, give a newborn infant the right to sue if a birth defect is proved to be the result of another's negligence.[90] This is granted by statute in England;[91] by the common law in Scotland. This suggests a legal presumption that even seriously handicapped life shall be allowed to continue. However, as we have seen from review of the English decisions in *Re B.*,[49] *McKay*[54] and *Baby C*,[72] there are limits to this. Parents and physicians will normally be left alone to decide on treatment where the child faces an intolerable or demonstrably awful existence[49] or where severe central nervous system abnormality and deficit exists.[72]

However, it is also clear that parents may not neglect or abuse their children.[93] Parents may not deliberately or recklessly deprive their children of needed medical care.[94] This to some extent begs the question, for in the case of severely handicapped newborns the question is what medical care is needed. It is one thing to fail to provide medical treatment needed, available and capable of preventing injury or death,[95] such as penicillin for pneumonia or a blood transfusion.[96] It is quite another to fail to resuscitate or tube feed a baby born without a brain.

Despite the absence of clear legal precedent in Scotland, the view remains that parents and physicians have the legal discretion to allow severely deformed newborns to die when it is reasonable and consistent with established medical practice standards to do so. The absence of any direct Scottish legal precedent supports this conclusion. The fact no prosecution has been taken against a Scottish physician for not treating an infant, despite common knowledge this occurs in severe cases,[2,23,28,94,97] may be the strongest evidence that the practice is accepted legally and socially, and has not given rise to perceived or actual abuses.

McCall Smith has stated that 'the propriety of non-treatment may be considered established, at least in those cases where there is no hope of any reasonable life for the infant.'[98] Cusine and Campbell have concluded that, 'if a doctor has done all that is reasonable in the circumstances, it is not neglect, and hence not a breach of duty, to allow an infant to die.'[94]

These cases are, of course, very infrequent. The vast majority of live births produce normal infants. Of those born with handicaps, many are readily treatable. Even as to those infants with severe handicaps, many parents will elect to actively treat the baby.[99] As Campbell has stated, more infants are being abused by high technology than were ever allowed to die without it.[100]

The physical and emotional changes that a developing pregnancy brings to the parents normally causes a strong emotional bond and attachment to the neonate. Thus, the parents are presumptively well situated to carefully consider the best interests of the neonate before deciding against active medical treatment. As we have seen before, the Scottish prosecutorial apparatus and courts do not lightly intrude into questions of medical treatment. Unless there is clear abuse, or departure from recognized standards, the courts see no need to intervene and do not do so. The doctor's duty to his or her patient under Scots law is to act as a doctor of ordinary skill and training would act, exercising ordinary skill, under the circumstances at hand.[101] This is the same standard as applies in England.[102]

Thus, there is no legal duty to act to prolong the life of a severely handicapped neonate in Scots law if it is not reasonable to expect a doctor exercising ordinary care to do so under the circumstances.[100,98,97,94,40,39] Gordon, for example, does not even mention the possibility in his text on *Criminal Law*. If there is no duty to treat, then there is no legal liability for not treating.[97] Of course it is for the medical profession to establish socially and professionally acceptable treatment standards so that a physician's decision not to treat further can be judged against those standards to determine its reasonableness.[40] While some steps have been made to articulate such standards, more open discussion to reach consensus is needed.[103]

Duff and Campbell have suggested grouping handicapped infants into three general treatment categories:[104] maximum treatment, where prognosis with treatment is good; limited treatment, consisting of essentially palliative care, where treatment is not likely to provide benefit overall;[105] and withdrawal of life-sustaining treatment, where the patient is dying and the intent is not to prolong unnecessary suffering.

I have suggested elsewhere, with Professor Mason, that treatment may properly be withheld where because of severe newborn handicaps: (1) death is highly probable, within 1 year's time or sooner regardless of treatment; (2) there exists no reasonable possibility the infant will be able to participate in human relationships with others requiring some interaction or response;[106] or, (3) the treatment cannot alleviate an intolerable level of chronic pain making further life-sustaining treatment inhumane.[40]

Such guidelines assume consensus. If disagreements exist between parents, between parents and physicians, or between physicians, then withdrawal of treatment is inappropriate pending resolution of this dispute. If this cannot be done, privately among the parties, with input from social workers, nurses, psychologists, or others interested in the case, then in such rare instances court guidance should be sought.[28] The appointment of a guardian,[107] or of a tutor-dative[108] to act in the best interests of the child would seem appropriate in such cases.

A Scottish court has made it clear that where treatment for a newborn is futile, there is no obligation to institute that treatment.[109] In the case a premature baby girl was born weighing only 700 grams. The doctor concluded the newborn was not viable and accordingly elected not to attempt resuscitation by placing her on a mechanical ventilator. A Fatal Accidents Inquiry was held in the Sheriff Court.[110] The Sheriff found the evidence supported the doctor's conclusion that the infant was not viable,[111] and there was thus no obligation to attach the infant to a ventilator.

In sum, in Scotland decisions on withholding or withdrawing life-sustaining treatment from severely handicapped newborns will likely continue, much as they have in the past, to be made by parents, physicians and other concerned caregivers. The child's best interest must remain the cornerstone of decision making.

The quality of life the child will enjoy must be evaluated, not what the parents want. It must also be recognized that quality of life should be evaluated in a physical sense. If the neonate has sufficient cognitive ability to relate in some minimal way interpersonally and to his environment, and he does not suffer from an intolerable or inhumane level of chronic pain and suffering, the goal and presumption should be to treat and to salvage the infant. Given the uncertainties of neonatal prognosis, where the patient is essentially totally incapable of expressing his preferences, in any marginal or uncertain cases the presumption and practice should be in favor of treatment.

At the same time, it should be recognized that this area of medical care is an intensely personal one, bringing together issues of clinical judgment, of concern for the future life of the infant, and of the impact of the infant's handicap on the parents, the rest of the family, and the available medical resources.[112] A certain amount of discretion must necessarily be afforded parents and physicians. Historically, this has not resulted in any reported abuse.

In Scotland, undoubtedly more so than in England, or in the United States where a more consumer oriented attitude toward health care exists, parents have and will continue to rely heavily on what their doctor feels is 'best' in deciding whether to forego treatment for their newborn. This more paternalistic attitude toward medical care in Scotland is the result of the respect enjoyed by the medical profession generally, a more conservative, accepting attitude among patients, few legal challenges to the conduct of medical practice by the profession, a recognition fostered by the delivery of medical care through the National Health Service that there are limits on the availability of medical resources, and the traditional private decision-making in this area by parents and physicians.

As more clearly articulated medical treatment guidelines are established, doctors will feel more secure in recommending against treatment they feel is not warranted and will not be productive. Parents will also be reassured their decision is right, as they will have a basis of comparison. In the last analysis, however, the law can be expected to continue to honor the non-treatment decision reached by parents and physicians where it is made in good faith, in the belief it is in the best interests of the infant, and the decision is supported by a responsible body of medical opinion as reasonable and proper.[113] The courts will, of course, remain available to act promptly to protect the child in cases of abuse, neglect, questioned medical care or motive, disagreement, or where, on occasion, they conclude a more stringent treatment standard is needed to protect the best interests of the infant than that adopted by the profession.[114]

D.   UNITED STATES

1.   *The important role of the parents and the child's best interests*

As in the United Kingdom, the parents play an important role in decisions to withhold or withdraw treatment from their handicapped newborn.[115] The United States Constitution has been interpreted as extending to the parents a qualified, but revered, right to raise and care for their children in the way that they deem best.[116] The Supreme Court has encapsulated the principle in the following way,[117]

> 'It is cardinal with us that the custody, care and nurture of the child
> reside first in the parents whose primary function and freedom include
> preparation for obligations the state can neither supply nor hinder.'

Strong as this principle is, it is rebuttable. It does not condone the parents' proposal to take an action that will expose the child to harm, abuse or neglect. The state, as *parens patriae*, or substitute parent, will intervene to protect the health of a newborn or unborn child where the parents fail to act *reasonably* to protect him or her from harm.[118] The state may compel medical treatment in such cases, remove the child from the custody of the parents, or prosecute the parents for child abuse, manslaughter, reckless homicide, or even murder if the child is allowed to die.[119]

Courts are empowered to act to protect the best interests of children by the *parens patriae* doctrine and by the power of wardship conferred upon them by statute in most states.[120] Reasonable apprehension of harm to the child is an adequate basis for state intervention.[121] It need not wait until that risk of harm has actually been realized. The courts will consider several factors before compelling medical treatment over the objection of the parents,

> 'Several relevant factors must be taken into consideration before a state
> insists upon medical treatment rejected by the parents. The state
> should examine the seriousness of the harm the child is suffering or the
> substantial likelihood that he will suffer serious harm; the evaluation
> for the treatment by the medical profession; the risks involved in
> medically treating the child; and the expressed preferences of the
> child. Of course, the underlying consideration is the child's welfare

and whether his best interests will be served by the medical treatment.'[122]

Nearly all of the decided cases have, however, involved the advisability of surgery, blood transfusions, or other forms of active medical treatment or management in young children whose parents, principally because of philosophical or religious beliefs, are opposed.[123] Few have involved decisions not to treat newborn infants because of the severity of their birth defects. The courts have made it clear that the parents' failure to provide food or basic medical care for their child will result in criminal manslaughter or murder liability if the result is the death of the child.[124]

Where the parents follow the advice of a responsible body of medical opinion in treating or not treating their child, their decision will in all likelihood be respected.[125] This is true even though the decision is not to actively treat a life-threatening affliction or handicap. If the treatment decision is one concurred in by a responsible body of medical opinion, then it is presumed to be a reasonable course of action. The parents in electing to follow it are, accordingly, acting reasonably and courts will rarely intervene to overrule or censure their decision. However, in limited circumstances, although the action of the parents is not deemed improper in refusing treatment for their child,[126] the courts will nonetheless order treatment where it is felt to clearly be for the best interests of that infant.[127]

One case will illustrate this principle. Phillip B. was born with Downs syndrome, complicated by a congenital heart anomaly. He was institutionalized by his parents. At age 12 the local authority sought to have him declared a ward of court for purposes of authorizing corrective heart surgery which the parents refused to permit.

There was some surgical risk of mortality (less than 10 per cent), but without surgery the boy's health would painfully decline, with death expected within 20 years. The court concluded this parental refusal did not amount to abuse or neglect and denied the wardship.[126] The best interests of the boy were not considered.

Several years later guardianship over the boy was sought by his foster parents. Their purpose was to authorize the surgery. The issue was the boy's best interests and, fortunately, the court had no difficulty in finding the surgery, and the guardianship to accomplish it, in the best interests of the boy.[127] The petition was granted.

2. *The traditional private decisionmaking process*

Traditionally, in the United States, as in the United Kingdom, parents and physicians have made decisions to allow seriously handicapped newborn infants to die by not providing life-sustaining medical care.[128] This practice has been judicially recognized.[129] However, it has been pointed out that this practice may be subject to abuse for several reasons: the medical prognosis may be uncertain and erroneous when dealing with a newborn; the parents' ability to decide rationally may be compromised by emotional distress, fear, disappointment, or guilt; the parents' decisions may be based on their economic, emotional and familial considerations, rather than from the point of view of the infant's best interests. For these reasons, it has been asserted these decisions should only be made openly,[130] in accordance with clearly articulated standards for selective nontreatment.[128] While this is an admirable goal, with which few would argue, such standards have not, at least until recently,[131] been forthcoming. In the meantime, severely handicapped children continue to be born, complicated of late by drug-dependent mothers and extremely premature infants born of mothers disenfranchised from needed prenatal medical care because of financial constraints.[132] The few court cases decided show that the decisionmaking process remains largely private and without any widespread abuse.

3.   *The American Court decisions*

There are a limited number of court cases which have addressed the legal standards for nontreatment of severely handicapped newborn. Many have been trial court decisions only, which lack precedent value. Some are unreported to protect the privacy of parents and child. Few have attempted to articulate any standards beyond dealing only with the specific and peculiar facts of the case before them. Some recognize quality of life as a proper component of the decisionmaking formula; others assert that it is impermissible to consider it. The result is a patchwork of decisions, with very little in common to hold them together, from which to discern the position of the law. Some conclusions may be ventured, but they must necessarily be tentative and without strong conviction.

a.   *cases refusing to order treatment.* American courts have in general allowed parents broad discretion in electing against treatment for their newborn infants where the physicians in attendance concurred in the decision and one or more serious congenital handicaps were present. Courts have refused to overrule the parents in the following instances:

1. where the child would be retarded due to Downs syndrome,[133] and suffered, it is believed, from a serious life-threatening, congenital heart defect which caused responsible physicians to be of mixed minds concerning the advisability of correcting an intestinal blockage (duodenal atresia) to permit the child to eat;[134]

2. where the child was in an irreversible coma, or persistent vegetative state due to brain injury or deprivation of oxygen and had no reasonable possibility of ever regaining consciousness;[135]

3. where the child was born with occipital encephalocele, a protrusion of brain tissue, poor response to stimuli, slow respiration and other aggressive medical treatment was declined;[136]

4. where the child was born with myelomeningocele, microcephaly and hydrocephalus, a malformed brain stem, 'weak face' and upper extremity spasticity, would probably only live two years without surgery, might live twenty years with corrective surgery involving closing her spinal opening and implanting a cerebral shunt to drain off fluid, but would be severely retarded, bedridden, epileptic, paralyzed and subject to frequent infections throughout her life, and where a responsible body of medical opinion opposed surgery and favored a conservative course of treatment for symptom relief;[137]

5. where the child was suffering from cancer (Hodgkins disease), was responding to a somewhat unconventional but recognized medical treatment program emphasizing nutritional and metabolic therapy, and the parents indicated a willingness to undertake conventional, but risky and invasive chemotherapy treatment if all else failed;[138]

6. where the infant is reliably diagnosed as suffering from a permanent, incurable and irreversible physical or mental abnormality that is likely to soon result in death.[139] A physician need not provide futile treatment.

b. *Cases ordering treatment.* Other courts have been more inclined to order treatment for handicapped newborns. At times the courts have looked at quality of life for the infant. At other times they have only considered the feasibility, not necessarily the productivity, of the treatment: if it is life-saving, it has been ordered by some judges without further consideration. These decisions are in the minority. Courts have ordered treatment undertaken,

1. where the infant suffered from spina bifida, but the defect was relatively low on the spine, it would likely cause incontinence and possibly lower extremity paralysis, but the case was not 'hopeless' and the child could expect normal intellectual development and to live a 'useful, fulfilling life;'[140]

2. where the infant suffered from a life-threatening congenital transposition of the aorta with the pulmonary artery, but no other gross abnormalities;[141]

3. where the infant suffered multiple birth defects from his mother's prenatal rubella, life-saving surgery had a 50–60 per cent mortality rate, and quality of life was deemed to be poor;[142]

4. where the infant suffered multiple birth defects including no left eye, disconnected vertebrae, malformed ear and thumb, tracheal-esophageal fistula preventing normal feeding and brain damage, but corrective surgery was life-saving and feasible to permit feeding;[143]

The apparent inconsistency between these court decisions, as well as the publicity surrounding several of the cases in particular,[134,137] prompted the Congress in 1985 to adopt certain legislative standards for treatment in the case of handicapped newborn. Federal regulations have been promulgated, but no court cases have interpreted their application to date.

4. *Legislatively-imposed treatment standards for handicapped newborn*

The U. S. Department of Health and Human Services has promulgated certain rules to carry out the intent of 1984 amendments to the Child Abuse Prevention and Treatment Act of 1974.[144] Hospitals are encouraged to establish Infant Care Review Committees to monitor the proper care of disabled infants and to help prevent medical neglect in any such cases. Withholding 'medically indicated treatment' is considered to be neglect. While the rules seek to limit the instances where treatment may be withheld, they do recognize that medical judgment must continue to play an essential role in treatment and nontreatment decisions.

Treatment need not be provided when, 'in the treating physician's reasonable medical judgment' (1) the infant is irreversibly comatose; (2) treatment would only prolong inevitable death and be futile in terms of the infant's survival; or, (3) treatment would be virtually futile,[145] in terms of the infant's survival and would, under the circumstances, be inhumane.[146]

Food and water is placed in a special category under the rules. It is to be provided, if 'appropriate', even in the hopeless instances mentioned. However, if the physician, in the exercise of reasonable and prudent medical judgment concludes even nutrition, hydration or medication is not 'appropriate', it apparently need not be given and may also be withheld.

Thus, these federal regulations are restrictive, yet at the same time enabling. They apply to virtually all hospitals, since all depend on Medicare reimbursement and other federal aid and must satisfy federal regulations to obtain it.

The regulations are recognized and likely set the standards for nontreatment of newborn infants. They do not, however, cover the situation where treatment will allow the infant to survive, but at what most would consider to be an unacceptable level of sapient, cognitive existence, or at an acceptable, 'humane' level of pain and suffering. This needs to be addressed more clearly in the regulations. Whether they have inhibited the traditional medical practice of accepting the hopelessness of the infant's condition in such cases where the parents and physician concur is not clear. As a result, the need for clear, legally acceptable, medically workable treatment guidelines and standards remains.

E.   CONCLUSIONS

1. *A common ethic*

What emerges from a review of the law and of medical practice in Scotland, in England, and in the United States is a sense of remarkable similarity.

What may be inferred from this similarity of law and medial practice is the existence of a moral and ethical consensus in these countries of similar origin and attitude. From this comparison comes the confidence that the present legal and medical environment, while not clearly articulated, is nonetheless sound, accepted, and acceptable. It then remains to try to fairly define the parameters and general principles that have evolved in the law and medical practice, so that the basic tenets may be recognized and the gaps identified for filling and definition. At the risk of perhaps over-simplifying the picture, the following conclusions seem to emerge.

2. *Parents and physicians are the decisionmaking norm*

In all three jurisdictions the accepted norm for decisionmaking is for the parents and physicians in attendance to do so. The advisability of an independent, expert consultation is clear, as it is in other areas of controversial medical care.[147]

Most handicapped newborns will present a clear treatment picture. Where physical defect exists, without serious mental impairment,[140,141] or where uncertain mental impairment exists, such as in cases of Down's syndrome,[49,148] treatment can and should be undertaken and may be legally compelled.

On the other hand, where severe brain or other neural tube defects are present, represented by cases of anencephaly, hydrocephaly and/or micro-cephaly, so as to make the infant's survival or ability to relate cognitively to his physical environment and others around him most unlikely, treatment is not and should not be legally compelled.[72,135-137,144-146]

Ambiguous cases that present no clear prognosis at birth should be treated until it can be determined with reasonable medical certainty whether treatment is proportionate; that is, whether it offers benefits to the child sufficient to outweigh the burdens it imposes upon him.[72,149] Some have suggested this determination should be made within some arbitrary time after birth.[150] However, no time limit should be imposed to discourage a full and reasonable clinical trial. Once prognosis is clear, whenever that may be, is the time to decide on withdrawal of further treatment.

3. *Reasonableness, not perfection, is the standard*

The law should not require more than reasonable conduct, for fear of discouraging compliance with unattainable or unfair standards of conduct. No one is better situated than parents and physicians to act in the best interests of the infant. The parents have conceived, carried, nurtured and given birth to the child and strong biological and emotional bounds presumptively exist to promote actions to save and benefit the child.[151] The physician, except perhaps in occasional cases of medical neglect, has motives to save life and to avoid any claim of abandonment, wrongful death or failure to do all required by good medical practice.

Fortunately, the law requires neither perfection or cure from parents or physician. It does require that they act as reasonable persons would, in the circumstances, act. As Robertson has stated,

> 'Parental duty is limited by what can reasonably be expected of parents, given their protective relationship to a child. Similarly, a physician's duty to undertake a medical procedure is determined by what can reasonably be expected in light of customary medical practice, the likelihood of success and the available alternatives.'[152]

The position at common law in Britain is the same. Glanville Williams has stated it as follows:

> 'A doctor must never do anything actively to kill his patient, but he is not bound to fight for the patient's life forever. His duty in this regard is to make reasonable efforts, having regard to customary practice and expectations, and in particular having regard to the benefit to the patient to be expected from future exertions.'[153]

Following this standard, where the treatment offers reasonable hope of benefit, without disproportionate pain, suffering or expense, it should normally be pursued. There remains, however, the task of determining benefit. It is here that guidelines and treatment standards are needed; they must be openly discussed, noted in the patients' chart when they are relied upon to discontinue treatment, and be flexible enough to admit of constant changes and advances in medical science, in treatment and diagnosis.

Duff and Campbell have pointed out that rigid guidelines cannot be set out in advance for treatment and nontreatment. Flexibility is essential. No two cases are exactly alike. 'Patients (when able), families and health professionals (physicians, nurses, social workers), together and usually in that order, should do this [decide treatment] instance by instance.'[154]

4.   *Treatment should be productive and beneficial to be compelled*

If treatment will allow the child to function in a conscious state, with some apprehension of those around him and of his environment and without intolerable pain, then it is productive, beneficial and should be presumptively required. If it offers this benefit without other attendant burdens of significantly greater impact, then it is 'appropriate' care.[72] But when are the burdens too great to warrant treatment? That remains to be articulated in many specific instances of patient care.

Treatment should not be required where, (1) death is highly probable within the immediate future, say within one year or less, regardless of treatment; (2) because of persistent coma or mental abnormality the child has no reasonable possibility of minimal interaction with his environment and those around him; or, (3) treatment cannot alleviate a chronic, hopeless condition of intolerable pain, making continuation of the treatment itself inhumane.[40,144-146,155]

These guidelines are intended to be flexible, restricted to the most severe cases, yet broad enough to cover the multitude of congenital conditions which may bring about such dire circumstances. While guidelines should not be overly rigid and while clinical judgment and parental disposition must be allowed some reasonable discretion in individual cases, it is also true, as the Canadian Law Reform Commission has stated that, '[w]hen human life is at stake, the law should do everything within its power to clarify the situation and to define as precisely as possible the minimal limits which our society considers acceptable.'[156]

5. *Difficult cases should be dealt with first by parents and physicians, second institutionally, and only last by the courts*

We have seen that parents and physicians have been and should remain the norm for decisionmaking. However, if medical neglect or ill motive is suspected, or any dispute or disagreement exists between parents, parents and physicians, or among physicians, the hospital or medical society should have a bioethics committee to serve as a forum to encourage discussion and resolution of these concerns.

If this fails, then the courts are available to make the child a ward,[49,72] to appoint a guardian or conservator,[127] or to authorize treatment.[118] In rare instances this will continue to be necessary in the future as it has in the past. Treatment guidelines are just that. As such they will inevitably be general and at times vague. They can never be a substitute for the clinical judgment of the physician and the compassion of the parent. The law must allow for some reasonable discretion in decisionmaking concerning these wrenching and intensely personal matters.

The law, although strictly prohibiting any action to take life as homicide, is much more flexible in practice. This is true in Britain and in the United States. A recent example involved a hopelessly brain-damaged, comatose 15 month old boy.[157] He was not brain dead however. As a result the hospital and physicians refused to disconnect him from an artificial respirator for fear of legal liability. The boy's father took things into his own hands, held hospital workers at gunpoint and disconnected his son, who died shortly thereafter. He was arrested, but the Cook County grand jury refused to return an indictment of murder. The father was convicted only of unlawful use of a firearm and placed on probation for one year. In imposing sentence the judge concluded, 'as far as punishment is concerned, I think you have suffered enough.' Similar situations have been treated with similar leniency by other courts.[158] It is perhaps best that the strict prohibition of the law remains, leaving it to be properly applied by compassionate judges and juries based on the particular evidence before them.

6.   *The best interests of the child*

In the last analysis, decisions not to treat must be based on subjective and imperfect human perceptions of what is best for the unrepresented infant who is unable to speak or decide for himself. While healthy adults will be deciding for unhealthy newborns, without the experience or point of reference of the newborn, and with much of life behind them, society has yet to devise a better system.

While some argue persuasively that non-life can never be in the infant's best interests as opposed to impaired life, the existence of at least the general outlines of a similar consensus in Scotland, England and the United States on selective newborn nontreatment suggests the existence of a common ethic and an accepted morality for this practice. It is not easy to acknowledge or implement for parents, physicians or, when called upon, the courts. However, it seems to have worked, at least in very large part, without evident abuse. For those one or two babies in every thousand who present these issues, the existing laws against homicide, child abuse and neglect seem strong enough, yet flexible enough in practice, to protect and promote the best interests of these infants to the greatest extent reasonably possible.[159]

NOTES

1 The first 28 days after birth. Mason & McCall Smith, *Law and Medical Ethics*, p. 102.
2 See Duff & Campbell, 'Moral and Ethical Dilemmas in the Special-Care Nursery,' 289 *N. Eng J. Med.* 890 (1973); Lorber, 'Selective Treatment of Myelomeningocele: To Treat or Not to Treat,' 53 *Pediatrics* 307 (1974).
3 Yu, et. al. 'Prognosis for Infants Born at 23 to 28 Weeks' Gestation,' 293 *Brit. Med. J.* 1200 (1986).
4 *Ibid*; see also, Bromwich, 'Late Abortion,' 294 *Brit. Med. J.* 527 (1987).
5 Reidinger, *Am. Bar Assn. J.*, July 1, 1988, pp. 66,69; Wells & Morgan, 'What Price a Baby's Life,' *The Independent* (London), Nov. 2, 1988, p.12.
6 Wells & Morgan, *loc. cit.*
7 Savage, 'Young Fetus "Viability" Unchanged, Court Told,' *Los Angeles Times*, April 1, 1989, p. 20.
8 *C. v. S.* (1987) 1 All E.R. 1230, (1988) Q.B. 135.
9 Meyers, *Medico-Legal Implications of Death & Dying*, Dec., 1988, Cum. Supp., §14:1, p. 231.
10 See the pioneering article by Robertson, 'Involuntary Euthanasia of Defective Newborns: A Legal Analysis,' 27 *Stan. L.R.* 213 (1975).
11 Lorber, *loc. cit.*
12 *In re Phillip B.* (1979) 92 Cal. App. 3d 796, cert. den. (1979) 445 U.S. 949 (Downs's syndrome with correctable congenital heart defect; not

neglect for parents to refuse consent to proposed corrective surgery); but compare, *Guardianship of Phillip B.* (1981) 139 Cal. App. 3d 407 (guardianship given to foster parents who wished boy to undergo surgery, as in his 'best interests'.)

13 *Re Cicero* (1979, N.Y. App.) 421 N.Y.S. 2d 965 (surgery ordered for newborn with myelomeningocele where evidence was that normal intellectual development was probable, with limited lower extremity paralysis).

14 Lorber, 'Results of Treatment of Myelomeningocele', 13 *Develop. Med. and Child Neurol.* 279 (1971; Lorber, 53 *Pediatrics* 307 (1974).

15 ie., incontinence, infections and significant paraplegia, hydrocephalus and/or blind, fits and obesity, although 60 per cent had a normal range I.Q. of 80 or above.

16 Incontinence and partial paraplegia.

17 Lorber, 'Ethical Problems in the Management of Myelomeningocele and Hydrocephalus,' 10 *J. Roy. Coll. Phys.* 47 (1975).

18 Lorber, 53 *Pediatrics* 308 (1973).

19 Involving coincidence of the following criteria: (1) leg paralysis, (2) vertebral lesions, (3) scoliosis, (4) grossly enlarged head, (5) intracerebral birth injury, and (6) some other gross congenital defect in the neonate. 53 *Pediatrics* 307; 13 *Develop. Med and Child Neurol.* 279.

20 289 *N. Eng. J. Med.* 890 (1973).

21 *Ibid.*, at p. 894.

22 Shaw, 'Dilemmas of Informed Consent in Children,' 289 *N. Eng. J. Med.* 885, 886 (1973).

23 Lorber, 10 *J. Roy. Coll. Phys.* 47, 56 (1975); accord, Campbell & Duff, 'Deciding the care of severely malformed or dying infants,' 5 *J. Med. Ethics* 65, 66 (1979).

24 5 *J. Med. Ethics* 65.

25 'Ethics and Selective Treatment of Spina Bifida,' 1975 *The Lancet* 85, 88.

26 *Gillick v. West Norfolk and Wisbech Area Health Authority* (1985) 3 All E.R. 402 (H.L.); *Sidaway v. Bethlem Royal Hosp. and Others* (1985) 1 All E.R. 643, 2 W.L.R. 480 (H.L.); *Cobbs v. Grant* (1972) 8 Cal. 3d 229; *Bouvia v. Superior Court* (1986) 179 Cal. App. 3d 1127.

27 *U. S. v. University Hospital* (1984, 2d cir.) 729 Fed. 2d 144; *Re Hofbauer* (1979, N.Y.) 393 N.E. 2d 1009; *R. v. Arthur, The Times*, 6 Nov. 1981, pp. 1, 12, 1981 *The Lancet* 1085, 1101.

28 Duff & Campbell, 5 *J. Med. Ethics* 65, 66–7 (1979).

29 289 *N. Eng. J. Med* 890, 893 (1973).

30 Meyers, *Medico-Legal Implications of Death and Dying*, §14:8, p. 444, §14.21, p. 465.

31 Campbell, AGM, 'Withholding or Withdrawing Treatment,' Univ. of Aberdeen, Faculty of Law, Nov. 2, 1988; 1981 *Brit. Med. J.* 1629.

32 Lorber, 10 *J. Roy. Coll. Phys.* 47, 58 (1975).

33 1975 *The Lancet* 85, 87.

34 See discussion on allocation of scare medical resources in Chap. 11, *infra*.

35 *Barber v. Superior Court* (1983) 147 Cal. App. 3d 1006; Brahams, 'No Obligation to Resuscitate a Non-Viable Infant,' 1988 *The Lancet* 1176.

36 1975 *The Lancet* 85, 88.

37 Robertson, 27 *Stan. L. R.* 213, 236 (1975).

38 Weir, *Selective Nontreatment of Handicapped Newborns: Moral Dilemmas in Neonatal Medicine.* Oxford: Oxford U. Press, 1984.

39 *Hunter v. Hanley* 1955 S.C. 200, 206; *Bolam v. Friern Hosp. Management Committee* (1957) 2 All E.R. 118, 122.

40 Mason and Meyers, 'Parental choice and selective non- treatment of deformed newborns: a view from mid-Atlantic,' 12 *J. Med. Ethics* 67, 70 (1986).

41 *Sidaway v. Bethlem Royal Hosp. and Others* (1985) 1 All E.R. 643 (H.L.); *The T.J. Hooper* (1932, 2d cir.) 60 Fed. 2d 737 (Learned Hand, J.), cert.den. 287 U.S. 662.

42 *Helling v. Carey* (1974, Wash.) 519 Pac. 2d 981 (superceded by statute), (simple pressure test to detect glaucoma in patient under 40 not excused because opthamology profession felt test unwarranted by low incidence of risk).

43 Duff and Campbell were threatened with prosecution by the state's attorney after their disclosure in 1973 of selective nontreatment practices at Yale–New Haven Hosp.

44 'Pediatricians and the Law' (ed.) 1981 *Brit. Med. J.* 1280–1281.

45 See discussion in Chap. 9, *infra.*

46 Mason and McCall Smith, *Law & Medical Ethics* (1st ed. 1983), p. 89.

47 Mason and McCall Smith, *Law & Medical Ethics* (2d ed. 1987), p. 115.

48 1981 *Brit. Med. J.* 1629.

49 *In Re B. (A Minor)*, (1981) 1 W.L.R. 1421 (C.A.).

50 The surgeon stated he believed the 'great majority' of surgeons faced with the parents' refusal to consent under similar circumstances would do likewise. (1981).

51 (1981) 1 W.L.R. 1421, 1423.

52 (1981) 1 W.L.R. 1421, 1424.

53 McCall Smith, *The Times*, 22 April 1988, p.16.

54 (1982) 2 W.L.R. 890, 2 All E.R. 777 (C.A.).

55 Abortion Act 1967, sec. 1(1)(b).

56 (1982) 2 W.L.R. 890, 902.

57 Dickens, 'Wrongful birth and life, wrongful death before birth, and wrongful law,' *Legal Issues in Human Reproduction*, pp. 80, 91.

58 (1982) 2 All E.R. 777, 781 (Stephenson, L.J.).

59 There are a number of accounts of the officially unreported case. See, for example, Gunn & Smith, 'Arthur's Case and the Right to Life of the Down's Syndrome Child,' 1985 *Crim. L.R.* 705; Poole, 'Arthur's Case: (1) A Comment,' 1986 *Crim. L.R.* 383; Brahams, 'The Arthur case – a proposal for legislation' 1983 *J. Med. Ethics* 12; Mason & Meyers, supra, 1986 *J. Med. Ethics* 67; 'Dr. Leonard Arthur: his AG trial and its implications,' 1981 *Brit. Med. J.* 1340.

60 The majority of parents, when faced with a fetal diagnosis of Down's syndrome, evidently opt for abortion. *Los Angeles Times Magazine*, April 23, 1989, pp. 12, 25 (reporting 91 per cent of California women did so, as shown by Dept. of Health statistics; the attitude of parents after birth has not been reported, but presumably it is much less.). See Simms, (1986) 12 *J. Med. Ethics* 72.

61 1981 *Brit. Med. J.* 1340.

62 Under the Criminal Attempts Act 1981, sec. 1(1), one is guilty of an attempt if he 'does an act which is more than merely preparatory to the commission of the offense.'

63 *R. v. Instan* (1893) 1 Q.B. 450 (niece convicted of manslaughter for failure to provide bed-ridden aunt with needed nourishment not being otherwise provided); *R. Gibbins & Proctor* (1918) 13 Cr. App. 134 (C.A.), (father and woman with whom living convicted of murder for withholding food from dependent young child with intent to cause death or grievous harm).

64 Dunn & Smith, 1985 *Crim. L.R.* 705, 710)11.

65 Brahams, 1983 *J. Med. Ethics* 12, 13.

66 *Hunter v. Hanley* 1955 S.C. 200, 206; *Bolam v. Friern Hosp. Management Committee* (1957) 2 All E.R. 118,122.

67 *Sidaway v. Bethlem Royal Hosp. and Others* (1985) 1 All E.R. 643 (H.S.); *The T.J. Hooper* (1932, 2d cir.) 60 Fed. 2d 737 (Learned Hand, J.), Cert. den. 287 U.S. 662.

68 Brahams, 'Putting Arthur's Case in Perspective,' 1986 *Crim. L.R.* 387, 388.

69 Children and Young Persons Act 1933, sec. 1 (see also, Children and Young Persons Act 1963), discussed in Poole, 1986 *Crim L.R.* 383, 385.

70 See discussion of the unsuccessful prosecutions of Doctors Adams and Carr in Chapter 10, *infra*.

71 Whitelaw, 'Death as an option in neonatal intensive care' 1986 *The Lancet* 2, 328; 1981 *Brit. Med. J.* (1) 925)6; 1981 *Brit. Med. J.* (2) 569)70; 1981 *The Lancet* 1085; Campbell & Duff, 1979 *J. Med. Ethics* 65.

72 *In Re C (A Minor) (Wardship: Medical Treatment)*, (1989) 3 W.L.R. 240; see also *The Times*, 17 April 1989, p. 9 (High Court, Leeds, Mr. Justice Ward); *The Times*, 21 April 1989, pp.3,36; Brahams, 'Court of Appeal Endorses Medical Decision to Allow Baby to Die,' 1989 *The Lancet* 969–970.

73 *Re B. (A Minor)* (1981) 1 W.L.R. 1421 (C.A.); *McKay v. Essex Area Health Auth.* (1982) 2 All E.R. 777, 781 (Stephenson, L.J.).

74 Palmer, 'Dr. Adams' Trial for Murder' 1957 *Crim. L.R.* 365, 375; see discussion in Chapter 9,C., *infra*.

75 The portion of the order deleted stated 'it shall not be necessary either to (a) prescribe and administer antibiotics to treat serious infection, or (b) to set up intravenous fusions or nasal gastric feeding regimes.' Note 72 above; *The Times*, 21 April 1989, p.36 (Law Report).

76 *In re D (A Minor) (Wardship; Sterilization)* (1976) Fam. 185, 196 (Heilbron, J.); see also, *In re B (A Minor) (Wardship; Sterilization)* (1988) A.C. 199 (Lord Hailsham, J.).

77 Mason and Meyers, 'Parental choice and selective non-treatment of deformed newborns: a view from mid-Atlantic,' *J. Med. Ethics* 67, 70 (1986).

78 Alexander McCall Smith, 'Life or death for a baby,' *The Times*, 22 April 1988, p. 16.

79 Arras, 'Toward an ethic of ambiguity,' 1984 *Hastings Center Report* 25.

80 Mason & McCall Smith, *Law and Medical Ethics* (2d ed.) p. 115; Brahams, 1983 *J. Med. Ethics* 12, 14–15.

81 Mason states only one Coroner's Court has claimed death resulted from want of proper medical care at birth, but there was no prosecution. Mason, *Human Life and Medical Practice*, p. 90.

82 *R. v. Hamilton, The Times*, 16 Sept. 1983, p. 1.

83 283 *Brit. Med. J.* 569, 570 (1981).

84 *R. v. Arthur*, note 59, *supra*; 1981 *The Lancet* 1085; Kennedy, 'Reflections on the Arthur Trial,' 1982 *New Society* No. 999, p. 13; Skegg, *Law, Ethics and Medicine*, p. 146.

85 Mason & Meyers, 1986 *J. Med. Ethics* 67, 70; Brahams, 1983 *J. Med. Ethics* 12, 14–15; 1975 *The Lancet* 85, 87.

86 See McLean, *Medicine, Morals and the Law*, p. 69.

87 Raphael, 'Handicapped infants: medical ethics and the law,' 1988 *J. Med. Ethics* 8, 9.

88 *Sidaway v. Bethlem Royal Hosp. and Others* (1985) 2 W.L.R. 480 (H.L.).

89 *Ibid.*; *R. v. Arthur, supra*, note 105; Skegg, *Law, Ethics and Medicine*, p. 131.

90 McLean & Maher, *Medicine, Morals, and the Law*. Aldershot: Gower, 1981, p. 69.

91 Congenital Disabilities (Civil Liability) Act 1976, sec. 1(2)(b.)

92 2 All. E.R. 777, 781 (Stephenson, L.J.).

93 Children and Young Persons (Scotland) Act 1937, as amended.

94 Campbell and Cusine, 'Focus: current issues in medical ethics,' 1981 7 *J. Med. Ethics* 5, 16.

95 *Isabella Martin* (1877) 3 Couper 379; *R. v. Senior* (1899) 1 Q.B. 283.

96 'Sheriff allows blood for baby', *The Scotsman*, 25 April 1973, p. 1.

97 See also, for example, 1981 *Brit. Med. J.* 569–70; Cusine, 1983 *J. Med. Ethics* 123.

98 Alexander McCall Smith, 'Life or death for a baby,' *The Times*, 22 April 1988, p. 16.

99 Lorber, 1981 *Brit. Med. J.* 1463 (letter).

100 Campbell, A.G.M., 'Withholding or Withdrawing Treatment', Univ. of Aberdeen, Faculty of Law, 2 Nov. 1988.

101 *Hunter v. Hanley* 1955 S.C. 200, 205 (Lord Pres. Clyde).

102 *Ibid.*; Williams, G., 'Euthanasia' 1972 *Medico-Legal J.* 19; see also, G. Williams, *The Sanctity of Life and the Criminal Law*, p. 291.

103 Wells & Morgan, *The Independent*, 2 Nov. 1988, p. 12; Campbell, 'The right to be allowed to die,' 9 *J. Med. Ethics* 136, 138 (1983).

104 'Deciding the care of severely malformed or dying infants,' 5 *J. Med. Ethics* 65, 67 (1979).

105 Presumably what is meant here is that the burdens imposed by the treatment will outweigh the benefits reasonably anticipated from the treatment. See *Barber v. Superior Court* (1983) 147 Cal. App. 3d 1006, 1019.

106 This would include the infant in chronic coma or persistent vegetative state, as well as those with such severe mental abnormality as to be unable to respond to or interact with others. See *U.S. v. University Hospital* (1984, 2d. cir.) 729 Fed. 2d 144.

107 Law Reform (Parent and Child) (Scotland) Act 1986,s.3.

108 Ward, 'Morris Petitioner, Revival of Tutors-Dative,' 13 Feb 1987 *S.L.T.* (News) 69.

109 Brahams, 'No Obligation to Resuscitate a Non-Viable Infant,' 1988 *The Lancet* 1176.
110 Fatal Accidents and Sudden Deaths Inquiry (Scotland) Act 1976.
111 Incapable of independent existence outside the womb, with or without artificial support medically.
112 1975 *The Lancet* 85, 87; Campbell, 9 *J. Med. Ethics* 136, 139 (1983).
113 McLean & Maher, *Medicine, Morals, and the Law*, p. 71; Meyers, *Legal Issues in Human Reproduction*, p. 126.
114 *R. v. Arthur*, 1981 *The Lancet* 1101 ('Whatever ethics a profession might evolve they could not stand on their own or survive if they were in conflict with the law' per Farquharson, J.).
115 See discussion in Chapter 6, part D., *supra*; Meyers, 'Parental rights and consent to medical treatment of minors,' Chap. 28 in Mason (ed.) *Paediatric Forensic Medicine and Pathology*. London: Chapman & Hall, 1989, p. 428.
116 *Pierce v. Society of Sisters* (1925) 268 U.S. 510; *Prince v. Massachusetts* (1944) 321 U.S. 158.
117 *Prince v. Mass.*, *supra*; see also, *Bowen v. American Hosp. Ass'n.* (1986) 106 S. Ct. 2101, 2113.
118 *Raleigh-Fitkin Paul Morgan Hosp. v. Anderson* (1964, N.J.) 201 A. 2d 537 (reaffirmed, *Matter of Baby M.* (1988, N.J.) 537 A. 2d 1227, 1254, note 13); *Application of Pres. and Dir. of Georgetown College* (1964, D.C. Cir.) 331 Fed. 2d 1000, 1008.
119 *Hall v. State* (1986, Ind.) 493 N.E. 2d 433; *People in interest of E.* (1982, Colo.) 645 Pac. 2d 271; *U.S. v. Repouille* (1947, 2d cir.) 165 Fed. 2d 152.
120 See, for example, Calif. Welfare and Institutions Code §300(a), which provides for wardship in the following broad terms: 'Any person under the age of 18 years who comes within any of the following descriptions is within the jurisdiction of the juvenile court which may adjudge that person to be a dependent child of the court: (a) who is in need of proper and effective parental care or control and has no parent or guardian, or has no parent or guardian willing to exercise or capable of exercising care or control, or has no parent, guardian or custodian actually exercising care or control.'
121 *Wisconsin v. Yoder* (1972) 406 U.S. 205, 233–34; *In re Eric B.* (1987) 189 Cal. App. 3d 996, 1004.
122 *In re Phillip B.* (1979) 92 Cal. App. 3d 796, 802.
123 *Jehovah's Witnesses of Washington v. King Co. Hosp.* (1967, W.D. Wash.) 278 Fed. Supp. 488, aff'd. (1968) 390 U.S. 598; *State v. Perricone* (1962, N.J.) 181 A. 2d 751, cert. den. 371 U.S 890; *People ex rel. Wallace v. Labrenz* (1952, Ill.) 104 N.E. 2d 769, cert. den. 344 U.S. 824; *Morrison v. State* (1952, Mo. App.) 252 S.W. 2d 97; *Matter of Jensen* (1981, Ore. App.) 633 Pac. 2d 1302; *In re Karwath* (1972, Iowa) 199 N.W. 2d 147; *In re Rotkowitz* (1941, N.Y. App.) 25 N.Y.S. 2d 624; *In re Eric B.*, *supra*.
124 *Walker v. Superior Court* (1987) 194 Cal. App. 3d 1090 (appeal granted); *R. v. MacDonald* (1904) St.R.Qd. 151; *R. v. Senior* (1899) 1 Q.B. 283.
125 *Matter of Hofbauer* (1979, N.Y.) 393 N.E. 2d 1009; *Weber vs. Stony*

Brook Hosp. (1983, N.Y.) 456 N.E. 2d 1186; *Infant Doe v. Bloomington Hosp.* (1982, Ind. unrptd.), cert. den. (1983) 464 U. S. 961.

126 *In re Phillip B.* (1979) 92 Cal. App. 3d 796, cert. den. (1979) 445 U.S. 949.

127 *Guardianship of Phillip B.* (1983) 139 Cal. App. 3d 407.

128 Robertson, 'Involuntary Euthanasia of Defective Newborns: A Legal Analysis,' 27 *Stan. L.R.* 213, 214 (1975); Duff & Campbell, 289 *New Eng. J. Med* 890 (1973).

129 *Amer. Academy of Pediatrics v. Heckler* (1983, D. C. Dist. Col.) 561 Fed. Supp. 395 (Gesell, J.); *Matter of Storar* (1981, N.Y.) 420 N.E. 2d 64 (Jones, J., dissenting).

130 283 *Brit. Med. J.* 1629 (1981).

131 Child Abuse Prevention and Treatment Act, 1985 Rules, 45 Code Fed. Regs. Part 1340, 42 U.S. C. S. 5100–5104 (1985), discussed *infra*.

132 It is estimated 35 million are uninsured and 50 million are underinsured in the United States. Those poor enough to qualify for state health insurance often are unable to find doctors to accept their care because of very low state reimbursement.

133 The degree of mental retardation in Downsian or other brain abnormal infants cannot be determined with accuracy at or shortly after birth. See *Iafelice v. Zarafu* (1987, N.J. Super.) 534 A. 2d 417.

134 *Re Infant Doe* (Monroe Co., Ind., No. 7GU8204)004A, 1982), (Cir. Ct.); *State ex rel Infant Doe v. Baker*, 482 S. 140 (1982), (Ind. Supreme Ct.); cert. den., *Infant Doe v. Bloomington Hosp.* (1983) 464 U. S. 961.

135 *In Re L.H.R.* (1984, Ga.) 321 S.E. 2d 716; *Guardianship of Barry* (1984, Fla. App.) 445 So. 2d 365.

136 *Matter of Baby F.* (1983) Coos Co. Cir. Ct. No. J 928 (reported in Meyers, *Medico-Legal Implications of Death and Dying*, Dec., 1988, cum. supp., p. 236).

137 *Weber v. Stony Brook Hosp.* (1983, N.Y.) 456 N.E. 2d 1186, cert. den. (1983) 104 S. Ct. 560. The U.S. Federal Court, addressing another issue in the case, observed in implicit recognition of the treatment decisions made – that, 'Due to [the birth defects] there was an extremely high risk that the child would be so severely retarded that she could never interact with her environment or with other people.' *U.S. v University Hosp.* (1984, 2d cir.) 729 Fed. 2d 144, 146.

138 *Matter of Hofbauer* (1979, N.Y.) 393 N.E. 2d 1009; compare, *Custody of a Minor* (1978, Mass.) 379 N.E. 2d 1053 (metabolic therapy rejected; chemotherapy ordered).

139 *Guardianship of Barry* (1984, Fla. App.) 445 So. 2d 365; *Maine Med. Ctr. v. Houle*, note 153, *infra*.

140 *Re Cicero* (1979, N.Y. App.) 421 N.Y.S. 2d 965, 967.

141 *Joswick v. Lenox Hill Hosp.* (1986, N.Y. App.) 510 N.Y.S. 2d 803.

142 *In Re McNulty* (1978) Mass. Probate Ct. No. 1960 (trial court decision, no appeal taken, surgical outcome unknown).

143 *Maine Med. Ctr. v. Houle* (1974) Cumberland Co. Super. Ct. No. 74)145 (trial court decision, no appeal taken, surgical outcome unknown).

144 45 Code Fed. Regs. 1340. 15(b)(3), (1985).

145 'Highly unlikely to prevent death in the near future.' *Fed. Register*, 50, No. 72, April 15, 1985, p. 14892.
146 'Inhumane' is defined to mean the treatment itself involves significant medical contra-indications and/or significant pain and suffering that clearly outweigh the very slight potential benefit to the infant. *Fed. Register, loc. cit.*
147 Transplantation of organs, abortion, pronouncement of death, termination of life-saving treatment for the terminally or incurably ill.
148 President's Commission, *Deciding to Forego Life-Sustaining Treatment*. Wash. D.C., U.S.Gov't. Printing Office, 1983, pp. 202,219.
149 *Barber v. Superior Court* (1983) 147 Cal. App. 3d 1006; President's Commission, *supra*, pp. 218–19.
150 28 days, Brahams, 1983 *J. Med. Ethics* 12, 14; 72 hours, Mason & McCall Smith; *Law and Medical Ethics* (1st. ed. 1983), p. 89 (removed in 2d ed. (1987).).
151 See, for example, Fletcher, 'Abortion, Euthanasia, and Care of Defective Newborns,' in Shannon (ed.) *Bioethics* (3d ed., 1987), pp. 99, 102; Campbell & Duff, 1979 *J. Med. Ethics* 65, 66.
152 27 *Stan. L.R.* 213, 236 (1975); see also, *Hunter v. Hanley* 1955 S.C. 200, *Friern v. Bolam, etc.* (1957) 2 All E.R. 118.
153 Williams, *Textbook of Criminal Law* (2 ed., 1983), p. 279.
154 Campbell & Duff, 1979 *J. med. Ethics* 141.
155 Rhoden, 'Treatment Dilemmas for Imperiled Newborns: Why Quality of Life Counts,' 58 *So. Cal. L.R.* 1283 (1985).
156 *Euthanasia, Aiding Suicide and Cessation of Treatment*. 1982, Working Paper No. 28, p. 30.
157 Green 'Teary Father Not Charged in Death of Comatose Boy,' *The Los Angeles Times*, 19 May 1989, p.1.
158 See discussions in Chapters 9 and 10, *infra*.
159 See Macklin, *Mortal Choices*. New York: Houghton Mifflin, 1987, pp. 128–9; Lipman, 'The Criminal Liability of Medical Practitioners for Withholding Treatment from Severely Defective Newborn Infants,' 60 *The Australian Law J.* 286, 297 (1986).

CONTROVERSIAL MEDICAL CARE DURING LIFE

5

Consent to Medical Treatment

A. INTRODUCTION

One of the foundations of the law is respect for individual autonomy. The law has long recognized that, subject to certain exceptions, a person's body and physical person are inviolate. The crime of assault and battery, and its more ancient predecessor, mayhem, was established to protect this physical inviolability and to punish any transgressions. Thus, in western society any physical intrusions against the bodily integrity of another person without consent are proscribed by both the civil and criminal law, save and except for the normal touchings and jostlings that are socially accepted as inherent in everyday life.[1] The latter include such things as handshakes, pats on the back, and the inevitable bumps and touchings which occur in the more crowded settings of society: public meetings and sporting events, subways, busy sidewalks.

A touching or other physical intrusion need not be hostile or intended to do harm to constitute a battery. Thus, medical treatment, if imposed without the consent of the patient, is a battery.[2] This is perhaps best explained by having reference to the early and often rather ghastly beginnings of medical treatment, which included such things as blood-letting and other unpleasant and arguably hostile procedures.

More importantly, however, considering medical treatment as a *prima facie* battery ensures to the individual freedom from bodily invasion unless he or she has consented to it. This not only protects against unwanted physical intrusions, but it recognizes individual autonomy and choice. Consent is the means by which an individual effects his or her right of self-determination. If a person must normally consent to any medical treatment, then that person is the one who has the power and the right to choose, to decide whether or not proposed treatment is a good thing, and whether it will be imposed on his or her body.

It is generally agreed that an aim of democratic society should be to maximize individual self-determination to the greatest extent feasible and not harmful to others.[3] Accordingly, the broad ethical and legal principle underlying medical treatment under Scots, English, and American law is that it may only be imposed, and continued, with the consent of the patient.[4] What we will see, however, is that there are a number of issues, often not clearly resolved, that are raised by this general principle. They include the following:

1. What is required for a consent to be valid?
2. What is done when the patient cannot consent due to age or infirmity?
3. Will consent justify any and all medical treatment?
4. What circumstances, if any, permit treatment without the consent of the patient?

The law of consent has evolved and developed to a greater degree in the United States than in England or Scotland. Divergent lines of development have occurred, but their review may assist evaluation of that development of the law to date in the UK.

B. UNITED STATES

1. *Bodily inviolability*

Medical treatment is presumed and is normally intended to be therapeutic, to benefit the patient. However, as in England and Scotland, it may not be legally imposed without the consent of the patient. This requirement ensures that the individual's body will not be tampered with unless authorized by him or her. As stated in a 1905 Minnesota decision,[45]

> 'Under a free government, at least, the free citizen's first and greatest right, which underlies all others – the right to the inviolability of his person; in other words, the right to himself – is the subject of universal acquiescence, and the right necessarily forbids a physician or surgeon, however skillful or eminent ... to violate without permission, the bodily integrity of his patient.'

2. *The advent of informed consent*

For many years the American courts were only concerned with whether the patient had consented to the treatment. Only in more recent times, co-incident to the post-World War II development of sophisticated medical technology and treatments, have the courts become concerned with the nature or quality of the consent given.[6] Courts have reasoned that if consent is to be valid, is to accomplish its purpose of protecting the bodily integrity of the patient from unauthorized or undesired intrusion, then it must be knowing, it must be 'informed' consent.[7]

Since the first articulation of this theory of informed consent, the courts have struggled with what the proper standard of information disclosure should be. Two divergent lines of opinion have developed.

a. *The reasonable physician standard.* The reasonable physician standard, which may still perhaps represent the majority view, is essentially the same as the rationale adopted by the Law Lords in *Sidaway v. Royal Bethlem Hospital*.[4] In the United States it has come to be known as the 'reasonable physician' standard of disclosure.[8] Under this standard the physician has a duty to disclose to the patient the risks, likely results and available alternatives to the proposed treatment that reasonable medical practitioners would, under the circumstances, disclose to the patient.

Under this standard, it is left to the physicians to determine the extent of required disclosure. This is not to say the physician need not take into account the individual circumstances of the patient. Under this standard the intention is to promote disclosure of information most patients in similar circumstances would receive from their physicians. Disclosure requirements are based upon the practice standards of reasonable physicians dealing with patients in similar circumstances.[9]

Even under this 'reasonable physician' standard of disclosure, the court reserves the right to overrule an established practice among reasonable and prudent physicians if the court, exercising its independent judgment, concludes the practice is not reasonable.[10] Courts are loathe to do this, substituting their judgment for a responsible body of competent medical practitioners, but will do so on rare occasion. In one case, opthamalogists had developed a practice of not performing a simple pressure test to detect glaucoma in patients under 40 years old. The court concluded such a test should be offered because it was simple and was an effective means of disclosing a potentially grave condition.[10] The low incidence of glaucoma in patients under 40 was not deemed to be a 'reasonable' basis for omitting such a test, or disclosure of its availability to the patient. The classic statement of this principle was made by Justice Oliver Wendel Holmes, when he stated,

> 'What usually is done may be evidence of what ought to be done, but what ought to be done is fixed by a standard of reasonable prudence whether it usually is complied with or not.'[11]

Nonetheless, courts rarely overrule an established medical practice. Judges normally do not feel competent to do so. The result is physicians may develop a standard of disclosure which does not really meet the needs of the patients to know. For this reason, the better-reasoned and growing weight of decisions in the U.S. has espoused a second criterion for disclosure of treatment information. It is referred to as the 'material risks' or the 'prudent patient' standard.

b. *The material risks standard.* The 'material risks' or 'prudent patient' standard of disclosure is one determined not by prevailing medical standards, but by the patient's need to know.[12] Under this standard, the physician has a duty to disclose any information that a *reasonable* patient in the particular circumstances would consider material, or significant, in deciding whether or not to undergo the treatment proposed. Thus, the physician must have regard to what the patient would want to know, not simply to what may be the common practice of his colleagues. However, the obligation to disclose is still one of reasonableness, since disclosure is what a 'reasonable' patient would want to know under the particular circumstances at hand.

Material risks must be disclosed. This does not mean everything that the particular patient would, subjectively, want to know, but rather what a reasonable patient in the same or similar circumstances would be likely to consider significant in deciding whether to undergo or forego the treatment proposed. This protects the physician by only requiring disclosure of what the average patient would want to know, but it is the reasonable patient, not the reasonable physician, that sets the scope of disclosure. Included among material risks and treatment alternatives is the alternative of no treatment. If the patient declines proposed treatment, he or she should do so only after being informed of the material risks of electing not to undergo the proposed treatment.[13]

Under the doctrine of informed consent, the physician is obligated to disclose to his or her patient 'all relevant information concerning a proposed treatment, including the material risks involved, alternative treatments, and hazards if the condition is left untreated, so that the patient's consent to treatment will be an intelligent one based on complete information.'[14] The physician is not required to disclose everything that a given patient would want to know because such an individualistic disclosure standard would unfairly require the physician to ascertain the subjective, unexpressed views of his patient about materiality in every case, which may vary widely. This would impose an unreasonable burden.[12]

Normally, to be successful the litigating patient must also show causation – that a *reasonable* person would not have undergone the treatment if the required disclosure of risk information had been made. However, a few courts have taken issue with this, finding that the purpose of informed consent – to effectuate a patient's right to self-determination – is served if the patient need only prove that he or she would not have undergone the treatment if properly informed.[15]

The 'material risks' standard of disclosure has been preferred to that of the 'reasonable physician' by many recent courts, for several reasons:

1. The existence of a medical consensus on disclosure may not always exist;

2. Non-medical factors, such as the patient's emotional condition and intelligence, may properly play an important role in determining the scope of disclosure;

3. Allowing physicians to set their own standards for disclosure is in-imical to patient self-determination;

4. The requirement that the patient prove negligent nondisclosure based on medical standards of practice may prove difficult because expert medical testimony will be required, but difficult to obtain.[16]

Some state legislatures have seen fit to limit or clearly define the require-ments imposed on the physician for obtaining an informed consent. Some adopt either the reasonable physician or the material risks standard of disclosure. Others require only that a general description of the proposed treatment be given. Still others require that certain specified risks only be disclosed. Louisiana, for example, requires the physician to disclose the nature and purpose of the treatment and any known risks, if any, of death, brain damage, paralysis, loss of function or distinguishable scarring associ-ated with it.[17]

3. *Exceptions to disclosure*

Under either standard of disclosure, the courts have recognized that certain risk need not be disclosed in soliciting consent to medical treatment. If it is unforeseeable or unknown it need not be disclosed.[17] If the risk of harm or complication is 'uncommon or remote' it normally need not be disclosed.[18] What may be difficult for physician or judge alike to gauge in this context is what is sufficiently remote to obviate the need for disclosure. If the risk of harm is serious, involving serious disability or death, disclosure would undoubtedly be required at a level of remoteness much greater than that requiring disclosure of a trivial or insignificant risk of harm. If a reasonable patient would consider the risk significant, or reasonable physicians would normally disclose it, then it would have to be disclosed regardless of its low incidence. The cases have reached different results. No definite rule can be set. However, what seems to have emerged, in general, is that risks of severe or permanent disability or death 1 percent or greater should normally be disclosed.[19] If less than that, even if very serious, they need not be.[20] If the harm risked is less severe, even higher likelihood may not require 'reason-able' disclosure.[21]

No disclosure need be made where the patient has waived the require-ment, or asked not to be informed.[22] The same is true where the risks are obvious to a lay person, such as the risk of infection from a wound.[23] If the risk is one not generally known to the medical profession, there is no obligation to disclose it.[24]

4. *The therapeutic exception to disclosure*

Perhaps the most important exception is the 'therapeutic exception' to disclosure. It obtains where the physician reasonably concludes that because of the patient's condition disclosure is not indicated from a medical point of view.[25] Where full disclosure, it is reasonably and professionally believed, would hinder the success of the treatment or interfere with the recovery therefrom, a sound medical reason exists not to provide it to the patient. However, care has to be taken so that this exception does not threaten to engulf the rule. In such instances, it is incumbent upon the doctor to show he relied on sound medical judgment in electing not to make a full disclosure.

Thus, even under the material risks standard, if the doctor shows he did what other reasonable physicians would have done under the circumstances in electing not to fully inform the patient, he is likely to be legally excused.[26] While the patient's right to make a decision that is informed is significant, where full disclosure poses a real risk of threatening the patient's health, it may properly be withheld. This may be most evident in the case of a particularly apprehensive, agitated or psychologically unstable patient.[27]

Some discretion must be allowed the doctor here and the professional standard seems appropriate, since the medical harm from disclosure must be measured against the patients right to be fully informed. One is a medical judgment, the other is not, but they are hard to segregate one from the other.

5. *Statutory limits on informed consent*

As mentioned above[17] in a number of states the medical profession has prevailed upon the legislature to impose statutory limitations on the common law development of the informed consent doctrine by the courts.[28] Some abrogate the informed consent doctrine entirely and in its place substitute an obligation only to inform the patient in general terms of the nature of the treatment. Others select either the reasonable physician or the material risks standard of disclosure. Still others establish a professional body to articulate what specific risks need to be disclosed in specific treatment situations.[29] Idaho allows a doctor to defend a claim he treated without consent *either* on the basis he disclosed what a reasonable physician would or all material information a reasonable patient would want to know.[30] Oregon has two levels of required disclosure.[31] The first requires disclosure of the general purpose and major known risks of treatment. Thereafter, further detail need only be given if the patient expressly requests it.[15] Finally, there are those statutes which only require disclosure of risks of serious harm, such as paralysis, permanent disability, or death.[17]

If the treatment is unconventional or experimental, specific disclosure requirements may be mandated. Where new drugs or medical treatments have not as yet received full approval for general use from the Federal Food and Drug Administration, the patient's consent must be in writing and include the following written provisions:

1. A fair explanation of the medical procedures proposed and their purposes;

2. Identification of any experimental procedures;

3. A description of attendant discomfort and any reasonably expected risks;

4. A description of any benefits reasonably expected;

5. An offer to answer any questions;

6. A disclosure of any appropriate alternative treatments or procedures that could benefit the patient.[32]

7. A statement the patient may withdraw his consent at any time without suffering prejudice in treatment;

The result of these statutory enactments is a patchwork of standards among the various states. Patients in California must be told more before surgery than patients in New York.

6.   *Causation: lack of disclosure and harm to the patient*

If liability is to be imposed on a physician for failing to properly inform a patient about the risks posed by the proposed treatment and the alternatives to it, the patient must show breach of duty by the physician, harm, and causation between the two. Even if the physician has breached his duty of proper disclosure to his patient, there is no liability if the patient suffers no harm. Similarly, if proper disclosure would not have dissuaded the patient from undergoing the treatment, there is no liability for failure to disclose since no legal causation exists. Most courts require the patient to prove not just that he, but also that a reasonable person in the patient's position would not have undergone the treatment if proper disclosure of its risks and alternatives had been made before allowing recovery against the physician.[33] A minority of courts have ruled causation established if it is proven the patient himself would not have undergone the treatment in question if properly informed.[34]

The latter test of causation, known as the subjective test because based on the decision of the particular patient, has been disfavored by courts principally concerned with its potential for abuse by disenchanted patients exercising 20/20 hindsight. It does give maximum effect to the patient's right to self-determination. Courts adopting it have cautioned that jurors are free to disregard the patient's own testimony on the subject if they find it unreliable or unpersuasive, particularly in light of evidence that other, reasonable patients would have consented even after the required disclosure of risks.

7.   *Implied consent*

Another important exception to the requirement of obtaining the patient's consent is implicated when an emergency need to treat a patient exists. Where the patient is unable to give an informed consent due to illness or injury, and treatment is immediately necessary to save life or limb, or to avoid serious harm or disability, the patient's consent is legally implied by the emergency circumstances. In such situations, the law presumes the patient, if able, would consent. Where the risk of harm posed by the treatment is less than the risk of harm posed from not undertaking treatment, it is logical, reasonable, and proper to treat.[35]

It might be said that implied consent really is based on the doctrine of necessity, which seems to provide the foundation for treatment in such cases in Britain.[36] However, necessity does not fully subsume implied consent, for the latter is found to exist also in non-emergency situations where the patient, by conduct, usually acquiescence, creates an inference that treatment is desired and authorized by him.[37] This is commonly relied upon by physicians in everyday treatment of their patients. In practice, common office procedures, including minor surgeries, are carried out by physicians without any discussion of risks or alternatives. This practice is protected by three closely-related principles. One, that consent in the circumstances is implied. Two, that disclosure of commonly understood risks is not required. Three, that disclosure of minor and remote risks is not required.[38]

8. *Incompetent patients*

Our discussion of consent has presumed the patient is capable of consenting. While a patient need not necessarily be competent in the legal sense to consent to medical treatment, he or she must be able to understand the nature and purpose of the treatment proposed, as well as its significant intended benefits and risks. If the patient is unable to comprehend this, as may often be the case with young children and the significantly mentally compromised, different rules of consent apply. We will consider those next in Chapter 6.

C.   ENGLAND

To a large extent our discussion of the legal status of consent to medical treatment in England will disclose the position in Scotland. In the chapter that follows we will see the position concerning parental rights to consent for their children is somewhat different in England and in Scotland. However, here we are dealing with adults. As to competent adults the position of the law appears to be essentially the same in England as in Scotland. The most legal development has occurred in England, much of it quite recent.

1. *The Sidaway case in England*

The seminal case on consent is *Sidaway*.[4] It holds that the same test of liability applies to a doctor's duty to disclose to his or her patient the risks inherent in proposed treatment as applies to the doctor's duty to diagnose and treat the patient. The test, known as the *Bolam* principle after a 1957 case of that name,[39] is whether or not the doctor, in disclosing whatever information he or she did to the patient, acted in accordance with a standard of practice recognized at the time as proper by a responsible body of medical opinion. This is not to say that the doctor may decide for the patient. English law recognizes the patient has the clear right whether or not to consent to medical treatment. In the words of Lord Bridge in *Sidaway*,

> 'It is clearly right to recognize that a conscious adult patient of sound mind is entitled to decide for himself whether or not he will submit to a particular course of treatment proposed by the doctor, most significantly surgical treatment under general anaesthesia.'[40]

Despite this recognition, the majority in *Sidaway* held that so long as the doctor discloses what ordinary skilled doctors would disclose under the circumstances, the doctor's duty to the patient has been fulfilled. It is somewhat difficult to reconcile these two principles, since ordinary skilled doctors acting to a standard accepted as proper by a responsible body of medical opinion may or may not disclose sufficient information for the patient to make a truly knowing decision whether he or she should consent to the treatment proposed.

One distinguished commentator, in criticizing the rationale of *Sidaway*, uses the example of a patient with breast cancer. If the doctor belongs to the school of thought that believes radical mastectomy (breast removal) is the appropriate course of treatment and explains it to the patient, including its significant risks, in accordance with what other doctors supporting such treatment would tell their patients he or she has seemingly satisfied the disclosure requirements of *Sidaway*. Yet, can the patient make a truly knowing decision? Probably not. Why? Because there are other forms of accepted treatment, including lumpectomy (removal of cancerous tumor tissue only), radiation therapy, chemotherapy, or a combination, which other surgeons may recommend, which the patient would want to know about, but which the doctor apparently has no obligation to disclose if others of his or her school of practice deem them to be inadequate or undesirable. *Sidaway* seems to allow doctors, not patients, to control patients' treatment choices, by controlling the information on treatment risks and alternatives that patients receive. It remains to be seen whether *Sidaway* will be flexible enough to avoid unfortunate applications which defeat the patient's right to know, to be informed, and to make a knowing decision to consent, or refuse consent.

2. *The courts may, rarely, overrule doctors*

The Law Lords wisely imposed a significant qualification in deciding *Sidaway*. It was an obvious effort to avoid 'abdicating' the responsibility to ensure the patients' consent is a knowing and voluntary one to the medical profession alone. Lord Bridge reserved power for the court to overrule what the medical evidence suggested was satisfactory practice in certain cases. He stated,

'I am of opinion that the judge might in certain circumstances come to the conclusion that *disclosure* of a particular risk was *so obviously necessary to an informed choice* on the part of the patient that *no reasonably prudent medical man would fail to make it*' (emphasis supplied).[42]

His Lordship then went on to give an example of such a case where disclosure should be compelled judicially, if not by prevailing medical practice,

'The kind of case I have in mind would be an *operation* involving a *substantial risk* of *grave adverse consequences*, as for example the 10 per cent risk of stroke from the operation which was the subject of the Canadian case of *Reibl v. Hughes* (1980) 114 DLR (3d) 1. In such a case, *in the absence of some cogent clinical reason why the patient should not be informed*, a doctor recognizing and respecting his patient's right of decision, could hardly fail to appreciate the necessity for an appropriate warning.' (emphasis added).[42]

This portion of the reasoning of the case is of great significance. It recognized the patient has a right to make 'an informed choice.' It recognized that standards of disclosure adopted by the medical profession may prevent this, unless overruled by the court. And, it recognized the so-called 'therapeutic privilege' not to warn of risks, if supported by 'some cogent clinical reason.' It can be argued that this exception could eventually engulf the rule.

For the judge to determine if a disclosure is obviously necessary to informed choice by the patient, the judge, it is submitted, must view the information customarily disclosed by the medical profession from the perspective of the patient being asked to consent. If the patient would perceive the risk of grave consequences to be 'substantial,' then it should be disclosed. This, it can be argued, leaves open to judges, the allowance of evidence of what reasonable or prudent patients would consider substantial risks under the circumstances at hand. This may well lead to a modified version of the 'informed consent' doctrine the Lords apparently were so anxious, for policy reasons, to avoid. Only time will tell. The use of the word 'substantial' in reference to risks used by Lord Bridge is ambiguous and would seem to give judges considerable leeway in deciding when to abide by and when to overrule medical practice standards of disclosure.

3. *Other cases usually support the physician*

Several other cases, decided both before and since the House of Lords decision in *Sidaway*, have applied similar reasoning. In *Gold v. Haringry*

Health Authority,[43] the Court of Appeals held the *Bolam* test (i.e., what ordinary skillful doctors would do in the circumstances) should be applied to determine what information concerning risks inherent in a 'non-therapeutic' procedure (contraceptive sterilization) should be disclosed to the patient. The court found no sound reason to distinguish between therapeutic and non-therapeutic procedures in terms of the test for disclosure. Some have suggested a higher standard of disclosure is appropriate in non-therapeutic procedures, since the clear benefit to health presumably present in therapeutic treatment does not exist to offset or justify the physical intrusion.[44]

It has been held that the patient should be warned 'if there was a *real* risk of misfortune inherent in the procedure' to be performed.[45] In another decision,[46] the *Bolam* test was again applied by the judge to determine the reasonableness of the doctor's challenged conduct. Obviously sensitive to the accusation that the standard left to the medical profession the unique discretion to set, by its own practice, its own standards of liability, the judge pointed out,

> 'I do not accept the argument of counsel for the plaintiff that by adopting the *Bolan* principle, the court in effect abdicates its power of decision to the doctors. In every case *the court must be satisfied* that the standard contended for on their behalf accords with that upheld by a *substantial* body of medical opinion, and that this *body of medical opinion* is both *respectable and responsible, and experienced* in this particular field of medicine.' (emphasis added.)[47]

Recently it was held a sex offender could consent to chemical castration, even if he did not understand the 'precise physiological process' of the treatment. A general understanding of the nature and likely effects of treatment was adequate to give consent.[48]

The effect of these decisions is that the courts will rarely second guess decisions made by doctors on how much to disclose to their patients. Few English courts have done so. Only in cases where serious, not commonly accepted risks are not disclosed by doctors will courts say they must do so.

In the absence of consent, medical treatment is normally both civilly and criminally actionable under English law. As Lord Scarman has stated,

> 'A doctor who operates without the consent of his patient, is, save in cases of emergency or mental disability, guilty of the civil wrong of trespass to the person; he is also guilty of the criminal offense of assault.'[49]

4. *Emergency*

Let us discuss the two referenced exceptions of emergency and mental disability. Mental disability resulting from lack of age, from childhood, will be considered in the chapter following. Emergency, as we discussed, normally presents the problem of the competent person who because of accidental injury or acute illness is unconscious, or otherwise incapable at the time of giving an informed consent. In addition he or she is in immediate need of treatment to prevent death or serious harm. Under such circumstances the law typically engages in a fiction known as implied consent. The patient is presumed to have consented since all reasonable persons would wish, the law presumes, to have treatment under such circumstances and would consent to it if they were able to do so. Alternatively, the doctrine of necessity may be relied upon, since it is recognized in such cases that the evil of treating the person without his or her consent is more than outweighed by the good of saving him or her from death, serious disability, or damage to health.

It may properly be questioned whether there is much difference, in the context of emergency medical treatment, between the doctrines of implied consent and necessity. Both simply justify treatment immediately needed to avoid death or serious harm. Both presume the patient has not, while competent, indicated opposition to any such treatment.

5. *Mental incompetence*

Where patient consent cannot be obtained because of mental disability, several alternatives present themselves. If an emergency exists, treatment may proceed as discussed above. If there is not an emergency, there are two bases on which to treat. The first and most desirable is where the patient while competent has clearly expressed his or her desire for such treatment.[45] If verified, this allows treatment which is presumed to be in the patient's best interests since it has been shown as wanted by him or her and thus effectuates the patient's important rights to autonomy and self-determination. British law, English or Scottish, at present provides no established procedure or mechanism to accomplish treatment based on prior, competently-expressed views of the patient. American law does, in the form of 'living wills,' or 'Durable Powers of Attorney for Health Care,' as we shall see in the Chapters ahead concerning termination of treatment. However, it has been recently opined that British Courts should follow competently expressed treatment views of the now-incompetent patient if there is no evidence of a change of mind by the patient.[50] Obviously concurrence by the family and the physician with the treatment choice of the patient would make the task that much easier for the court.

British cases decided to date authorizing treating for mentally disabled adults (and children) have done so by use of the 'best interests' or 'welfare' standard. Where minors are involved, wardship proceedings are available. The child may be made the ward of the court which, exercising traditional jurisdictional powers over the minor, may authorize treatment determined to be in the best interests of the minor.[51] Or, the court may conclude the treatment proposed is not in the best interests of the child and refuse to authorize it.[52] Care of children and power of consent may be transferred in appropriate cases to the local child welfare authority.[53]

Where the mentally incompetent is an adult, the traditional prerogative powers invested in the Crown as *parens patriae* do not presently extend. A recent case wherein consent for abortion and contraceptive sterilization was sought from the court for a 19 year old mother by the medical consultants, and granted after considerable soul-searching analysis by the Family Division, the Judge encouraged the restitution of prerogative jurisdiction whereby the Crown may act as *parens patriae* for incompetents.[54] This would entitle the courts, similar to wardship proceedings for children, to decide questions of medical treatment for incompetents of any age based simply upon their best interests.

As a practical matter, this is undoubtedly what occurs in the day-to-day treatment decisions for incompetents where the surgery is determined, based on good medical judgment, to be in the patient's best interests. It is considerably less clear in England when the treatment is unusual and very intrusive such as abortion or sterilization.

It should be pointed out that the mere fact a person is mentally ill, or incompetent to manage his or her own affairs or property, does not necessarily mean he cannot give a valid consent to medical treatment. If patients can understand the nature and purpose of the proposed treatment and come to a decision whether or not they wish to have it then they should not be robbed of the right and the power to grant or refuse consent.[55] The patient's decision on consent is not required to be wise or reasonable to be valid. It need only be knowing and voluntary. Consent is intended to protect the patient's right to individual choice, however unwise or foolish others may think the decision may be. Doctors are accused of overruling unwise or unreasonable consent, seeing it as synonymous with an inability to give a competent or knowing consent.[56] However, the two should be kept separate to the greatest extent possible in order to maximize individual self-determination in medical care.

Apparently there no longer exists in England any residual jurisdiction under the ancient *parens patriae* doctrine with which to deal with such situations.[57] Further, there is not anyone with clear authority to exercise such powers over an incompetent adult.[58] The Crown's ancient prerogative powers over the mentally disabled were traditionally delegated to the Lord Chancellor, but were revoked when the Mental Health Act 1959 became operative. Under its successor, the Mental Health Act 1983, the guardian can only consent to treatment for the mental disability itself, not to treatment in general. Thus, no express authority presently exists for such treatment.

However, the House of Lords has recently confirmed that there is residual jurisdiction in the courts to decide upon treatment for incompetent adults based on their best interests. Trial judges have granted declarations that sterilization and abortion[59] procedures may be lawfully carried out on severely mentally handicapped women when shown by medical evidence to be in their best interests. The House of Lords recently, in *F v. West Berkshire Health Authority*,[57] confirmed that a 36 year old severely mentally handicapped woman could be sterilized where the evidence showed it was in her best interests to do so. The case is significant, for it fills a gap in English (and arguably in Scottish) law concerning treatment of an incompetent patient. The standard is best interests, which the Lords interpreted to mean only that treatment which is life-saving or is carried out to improve, or to avoid deterioration of, the patient's physical or mental health. It was held that doctors could properly decide if the treatment was of such a permissible nature by applying ordinary standards of common medical practice under the so-called *Bolam* standard.[39]

The House of Lords, by recognizing this common law 'best interest' right of the physician to treat the incompetent, cleared up considerable uncertainty in the law as we have seen. The Lords made it clear that routine court approval was neither necessary nor desirable in such cases. Lord Brandon concluded,

'The application of the principle which I have described means that the lawfulness of a doctor operating on, or giving other treatment to, an adult patient disabled from giving consent, will depend not on any approval or sanction of a court, but on the question whether the operation or other treatment is in the best interests of the patient concerned. That is, from a practical point of view, just as well, for, if every operation to be performed, or other treatment to be given, required the approval or sanction of the court, the whole process of medical care for such patients would grind to a halt.'

However, their Lordships made it clear that in cases involving irreversible loss of reproductive function, as by sterilization, it was 'highly desirable as a matter of good practice' to obtain prior court authorization. This was not legally required, but with such a strong recommendation it is sure to be followed. It is also probably appropriate in other 'special operations' alluded to but not identified by the Court. Surely among them are abortion, experimental treatment or transplantation of a vital organ.[60]

The case is a significant example of the adaptability of the common law. It legitimates what has be prevailing medical practice in Britain for many years.[61]

6. *Proportionate treatment*

In general, it can be said that treatment is in the 'best interests' of the patient if it is proportionate treatment. By that is meant that the benefits the treatment offers the patient in terms of improving health are greater than and outweigh the burdens attendant upon the treatment, such as pain, discomfort, disability, embarrassment or cost.[62] Mason & McCall Smith prefer to refer to it in terms of productive as opposed to nonproductive treatment.[63] However, the treatment must be looked at not solely in terms of what result it is intended to produce, but also at what burden to the patient, mentally, physically, and financially. Using this principle ensures the patient a choice when he or she is unable to choose. It may not be precisely their choice, but the odds are it will be. If not, it is a reasonable solution. It also is preferable to exercising no treatment choice at all for the patient when incompetent.[64]

An interesting question is raised where consent is sought to a procedure that involves no serious risks of physical harm, but may nonetheless carry adverse consequences for the patient of a social or mental nature. For example, it would seem a doctor or laboratory taking blood for testing from a patient must disclose testing for the AIDS (HIV) virus if such is planned.[65] However, the issue is unsettled and there are those who claim that since there is no significant risk from the procedure itself to the patient, it is governed solely by accepted medical practice under *Sidaway*. Thus if doctors elect not to disclose as a matter of practice, they need not so do. This seems highly dubious, given the significant implications of a physical, mental and social nature arising from a positive HIV blood test. Nonetheless, it points out rather vividly the shortcoming of the *Bolam* test adopted by the majority of the Law Lords in *Sidaway*. Certainly it is hard to imagine, from the patient's point of view, a more obvious case calling for disclosure of this material purpose of the diagnostic procedure. Yet, under *Sidaway* it remains an open question about which reasonable doctors can differ and, in fact, a BMA committee recently voted to leave the matter for the individual doctor to decide on his own.

It seems that most activity in English law concerning consent to medical treatment, for the time being, is likely to focus on refining, applying and defining the scope of *Sidaway*, particularly with respect to clarifying the criteria for court acceptance, or overriding, of ordinary medical practice standards. It is also likely to struggle with the means of giving consent to treat the incompetent patient who cannot consent and the criteria to be applied in deciding to grant or refuse consent on his or her behalf.

D.   SCOTLAND

1. *The nature of consent*

Unless the patient has freely consented under Scots law medical treatment is an assault, resulting in criminal and civil liability.[66] Consent may be expressly given, or it may be manifested by conduct, as by acquiescence following an explanation or other understanding of the treatment to be undertaken.

Consent, of course, must be freely given. If it is not voluntary, but rather is the result of coercion, undue influence, or deceit, then it is not valid. In such situations its purpose is frustrated, for it does not represent a conscious, volitional exercise of the patient's right of self-determination.

As well as being freely given, the patient's consent must also be a knowing consent. It seems one may not exist without the other. If the patient does not know or understand what he or she is being asked to consent to, then while perhaps freely given the consent is not volitional. The patient's right to choose, to decide, is only meaningful if the patient knows what the effect of his or her consent is; that is, to what exactly is he or she being asked to consent.

The patient has a right to know what is expected to happen if consent to treatment is given, and if consent is refused. But who decides what information the patient should be given to help him or her decide? While still an open legal question in Scotland, it appears likely the courts will leave it to the doctor to decide what the patient should be told before his or her consent is given or refused. The reason for this conclusion is the modern recognition that a doctor's duty to disclose information to his or her patient before rendering treatment should be evaluated by legal standards of negligence. The same standard that is applied to evaluate treatment is to be applied to evaluate disclosure of information by the physician.

Two Scottish cases illustrate this. In the first, an unreported decision rendered well before *Sidaway*,[67] the patient claimed he did not consent to removal of a carotid body tumor when he consented to surgery to eliminate a suspected bronchial cyst. The written consent form authorized 'any operation the surgeon considers necessary.' Their Lordships concluded this left it up to the surgeon to do what he determined, in the exercise of sound clinical judgment, was 'in the patient's interest to be done at the time.' The court appeared to apply the traditional negligence standard to determine if adequate disclosure had been made to the patient and permission obtained to justify the surgery in question. While the case is unreported, it appears however that the Law Lords were more concerned with the best interests of the patient and the scope of the consent given, than with the degree of disclosure given the patient before eliciting the rather generic written consent.

In a recent case, *Moyes v. Lothian Health Board*,[68] the Court of Session had opportunity to more fully set out the expected level of disclosure to the patient by the physician. The patient asserted she had not been properly informed of all the risks involved with exploratory angiography surgery to diagnose the cause of severe facial pain. She evidently suffered a serious neurological reaction and it was agreed her damages would be limited to

£8,000 if she prevailed. However, Lord Caplan in his judgment rejected her claims. His Lordship suggested that causation was missing; namely, that given the patient's severe symptoms and the low probability of complications of the kind that followed, that the patient would have consented even if full disclosure had been made. The patient, the Judge suggested, was being 'wise after the event.' Unstated was whether causation was to be judged by whether a reasonable patient under the circumstances would have consented after the required disclosure (the so-called 'objective' test), or by whether the particular patient herself would have consented (the so-called 'subjective' test).[15] However, this was not critical to the outcome because the Judge found that disclosure had been adequate.

The risk of neurological complication complained of was found to be 'slight,' only 0.2 percent or 0.3 percent. The Judge concluded such a small risk fell into the category of cases where the decision to disclose it became one of 'fine clinical judgment.' Absent a showing it was negligent not to disclose it – that no physician of ordinary skill exercising ordinary care would not, in the circumstances, disclose it – there was no liability for the physician's failure/election not to disclose it. His judgment was to be respected, for he was strongly presumed to be in the best position from which to judge what the patient should safely be told, given the physician's knowledge of the inherent risks, those peculiar to the patient and the patient's ability to absorb and be aided in deciding by the information disclosed.

2.   *Doctors normally decide what to disclose*

It appears that courts in English, Scottish, American and Commonwealth jurisdictions have largely concluded that assault and battery liability, based on intentional wrongdoing, should be limited to cases where the doctor fails to obtain consent for a particular treatment or procedure. Where consent is solicited and obtained, but questions are raised as to whether it was knowing, negligence principles are felt to more appropriately apply to judge the doctor's conduct.[66-69] In such situations there is normally no implication of intentional wrongdoing or of harmful intent.

In Scots law, the test for negligent medical treatment was clearly and authoritatively laid down by Lord President Clyde in the 1955 case of *Hunter v. Hanley*.[70] There are three requirements: (1) there must be a usual and normal medical practice; (2) the doctor must have deviated from it; and, (3) the course undertaken by the doctor must have been one 'which no professional man of ordinary skill would have taken if he had been acting with ordinary care.'

Under this well-established standard, a doctor is not negligent in the treatment of his or her patient if that treatment is supported as proper in the circumstances by a responsible body of professional medical opinion. There will not uncommonly be more than one responsible body of medical opinion or practice. Unless no reasonably prudent doctor of ordinary skill would have treated the patient similarly, there is no showing of negligence.

This standard has several underpinnings. First, that paternalism continues to play a strong role in British,[56,71] and in particular in Scottish,[72,67,68] medical practice. Although times are changing, most patients, it seems, still want to do what the doctor thinks is best and to leave it up to him or her to decide. Second, that medical science is a technical, evolving field, where courts and juries are often ill-equipped to judge what should be done under the highly individualized circumstances of patient care. Third, akin to the first, that physicians are a responsible body who have evolved generally acceptable standards of care and treatment and no widespread abuse suggests the law should do other than support good medical practice as that defined by the profession. As pointed out by Lord President Clyde in the *Hunter* case referenced above,

'It is a tribute to the high standard in general of the medical profession in Scotland that there are practically no decisions on this question [standards by which to judge physician negligence in diagnosis and treatment] in the reported cases.'[73]

This Scots law standard for determining medical negligence was approved and applied in a consent case two years later by an English court. In *Bolam v. Friern Hosp. Mgt. Committee*[74] the patient was a voluntary patient in a mental hospital who sustained fractures during electroconvulsive treatment. The patient claimed the medics failed to properly warn him of the risks of such treatment. In summing up to the jury, the judge stated the standard to be followed by the doctor in informing the patient about proposed treatment. He stated,

'The test is the standard of the ordinary skilled man exercising and professing to have that special skill . . . it is sufficient if he exercises the ordinary skill of any ordinary competent man exercising that particular art.'[75]

The standard of the 'doctor of ordinary skill . . . acting with ordinary care' adopted by the Scottish Court of Session in 1955 has not yet, as in England, been applied to an officially reported case involving whether or not a patient was properly informed about treatment before being asked to consent. However, the decisions we have discussed,[67,68,70] as well as other reasons strongly suggest the same standard will be applied to disclosure of treatment information as that applied to judge the propriety of the treatment itself: negligence.

3. *The Sidaway case in Scotland*

The idea that doctors should normally be allowed to decide what to tell their patients was approved by the House of Lords in the important case of

Sidaway v. Bethlem Royal Hospital Governors.[4] Since the House of Lords expressly relied upon the test approved by *Hunter v Hanley* and since it is the court of last resort in Scottish civil matters, *Sidaway* would seem to state the legal standard for review of doctors' conduct in obtaining their patients' consent to treatment in Scotland,[76] as well as in England.

A Scottish judge has succinctly summarized the importance of the *Sidaway* case as follows:

> 'it establishes that the advice-giving component of the doctor's activities constitutes an exercise of medical skill on a par with diagnosis and treatment and, as such, is to be assessed, from the point of view whether negligence has taken place, on the same standard as diagnosis and treatment.'[77]

The recent case of *Moyes v. Lothiun Health Board*[68] points out the continued, strongly paternalistic deference paid to the medical profession by the Scottish judiciary. In dismissing claims that disclosure of surgical risks by the physicians was inadequate, Lord Caplan had this to say,

> 'When the patient entrusts himself to the doctor he expects and is entitled to be kept fully informed about decisions which have to be taken, and which may concern his welfare. But the paramount expectation is that the doctor will do what is best to care for the patient's health.'

One cannot help but wonder if the qualifying language here does not largely eviscerate the protection offered in the opening sentence. While patients should not be unduly agitated with inadvisable disclosure of commonly understood or remote and slight risks, being 'fully informed' should mean being told what most patients would want to be told, not what most doctors decide they should be told, if there is in fact a difference between the two.

It is one thing to allow doctors to determine what is good treatment for a specific set of symptoms or malady, matters particularly within their expertise and training. It is quite another to allow doctors to decide what a patient should or should not be told before consent to treat is solicited and obtained. Do doctors have any particular skill in communication or in intuitively knowing what the patient should be told or needs to know about the treatment? If consent serves to promote the patient's right to autonomy and self-determination, should not the test of what information to disclose be grounded on what most ordinary patients in such circumstances would want to know, not what most ordinary doctors in such circumstances would want to disclose?

These questions are at the heart of the debate over 'informed consent.' The Law Lords in *Sidaway* considered and rejected imposing on doctors the legal obligation to disclose what the ordinary patient would want to know and instead imposed the obligation to disclose only what ordinary doctors, exercising ordinary skill, would disclose before acting on their patient's consent. Lord Scarman was of the mind that the 'patient-oriented' standard was preferable. First he pointed out,

> It would be a strange conclusion if the courts should be led to conclude that our law, which undoubtedly recognizes a right in the patient to decide whether he will accept or reject the treatment proposed, should permit the doctors to determine whether and in what circumstances a duty arises requiring the doctor to warn his patient of the risks inherent in the treatment which he proposes.'[78]

From this he then concluded,

> 'If one considers the scope of the doctor's duty by beginning with the right of the patient to make his own decision whether he will or will not undergo the treatment proposed, the right to be informed of significant risk and the doctor's corresponding duty are easy to understand, for the proper implementation of the right requires that the doctor be under a duty to inform his patient of the material risks inherent in the treatment.'[79]

The majority did not adopt this reasoning. The doctrine of 'informed consent' adopted by several respected American Courts[80] and by the Canadian Supreme Court[81] was rejected. Three principal reasons to do so were offered by Lord Diplock. First, it does not give sufficient weight to the subtle judgment factors the doctor must consider in deciding what disclosure is necessary for the patient to make an 'informed decision.' Second, it is unwise to deny the court the benefit of expert medical evidence on the issue of information disclosure need and practice. Third, the standard of what 'a reasonable person in the patient's position' would consider important to know is too imprecise to be useful.[82]

The holding in *Sidaway* does not answer fully what the doctor has to tell his or her patient. It will be developed further by English and Scottish decisions. Fortunately, it does not leave the determination of duty to disclose exclusively or conclusively to the medical profession. Rather, it may be viewed as creating a rebuttable presumption that what doctors tell their patients to get their consent is adequate. However, there must be room for exceptions. The Lords recognized one important exception, that the court may be compelled to find a duty to disclose even when the prevailing medical practice is one of non-disclosure. If the standard of the profession is unreasonable, then the court may overturn it. The disclosure standard remains a legal one, not one imposed by the profession alone.

In addition, Lord Bridge concluded that if the patient asks specifically about risks involved with the proposed treatment the doctor must 'answer both truthfully and as fully as the questioner [patient] requires.'[83]

It may be that in practice Scottish courts will recognize the normal rule is to accept that the doctor need only disclose what reasonably skilled doctors would, but that it is the court that must ultimately safeguard the rights of the patient by determining if that ordinary medical practice is proper. When, for example, the Glasgow Sheriff's Court was called on to apply the *Sidaway* holding, it stated its understanding of the rule in the case as follows:

> 'The rule in *Sidaway* may, therefore, with respect, perhaps be summarized as follows, that before an operation (other than in emergency conditions) be decided upon the patient must be given an explanation of the nature of the procedure including an estimate of the amount of risk; *only the court can determine if the doctor has erred in deciding what to disclose to the patient but the court will have regard to the general practice of the profession* in deciding how much disclosure should have been made and will not normally over-ride a generally accepted practice which has become well established.' (emphasis supplied.)[84]

This seems to be very sensible reasoning of *Sidaway*. It is submitted that it is one that should be accepted and applied. Normally there should be no need to look beyond established medical practice. But court review and acceptance of such practice is necessary in order to prevent the medical profession adopting an unreasonable, purely defensive, or self-protective standard of disclosure to the detriment of the patient.

In the recent *Moyes* case,[68] a Scottish Court of Session judge, presumably having *Sidaway* very much in mind, pointed out that what to tell the patient may largely depend on factors which normally are best evaluated by the physician in the exercise of his prefessional judgment and experience. These factors were said to include the nature of the risks inherent in the proposed medical procedure, the manner in which the treatment could affect or harm the particular patient, and the ability of the patient to absorb the risk disclosure information without doing damage to his health or the chances for success of the procedure.[85]

In summary then it can be seen that normally patients will have to rely in Scotland and in England on their doctors to tell them what they should know before deciding whether or not to consent to proposed medical treatment. Surely this will mean that the patient must at least be told the nature and purpose of the treatment in general terms and any significant, not commonly-appreciated risks associated with the treatment. As Lord Justice Lawton has stated,[86]

> 'A person consents to treatment if he knows what is going to be done to him and what are reasonably likely to be the consequences and risks of what is proposed to be done.'

It seems correct to say that only risks reasonably likely to occur need be disclosed. This, of course, is not free from doubt. A 1 per cent or less risk of spinal damage did not need to be disclosed in *Sidaway*, though a 10 per cent risk of stroke required disclosure.[87] A 0.2 per cent to 0.3 per cent risk of serious neurological reaction did not need to be disclosed in *Moyes*,[68] such slight or remote risk disclosure being a matter of 'fine clinical judgment' for the physician to decide.

4. *The patient must ask, to be fully informed*

The only way the patient can ensure that he or she is given all the information he or she wants to know about the risks of treatment, its nature and purpose, or alternatives to it, is to actually ask these questions directly of the doctor. Then, the doctor will be required to answer 'truthfully and . . . fully' those questions.[88] However, even in such situations the doctor may be able to rely on the so-called 'therapeutic privilege' to disclose less than the full truth about the procedure contemplated and all its risks. In such cases the burden would be on the doctor to show that the patient's medical condition was such that it was consistent with ordinary and reasonable medical practice for the doctor to conclude that full disclosure would be more harmful to the patient's condition and his or her prospects for recovery than only selective or partial disclosure.[89]

Obviously, the more serious the risk of harm, the less likely need be its occurrence, for it to be significant. Prudent medical practice will be likely to disclose a relatively small risk of death or severe permanent disability, such as paralysis, even though its incidence is quite low (as, for example, with coronary angiography where risk of death from cardiac arrest is in the neighborhood of 1–2 per cent). Contrariwise, commonly understood risks, such as infection, though more likely, will normally not be disclosed. The same disclosure standard will probably apply to the doctor when the treatment proposed is of a non-therapeutic as opposed to a therapeutic nature, as, for example, with a contraceptive sterilization procedure.[90]

We have been discussing thus far the competent adult patient. We have considered what he or she must be told before he or she will be legally deemed to have consented to medical treatment. We started from the proposition that medical treatment constitutes an unauthorized invasion of bodily integrity unless excused, condoned, or justified by the patient's consent. The physician is presumed liable, in the absence of an emergency, if he or she treats the patient without consent, for civil assault and trespass against the person and for criminal assault and battery.[91]

Are there any situations, where this presumption does not obtain, where the doctor is entitled to treat without the patient's consent? Yes. As mentioned, emergency is one. This typically occurs where an injured or acutely ill patient is presented to a physician or at a hospital in immediate need of treatment to avoid death or to minimize the risk of serious disability or harm. Often such patients will be unconscious, delirious, or otherwise mentally unable to give consent.

5. *Incompetent patients*

In Scots law, no one is authorized to decide medical treatment for another who is incompetent, except perhaps the parent of a pupil (girls under 12, boys under 14) child,[92] or a court appointed tutor for an older incompetent.[93] Absent such a relationship, there is no one with expressly conferred authority, absent court order,[94] to give consent for treatment on behalf of the unconscious or otherwise mentally incompetent patient.

a. *The consent of the family.* There are three potential ways of dealing with the problem. One is for the courts to accept that the closest available relative may consent for the patient.[95] This may not be particularly satisfactory because no such relative may be available, nor have any idea whether or not the patient would want to consent.

However, as a practical matter, in the majority of situations it is the family, in conjunction with the physicians, who do make decisions for an incompetent family member. These decisions are the norm[96] and do not involve the courts, unless there is disagreement or dispute between the family, or the family and the doctors, the treatment is non-therapeutic or involves irreversible loss of function (sterilization, psychosurgery) or is socially controversial (abortion).[97]

b. *Implied consent.* Another way to deal with the incompetent patient is to rely on the legal fiction of implied consent. This holds that since express consent cannot be given and that since most people would want treatment to avoid death or serious disability, that consent will be implied from the patient's circumstances. Implied consent derives from the 'welfare' or 'best interests' principle; to wit, that patients who are incompetent will be *presumed* to have given consent to treatment that is in their best interests or for their welfare.

The problem with these welfare principles is that others are left to define what is in the patient's best interests. Normally, this will mean what most people would want done. What most people would want done is not necessarily what the particular patient would want done. Arguably it is the next best standard by which to treat someone. It is based on how most people in the society would want to be treated under the circumstances when actual preferences are unknown.[98] However, its practical application is limited to the emergency situation where treatment is immediately necessary to avoid death or serious disability, since it is here that what most people would want done, presumably including the patient, is most clear. It is hard to imagine use of the doctrine elsewhere, as, for example, in cases calling for abortion, sterilization, or psychosurgery in incompetent patients.

c. *Necessity.* The third way of dealing with the patient unable to consent is to rely on the principle of necessity. Walker states it this way,

'In emergency, as where an injured person is brought unconscious into hospital, the *necessity* in the circumstance of emergency treatment probably justifies surgery without consent.' (emphasis supplied)[99]

The doctrine of necessity applies in both the civil and criminal law. It provides a defense to conduct that otherwise would be wrongful on the rationale that the good resulting from the conduct so materially outweighs the bad consequences from strict adherence to the law as to legally condone the conduct.[100] The idea is that the benefit to the patient – avoidance of death or serious disability – is so great that it excuses the wrong – non-consensual medical treatment. This assumes at least two factual circumstances are operative. First, that the treatment clearly offers the benefit of avoiding death or serious disability without serious concomitant risk. Second, that the patient while competent has not let it be known that he or she would not want such treatment.

Even with these two factors operative, the necessity doctrine is still rather vague in outline. In a recent English case raising the issue of whether a severely handicapped pregnant adult should be aborted and sterilized to avoid a pregnancy and birth she was incapable of understanding and tolerating, the Judge concluded necessity was not applicable.[97] 'I do not find the use of that word to be sufficiently precise as a test of what the courts would consider to be a justification for the operative procedures anticipated in the present case.'

Necessity thus is seen as a narrower criterion than 'best interests.' A treatment may be in the patient's best interests, but it does not seem necessary unless it is required to save the patient's life or avoid serious disability.[101] In the important English case of *Re B (a Minor)*,[102] the House of Lords authorized sterilization for a 17 year old mentally handicapped girl incapable of caring for a child, or taking other birth control measures, and who was expected to do herself physical harm during pregnancy and childbirth. However, the court did not rely upon necessity, but rather upon the so-called 'welfare' principle; to wit, that the treatment proposed would be in the best interests of the girl.

Granted, the line is not distinct between what treatment is not necessary, but in the best interests of the incompetent patient, and that which is necessary for the life or health of the patient. The difference will often be a matter of judgment. There is no clear distinction evident. There are no Scottish cases to rely upon. Mason and McCall Smith[100] rely upon two Canadian cases to illustrate the difference between 'necessary' and only 'convenient' treatment. In one, it was 'necessary' to remove a diseased organ discovered during surgery 'for the protection of the patient's health and possibly his life.'[103] In the other, it was convenient to sterilize the patient during the first surgery to avoid the risk of a future pregnancy, but no immediate health hazard was presented by postponing the surgery.[104]

d. *Only one good available treatment.* There may actually be a fourth way of dealing with treatment for an incompetent patient who has no one authorized by parentage or appointment to consent for him. Wood, J. suggested it in the recent English case of *T. v. T.*[97] He suggested treatment may proceed without consent where it is so clearly in the best interest of the patient that there exists only one recommended course of treatment dictated by 'good medical practice.' This is sort of an uncontested or 'clear and convincing'[105] best interests or welfare test. It must be so clearly beneficial treatment that, in the words of Wood, J., it is what good medical practice 'demands'. It is treatment 'positively' in the patient's best interests.

While at first blush this may seem a rather vague and ill defined concept upon which to rely to dispense with the requirement of patient consent, it might well be the unstated, but practical basis for most incompetent adult treatment decisions in Scotland. There are no adult guardianship or conservatorship proceedings in Scotland by which individuals may be authorized to consent to medical treatment for minor (non-pupil) or adult incompetents. Although the tutor-dative procedure is apparently available to appoint a conservator in such cases, it has been rarely relied upon in Scotland.[93]

6. *Doctors are rarely questioned*

Despite this lack of authority, medical treatment of adult incompetent patients goes on daily in Scottish hospitals, medical clinics and surgeries. Many aged will become incompetent at some point in the progression of a terminal or incurable illness due to a combination of age, infirmity, stress, and/or medication. These people are commonly treated without any express consent being given by the patient.[96] In practice, doctors are relying upon their own good faith determination of what treatment is indicated for the patient, what good medical practice dictates, what are the wishes of the family, and any known preferences of the patient. It may also be that in such cases the public continues to have a greater trust and confidence in the medical profession than in either England or America, a greater willingness to abide by what the doctor feels is 'best.'[106]

Although beyond the scope of this book, it seems safe to say that social and cultural factors play a strong role in the development and interpretation of the law, and in the reliance placed upon it by the citizens of a country. In this instance those involved are doctors, patients, and their families. A more paternalistic medical climate prevails in Scotland, as well as one that generally seems to be less litigious than that south of Hadrian's Wall and, more particularly, across the Atlantic. Whereas Americans tend more and more to approach the medical establishment as consumers looking for the best service available to them and often with a certain amount of skepticism about doctors' motives and skills, such is not the case in Scotland. The

Scottish patient, by and large, respects the doctor treating him or her, accepts whatever treatment is recommended, and normally does not insist upon treatment not offered. United Kingdom doctors also operate in a health delivery system accustomed to limited availability of expensive technology.

An eminent Scottish physician was comfortable stating recently that most Scottish physicians do not feel it necessary to even consider the law in treating their patients. They decide what is best for the patient and proceed accordingly.

It is also true that there is a broad latitude given to prosecutorial authorities in Scotland, who have a history of not prosecuting doctors over treatment or nontreatment decisions. Absent some clear reported abuse, this attitude is likely to continue. The same holds true, it appears in very large degree for England and for America, where despite considerably more litigation, the vast majority of treatment decisions for adult incompetents seem to be taken on an informal 'best interests' sort of approach agreed upon by the doctors and the available family, or legal guardian, so long as this does not run counter to any known, competently-expressed views voiced previously by the patient.[107]

As we have seen, consent, necessity, and patient best interests, are the justifications for medical treatment. These justifications are not always adequate. Public policy may intervene. The traditional position of the common law has been that certain bodily invasions are so antisocial, or against public policy, that consent does not justify the intrusion, nor provide a defense to the perpetrator. Sports likely to maim or kill, such as bare-handed boxing, fall into this category.[108] While contraceptive sterilization is now an accepted practice, it was not always so and in fact quite recently was not.[109] Abortion is unlawful, except under certain limited conditions which provide a defense to the doctor, now recognized by statute.[110] Apart from these limited exceptions, the law has seen fit to leave consent to the patient (when competent), the family (when the patient is incompetent), and the physicians to resolve. Unless the treatment is not deemed to be in the best interests of the patient, few problems arise. This has been the case in Scotland.[96]

E. CONCLUSIONS

The law in United States, in England and in Scotland is, to large degree, very similar. The doctrine of consent protects bodily integrity against unwanted intrusions, whether by physician, assailant, or unwanted suitor. All jurisdictions expect the consent to be informed. That is, consent should be voluntary and knowing. Informed consent means nothing more than that.

In fact, despite suggestions to the contrary, informed consent is part of both English and Scottish law. However, rather than requiring that all material information be disclosed to the patient, as do the more progressive American decisions which many equate with 'informed consent,' the British cases to date, following the lead of *Sidaway*, require that only information reasonably and customarily disclosed by physicians be given the patient. This is merely one standard of informed consent. It remains the rule in many of the United States. It is known as the 'reasonable physician' or 'professional' standard of disclosure.

Its disadvantage is that the patient's needs may not be addressed by this standard. It allows physicians, with rare exception, to decide what patients should be told. It is a paternalistic practice in the increasingly autonomous modern relationship between doctor and patient.

There is an interesting correlation suggested here. It appears those jurisdictions most paternalistic in their approach to medical care are most happy with the 'professional' standard (viz. Scotland). Those most consumer-oriented in medicine, with the strongest value placed on the autonomy of the patient, support the 'patient' standard, requiring disclosure of all material risks (viz. California, Oregon, Washington D.C., New Jersey, etc.). England is perhaps somewhere in between. It resolves these competing values legally by acceptance of the professional standard, but leavened by the articulated right of judges to overrule it where necessary to protect the patient. One may well ask how and when judges will know what all reasonable doctors disclose is not adequate and more need be disclosed? What qualifies judges to say disclosure of a 5 percent risk of paralysis is a matter of professional judgment, but a 6 percent risk must be disclosed regardless of the prevailing practice?

It is unclear which approach to informed consent is best. Patient autonomy is an ethical and desirable objective, but patients must still rely essentially, as they have before, on the ethics and professional competence of the physician to deal with their illness or injury. The doctor may normally know what is best, but the law has a place to play in regulating medical practice to ensure that penalties – discipline, damages, or other censure – play a useful role in encouraging quality of care.

In discarding the 'reasonable physician' standard of disclosure recently, the New Jersey Supreme Court concluded that it smacked of 'an anachronistic paternalism that is at odds with any strong conception of a patient's right of self-determination.'[16] The idea here is we rely on a doctor's skill to treat us, but *we* want to know what it involves before deciding whether to consent.

All jurisdictions clearly recognize that the competent patient generally has a right to know the nature and purpose of the procedure and its significant risks and alternatives. All the patient's questions must be answered truthfully. In rare instances the patient's condition may warrant withholding information, but rarely will this be so when the question eliciting it is expressly asked.

Patients are demanding to be told more by their doctors. Medicine offers many more choices now than it once did. Decisions have to be made. Alternative therapies are available and must be selected. A staggering array of technology requires constant decision-making as to its availability, suitability and effectiveness.[111] As a result, the burden on both patient and doctor to decide on appropriate treatment – when to institute it and when to withdraw it – is much greater. Quality of life issues enter the picture and doctors may, at least at times, welcome the involvement of others in the treatment decisionmaking process.[112]

Autonomy and self-determination should remain the touchstone. They protect the bodily integrity of the patient. Their role should be maximized to the greatest extent possible in a free society. Given this, consent emerges as an increasingly important prerogative of the patient in an increasingly complex and technological medical treatment environment.[113] There may be times when full disclosure will only unduly agitate the patient. In these occasional circumstances reasonable doctors will elect not to tell and reasonable patients will not want to be told. This therapeutic privilege exception is valid, but it should not be used to protect physicians at the expense of patients.

The objective should be to fully and properly inform the patient so that his or her decision – whether to give or to refuse consent – is made with full understanding of the consequences. Reasonable medical practice standards should strive to meet this goal, so that as a practical matter there exists little or no significant difference between what reasonable doctors elect to tell their patients and what reasonable patients want their doctors to tell them.

If consent is not given, treatment cannot be given. If an emergency exists, the patient cannot freely consent and serious harm is threatened, either necessity or implied consent provide legal justification for treatment. Where no such emergency exists, the question is how and by whom is the treatment decision made for the patient unable to consent for himself? We now turn to consider treatment of children and incompetents to answer this question.

NOTES

1 It is not feasible nor necessary for the law to protect against such touchings. There is no harm or damage. Some are inevitable.
2 Walker, *The Law of Delict in Scotland*, Edinburgh: W. Green & Son, Ltd., 1981 (2d ed), p.493
3 *Erickson v. Dilgard* (1962, N.Y. App.) 252 NYS 2d 705, 706; Ian

Kennedy, 'The Patient on the Clapham Omnibus,' 47 *Mod. L.R.* 454 (1984); John Stuart Mill, *On Liberty*.

4 *Sidaway v. Bethlem Royal Hospital Governors* (1985) 1 All E.R. 643 (H.L.); *Re Spring* (1980 Mass) 405 N.E. 2d 115.

5 *Mohr v. Williams* (1905, Minn) 104 N.W. 12 (reversed later on other grounds.)

6 The first such case appears to be *Salgo v. Stanford University Board of Trustees* (1957) 154 Cal. App. 2d 560.

7 *Natanson v. Kline* (1960, Kan) 350 P. 2d 1093; *Canterbury v. Spence* (1972, D.C. App.) 464 F. 2d 772 (cert. den., 409 U.S. 1064); *Cobbs v. Grant* (1972) 8 Cal. 3d 229.

8 *Ouellette v. Mehalic* (1988, Me) 534 A. 2d 1331; *Guebard v. Jabaay* (1983, Ill. App.) 452 N.E. 2d 751; *Buckner v. Allergan Pharmaceuticals, Inc.,* (1981, Fla. App.) 400 So. 2d 820 (pet. den., 407 So. 2d 1102); *Nishi v. Hartwell* (1970, Haw) 473 P. 2d 116.

9 *Crisher v. Spok* (1983, N.Y. App.) 471 N.Y.S. 2d 741.

10 *Helling v. Carey* (1974, Wash.) 519 Pac. 2d 981 (superceded by statute.)

11 *Texas and P.R. Co. v. Behymer* (1903) 189 U.S. 468, 470.

12 *Largey v. Rothman* (1988, N.J.) 540 A.2d 504; *Canterbury v. Spence* (1972, D.C. App) 464 Fed. 2d 772; *Cobbs v. Grant* (1972) 8 Cal. 3d 229; *Wilkinson v. Vesey* (1972, R.I.) 295 A. 2d 676; *Sard v. Handy* (1977, Md.) 379 A. 2d 1014; *Plutshack v. University of Minn.* (1982, Minn.) 316 N.W. 2d 1; *Wheeldon v. Madison* (1985, S.D.) 374 N.W. 2d 367; *Phillips v. Hull* (1987, Miss.) 516 So. 2d 488; *Cook v. Trout* (1987, Id.) 747 Pac. 2d 61.

13 *Truman v. Thomas* (1980) 27 Cal. 3d 285 (patient who declines 'pap smear' diagnostic test for cancer should be told of the risks of undetected cancer). See also, *Haughian v. Paine* (1987, Sask. Ct. App.) 4 W.W.R. 97 (risk of paralysis in disc surgery; alternative of no surgery should have been explained); 1987 *The Lancet* ii, 1474.

14 Seidelson 'Lack of Informed Consent in Medical Malpractice and Product Liability Cases: the Burden of Presenting Evidence,' 14 *Hofstra L. Rev.* 621 (1986).

15 *Arena v. Gingrich* (1988, Ore.) 748 Pac. 2d 547; *Scott v. Bradford* (1879, Okla.) 606 Pac. 2d 554.

16 *Largey v. Rothman* (1988, N.J.) 540 A. 2d 504, 508–9.

17 LSA.R.S. 40: 1299.40; *Douget v. Touro Infirmary* (1988, La.App.) 537 So. 2d 251, 257.

18 *Slate v. Kehoe* (1974) 38 Cal.App. 3d 819; *Cobbs v. Grant, supra.*

19 *Canterbury v. Spence, supra,* (1 per cent risk of paralysis up to finder of fact to decide); *Scott v. Wilson* (1966, Tex.) 412 S.W. 2d 299 (1 per cent risk of loss of hearing must be disclosed); *Bowers v. Talmage* (1963, Fla. App.) 159 So 2d 888 (3 per cent risk of paralysis or death must be disclosed).

20 *Starmes v. Taylor* (1968, N.C.) 158 S.E. 2d 339 (1/250 to 1/500 risk of esophageal perforation); *Stottlemire v. Cawood* (1963 D. C. Dist.) 213 Fed. Supp. 897 (1/800,000 risk of aplastic anemia).

21 *Slater v. Kehoe, supra* (less than 5 per cent risk of non-lethal condition); *Collins v. Itoh* (1972, Mont.) 503 P. 2d 36 (less than 3 per cent risk of hypoparathyroidism).

22 *Mroczkowski v. Straub Clinic and Hospital, Inc.* (1987, Haw. App.) 732 P. 2d 1255.

23 *Wilkinson v. Vesey, supra.*

24 *Srogun v. Fruchtman* (1973, Wis.) 207 N.W. 2d 297.

25 *Canterbury v. Spence, supra,* 464 Fed. 2d 772, 789.

26 *Pardy v. United States* (1986, 7th cir.) 783 Fed. 2d 710.

27 *Wilkinson v. Vesey, supra,* 295 A. 2d 676, 689; *Cobbs v. Grant, supra,* 8 Cal. 3d 229, 246.

28 See, for example, Georgia Medical Consent Law, §88–2906 (1971); Florida Statute §758.46 (1983); Iowa code Ann. §147.137 (1977); Ohio Rev. Code Ann. §2317.54(A), (1977).

29 Hawaii (see *Mroczkowski v. Straub Clinic and Hospital, Inc.* (1987, Haw. App.) 732 Pac. 2d 1255.

30 Idaho Code §39–4301, et seq.(1975); see *Rook v. Trout* (1987, Id.) 747 Pac. 2d 61.

31 Ore.R.S. §677.097

32 40 Fed Reg. 11, 854, §46.3(c), (1975)

33 *Canterbury v. Spence, supra; Bartsch v. Brewer* (1982, Wash.) 640 Pac. 2d 711; *Harnish v. Children's Hospital Med. Ctr.* (1982, Mass.) 439 N.E. 2d 240. *Adams v. El-Bash* (1985, W.Va.) 338 S.E. 2d 381.

34 *Arena v. Gingrich* (1988, Ore.) 748 Pac. 2d 547; *Shenefield v. Greenwich Hosp.* (1987, Conn. App.) 522 A. 2d 829; *Cheung v. Cunningham* (1987, N.J. Super.) 520 A. 2d 832.

35 *Canterbury v. Spence, supra,* 488 Fed. 2d 772, 788; *Stafford v. Louisiana State University (1984, La. App.) 448 So. 2d 852.*

36 See *T. v. T.* (1988) 2 W.L.R. 189; *Re B* (1987) 2 W.L.R. 1213; *R. v. Bourne* (1939) 1 K.B. 687.

37 *Busalacci v. Vogel* (1983, La. App.) 429 So. 2d 217; *Younts v. St. Francis Hospital and School of Nursing, Inc.* (1970, Kan.) 469 P. 2d 330.

38 *Cobbs v. Grant, supra,* 8 Ca. 3d 229, 244)5.

39 *Bolam v. Friern Hosp.Mgt.Committee* (1957) 2 All E.R. 118.

40 (1985) 1 All E.R. at 660.

41 Ian Kennedy, 'The Patient on the Clapham Omnibus' 47 *Mod.L.R.* 454 (1984).

42 (1985) 1 All E.R. 643, at 663

43 (1987) 2 W.L.R. 649 (C.A.); see also, *Eyre v. Measday* (1986) 1 All E.R. 488 (C.A.), (no warranty of sterility implied in sterilization procedure.)

44 Grubb, 'The Emergence and Rise of Medical Law and Ethics,' 50 *Mod L.R.* 241 (1987), 254.

45 *Chatterton v. Gerson* (1981) 1 All E.R. 257, at 266 (emphasis added).

46 *Hills v. Potter* (1983) 3 All E.R. 716, (1984) W.L.R. 641.

47 (1984) 3 All E.R. 716, at 728.

48 (1988) *The Lancet* 1291 (*R. v. Mental Health Commission, Ex Parte Witham*)

49 *Sidaway* (1988)1 All E.R. 643, 649; *T. v. T.* (1988) 2 W.L.R. 189, (Wood, J.)

50 See Gillon (ed.), 14 *J. Med. Ethics* 60 (1988)

51 *Re B (A Minor)* (1987) 2 W.L.R. 1213 (H.L.), (sterilization authorized for 17 year old); *Re B* (1981) 1 W.L.R. 1421 (C.A.), (Intestinal

blockage correction surgery authorized over parental refusal for new-born with Down's syndrome).

52 *Re D. (A Minor)*, (1976) 1 All E.R. 326, (Heilbron, J.).
53 See Children and Young Persons Act 1969, s. 23.
54 *T. v. T.* (1988) 2 W.L.R. 189, (Wood, J.).
55 See Skegg, *Law, Ethics and Medicine*. Oxford: Clarendon Press, 1984, p. 56. See also, Kennedy, 'The Patient on the
Clapham Omnibus,' 47 *Mod. L.R. 454* (1984).
56 Kennedy, 'Legal Effect of Requests by the Terminally Ill and Aged not to Receive Further Treatment from Doctors,' 1976 *Crim L.R.* 217.
57 *In re F (Mental Patient) (Sterilisation)*, (1989) 2 W.L.R. 1025, 1069 (Lord Brandon); see Brahams, 1989 *The Lancet* 340, 1089.
58 See Dyer, 'Consent and the mentally handicapped,' 295 *Brit. Med .J.* 257 (1987).
59 *T. v. T.* (1988) 2 W.L.R. 189 (Wood,J.).
60 See discussion in Chapters 2, 7 & 9.
61 See Skegg 'Consent to Medical Procedures on Minors' 36 *Mod.L.R.* 370 (1973); Brahams, 1987 *The Lancet* i, 1386)7; *In re X* (June 3, 1987, Fam.Div., Reeves, J.)
62 See *Barber v. Superior Court* (1983) 147 Cal App 3d, 1006; Strong, 1981 *J. Med. Ethics* 83.
63 Mason & McCall Smith, *Law & Med. Ethics*, London: Butterworths, 1987 (2d.ed.) Chap. 15.
64 *Conservatorship of Drabick* (1988) 200 Cal App 3d 185.
65 General Medical Council, *HIV Infection and AIDS: The Ethical Considerations* (1988), para.13 (specific consent essential); cf. Dyer, 'Another judgment on testing for HIV without consent,' 296 *B.M.J.* 1791 (1988).
66 Walker, *supra*; Gordon *The Criminal Law of Scotland*. Edinburgh: Green, 1978 (2d ed), p.429.
67 *Craig v. Glasgow Victoria & Leverndale Hospitals Bd. of Management* (March 22, 1974), Court of Session, 1st Div.).
68 *Moyes v. Lothian Health Board* (July 6, 1989), *The Scotsman*, July 7, 1989, p.8.
69 See *Freeman v. Home Office* (1983) 3 All E.R. 589 (Q.B.); *Riebl v. Hughes* (1980) 114 D.L.R.(3d) 1 (Can SC).
70 *Hunter v. Hanley* 1955 S.C. 200, 206.
71 Kennedy, 'Legal Effect of Requests by the Terminally Ill and Aged not to Receive Further Treatment from Doctors,' 1976 *Crim L.R.* 217.
72 AGM Campbell, 'The Right to be Allowed to Die,' 9 *J. Med. Ethics* (1983).
73 1955 S.C at 205
74 (1957) 2 All E.R. 118, (1957) 1 W.L.R. 582.
75 (1957) 1 W.L.R. at 586.
76 Walker, *supra*, p.1059, states the doctor's failure to disclose must be shown to be a failure to comply with proper professional standards (i.e., negligence) to be actionable.
77 James McAlpine Fatal Accident Inquiry (Sheriff Kierney 1/17/86, Glasgow, unreported), p. 46.
78 (1985) 1 All E.R. at 649.
79 (1985) 1 All E.R. at 654.

80 *Canterbury v. Spence* (1972, D.C. Cir) 464 Fed. 2d 772, cert. den. 409 U.S. 1064; *Cobbs v. Grant* (1972) 8 Cal.3d 229.
81 *Reibl v. Hughes* (1980) 114 D.L.R. (3d) 1, (Can S.C.); accord, *Haughian v. Paine* (1987, Sask. Ct. App.) 4 W.W.R. 97.
82 (1985) 1 All E.R. 662
83 (1985) 1 All E.R. 661
84 *James McAlpine Fatal Accident Inquiry, supra*, pp. 45–48.
85 This so-called 'therapeutic privilege' not to disclose is narrowly construed by most American court decisions.
86 76 *J. Roy Soc. Med.* 298 (1983).
87 (1985) 1 All E.R. at 663, referencing the Canadian decision in *Reibl v. Hughes, supra*.
88 (1985) 1 All E.R. 661.
89 While not clearly developed in Scots law, if the scope of the duty to disclose is normally to be set by prevailing reasonably prudent medical practice, then exceptions to that duty, based on evidence of the patient's mental and emotional condition, would normally be similarly set by prevailing prof. practice. See, Edmund Davies, L.J., 'The Patient's Right to Know the Truth,' 66 *Proc. Roy. Soc. Med.* 533 (1973).
90 *Gold v. Haringey Health Authority* (1987) 3 W.L.R. 649, (C.A.).
91 *Sidaway, supra* (1985) 1 All E.R. 643, 648 (per Lord Scarman).
92 See Norrie, 'The Gillick Case and Parental Rights in Scots Law' 1985 *S.L.T.* 157.
93 Ward, 'Morris, Petitioner, Revival of Tutors-Dative,' 1987 *S.L.T.* (News) 69.
94 See Law Reform (Parent and (Child)(Scotland) Act 1986, s.3.
95 See, for example, the Californian precedent *Cobbs v. Grant* (1972) 8 Cal 3d 229, *244*.
96 Campbell, A.G.M., M.D., Norrie, K. McK. and Meyers, D.W. 'Withholding or Withdrawing Treatment,' Univ. of Aberdeen Faculty of Law, Nov.2,1988; Brahams, 1989 *The Lancet* 1, 969–70.
97 See Brahams, 'Legal Power to Sterilise Incompetent Women,' 1989 *The Lancet* 854; *T. v. T.*(1988) 2 W.L.R. 189; see Mental Health Act (1983), §57.
98 See Pres. Comm., *Deciding to Forego Treatment*. Wash D.C., U.S. Govt. Print.Off. 1983; *Drabick & Drabick* (1988) 200 Cal.App. 3d 185. In *T. v. T.* (1988) 2 W.L.R. 189, Judge Wolf held implied consent unavailable because the patient had never been competent to decide. The doctrine does not require prior competency for its application, since it is based on what others decide should be done, not what the patient wants or has expressed previously.
99 Walker, *The Law of Delict in Scotland, supra*, p. 345.
100 Mason & McCall Smith, *Law and Med Ethics*, p.143.
101 Perhaps 'necessity' can be more properly equated, in the medical treatment context, with 'emergency' rather than 'best interests.' See *Thomson v. Devon* (1899) 15 Sh. Ct. Rep. 209; Walker, *Delict, supra*, p. 345.
102 (1987) 2 W.L.R. 1213.

103 *Marshall v. Curry* (1933) 3 D.L.R. 260. See also the unreported Scottish case of *Craig v. Glasgow Victoria and Leverndale Hospitals Bd. of Management* (March 22, 1974, Court of Session, 1st Div.), note 67, *supra*, also discussed in Mason & McCall Smith, *Law and Medical Ethics*, p.144.
104 *Murray v. McMurchy* (1949) 2 D.L.R. 422.
105 More compelling than merely the balance of probabilities or the preponderance of the evidence, but not rising to the strict criminal evidentiary standard of 'beyond a reasonable doubt.'
106 Campbell, 'The right to be allowed to die' 1983 *J. Med. Ethics* 136, 137.
107 See *Amer. Acad. of Pediatrics* v. *Heckler* (1983, D.C. Dist. Ctl.) 561 Fed. Supp. 395 (Gesell, Jr.)
108 *R. v. Donovan* (1934) 2 K.B. 498, 507.
109 See *Bravery v. Bravery* (1954) 1 W.L.R. 1169.
110 See Chap. 3 and in particular, Abortion Act 1967.
111 See discussion in Chapters 9,10,& 11, *infra*.
112 The Baby C. case is a recent example, *In re C (A Minor) (Wardship: Medical Treatment)*,(1989) 3 W.L.R. 240; (*The Times* 21 April 1989, pp.3, 36), (discussed in Chapter 4, *supra*).
113 A recent example is found in *Moore v. Regents of University of California* (1988) 202 Cal. App 3d 1230. There it was alleged Defendant physicians and researchers removed the Plaintiff's spleen, but failed to obtain his consent to use of the spleen tissue for commercial, pharmacological purposes. A claim for conversion of body tissues and the right to sue for damages in tort was upheld on appeal.

6

Treatment of Children and Incompetents

A. INTRODUCTION

We have seen that the law in Scotland, England, and the United States explicitly recognizes the rights of a competent adult to consent to, or refuse, proposed medical treatment.[1] The autonomy and bodily integrity of the individual are seen as fundamental tenets of a democratic society,[2] long established in the history and legal foundations of each country. With few exceptions, the competent adult may refuse any kind of medical treatment, even life-saving treatment.[3] If the individual does not give express consent, or it is not legally implied by the necessity of the circumstances at hand,[4] surgery or other treatment is illegal and cannot be imposed. Although there may be instances where the consent or refusal of consent to treatment by a competent adult may be overridden, if brought to the attention of the courts, for violating certain basic tenets of public policy, such instances are exceedingly rare.[5]

Where, however, the patient is deemed legally incompetent due to age or infirmity, a much different and more complicated picture emerges. If such a patient cannot understand the nature and purpose of the proposed medical procedure, then he or she is not able to knowingly consent, or refuse consent.[6] If the patient is unable to give or refuse a knowing or informed consent, then he or she is not personally able to exercise rights to individual autonomy and bodily integrity.

The law, in such situations, has had to find a substitute for the individual's right to decide. In the case of children, the normal response has been to entrust this right and responsibility to the parents. However, as we will see, limitations have been imposed on the parents' freedom of action in an effort to protect the welfare and best interest of the child. In the case of other incompetents, legal mechanisms have been provided (guardianship, conservatorship, the tutor-dative) but in practice they are often not utilized. The courts have been available to assert a protective role, when petitioned to do so.

Treatment decisions for children and incompetents have similar objec-

155

tives in Scotland, England, and the United States, although the legal foundations for such substitute decision making may be different. The Law seeks to reconcile the rights and responsibilities of patient, parent or other surrogate, and state, which may well conflict.

B.   SCOTLAND

1.   *Children*

In Scots law a child is a pupil until puberty (12 for girls, 14 for boys). Thereafter, until age 18 the child is a minor. The pupil child has historically been considered to have no legal capacity to decide, pupillarity being 'a state of absolute incapacity.'[7] Rather, the parent is vested with full control over the pupil.[8] During this period of pupillarity, traditionally the father exercised the power of *patria potestas* over his children.[9] This carried with it powers of custody, residence, education, general upbringing, religious training, legal representation, and *medical treatment* decision-making.[10] These powers must still be exercised for the welfare of the child.

Upon attaining the presumed age of puberty in Scotland, the child becomes a minor. Minority brings with it a substantial increase in the rights of the child and a substantial lessening in the powers and control of the parent. Instead of having control over the person of the child, the control of the parents extends only to the property or estate of the minor, to his affairs, but not to his body. While the parent of a pupil is known at common law as a tutor, upon attaining minority the child's parent becomes known as a curator, or in effect, a caretaker.[11]

Thus, in Scots law, unless changed by statute, the *presumption* is that a child upon reaching puberty can decide for him or herself. This includes the right to consent to medical treatment. However, to exercise this right the minor must be capable of understanding the nature and purpose of the proposed treatment, for absent that capacity the minor is unable to give a valid consent.[12]

The Scottish courts have recognized that no hard and fast rule can be laid down prior to majority at age 18, and that no particular age necessarily implies an ability to understand – and therefore to consent to – a particular type of treatment. Obviously simple procedures of first aid, immunization against known illness and other common medical procedures can be understood by children of tender years.[13] On the other hand, complicated procedures, those of esoteric or little-known nature, or those calling for a reasoned balancing of risk or intrusiveness against anticipated benefit may not be well understood until the child is much older, perhaps not until an age nearing majority in some cases.

Several older Scottish cases point up this flexible and imprecise relationship between age and capacity. In one,[14] the fact the girl was under 16 did not alone cause the conclusion she was unable of consenting to sexual intercourse. In another,[15] it was concluded a boy of 16 or 17 was unlikely to fully comprehend the implications of consenting to be fingerprinted; social consequences of a long-term nature, as well as physical intrusion, may be inherent in such a procedure.

In general it can be said that boys under 14 and girls under 12 cannot consent to treatment in Scotland. However, this should not be conclusive. The issue is ability to understand the nature or purpose and the consequences of the procedure; the lower age limits of understanding have not been tested in relation to medical treatment.

To clarify the uncertainty in this area, the Scottish Law Commission has proposed replacing the pupil – minor – adult progression with a system making 16 the age of capacity to consent.[16] This is the statutory age of consent to medical treatment in England and Wales,[17] although younger children may have power to consent if able.[18] So far, this proposed change has not been adopted in Scotland. Legislation would be required to do so.

In Scotland, regardless of age, it appears the child can consent to therapeutic treatment (treatment reasonably thought to be medically beneficial) if he or she understands the general nature and consequences of the treatment proposed. Although traditional legal authorities suggest a pupil child does not have any legal capacity to consent, regardless of actual capacity,[19] the more likely modern view should be that pupillarity raises a clear presumption of lack of capacity, but it may be overcome by proof of an actual knowing and understanding consent having been given to treatment in a particular case. If the child's welfare and autonomy is the foundation of the law in this area,[20] then should not anyone capable of consenting to treatment be accorded the opportunity to do so (and those relying on that consent deemed entitled to do so) regardless of age? A Scottish court has yet, however, to answer this question with regard to a pupil child who is shown to understand the treatment in issue. As to a minor it is certainly true.

Where, however, the child cannot consent, is unable to do so, then another must consent for him. The parent is normally the person to do so.[21] In some instances the local authority because of parental abuse or neglect, or because the child's welfare otherwise requires it, may have assumed parental rights of control and consent.[22] In such instances, it will have the right and the obligation to consent (or refuse consent) to treatment for the child.

At times the judiciary, yet a third institution, may exercise consent powers on behalf of the child. In Scotland the court of Session has historically exercised its powers of 'inherent protective jurisdiction' over the welfare of children to order, or restrain, certain treatment deemed to be, or not to be, in the best interests of the child.[23] The Scottish judiciary, in compelling circumstances, has 'the overriding power of the court to exercise the *patria potestas* in the interests of a child.'[24]

The authority of the parents to consent is a *prima facie* or *presumptive* right. Even during pupillarity, the parents must exercise their rights in the best interests of the child. No power – of parents, local authority, or court – transcends the best interests of the child. All surrogate decision-makers must exercise their power to consent consistent with the best interests of the child.[25] This is a standard that seeks to maximize the welfare of the child, above all else.

A parent, does not have authority to compel treatment that is contrary to the child's best interests.[26] As a practical matter, physicians are unlikely to propose, or acquiesce, in any such treatment, rendering its occurrence unlikely. A doctor has no obligation to follow the treatment wishes of a parent which are antithetical to the best interests of the child.[27] Necessity will justify a physician disregarding the wishes of the parents where necessary to protect the best interest of the child.[28] However, absent an emergency, the lack of clear authority in Scots law makes prudent the referral of such cases to the attention of local authority, or court, for treatment authorization.

Scots law has not attempted to grapple with what medical treatment is, or is not, in the best interests of the child. Obviously, this depends on the particular circumstances of a given case. With few exceptions the physician will provide the answer. If he or she feels the treatment appropriate, given the dictates of the Hippocratic Oath to heal and to 'do no harm,' neither local agency nor court is likely to become involved. Even if involved, neither is likely to intervene, or take issue with the views of the physician.

Where the treatment proposed is of a radical and irreversible nature, such as sterilization, one Scottish commentator has opined a court order authorizing such treatment is likely necessary,[29] whereas another has said parents and physicians can decide such treatment like any other, absent uncertainty or disagreement.[30] The latter view seems more correct, particularly in light of the great deference given the medical profession by the Scottish courts.[31]

2. *Incompetents*

The patient may be incompetent to consent to treatment not because of age, but because of infirmity or illness. It is generally true in Scotland that the law has not provided that another may decide on medical treatment for one who is not competent. However, a family member, or the local authority, may petition the Court of Session to be appointed tutor dative for an adult incapax.[32] Such a procedure, similar to guardianship or conservatorship, allows the appointee to make treatment choices for the incompetent, subject to court supervision.

While such procedure exists, it is rarely used. As a practical matter there is rarely need for it. Everyday, parents or other family members seek medical attention for adult incompetents, without judicial or statutory authorization to do so. Doctors in turn treat those patients where they feel it is in their best interests to do so. Where such occurs there is little risk of legal liability, unless the physician has failed to exercise ordinary skill and care in the treatment of the patient,[31] or has acted contrary to the patient's welfare and best interests. Where the physician acts at the request of the parent or other immediate family member, there is little risk of suit. Where, however, the family of the incapax is not in agreement, or the course consistent with the patients best interests is unclear, the physician would be best advised to seek prior court authorization to treat. If the circumstances make treatment a necessity to avoid serious harm to the patient, the physician may proceed, with or without consent of the family, although there is no clear Scottish legal authority on point.[33]

C. ENGLAND

1. *Children*. England does not recognize the Roman law distinction of pupil and minor, as does Scotland, A child in England is a minor until adulthood at age 18. However, at 16 children are given the power and right, by statute, to consent to medical treatment.[34] This impliedly carries with it the right to refuse consent, since the power to give consent only has force and meaning if consent can be withheld.

While legislation has given children in England of 16 or older the power to consent to treatment, the common law ties the younger child's right to consent, as in Scotland, to his or her ability to comprehend and understand the nature of the proposed treatment.[35] If the child has sufficient understanding and intelligence to make up his own mind, then child, not parent, may make the decision. As stated by Lord Scarman in the well-known *Gillick* case,

'. . . I would hold that as a matter of law the parental right to determine whether or not their minor child below the age of 16 will have medical treatment terminates if and when the child achieves a sufficient understanding of what is involved to give a valid consent in law.[36]

This clear statement of the law – that the child may consent if he or she knows what is going to be done and what are 'reasonably likely to be the consequences and risks of what is proposed to be done'[37] – is muddied by what follows in the *Gillick* decision. The Law Lords appear to adopt a special standard of understanding to control decisions concerning treatment involving contraception and abortion. Lord Scarman, for example, concludes that an understanding of the contraceptive advice given by doctor to patient is not adequate for a minor to consent. She also must have 'sufficient maturity' to 'appraise' the moral and family questions involved in contraceptive decisions, the long-term emotional impacts from pregnancy and its termination, and the risks to health from sexual intercourse before age 16.[38] These requirements smack more of value judgments than of prerequisites to a knowing consent to medical treatment.[39]

It may be *Gillick* has established a higher standard of maturity as necessary before a minor can consent to an abortion[40] or to other contraceptive treatment and advice. If so, it has created some uncertainty for physicians in providing such treatment or advice to minors, even though they seem to understand its nature and consequences. Such an understanding should be adequate.

It does not seem the courts are charged with allowing a minor to consent only if the decision they reach is wise or intelligent. Many people, even as adults, are neither wise nor intelligent. However, they are free and able to consent if they can understand, at least in broad terms, the nature of the treatment, its consequences, and its material, reasonably likely risks.[41] It does not seem that more should be required of a child. The only exception might be where a strong social policy, as expressed in legislation, mandates an awareness of certain other information, or attainment of a certain age, is required before the consent of the minor alone will be deemed adequate. Society has determined that a minor must be a certain age in order to legally (consent to) drink, smoke, or be tattooed. Some suggest this reasoning should be applied to contraceptive treatment,[42] but to do so may impinge on a fundamental personal right of a woman to reproduce.[43]

Absent such legislation, consent to contraceptive or reproductive treatment should be grounded on the same basic understanding as other consent issues. This requires the physician to exercise due care in disclosing all information about the nature, consequences and risks of the treatment that other reasonable and prudent practitioners would disclose to their patient.[44] Practitioners are likely to be very clear in their disclosure to the patient in such cases, and in concluding that consent is freely and knowingly given, given the uncertainty in the law to be applied created by the different and unsettled viewpoints expressed by the Law Lords in *Gillick*.[45]

Prior to the *Gillick* decision, English courts found children capable of consenting or not consenting based on their ability to understand, not by reference to any particular age they may have attained. For example, in one very old case the court found a 9 year old boy capable of consenting to touchings of a sexual nature, thereby providing a defense to a charge against the offender of assault.[46] This seems an unlikely, if not impossible, conclusion in modern times, where a much heightened concern of sexual abuse of children exists. Duff, however, has said that it is 'conceivable, although unlikely,' that a child's wishes concerning treatment might be decisive as early as age 7, and likely will be by age 11, if they are reasonably competent.[47] By the age of 14 he states that children are ordinarily 'capable of making their own decisions about treatment, including the decision to live or die.'

Such comments can only be viewed as presumptions, or general guidelines. One child may understand the treatment proposed, another at the same age may not. The same child may understand some treatments, but not others. One physician may be a better, more lucid communicator than the next one. In one English case a boy 13 was held not capable of consenting to a tattoo because he could not understand the consequences.[48] In another case a boy 13 was found capable of consenting.[49] Soon thereafter Parliament passed legislation to prohibit tattooing on those under 18.[50]

Where the child cannot consent due to incapacity, the power to consent is transferred to the parent or legal guardian, who is presumed to act in the best interests of the child.[51] Just as in Scotland, 'while great weight ought to be given to the views of the parents [concerning treatment] they are not views which necessarily must prevail.'[52] If it is manifest that the treatment choice (be it to consent or refuse consent) of the parent is not consistent with the welfare of the child, the English courts in the exercise of their wardship powers will overrule the parents. The courts will direct treatment shown to be in the best interests of the child. The cases reaching the courts for resolution are likely to involve controversial or emotionally-charged treatment issues, such as opening an intestinal blockage so a child suffering from Down's Syndrome may be fed,[53] ordering abortion and placement of an uterine contraceptive device for a 15 year old girl,[54] or ordering sterilization of a 17 year old girl with a mental age of 6 to avoid serious risk of harm to her and child in the event of childbirth.[55]

In the last case mentioned, the principle involved was well stated by Lord Hailsham:

'There is no doubt that, in the exercise of its wardship jurisdiction the first and paramount consideration [of the court] is the well being, welfare, or interests (each expression occasionally used, but each, for this purpose, synonymous) of the human being concerned, that is the ward herself or himself. In this case I believe it to be the *only* consideration involved.'[56]

The law has long recognized that as the child matures, the parent's right of custody over the child evolves from control during the tender years to little more than advice as the child approaches majority.[57] In England, as in Scotland, parents only enjoy the qualified 'right' to consent to treatment for their children if it is in their best interests. The right vanishes if it is not. It is not balanced against the child's best interests; the latter is the only criterion the courts apply. The parents, more accurately, enjoy the privilege and responsibility of seeing to it that their child receives treatment that will promote his or her welfare, not hinder or detract from it.

The clearest welfare interest of the child is survival. The parent must consent to treatment to allow the child to survive.[58] If the child needs a blood transfusion, the parents cannot object because of their religious views, no matter how genuine. Other interests of the child will depend on the facts of a given case, but will likely include the right to receive treatment to be free of pain, physical, or mental harm.[59] In some situations this may mandate ending a pregnancy,[60] in others allowing it to continue.[61]

Where the parents' refusal to consent exposes the child to immediate risk of serious harm, a physician can undoubtedly proceed to treat without consent. Necessity provides the legal justification for such action.[62] If necessity will justify destroying a fetus to preserve the life of the mother, as held in the famous case of *Rex v. Bourne*,[63] then it appears clear that it will justify disregarding the wishes of the parents in order to do what is clearly necessary to protect the best interests of the child.[64]

Some courts are troubled by reliance on the doctrine of necessity in other than life-saving situations, finding it to be insufficiently precise to provide a reliable test in most cases.[65] A reasonable definition of medical 'necessity' might be any treatment necessary, or reasonably required, to avoid death, serious physical harm or disability.[66] Perhaps it should also be treatment needed to avoid serious or permanent mental or emotional disability.[67]

One court has suggested treatment justification in such cases may be found not on the basis of necessity, but rather where good medical practice standards 'demand' it in the sense that 'there are really no two views of what course is for the best.'[68] If anything, however, this test is more imprecise and amorphous than that of necessity.

Often what is in the child's best interest will be a much broader and more flexible concept than what treatment is necessitated to avoid serious harm, or 'demanded' by good medical practice. The wardship jurisdiction of the English courts allows them to intervene as *parens patriae*, or substitute parent, for the child when and as necessary to protect the child's welfare. The rights of the natural parents will be deferred to where no clear harm is threatened, where the parents are acting reasonably, or where no course of treatment is clearly indicated. In this way the law seeks to intervene in the parent-child relationship only when compelling reasons exist to do so. The law recognizes that parents, not courts, should guide and raise their children wherever possible.

Doctors and parents will normally resolve treatment issues concerning children too young to consent between themselves. Where, however, a course of treatment is clearly indicated or not indicated, if the parents do not concur, the child abuse or neglect machinery of the state is available. The relative paucity of such reported cases shows most decisions can and should be made privately, and that there are few instances of reported abuse. By and large, only cases involving the most wrenching and controversial treatment issues – such as selective non-treatment of deformed newborns and sterilization or abortion – proposed for children or incompetents unable to consent have reached the courts.

2. Incompetents

The fact persons are mentally ill or incompetent to manage their own affairs does not necessarily mean they cannot consent to treatment. If they can understand the nature and general consequences of the proposed treatment, what it means for them, and can come to a decision based on that understanding, they may consent.[69] If they are mentally ill and unable to consent, the Mental Health Act 1983 authorizes treatment necessitated by their mental illness, but not other treatment that is indicated, but unrelated.[70] No prerogative powers of the Crown as *parens patriae* remain to care for incompetent adults, akin to the wardship jurisdiction of the courts for children.[71] This seems a strange and unwelcome situation. If courts may order treatment to protect the best interests of children who cannot consent, there seems no sound reason not to provide similar relief to adults also incompetent to decide. Authority for court appointment and supervision of a guardian to act in the patient's best interests is one reasonable means of dealing with such cases when needed.

As a practical matter, day-to-day treatment decisions are made for incompetents by family or others caring for them in reliance on recommendations of the attending physician. Court orders are rarely involved. Justification is provided by the best interests or welfare standard, which is expressly applicable only to treatment decisions for minors. Where the best interests of the patient are served, the treatment is consistent with good medical practice, and those closest to the incompetent, or having custody of him, consent, there seems no actionable legal harm or violation of legal right involved.[72] Of course, if the patient, while competent, expressed a preference concerning treatment it should be honored if reasonably possible. If no preferences exist, the best interests standard should be applied.[73]

If treatment is necessary to prevent serious injury, necessity or implied consent, two sides of the same legal coin, exists to justify it and provide a defense to the doctor, just as with children too young to consent.

The recent actions by the Court of Appeal and House of Lords shows that the courts are quite willing to find a means of approving what is felt, based on the evidence at hand, to be best for the incompetent. Whether it is called necessary or best interests treatment, or treatment demanded by good medical practice standards, the courts have inherent equitable powers to protect the incompetent.[74] The result in England is essentially the same as in Scotland. American law also reaches a similar result, but the formalized mechanism of guardianship is available, as well as the common 'best interests' approach, also carried out paternalistically by care givers and custodians as a common practice in daily decision making for incompetent patients.

D.   UNITED STATES

1.   *Children*

American law traditionally has vested substantial discretion in parents to consent or refuse consent to treatment for their children.[75] In part this derives from the impracticality of trying to regulate the parent-child relationship, particularly given the many divergent philosophies of child-rearing, religious viewpoints and social-cultural orientation among a polyglot population. In addition, constitutional rights of privacy, individual liberty, and free choice are implicated in parental decision making for their children. While not expressly mentioned in the United States Constitution, the Supreme Court has long held that certain 'fundamental' personal rights are protected from government regulation. Such rights include the right of parents to rear and educate their children in the way they see fit.[76] The state must show it is acting to further a 'compelling interest' before it can intrude into 'matters relating to marriage, procreation, contraception, family relationships, and child rearing and education.'[77]

Weighing against this general 'hands off' presumption imposed by the Constitution is the strong interest of the state in protecting and promoting the health and safety of children. The state, in its role as *parens patriae*, or substitute parent, has an obligation, imposed by the common law, to see that actions effecting children and other incompetents are consistent with their welfare and best interests.[78]

These conflicting values are accompanied by a judicially-developed 'balancing' test. Parental choice is balanced against the welfare of the child. Where reasonable minds may differ over the proper course of action, that which is in the best interests of the child, the courts will rarely intervene and overrule the decision of the parents. For example, where two reasonable and responsible bodies of medical thought exist as to the care of a minor, even one terminally ill, the parents normally may legally select either[79]. Where, however, the action or inaction of the parents exposes their child to the clear risk of serious harm, the state and the courts will not hesitate to intervene to protect the welfare of the child.[80]

The parents may not prejudice the health of their child by imposing their views upon him or her. Jehovah's Witnesses, deeply believing it is a mortal sin to accept a blood transfusion, may not prevent blood being given to their child to save his life.[81] Parents may not rely solely on their belief in faith healing to cure their acutely ill child when all reasonable medical opinion supports active treatment.[82]

The child's health need not be in imminent danger for the state to intervene. The *parens patriae* power allows intervention both where treatment is needed because of an existing health problem, and where treatment, or observation, is recommended to reduce the risk of threatened harm.[83] A Californian court, for instance, justified medical monitoring of a young boy to test for the possible (40 per cent) recurrance of his cancer, despite parental opposition. The factors enumerated by the court to justify this intervention were as follows:[84]

'[1] Erich faced an appreciable risk of harm from a deadly disease. [2] Medical testimony was uncontradicted on this point. [3] The risks entailed by the monitoring are minimal, although a certain amount of physical discomfort might be expected. [4] The parents concede that Erich is too young to express his own preference regarding Christian Science or conventional medical treatment.'

The courts generally consider several factors before deciding whether to compel medical treatment over the objection of the parents. These include, (1) the degree of likelihood of the risk of harm to the child, (2) the seriousness of the harm risked, (3) the existence of a medical consensus on appropriate treatment, (4) whether the parents have elected to pursue a 'reasonable' course of action, one supported by a reasonable body or school of medical opinion, (5) the intrusiveness posed by the recommended treatment, (6) the likelihood of success of the treatment proposed, (7) the sincerity of the parents' views in opposition to the treatment, and (8) the degree and maturity of the child's expressed preferences for or against treatment.[85]

Here it should be made clear that a child may consent to medical treatment (or refuse consent) if competent to do so. Minority is not a bar. There is no minimum age below which a child is deemed legally incapable of giving consent. For example, a 12 year old boy has been held capable of refusing consent to treatment proposed for grand mal seizures, though they were not considered life-threatening.[86] A 14 year old boy has been held capable of refusing consent to surgery to correct a cleft palate and hairlip.[87] Satutes in many states require the consent of children over 14 to treatment, absent a life-threatening emergency.[88] Minors approaching the age of majority have frequently been found by the court to be capable of deciding on complex treatment proposals – such as spinal fusion surgery or excision of a herniated spinal disc[89] – regardless of the views of their parents or physicians.

The test in all these cases is whether the minor is able to give an informed consent. If he is, then he may consent, or refuse consent, even if the procedure is a highly technical one,[90] or involves a controversial value judgment such as abortion.[91] If the minor understands the nature and purpose of the treatment, its significant risks, and the available alternatives to it, then he or she is capable of giving or refusing consent to the treatment, regardless of his or her age.[92]

Thus, where the child is mature enough to decide, he or she is accorded that right. Where that is not the case, the law imposes a strong presumption that the decision of the parents is correct and proper. 'The decision to *provide* or *withhold* medically indicated treatment is, *except in highly unusual circumstances*, made by the parents or legal guardian.'[93] The United States Supreme Court has stated the rule to be that,

> 'There is a presumption, strong but rebuttable, that parents are the appropriate decision-makers for their infants [and children unable to give consent.] Traditional law concerning the family, buttressed by the emerging constitutional right of privacy, protects a substantial range of discretion for parents.'

Several cases decided by the state courts show the degree of deference generally given to parental decisions concerning medical treatment proposed for the care of their children. Courts have refused to order the correction of a heart defect that was likely to bring about death in less than 20 years in a 12 year old Downsian boy,[95] refused to order amputation of a grossly deformed arm because of a health-endangering affliction in an 11 year old girl who desired the surgery,[96] refused to order a spinal fusion recommended to allow a 17 year old boy crippled by polio to stand and walk,[97] and refused to order chemotherapy for an 8 year old boy suffering from Hodgkin's disease (cancer) undergoing only nutritional treatment, the value of which was disputed by the medical experts who testified in the case.[98]

While no clear trend in United States cases is clear, and despite the case decisions mentioned above, it seems that the weight of modern decision is more of favor of intervening and compelling treatment where benefit to the health of the child is shown to be likely from the proposed treatment, the risks or burdens of the treatment are clearly less than its expected benefits, and the evidence is that the parents are not following reasonable medical advice.[99]

The American courts have concluded that so long as the parents have selected a reasonable treatment (or nontreatment) alternative, the state may defer to the wishes of the parents without doing violence to its duties as *parens patriae*.[100] That the parents must pursue a reasonable course of treatment when the life or health of the child is at stake is a means of striking a balance between parental autonomy and child best interests. In such circumstances there is no abuse or neglect sufficient to override the wishes of the parents as to how to care for their child. The general rule has been summarized as follows:[101]

> 'Inherent in the preference for parental autonomy is a commitment to diverse lifestyles, including the right of parents to raise their children as they think best. Legal judgments regarding the value of child

rearing patterns should be kept to a minimum so long as the child is afforded the best available opportunity to fulfill his potential in society.

Parental autonomy, however, is not absolute. The state is the guardian of society's basic values. Under the doctrine of parens patriae, the state has a right, indeed, a duty, to protect children. (citation) State officials may interfere in family matters to safeguard the child's health, educational development and emotional well-being.

One of the most basic values protected by the state is the sanctity of human life. (U.S. Const., 14th Amend., §1.) Where parents fail to provide their children with adequate medical care, the state is justified to intervene. However, since the state should usually defer to the wishes of the parents, it has a serious burden of justification before abridging parental autonomy by substituting its judgment for that of the parents.

Several relevant factors must be taken into consideration before a state insists upon medical treatment rejected by the parents. The state should examine the seriousness of the harm the child is suffering or the substantial likelihood that he will suffer serious harm; the evaluation for the treatment of the child; and the expressed preferences of the child. Of course, the underlying consideration is the child's welfare and whether his best interests will be served by the medical treatment.

In the last analysis, American judges are possessed of substantial discretion to decide what they think is best for the child where his or her health is at risk.[102] If serious harm is risked and reasonable treatment is not being pursued, the courts will not hesitate to order treatment and to remove custody from parent to public agency to accomplish it. If, however, the harm risked is not significant, or is significant, but a reasonable course of treatment is being pursued, the public agencies are unlikely to intervene and unlikely to be sustained by the courts if they do so.

The courts are the final arbiters of the child's best interests. Just as the courts ultimately decide what is reasonable medical treatment,[103] so, too, they decide what is in the best interests of the child. Nonetheless, cases in which courts intervene to compel treatment over the wishes of the parents are rare in American law. Save for the blood transfusion cases, motivated by a particular and fervent religious viewpoint, where treatment is almost always ordered, there are few cases reaching the courts for the resolution of such matters. This is explained in large part by the natural affinity of parents to want what is best for their children, by a medical profession normally effective in convincing parents to do what is medically indicated, by an attitude of the law only to intervene in cases of clear abuse or neglect, and by the positive influence of social service agencies in promoting proper care where instances of potential neglect are brought to their attention.

2. *Incompetents*

Minority makes children incompetent to decide at a tender age, but as they mature we have seen they are more and more capable of deciding for themselves. Maturity normally removes the bonds of legal incompetence. However, others may be incompetent not because of their young age, but because of congenital abnormality, illness, trauma, old age, or even medication given to relieve symptoms. Who decides treatment questions for these people and on what basis?

First of all, different standards of legal competence may be applied depending upon the right to be exercised. To be competent to execute a will, a person must know, generally, what property he or she possesses to dispose of and who are the natural objects of his or her bounty. A person may be incompetent to manage his or her affairs if he or she cannot comprehend the basics of income and expenses and avoid the designs of artful or deceitful people seeking to influence improperly. In such cases a guardian or conservator 'of the estate' of the person is in order. If the person is mentally alert, but cannot physically care for himself or herself, so as to avoid harm to themselves or to others, then a guardian or conservator 'of the person' may be appointed to ensure proper care and treatment.

While any one or more of these incapacities may apply in the case of a particular patient, the patient will not necessarily be precluded from giving consent, or refusing consent, to proffered medical treatment. If a person can understand the general nature and purpose of the treatment, as well as its material risks and such alternatives to it as are reasonably available, he or she can give an informed consent (or refusal). If the patient, at the time, can give an informed consent, it matters not that they are legally incompetent in other ways, that they cannot contract, make a will, manage their personal affairs, take care of their physical needs, or that he or she is under a court-approved guardianship or conservatorship.[104]

All patients are presumed competent to decide their own treatment. The precept of personal autonomy is so deeply-rooted in American law that many courts require a showing that the patient cannot make such decisions to be made by 'clear and convincing' evidence.[105]

What must be remembered is that the patient need only understand what he is consenting (or refusing consent) to, as defined by the requirements of informed consent. The decision need not be reasonable, wise, or one that family, friends, or attending physician would make.

Where the patient cannot give a valid consent, someone must presume to consent for him. Historically, in American law, this responsibility has been that of the family, the next of kin. While until recently there was little express recognition of this in the law,[106] it has long been the practice adhered to in American medicine and has been accepted as proper for pragmatic reasons. Normally this has involved little controversy as the physician felt treatment was indicated for the patient, he or she recommended it to the family and they in turn, wanting to help the patient, almost always gave their consent. In many instances their consent was probably legally unnecessary, since the doctrine of implied consent or necessity[107] was operative to permit the physician to impose treatment because of its expected benefit to the patient's health.

However, in more recent times, with the advent of increasingly expensive, often highly invasive, technological means of prolonging life, family members at times refuse consent when asked to give it. Such situations have highlighted the need to define the scope and the limitations upon 'proxy' decisionmaking for an incompetent patient, whether by family members or legal guardian.[108]

First, it does not seem appropriate to allow a spouse or other family member (or guardian) to refuse consent to treatment that is beneficial to the patient unless the patient has clearly expressed a desire, while competent, not to have it. The welfare, or best interests principle applicable to decide treatment for minors not yet old enough to express themselves is presumptively applicable to adult incompetents as well.[109] The state's role as *parens patriae* applies to offer protection to anyone in need of treatment who cannot decide for himself. Inability to act for oneself, to protect one's self-interest, is the justification for exercise of this power by the state, not an arbitrary age limitation, such as reaching adulthood.[110] One at 19 or 29 may be no less in need of the protection of the state and its legal machinery than one who is 9 months or 9 years old.

If treatment is futile, or offers a limited benefit that the attending physicians and available family reasonably believe can only be imposed with a disproportionate physical burden or risk of harm to the patient, then the presumption the patient would want the treatment because it is in his or her best interest does *not* ordinarily arise.[111] Such treatment is not proportionate or beneficial when its attendant burdens clearly outweigh its expected benefits.

Nonetheless, even in such cases of disproportionate treatment, the goal of the surrogate decisionmakers – whether family or appointed guardian – is to decide what the patient would want done under the circumstances. If the treatment is futile, will provide no benefit, then the physician need not offer it and may reject the wishes of the patient or his surrogate to have it.[112] The patient has a right to demand treatment, but not mistreatment.[113]

Deciding based on what, it is thought, the patient would have wanted is called exercising 'substituted judgment.' The goal here is to maximise the personal autonomy and self-determination of the patient by carrying out his wishes and preferences, despite his or her inability to express them due to incompetence. It obviously only works where, (1) the patient has at one time been competent; and, (2) during that time has expressed views and preferences relevant to the treatment decision at hand. Where the patient has never been competent, or never expressed his preferences in a relevant way while competent, the idea of 'substituted judgment' is a myth and some other standard of surrogate decisionmaking must be utilized.

American courts have struggled with the application of the 'substituted judgment' rule, most frequently of late in the context of the terminally ill. Some courts have concluded the patients' wishes not to have treatment – particularly life-sustaining treatment – withheld or withdrawn must be shown by clear and convincing evidence,[114] so as to avoid the error of denying treatment the patient really would have wanted.[115] Other courts have held such a strict standard may detract from patient self-determination,[116] since many will not wish or have the opportunity to express themselves clearly on such an unpleasant subject.

It may also be asked if a view about medical treatment, particularly one opposed to treatment which sustains life, expressed while one is healthy, is meaningful when one is facing, often reluctantly, the reality of departing this life? The standard is not an easy one to apply, often aided by only general, off-hand, or not directly relevant remarks. And what of a change of heart as one's condition either slowly or dramatically changes?

Courts have encouraged competent individuals to express their views about treatment in writing. This can be done by appointing an agent to make treatment decisions after the onset of incompetence,[117] by drawing a 'living will' opposing life-prolonging treatment after diagnosis of a terminal and incurable condition,[118] or merely by expressing one's views in a hand-written note or letter (preferably witnessed).

Absent such clear expressions of intent and treatment preferences in writing,[119] courts will consider orally expressed intentions, such as 'I don't want to be a vegetable'[120] 'I don't want to be another Karen Ann Quinlan,'[121] or, 'I don't ever want to be on a life-support system.'[122] Other evidence that may be helpful includes the patient's attitude toward medical treatment for himself, or others, while competent, his religious beliefs, the invasiveness of the treatment, the cost of the treatment, the risks attendant to the treatment, the likelihood of success of the treatment (will it cure, relieve pain, return consciousness, allow independent functioning, or only briefly prolong life?), the impact on the family, the prognosis and pain without the treatment, and the humiliation, loss of independence or dignity in undergoing the treatment.[123]

Obviously, the more clear, immediate and relevant the expressions of the patient, while competent, the more compelling adherence to them becomes in the interest of perpetuating the autonomy and self-determination of the patient. That is not to say, however, that the views of the incompetent should be disregarded. They are entitled to consideration and may will represent the best indication of what the patient wants done.[124] This may be particularly so when the patient has never competently expressed himself on the treatment being undertaken or proposed.

Where the treatment preferences of the patient have never been competently expressed, or any expression is deemed unpursuasive,[125] the commonly articulated, modern standard of surrogate decisionmaking is the 'best interests' of the patient.[126] This is a paternalistic concept. It means what the majority of other 'reasonable' people think they themselves would want done in the patient's circumstances. This may have little bearing on what the true, unexpressed wishes of the patient are, since he or she may not be a 'reasonable' person, or want done what most 'reasonable' people would under the circumstances.[127] Nonetheless, many feel it is the only decisionmaking standard available in the circumstances, it prevents a situation where no decision is made, or others make the decisions by default, thereby diminishing the patient's right to self-determination,[128] and it represents a genuine choice, reasonably imposed, in an effort to do what the patient would, presumably, want done.[129]

Where the courts permit the 'best interests' standard to justify withdrawal of life-sustaining treatment, as with seriously abnormal newborn,[130] or terminally ill elderly,[131] the question may be asked why death is ever in the patient's 'best interests,' at least absent unremitting intolerable pain? The 'best interests' standard seems to be evolving into a weighing of the benefits offered by treatment – remission or cure of symptoms, relief of suffering, prolongation of conscious life without intolerable pain – against the burdens imposed by treatment – pain, invasiveness, risk of harm, humiliation, impact on family, cost.[132]

This is where the emphasis should be. The patient's best interests are served by productive or beneficial treatment. This is a socio-medical evaluation, but one with relatively definable parameters to avoid abuse. One court has suggested it is essentially a decision made by a surrogate for the patient, acting *in good faith*, based on *medical advice*, that the treatment is *necessary*.[133]

This test may be a little too narrow, a little too medically oriented, for those who believe quality of life is a necessary element in humane substitute decisionmaking. While courts are properly nervous of descending the 'slippery slope' when making treatment decisions, it is also evident that many modern decisions recognize that quality of life must enter into nearly every medical treatment decision and cannot be ignored.[134] If quality of life to the patient – the primary component of which would seem to be conscious existence without intolerable pain – is the keynote, the inquiry is a valid and humane component of treatment decisionmaking. I have stated it elsewhere in these terms,[135]

'Whether the decision is to commence, continue or terminate treatment, it seems quality of life is the fundamental determinant where prognosis is negative. Courts would be honest to recognize this. Courts, however, need to recognize quality of life is only relevant as a *patient-centered* standard. That is, what is best for the patient. It is not what is best for others. It is not a *socially-centered* standard. Quality of life does not connote what social worth a patient's life has, what value he or she has to others, or to society. That is irrevelent. Quality of life should not be confused with the value or worth of someone's life to others, to society, or based on the standards set by others.

The family or guardian in caring for an incompetent has the same burden as parents for their child; each should act in the patient's best interests by authorizing treatment that promises to be beneficial, to produce benefits to the patient without undue burdens of pain, discomfort or risk of further harm. Most decisions are made privately, between surrogate and physician, having due regard to the expressed, and in some cases only the presumed, preferences of the patient. This system of having those most familiar with and most interested in the welfare of the patient decide for him or her seems to have worked well, with few instances of reported abuse.

In the event of disagreement, uncertainty, suspected ill motive or improper care, the courts are and should be available to resolve such disputes and to act to safeguard the interests of the patient. However, these instances are the exception, not the rule. The courts have no business in the intensive care ward, nor in invading the physician-patient-family decisionmaking relationship, absent some maifest abuse by one party or the other to this intensely private and uniquely personal relationship.

E.   CONCLUSION

With relatively few exceptions, the legal and medical climate in which treatment of children and incompetents is carried out yields few substantive differences as between Scotland, England, and the United States. There are procedural differences to be sure, such as the distinction legally between pupillarity and minority among children in Scotland, and the absence of guardianship over the person of minors, but the availability of Tutor-Dative appointment where necessary. Expectedly, English and American common law more closely approximate each other procedurally as well as in substance, although surprisingly in the former the *parens patriae* power of the state to act to protect and authorize treatment for incompetents over 18 has been eliminated, at least for the time being, by statute.[136]

In all three jurisdictions parents enjoy great deference as to the manner in which they raise their children, including arranging medical care for them, absent some clear threat to the health or well-being of the child brought to the attention of the local health or social-welfare authorities.

Several other general principles emerge: The older the child the less deference paid to the 'rights' of the parent to control or decide for the child; children may decide upon their own treatment, or refuse it, if they are able to comprehend the nature and consequences of the treatment, or its refusal; the best interest or welfare of the child is preferred over the custodial rights or prerogatives of the parent if any serious harm is threatened; where honest differences of opinion exist, a course of parental conduct perceived to be reasonable is unlikely to be disturbed; lack of standards of acceptable conduct, particularly as regards the care and treatment of significantly abnormal newborn children, contributes to results in some instances which are arguably unpredictable and inconsistent, depending on the manner in which the legal machinery reacts;[137] society, parents, and the law normally find acceptable what the medical community recommends as good medical practice; informal decisionmaking for incompetents has traditionally been done paternalistically by physicians and family, but increasingly complicated medical technology is requiring a greater scrutiny and evaluation of the productivity of medical treatment in many cases, particularly those involving chronically unconscious or terminally ill patients; the informal decisionmaking of physicians and family has worked well and should continue to be the norm; and, in all three jurisdictions, the courts are ready if called upon to resolve treatment disagreements, deter patient abuse, or strike the proper balance between the sometimes competing interests of the parties involved: patient, parents, physician, or family.

NOTES

1 See discussion in Chapter 5, *supra.*
2 *Re Osborne* (1972, D.C. App) 294 A.2d 372.
3 See discussion in Chapter 10, *infra; Bouvia v. Superior Court* (1986) 179 Cal. App. 1127; Mason and McCall Smith, *Law and Medical Ethics.* London: Butterworths, 1987 (2d ed),pp. 235)6
4 Walker, *The Law of Delict in Scotland.* Edin: W. Green and Son, Ltd., 1981 (2d ed), p.345.
5 See discussion in Chapter 10, *infra.*
6 *Chatterton v. Gerson* (1981) 1 All E.R. 257,265 (Bristow, J.)
7 Bell (Prin., s.2067); see, *Hill v. City of Glasgow Bank* (1879) 7 R.68.
8 *Harvey v. Harvey* (1860) 22 D. 1198, 1208, discussed in Norrie, 'The Gillick Case and Parental Rights in Scots Law,' 1985 *S.L.T.* (News) 157,161. *Finnie v. Finnie,* 1984 *S.L.T.* 439,441.
9 Smith, T.B., *A Short Commentary on the Law of Scotland* (hereafter, *Short Commentary*). Edinburgh: W. Green and Son, 1962, p.370. Not until the Guardianship Act 1973 did the mother enjoy similar powers over her pupil children. See Thomson, 'Prima Facie Parental "Rights",' 54 *Scottish Law Gazette* 71 (1986)
10 Smith, *Short Commentary, loc.cit*; Thompson, *supra,* p.72.

11 The Scottish institutional writers acknowledge this historical distinction. Stair (I.vi.35); Erskine (I.vii. 1,33); Bell (Prin., s.2090); Fraser (p.74).

12 Norrie, 1985 *S.L.T.* (News) 157, 162, ('while there is no rule that a minor cannot consent, neither is there a rule that all minors can consent. Rather it is the case that those minors who possess sufficient knowledge and understanding of the nature of the treatment proposed will be able to consent.'); Smith, *Short Commentary, loc.cit.*

13 See Duff, 'Guidelines for Deciding Care of Critically Ill or Dying Patients,' in Shannon (ed.), *Bioethics* (3d ed), p.141.

14 *Murray v. Fraser*, 1916 S.C. 623; accord, *R. v. Howard* (1966) 1 W.L.R. 13.

15 *Adamson v. Martin*, 1916 S.C. 319.

16 Scottish Law Commission, 'Legal Capacity and Responsibility of Minors and Pupils (Consultative Memo. No. 65), 53 *Scottish Law Gazette* 67 (1985)

17 Family Law Reform (England) Act 1969, s.8(1).

18 *Gillick v. West Norfolk and Wisbech Area Health Authority* (1985) 3 All E.R. 402, 2 W.L.R. 413(H.L.), (hereafter, *Gillick*)

19 *Finnie v. Finnie, supra* ('in our law a pupil is without legal personality' per Cameron, J.); note 7, *supra.*

20 Gordon, *The Criminal Law of Scotland.* Edin.: W. Green and Son, 1978 (2d ed.) p.828; Walker, *The Law of Delict in Scotland, supra*, p.493; *Harvey v. Harvey* (1860) 22 D. 1198 (concerning a minor, but welfare principle also applicable to pupil).

21 Thomson, 'Sterilization of Mentally Handicapped Children,' 1988 *S.L.T.* (News) 1,3.

22 Social Work (Scotland) Act 1968, s.16.

23 See *Docherty v. McGlynn*, 1983 *S.L.T.* 645,648 (Lord Pres. Emslie), (blood test to determine paternity in best interests of pupil child).

24 *Docherty v. McGlynn, supra* 1983 *S.L.T.* at 651 (Lord Grieve, Concurring).

25 *Porchetta v. Porchetta* 1986 *S.L.T.* 105 (father must prove presumed right of access to child is in best interests of child)

27 Thomson, *supra*, 1988 *S.L.T.* (News) at 3; Law Reform (Parent and Child), (Scotland) Act 1986, s.3(2)

28 See *Gordon, Criminal Law of Scotland*, p.428; *Minnie Graham* (1897) 2 Adam 412; *Tudhope v. Grubb*, 1983 S.C.C.R. 350 (Sh. Ct., Glasgow).

29 Thomson, *supra* 1988 *S.L.T.* (News) 1,4.

30 Norrie, 'Sterilization of the Mentally Disabled, Minor or Adult,' (1988 unpublished paper, planned for 1989 publication).

31 See, for example, *Hunter v. Hanley* 1955 S.C. 200,205 (Lord Pres. Clyde), 'It is a tribute to the high standard in general of the medical profession in Scotland that there are practically no decisions on this question [medical negligence] in the reported cases.'; *Moyes v. Lothian Health Board* (1989), The *Scotsman*, July 7, 1989, p.8 (Lord Caplan).

32 *Dick v. Douglas* 1924 *S.L.T.* 578 (S.C.), (eldest son appointed and authorized, on expert advice, to decide on appropriate care and treatment for his 72 year old, senile mother); A.D. Ward, 'Revival of Tutors)Dative (*Morris, Petitioner*),' 1987 *S.L.T.* (News) 69 (parents

appointed by Session Court tutors-dative for mentally retarded 20 year old adult son's care).

33 Smith, *Short Commentary, supra,* pp.139–141; Gordon, *The Criminal Law of Scotland, supra,* p.428; on the defense of necessity, see one of the very few modern Scottish cases to accept it, *Tudhope v. Grubb* 1983 S.C.C.R.350 (Sh.Ct.). See also, *Re B (a Minor)* (Wardship: Medical Treatment), (1981) 1 W.L.R. 1421.

34 Family Law Reform (England and Wales) Act 1969, s.8(1).

35 *Gillick, supra,* note 18.

36 *Gillick, supra,* (Lord Scarman).

37 Lord Justice Lawton, 76 *J.Roy. Soc. Med.* 289(1983); see also, *Johnston v. Wellesley Hosp.* (1970) 17 D.L.R. (3d) 139, (minor may consent if capable of fully understanding the nature and the consequences of the particular treatment proposed)

38 *Gillick, supra.*

39 See criticism by Proffessor Glanville Williams in, 'The Gillick Saga-II' Vol.135 *New Law J.* 1179, 1180 (1985), and Parkinson in 'The Gillick Case – Just What Has It Decided?' 1986 *Family Law* 11,14.

40 See discussion in Chap. 2 on Abortion.

41 *Sidaway v. Bethlem Royal Hosp.* (1985) 2 W.L.R. 480 (H.L.); *Chatterton v. Gerson* (1981) 1 All E.R. 257; *Johnston v. Wellesley Hosp.* (1970) 17 D.L.R. (3d) 139.

42 Parkinson, *loc.cit.,* note 39

43 *Re D (A Minor),* (1976) Fam 186 (request to sterilize 11 year old girl denied per Heilbron, J.); see also, European Convention on Human Rights, Arts.2,3,8,12.

44 *Sidaway, supra,* note 41; *Gold v. Harengey H.A.* (1988) Q.B. 481.

45 Lord Fraser, for example, suggested a doctor is 'justified' in providing contraceptive treatment to a girl under 16 only if, (1) she understands the treatment, (2) she will not consent to informing her parents, (3) she is expected to continue to be active sexually, (4) she is at risk for physical or mental harm without contraceptive treatment, and (5) she should have the treatment to further her best interests.See also, Brahams, 'Cosmetic Surgery: Greater Duty to Warn of Risks,' 1988 *The Lancet* 1434.

46 *R. v. Banks* (1838) 8 C&P 574; *R. v Martin* (1840) 9 C&P 213.

47 Raymond Duff, M.D., *supra,* note 13.

48 *Burrell v. Harmer* (1967) *Crim. L. R.* 169.

49 Dilks (1964) 4 *Med. Sci. and Law* 209.

50 Tattooing of Minors Act 1969.

51 Skegg, 'Consent to Medical Procedures on Minors,' 36 *Mod. L.R.* 370, 381 (1973); de Cruz, 'Sterilization, Wardship and Human Rights,' 18 *Family Law* 6 (1988).

52 *Re B (A Minor),* (1981) 1 W.L.R. 1421, 1422 (C.A.), (Templeman, L.J.).

53 *Re B (A Minor), supra,* note 52.

54 *Re P (A Minor),* (1981) 80 L.G.R. 301.

55 *Re B (A Minor),* (1987) 2 W.L.R. 1213 (H.L.)

56 *Ibid,* 2 W.L.R. at 1214 (emphasis supplied.)

57 *Hewer v. Bryant* (1970) 1 Q.B. 357, 369 (Denning, MR)

58 except possibly where the child's existence will be intolerable. *Re B.,*

supra (1981) 1 W.L.R. 1421, at 1424. See, generally, nontreatment of deformed newborns discussed in Chap. 4.

59 *Re B, supra,* (1987) 2 W.L.R. 1213

60 *T. v. T.* (1988) 2 W.L.R 189.

61 *Re D (A Minor),* (1976) Fam. 185.

62 Skegg, *Law, Ethics and Medicine.* Cambridge: Oxford Univ. Press, 1984, p.72.

63 (1939) 1 K.B. 687; see Williams, *The Sanctity of Life and the Criminal Law.* London: Faber & Faber, Ltd., 1958, pp 151–2.

64 See notes 52,54–55, 28 *supra; Rex v. Bourne* (1939) 1 K.B. 687, (1938) 3 All E.R. 615.

65 *T v. T* (Fam.D.) (1988) 2 W.L.R. 189. see also, Gordon, *The Criminal Law of Scotland, supra,* p.428.

66 Fortin, 'Sterilization, the Mentally Ill and Consent to Treatment' 51 *Mod. L.R.* 634 (1988)

67 *Rex v. Bourne, supra.*

68 *T v. T, supra*

69 Skegg, *Law, Ethics and Medicine, supra,* p.56.

70 Part IV (1983); see Fortin, *supra,* 51 *Mod. L.R.* 634 (1988).

71 *T v. T, supra,* note 65

72 See generally, McLean, Sheila A.M., *Legal Issues in Medicine.* Aldershot: Gower, 1981, pp. 103–08; Walker, *supra,* p. 493.

73 *F. v. West Berkshire Health Authority and another* (May 4, 1989, House of Lords), (Feb. 13, 1989, Court of Appeal, Lord Donaldson, MR); see Brahams, 1989 *TheLancet* 340, 1089; see *Times,* 25 May, 1989, L.R.

74 *T v. T (Fam. D.)* (1988) 2 W.L.R. 189 (Wood, J.).

75 See Meyers, 'Parental Rights and Consent to Medical Treatment of Minors,' in Mason (ed.) *Pediatric Forensic Medicine & Pathology.* London: Chapman & Hall, 1989.

76 *Pierce v. Society of Sisters* (1925) 268 U.S. 510; *Prince v. Massachusetts* (1944) 321 U.S. 158.

77 *Paul v. Davis* (1976) 424 U.S. 693.

78 *Bowen v. American Hospital Association* (1986) U.S. , 109 S.Ct. 3040.

79 *Bowen v. American Hospital Association, supra; Re Hofbauer* (1979, N.Y.) 393 N.E. 3d 1009.

80 The decision of the parents must not 'expose the child . . . to ill health or death.' *Prince v. Massachusetts, supra.* The decision may not 'jeopardize the health or safety of the child.' *Wisconsin v. Yoder* (1972) 406 U.S. 205.

81 *Jehovah's Witnesses of Washington v. King County Hospital* (1967, W.D. Wash) 278 F. S. 488, aff'd. 390 U.S. 598; *Interest of J.V. v. State* (1987, Fla App) 516 So. 2d 1133; *Santos v. Goldstein* (1962, NY App) 185 N.E. 2d 904.

82 *People in Interest of E.* (1982, Colo) 645 Pac. 2d 271; *Hall v. State* (1986, Ind.) 493 N.E. 2d 433 (parents convicted of reckless homicide.)

83 *In re Eric B.,* (1987), 189 Cal. App. 3d 996.

84 *In re Eric B., supra,* 189 Cal. App. 3d at 1006.

85 *In re Philip B.* (1979) 92 Cal. App. 3d 796, 802, cert. den.(1980) 445 U.S. 949.

86 *People in Interest of E., supra,* 645 Pac. 2d 271.

87 *Re Seiferth* (1955, N.Y.) 127 N.E. 2d 820.
88 See, for example, Calif. Probate Code s.2353. Duff has concluded, 'Children over the age of 14 ordinarily are capable of making their own decisions about treatment, including the decision to live or die.' Duff, 'Guidelines for Deciding Care of Critically Ill or Dying Patients,' in Shannon (ed.) *Bioethics* (3d ed., 1987), pp. 135, 141.
89 *Re Green* (1972, Pa) 292 A. 2d 387; *Cardwell v. Bechtol* (1987, Tenn) 724 S.W. 2d 739.
90 See cases cited in notes 87 and 89, *supra*.
91 *Planned Parenthood Association v. Ashcroft* (1983) U.S., 103 S. Ct. 2517; *Ballard v. Anderson* (1971) 4 Cal. 3d 873.
92 Meyers, *Medico–Legal Implications of Death and Dying, supra*, Dec., 1988, Cum.Supp., s.6:2; see also, *In re E.G.* (1987 Ill.) 520 N.E. 2d 385 (17 yr. old could refuse blood transfusion).
93 50 Fed. Reg. 14880 (1985), (final rule indementing Child Abuse Amendments of 1984), (emphasis supplied).
94 *Bowen v. American Hospital Association, supra*, note 79.
95 *In re Phillip B*. (1979) 92 Cal. App. 3d 796. The U.S. Supreme Court allowed this decision to stand (1980) 445 U.S. 949, since it was based on a decision that the parents were not neglecting to provide 'basic medical care' by refusing consent to the heart repair surgery. However, in later guardianship proceedings, where the test was what was in the best interests of the boy, another court appointed foster parents as guardians with authority to order the corrective surgery. *Guardianship of Philip B*. (1983) 139 Cal.App. 3d 407.
96 *Re Hudson* (1942, Wash) 126 Pac. 2d 765. There was, however, a 'grave possibility' that the child would not survive the corrective surgery, which appeared to be very persuasive to the court.
97 *Re Green* (1972, Pa) 292 A. 2d 387 ('We are of the opinion that as between a parent and the state, the state does not have an interest of sufficient magnitude outweighing a parent's religious beliefs when the child's life is not immediately imperiled by his physical condition.' A strong factor here was the child's wishes, which were unclear, so the case was remanded to the trial court to determine them).
98 *Re Hofbauer* (1979, N.Y.) 393 N.E. 2d 1009. The attending physician testified, however, that the boy was responding well to the treatment, and chemotherapy had not been ruled-out if it became necessary. Cf., *Custody of a Minor* (1978, Mass) 379 N.E. 2d 1053 (chemotherapy ordered for 3 year old boy suffering from leukemia whose parents wished to treat him with ineffective laetrile therapy.)
99 *Guardianship of Philip B*. (1983) 139 Cal.App. 3d 407; *In re Baby Girl M*. (1987) 191 Cal. App. 3d 786; *Custody of a Minor* (1978, Mass) 379 N.E. 2d 1053; *In re Eric B*. (1987) 189 Cal.App. 3d 996; *Re Cicero* (1979, N.Y. App) 421 NYS 2d 965.
100 *Weber v. Stony Brook Hospital* (1983, NY) 456 N.E. 2d 1186, cert. den. (1985) U.S., 104 S.Ct. 560; *Re Hofbauer* (1979, NY) 393 N.E. 2d 1009; *Bowen v. American Hospital Association* (1986) U.S., 106 S. Ct 2101.
101 *In re Philip B*. (1979) 92 Cal.App. 3d 796, at 802.
102 *Weber v. Stony Brook Hospital, supra*; *Infant Doe v. Bloomington Hospital* (1982, Ind.) No. 4825140, cert. den. (1983) 464 U.S. 961

(surgery to remove intestinal blockage necessary for survival not required in multiply-impaired Downsian newborn).

103 *Texas and P.R. Co. v. Behymer* (1903) 189 U.S. 468; *Helling v. Carey* (1974, Wash) 519 Pac. 2d 981; see also, *Sidaway v. Board of Governors of the Bethlem Royal Hospital* (1985) 2 W.L.R. 480 (H.L.).

104 *Guardianship of Roe* (1981, Mass.) 421 N.E. 2d 40; *Riese v. St. Mary's Hospital and Medical Center* (1987) 196 Cal.App. 3d 1388 (review granted (Cal) 245 C.R. 627, 751 Pac. 2d 893); *Rivers v. Katz* (1986, N.Y.) 495 N.E. 2d 337; *Rogers v. Comm'r. Dept. Mental Health* (1983, Mass) 458 N.E. 2d 308; Cal. Wel. & Inst. Code ss.5331, 5326.5.

105 *Conservatorship of Valerie N.* (1985) 40 Cal. 3d 143, 168; *Re M.* (1981, Alaska) 627 Pac. 2d 607; *Re Grady* (1981, N.J.) 426 A. 2d 467; *Re Guardianship of Hayes* (1980, Wash) 608 Pac. 2d 635 (all sterilization requests for incompetent patients).

106 *Cobbs v. Grant* (1972) 29 Cal. 3d 229; Relman, 298 *N.Eng J. Med.* 508 (1978).

107 See discussion in Chap. 5, *supra*, Consent.

108 See discussion in Chaps. 10 and 11, *infra*, Termination of treatment.

109 President's Commission, *Deciding to Forego Life)Sustaining Treatment* (Wash., D.C.: U.S. Gov't. Printing Office, 1983), pp. 123–128.

110 Cf. *T v. T (Fam.D.)* (1988) 2 W.L.R. 189 (discussing the dilemma posed by terminating the *parens patraie* power at age 18); see also, *Re B (A Minor)* (1987) 2 W.L.R. 1213 (H.L.), (did court act without due diliberation in authorizing sterilization due to fear of loss of jurisdiction to act because of impending age of majority of incompetent woman?)

111 *Barber v. Superior Court* (1983) 147 Cal. App. 3d 1006; *Guardianship of Grant* (1987, Wash.) 747 Pac. 2d 445.

112 *Barber v. Superior Court, supra.*

113 *U.S. v. George* (1965, D.C. Conn.) 239 F.S. 752.

114 Evidence with a high probability of truth, leaving no substantial doubt as to its conclusiveness. See, *Lillian F. v. Superior Court.* (1984) 160 Cal. App 3d 314, 324.

115 *Re Conroy* (1985, N.J.) 486 A. 2d 1241. *Re Gardner* (1987, Maine) 534 A. 2d 947.

116 *Conservatorship of Drabick* (1988) 200 Cal.App. 3d 185, cert. den. (U.S.S.Ct.).

117 *Re Conroy, supra*; *Re Peter* (1987, N.J.) 529 A. 2d 419.

118 *John F. Kennedy Mem. Hospital v. Bludworth* (1984, Fla) 452 So. 2d 921.

119 Virtually all American states now provide, by statute, for the execution of a 'Durable Power of Attorney' appointing a health care proxy decisionmaker to act after the patient becomes incompetent, and/or 'Declarations,' 'Directives,' or 'Living Wills' to specify treatment not desired if incompetent to so state. Se Meyers, *Medico-Legal Implications of Death and Dying, supra*, Chap. 16 (Dec., 1988, Cum. Supp.).

120 *Matter of Quinlan* (1976, N.J.) 355 A. 2d 647.

121 *Matter of Eichner* (1981, N.Y.) 420 N.E. 2d 64.

122 *Brophy v. New England Sinai Hospital* (1986, Mass) 497 N.E. 2d 626.

123 See generally *Re Conroy, supra; Barber v. Superior Court, supra; Re Guardianship of Roe* (1981, Mass) 421 N.E. 2d 40.
124 *Re Hier* (1984, Mass.App.) 464 N.E. 2d 959; *Saikewicz v. Supt. of Belchertown State School* (1977, Mass) 370 N.E. 2d 417.
125 *Cruzan v. Harmon* (1988, Mo.) 760 S.W. 2d 408; *Matter of Westchester Co. Medical Center (O'Connor),* (1988, N.Y.) 534 N.Y.S. 2d 886.
126 President's Commission, *supra, Re M.* (1981, Alaska) 627 Pac. 2d 607; *Guardianship of Eberhardy* (1981, Wisc.) 307 N.W. 2d 881.
127 *Re Grady* (1981, N.J.) 426 A. 2d 467.
128 *Conservatorship of Drabick, supra,* 200 Cal. App. 3d 185.
129 *Re Grady, supra,* 426 A. 2d at 480–81.
130 See discussion in Chap. 4, *supra.* Se *F v. West Berkshire Health Authority* (H.L.) *The Times,* 25 May 1989 (Law Report).
131 See discussion in Chaps.10 and 11, *infra.*
132 *Guardianship of Grant, supra,* 747 Pac. 2d 545; *Barber v. Superior Court, supra,* 147 Cal. App. 3d 1006.
133 *Conservatorship of Drabick, supra,* 185 Cal. App. 3d at 200–201, 204.
134 *Guardianship of Grant, supra; Bouvia v. Superior Court* (1986) 179 Cal. App. 3d 1127; *Barber v. Superior Court, supra; Rasmussen v. Fliming* (1987 Ariz.) 741 Pac. 2d 674; see also, Ruark, et. al, 318 *N. Eng. J. Med* 25 (1988), Tomlinson & Brady, 318 *N. Eng. J. Med.* 43 (1988).
135 Meyers, *supra,* Dec., 1988, Cum. Supp., pp. 208)9.
136 See *T v. T (Fam. D.)* (1988) 2 W.L.R. 189.
137 Cf. *R. v. Arthur,* 1981 *The Lancet* 1101 with *Re B (A Minor),* (1981) 1 W.L.R. 1421, discussed in Chap. 4, *infra,* and in Mason & Meyers, 'Parental Choice and Selective Non)Treatment of Deformed Newborns: A View from Mid-Atlantic,' 12 *J. Med. Ethics* 67 (1986).

7

Transplantation of Organs

A. INTRODUCTION

The transplantation of body parts or substances can be carried out, with varying degrees of success, from animal to human being (heterotransplantation), from one to another, unrelated human being (homotransplantation), from one human twin to another (isotransplantation), or from the patient himself (autotransplantation).[1] While legends have described early efforts at human transplantations, it took the development of modern surgical procedures over the past century to make such efforts practical. The first transplants involved skin grafts, bones, teeth and corneas and by the time of World War II blood transfusion was widespread.[2] In 1954, history was made at Peter Bent Brigham Hospital in Boston with the successful transplantation of a kidney from a healthy twin into the other twin who was gravely ill with kidney failure.[1] Kidney transplants in the interim have become almost commonplace. Those in need still greatly outnumber donors.

In the U.S. some 20,000 are waiting for kidneys. In Britain the shortfall for kidneys is shown by a waiting list for the organ of more than 3,500.[3] It is said that the passage of a mandatory seatbelt law has saved many lives, but has greatly increased the wait for a cadaver kidney. Most cadaver donors come from those approximately 4,000 brainstem deaths that occur each year in the U.K.[3] These people can be kept on a heart-lung machine after they are diagnosed as dead, which protects the viability of the organ until removal and transplantation can occur.

Heart transplantation was first attempted in 1967. The recipient lived for eighteen days.[4] The second recipient lived for eighteen months.[5] Within the next three years more than 100 heart transplants were performed in America alone, at some 15 centers, as well as elsewhere in the world. Rejection, the body's natural immune reaction to foreign tissue, continued to plague the success of heart transplants. Due to the high cost and demand on personnel and resources, many hospitals and medical centers elected not to continue or commence such procedures. However, by 1981, the development of 'anti-rejection,' immunosuppressive drugs such as cyclosporin greatly improved the survival rate of heart transplant recipients. This resulted in both U.S. government and private medical insurers electing to cover the expenses of such procedures as no longer experimental.

There are now some 90 heart transplant centers in the U.S. Five year survival rates are now approaching 50 percent. Nonetheless, the cost remains prohibitive to many, in excess of $100,000 for hospitalization alone.

The first liver was transplanted in 1960. As with the early kidney and then heart recipients, initial survival rates were poor. With improvements in immunosuppression therapy and technique came big changes. Although the operation remains one of the most technical and difficult in medicine, taking up to eight hours and using a staff team of 20 physicians, nurses and technicians, its success rate has improved dramatically. In 1987 some 1,200 patients received new livers from cadaver donors at 50 U.S. transplant centers. Whereas hemodialysis may substitute for a non-functioning kidney, there is no replacement for the liver. Eighty percent of liver recipients now survive indefinitely with appropriate immunosuppressive drug therapy. Hospital costs average $150,000 to $200,000, but are now also accepted as medically proper expenses by the majority of health insurance programs.

There had been discussion on the advisability of lung transplants, especially as incidental to heart transplantation, even before Professor Barnard's pioneering heart transplant operation was carried out in 1967.[6] Shortly afterwards, a one-lung transplant, Britain's first, was carried out in Edinburgh, but it appears that the implanted lung never functioned.[7] Again, the procedure was plagued by tissue rejection, but by 1981 five combined heart and lung transplants were carried out at Stanford University Medical Center alone. Four of the five were still alive almost a year later. There are now some 15 heart/lung transplant centers in the U.S.

Although immunosuppressive drugs have made great inroads on transplant tissue rejection, 'incompatibility' of tissue remains a significant problem. The drug has to be taken very often for life and may be toxic. By suppressing immune reaction, it lowers normal resistance to bacteria and other infections. Incompatibility means that the human body regards tissue transplanted from another individual as a foreign substance and consequently, as in bodily infections by bacteria or viruses, it reacts with a cellular or humoral response seeking to produce lymphocytes or antibodies that seek to reject the foreign invader. This rejection process or immunological opposition usually takes place soon after a transplantation and the greater the genetic difference between donor and recipient of the tissue involved, the more rapid and vigorous this rejection reaction will be. As a result, transplants from a twin (isotransplantation) or from the patient himself (autotransplantation) will normally not involve any risk of rejection due to incompatibility. The use of blood relatives will substantially improve the chances of a successful kidney transplant over the use of non-related donors.

The use of non-related transplant donors is becoming more feasible because of two developments: the use of immuno-suppressive or anti-rejection reaction drugs and the improvement in methods of cross-matching or typing the tissue of donor and patient,[8] as has long been done in blood typing. The use of monoclonal antibodies to elicit life-long acceptance of a transplanted organ has been successfully reported in animals and may eventually cause us to conquer the rejection problem. Where only in-compatible donors are available, autologous transplantation may permit use of the patient's own tissue. This is being done with some leukemia patients, whose own bone marrow is harvested and frozen, then thawed, cleansed and injected into the patient.[9]

While some naturally replaceable tissue such as blood or skin may normally be taken from a living donor, as well as one of two paired organs such as kidneys, without a substantial detriment to his health, the same is obviously not true of the vital organs – liver, heart and lungs. For these organs, as well as corneas, blood vessels and bone, the only practical source is a dead donor, a cadaver. However, this poses serious difficulties of time. While 'non-critical' tissues such as skin (within twelve hours after death) and corneas (within six to twelve or even eighteen hours after death) may be leisurely removed after the donor's death, 'critical' tissue such as the kidney, the liver and the heart must, at present, be removed within about thirty minutes of the arrest of circulation.

The problem of organ storage may largely be a technical one of simulating body circulation in a cadaver kidney or other tissue. New techniques such as vitrification, or high pressure cooling, immersion of vital organs in a blood substitute cooled to 50°F and other procedures are significantly expanding the ability of medical science to harvest and bank organs for future use.[10] Kidneys stored at 5°C may be kept viable for up to six hours. The same is true of the liver, when stored at between 6° and 12°C and supplied with blood by a miniature heart-lung type of machine. A preservation chamber developed as an interim means of maintaining the viability of heart and lung tissue pending transplantation has been used to keep a dead man's heart and lungs alive for twenty-two hours after his death.[11]

The precious time factor in the utilization of cadaver tissues for trans-plantation is not the only difficulty to overcome. It is, however, at least one that can be overcome by medicine. Other, perhaps less soluble problems in the use of cadaver donors for transplants are created by the law dealing with the status, treatment and disposal of dead individuals. There are many who feel that these and other legal problems are the greatest present impediment or roadblock to progress in human organ transplantation. Whether or not this is true cannot be appreciated without an analysis of the legal difficulties in this area.

Where replaceable tissue is involved – blood and skin – there are few legal problems with the use of a living donor, provided the consent of the donor is clear. With certain paired organs like the kidneys, living donors are used, but the legal issues are more complex and warrant more careful attention. For the vital organs – heart, lungs, liver – and for other essential tissue – such as the corneas – the living donor is not a realistic alternative. Cadaver donors are looked to for these tissue and organs. That brings us to who may deal with the dead body and its parts, and in what manner.

B.   THE USE OR TREATMENT OF DEAD BODIES AT COMMON LAW

Granted that cadaver donors are likely to be the only large source of tissue for homotransplants, the law regulating their use must be ascertained. We can start from the proposition that, barring the enactment of relevant statutory guidelines, the common law limits the individual's power to give valid directions regarding the disposal of his body or selected parts thereof after his death. In the United States, for example, there are no judicial cases specifically granting an individual absolute control over the disposition of his body, or any parts thereof, after his death.[12] What statutory material does exist in this area, and it is growing, will be discussed subsequently. Here, for the moment, however, we are concerned with the operation of the common law. Once that is ascertained, we can more clearly superimpose those legislative enactments that are relevant and thereby more clearly gauge their application and scope.

That the individual has only a limited power under English common law to prescribe disposition of his cadaver probably stems from the fact that originally in England the Church and the ecclesiastical courts exercised jurisdiction over matters involving dead bodies.[13] Lord Coke recognized such jurisdiction and stated that such matters were generally not within the cognisance of the common law courts. When, in the seventeenth century the common law began to take jurisdiction of religious offenses, it was accepted that no property rights existed in a dead body, the corpse was *res nullius*.[2] There was probably apprehension that recognition of a property right in a dead body would result in undesirable sale, trade, attachment, or some other disposition of the cadaver in a commercial manner.[12] While no property right existed in the traditional sense, the courts nonetheless recognized a right of possession for purposes of burial in the surviving spouse, the children or the next of kin (in that order).[14]

Whoever took charge of the dead body after death was not considered the owner, but merely held it 'as a trust' for those with an interest in the body, subject to the protection of the public.[15] The very early American decisions adopted this trust concept, but they subsequently developed the theory that a quasi-property right in dead bodies vested in the nearest relatives because of their duty to bury their own dead.[16] This quasi-property right included the right to custody of the body for proper burial and the right to bring an action for damages if any outrage, indecency or injury were caused the body of the deceased.

While Scots law did not recognize any property rights in a dead body after it was committed to the grave, it is not so clear what rights remained in the relatives before interment of the deceased, for during that time an indictment could be raised for abstraction of the corpse.[17] There is some theoretical difficulty in concluding that a corpse is property before burial, but not after interment. Nonetheless, modern authority in Scots law appears to support the contention that a corpse could be owned by those entitled to it for burial and that an improper taking of the corpse is theft.[18]

Generally, the person with the legal right to possession of the cadaver is entitled to receive it in the same condition as when death occurred.[19] While the public interest may justify mutilation by autopsy, the person entitled to post-mortem possession of the body – be it spouse or next of kin – may sue for damages for unlawful mutilation of or injury to the corpse. The action is not, however, to recover damages for harming the corpse, but rather as solatium for the injured feelings of the affected relative.[20] In other words, the basic interests in the surviving spouse, children or next of kin of the deceased are emotional interests connected with the dignity of the disposition of the body and their own peace of mind.

The legal right to bury a corpse as a practical matter vests in the nearest relative of the deceased who is in a position to be able and is willing to perform that duty. However, in the absence of other instructions by the deceased, the legal duty and liability for costs of interment rests upon the surviving spouse.[21] The courts generally recognize the quasi-property right to possession of a dead body for the limited purpose of determining who shall have its custody for burial.[22] If need be, this duty of burial may be imposed upon the executor or administrator of the deceased's estate.

If the party entrusted with the duty to bury the dead body either attempts to sell it or make any other disposal of it which offends public feelings or endangers public health, he may well be subject to criminal prosecution for commission of a common law crime as well as a civil wrong.[23] Any disposal of a dead body which is contrary to common decency is an offense at common law.[24]

In the Scottish case of *Dewar v. H.M. Adv.*[25] the panel (accused) received a severe sentence for the theft of coffin lids of those deceased entrusted to him for cremation. Lord Justice-General Normand held such action to be 'inhuman disrespect for the dead' as well as 'callous indifference' to the rights and feelings of the surviving relatives.

A further charge of 'shameless, shocking and irreligious' conduct for mishandling of the corpses assigned to Dewar for cremation was preferred by the police, but the Crown did not proceed on it in the case.[26]

Thomson v. State[27] held it an offense for an undertaker to attempt to sell the body of a pauper entrusted to his care for burial. In *Baker v. State*,[28] the defendant exposed a boarder's dead body to public view for several days, propping it up and concealing the fact of death, in order to collect her monthly welfare check. Without statute, she was convicted of a common law crime for indecently treating a corpse.

The rights of the relatives to immediate possession of the corpse in the same condition as when death occurred must, at times, give way to the public interest. It may be necessary to detain and examine the body because of its evidentiary value in litigation. One obvious instance is a life insurance policy or a worker's compensation award dependent for resolution on cause of death and surrounding circumstances. Not infrequently, life insurance policies will contain autopsy clauses. Another such instance is when death occurs under suspicious circumstances, and an autopsy or post-mortem examination is ordered by the public medical examiner or coroner to ascertain the cause of death or to make some contribution to medical science. Such may be the case where death occurs suddenly, violently, unexpectedly, with no physician in attendance, or while the patient is under an anaesthetic. In Scotland, such deaths are referred to the Procurator Fiscal for inquiry and the performance of a post-mortem dissection of the corpse is within his discretion.[29] The coroner or medical examiner has similar jurisdiction in England[30] and America.[31]

If, however, an autopsy is unauthorized, the next of kin may sue for damages. Their right to possession of the body for burial is normally a right to the body intact: an unauthorized autopsy and dissection interferes with proper burial.[31]

The person with the burial right of the corpse may grant permission for an autopsy as well as sue for an unauthorized dissection.[1,31] It is also true that generally the deceased may consent by written authorization during his lifetime or by will, to the performance of an autopsy.[13] However, in the absence of enabling statutes, this power in the decedent is not without question. In the United Kingdom, at common law, such a declaration is of doubtful enforceability in the face of opposition from next of kin. Some states would allow the inconsistent wishes of close relatives to prevail. Massachusetts law, for example, until 1968 did not give binding effect to the decedent's directive for consignment of his corpse to science for anatomic dissection or post-mortem examination, but rather allowed the next of kin to deny such a disposition.[32] This rule was judicially weakened in the case of *O'Dea v. Mitchell*,[33] wherein the Supreme Judicial Court of Massachusetts dismissed an action brought against an undertaker by the decedent's next of kin for alleged misconduct in handling the corpse and improper burial. Addressing itself to the fact that the undertaker had apparently followed the decedent's ante-mortem instructions in so acting, the Court stated:

> 'The plaintiff's standing [to bring the action] rests on the statement that they are 'next of kin' to the decedent, and therefore have the right to possession of the decedent's body. That right rests however in the next of kin only when there is no surviving spouse or no contrary provision by the decedent concerning the disposition of his remains . . .
> The absence of . . . contrary directions by the decedent must be alleged by the next of kin in order to establish their standing to sue.[34]

In 1968, Massachusetts changed its law to prevent repudiation of a deceased's express ante-mortem gift of his cadaver to medical science by the next of kin withholding consent.[35] The person should be able to decide what will be done with his body after death, unless public interest, not merely preferences of relatives, requires otherwise.

Whether consent for autopsy has been given ante mortem by the decedent or post mortem by those with the right to burial of the corpse, the dissection must be carried out within the scope of the consent given and, more importantly for purposes of transplantation, does not include the removal and retention of organs.[1,31] There are several Scottish and American cases in point. *Hughes v. Robertson*[36] involved a damage action for unlawful post-mortem examination of the widow's deceased husband, which autopsy included removal of several vital organs from the corpse before it was returned to her. In an earlier Scottish case, *Conway v. Dalziel*,[37] the court stressed that the unauthorized retention of organs from the dead body examined is another and more serious wrong than the unlawful post-mortem itself.

In *Hill v. Travelers Ins. Co.*,[38] defendants were held liable for violating the stipulation of the decedent's surviving spouse that the autopsy should not be performed in a public place and should not involve mutilation of the body. The defendants had removed decedent's heart for use as evidence to defeat an insurance claim. In *Korber v. Patek*,[39] a physician was held liable for removing the corpse's stomach and refusing to return it when he had been authorized only to 'examine' the body. In *Hassard v. Lehane*,[40] an action was brought against the coroner who, during the course of an authorized autopsy, had removed the corpse's heart and spleen without satisfactory explanation. Similarly, in *Bonilla v. Reeves*,[41] the next of kin were held to have a valid cause for action against the pathologist for failing to return the decedent's brain removed pursuant to a coroner's authorized autopsy where death had resulted from a skull fracture.

Once the body has been buried, the state still exercises a protective function over it against unauthorized removal. The improper unearthing of a dead body was early recognized in an English case as an offence 'highly indecent and *contra bonos mores*' and as cognisable in the criminal courts.[42] The fact that the exhumation was for scientific purposes (dissection) did not change its characterization as a criminal offence. However, later Scottish practice and commentary indicates if the body was unearthed for personal, medical study, rather than for profit or perverted ends, the punishment would be much milder.[43] The removal of a body from the grave was not in Scotland considered as theft, but as a separate common law offence of *crimen violati sepulchre* (violation of sepulchre).[17,44] The court in the *Dewar*, case[25] concluded:

> 'In our law, the crime of disinterring human remains after interment is not punishable as theft, but as the crime of violation of sepulchres.'

The essence of the Scottish crime, applicable only once the corpse has been buried or otherwise removed from the protection of the law of theft, is disturbance of the dead body without permission of the relatives, executor or authority otherwise in charge of the corpse and interested in its undisturbed repose.[45] The English position, somewhat artificially, apparently considered the offence as theft when the body's clothes were taken from the grave along with the cadaver.[44]

It appears that Roman-Dutch law is quite similar to the Scots law and Anglo-American common law in matters involving dead bodies, postmortems and related legal rights and duties. In Roman law, the rights of custody, control and disposal of the corpse was in the hands of the heirs, who were to dispose of it in accordance with ideas of decency and religion.[46] This was also the position in Roman-Dutch law, the heirs or executor being required to carry out the terms of the deceased's will regarding burial as faithfully as possible – probably a greater burden than the English law would have imposed.[46] It is likely that the unauthorized conduct involved in the *Hughes* case, for example, would render the perpetrator liable to the relative possessing the burial rights (*actio injuriarum*).[47]

However, this is not to say that the Roman-Dutch common law would hold any cutting into a dead body as *prima facie* actionable in the absence of enabling statute. The position is more flexible, so that

> 'Any operation on a dead body which is generally accepted by custom is legal. This includes not only the activities of undertakers and embalmers, but also the long accepted customary practices of the medical profession in regard to post-mortem examinations and dissections of any kind made for *bona fide* medical or scientific purposes, provided that due attention is paid to the testamentary wishes of the deceased, or failing these, to the wishes of the next-of-kin or executor (if there is no next-of-kin).'[48]

The Roman-Dutch law would apparently allow for cadaver tissue to be removed during statutory autopsies, 'provided that is done *bona fide* and decently for medical or scientific purposes in accordance with long established custom in the medical profession.[46]

This is probably the common law position also, if 'medical purposes' is not interpreted to include the use of such removed tissue for purposes of transplantation.

This brings us to the question of whether and under what circumstances tissues may be removed from dead bodies for use in transplants. Some years ago, several American writers in the field stated carefully that

'It would seem to be fair to conclude that a person at the present time in the United States probably has the right to control the disposition of his body after death so long as no public policy is contravened, and it seems to follow that an individual, in his lifetime can give permission for the taking of tissue from his body after death.[49]

It is true that the Anglo-American common law, in the absence of statutory provision, requires permission for the removal of organs from the corpse to be obtained from the person who possesses the right to burial. While a post-mortem consent from such a relative will suffice, in the absence of an explicit direction for a contrary disposition by the deceased during his lifetime, it is often difficult to obtain this in time to utilize rapidly deteriorating tissues.

If the deceased himself during his lifetime has executed a gift[50] or direction in proper form of his organs for transplant purposes, it will normally be upheld as a matter of common law, just as his ante-mortem right to direct an autopsy for any reasonable purpose will normally be.[51] However, opposing next of kin may prevent this, as mentioned, in some jurisdictions.

Where the deceased did not while alive authorize post-mortem organ or tissue removal, the position at common law was unclear when the physician wished to remove an organ. No harm could be done to the deceased. As stated in an early case, 'the dead have no rights and can suffer no wrongs.'[52] This is overstated, however, since the living have a right to assume peaceful repose of their remains after their death unless they provide otherwise while alive. The deceased can obviously not enforce this expectation, but the heirs could. The heirs were also entitled, as we have seen, to the prevention of their own injured feelings and mental distress that would naturally result if the corpse were maimed or mistreated without their consent. As stated by a Scottish judge in a case at the turn of this century,

'I have no doubt that the cutting up or dissecting, or other unauthorized mutilation of a near relative's body, constitutes a wrong of which a near relative has a title to complain.'[53]

While the common law gave a remedy of damages to relatives when the decedent's corpse was mistreated or mutilated, it never recognized explicitly the individual's right to control the disposition of his remains after death.[54] Thus, he or she had to rely on the next of kin, or those in lawful possession of his or her body after death to carry out his or her wishes. This discouraged the use of the dead body, whether for scientific, education, or transplantation purposes. Those charged with burial were not secure of their rights to authorize any uses of the corpse. Those interested in the examination or use of body parts were fearful of liability. Modern cases continue to show this fear by physicians of legal liability for mishandling the deceased was well-founded. In one recent case a Georgia widow was awarded $150,000 for emotional distress suffered upon learning physicians had removed her husband's brain during autopsy without authorization to do so.[55] In another, a hospital was found liable for injuries sustained by the parents of a brain dead young man who was improperly kept connected to a respirator for two and one half days after the diagnosis was made and the request was made by his parents to remove the respirator.[56] The hospital was held to have wrongfully interfered with proper burial. The case, as others we will review, shows the continuing confusion among many medical care providers concerning brain death.

As can be seen, at common law the living had little encouragement that what they wished to authorize would be honored after their death. The result of this uncertainty was a recognition of the need for regulation to control the uses and disposition of dead bodies. The result was statutory enactments both in Britain and in the United States. In Britain the Human Tissue Act was passed in 1961. In the United States, the Uniform Anatomical Gift Act, which has now been adopted in all states, was introduced in 1968.

However, prior to introduction of these rather comprehensive statutes, earlier statutory enactments had occurred, albeit on a more piecemeal basis.

C. LEGISLATION IN BRITAIN DEALING WITH USE OF THE BODY AND
ITS PARTS FOR MEDICAL OR SCIENTIFIC PURPOSES

The criminal law in England and Scotland early dealt with the unlawful taking and use of a cadaver as we have seen. However, it took the abominable, wholesale murders of the notorious Burke and Hare, which came before the Scottish courts in 1828, to prompt legislation dealing with post-mortem treatment of human bodies. As a direct consequence of public indignation at Burke and Hare's unsavory trafficking in corpses, the Anatomy Act of 1832[57] was passed and remained law until its repeal in 1984. The Anatomy Act provided for the deceased to direct, *ante mortem*, that his body undergo anatomical examination after his death, so as to facilitate the carrying on of anatomy in the medical schools.

The Human Tissue Act 1961 was adopted to regulate transplantation of tissue and organs after death. Under the Act an individual can donate his organs after death for therapeutic, educational or research purposes by executing a written request while alive. If no such request has been made by the decedent, the person 'lawfully in possession of the body' may authorize the transplant after making reasonable inquiry to verify that neither the decedent, a surviving spouse nor any other surviving relative objects to it. This in effect means a relative may prevent transplantation where the decedent did not expressly authorize it before his death.

Since most people die in hospitals or medical facilities, not at home, the Act raises a further question as to who is the person 'lawfully in possession' of the decedent. The Anatomy Act is of importance in the transplantation field, despite its repeal, for the light it sheds on the words 'party having lawful possession of a dead body,' which were borrowed from the earlier Act and incorporated into the Human Tissue Act 1961, as 'person lawfully in possession of the body.' The words presumably have a similar meaning under both Acts, and cases interpreting their use in the Anatomy Act may be helpful in clarifying their presently uncertain meaning in the Human Tissue Act. In *Rex v. Feist*,[59] the master of a workhouse was held, for purposes of the Anatomy Act, to be the party 'having lawful possession' of those dying in the institution.

From this case, Lord Kilbrandon has reasoned that the Board of Management of the hospital where an individual dies is likewise the 'person lawfully in possession of the body' under the Human Tissue Act. If such is the case, then a more expeditious use for transplant purposes could be made of tissue from persons not expressly donating their organs under The Human Tissue Act.

Other authorities have suggested that the 'person lawfully in possession' of the cadaver for purposes of the Human Tissue Act is the executor or close family of the deceased. From this it is argued that it is they who must authorize removal and who may veto the deceased's ante-mortem donation under the Act. A careful distinction needs to be drawn here between the person with *right to possession* of the corpse – almost certainly the surviving spouse or next-of-kin under common law – and the person *in possession* of the deceased's corpse – almost certainly the institution where he expires. The Act is concerned with the latter, tangible possession, which the hospital clearly has, though it may well be otherwise bound to transfer the possession to the relatives.

The Human Tissue Act of 1961 has been criticized because, even presuming that the person lawfully in possession of the body is ascertained, the Act merely authorizes but does not require him to carry out the deceased's donative direction. Absent an express *ante mortem* donation by the decedent, the surviving spouse or next-of-kin may bar a donation with which the person lawfully in possession of the body wishes to comply. Even if the spouse or other family are not opposed, the wording of the Act is such that their consent must reasonably be sought by the hospital authorities concerned, which will often involve a time-lag fatal to the success of a proposed transplant. No such time-consuming procedure is necessary if the decedent has expressly provided, *ante mortem*, for use of his cadaver under Section 1(1) of the Act. Public education and acceptance is essential here.

It has been suggested that much of the problem posed by the Human Tissue Act (and the same problem exists under the Uniform Act in the U.S.) would be cleared up by allowing the hospital where a patient dies to direct removal of tissues needed for medical (transplantation) purposes, unless there is reason to believe the deceased or his next-of-kin would object to such a use.[60] Legislation has for many years been proposed to accomplish this at various times. One early bill, on renal transplantion, stated:

> 'It shall be lawful to remove from the body of a human person, duly certified as dead, any kidney or kidneys required for medical purposes unless there is reason to believe that the deceased during his lifetime had instructed otherwise.'[61]

The idea of such legislation is to create a presumption of consent, such as was contained in the Corneal Grafting Act 1952.[62] Under this Act, the 'party in lawful possession' of the dead body could authorize the transplant in the absence of any reason to believe that the deceased, surviving spouse or next-of-kin objected. While the Corneal Grafting Act was repealed by the Human Tissue Act, this presumption has not been carried over. The burden of 'reasonable enquiry' imposed by the Human Tissue Act requires, as a practical matter, the consent of the deceased's next-of-kin.

Despite the existence of the Human Tissue Act for nearly two decades, the supply of organs for transplants is still far outpaced by the demand. Although kidney transplantation is now commonplace, the waiting list for these organs has increased in recent times.[63]

Although 75 percent of the surveyed British public express a willingness to donate their organs after death to aid others, only 20 percent carry organ donor cards to readily identify this intent in the event of their death.[64] A number of reasons are offered for this shortfall: the lack of effective public education, a reluctance of people to clearly and unequivocally provide for organ donation,[65] time constraints which limit the viability and usefulness or organs, a reluctance of doctors to discuss the subject with patients and their family, lack of experience in diagnosing brain death (a discussion of which will follow), and limited intensive care facilities to maintain donor respiration and circulation mechanically after brain death has been diagnosed.

The shortage of these vital organs in Britain has brought allegations that impoverished donors from India or Turkey have been arranged by a middleman and delivered to certain hospitals for live kidney donation to a wealthy recipient in return for cash.[66] The sum paid was alleged to be £2,000–£3,000 to the donors, with more paid to the procurer. This practice is unethical. The British Medical Association has concluded that doctors should not participate in organ transplantation from a living donor unless they are assured that consent was obtained without any undue influence. Brahams has suggested that legislation similar to the Surrogacy Arrangements Act 1985 should be enacted to prohibit the commercialization of organ or tissue donation for transplantation.[67]

A court could well find such an arrangement *contra bonos mores* (against good morals) and not legally enforceable.[68] Consent, even if given, might not absolve the physician of criminal liability for battery or maiming.[69] Consent is no defense to a criminal act. One is still guilty of homicide, even if the victim because of pain and suffering asked to be killed.[70]

What this points out, however, is that legislation to date has not been adequate to provide the organs needed for transplants. A statute creating a presumption of intent to donate organs after death, that would control in the absence of direct evidence to the contrary, would undoubtedly be more effective in producing a supply of organs. Various European countries have elected to do this.[71] Britain has not. There could be a requirement that consent be sought from the family of all hospital terminally ill patients before the removal of life supports. This would overcome a reluctance of many doctors to raise the subject.[72] Even if it did, the question is raised as to how many resources can be devoted to transplantation. The state of Oregon recently, for example, elected to spend available health care funds on pre-natal care, rather than on transplants of any organs other than corneas and kidneys. We will explore these issues further in Chapter 12 when we discuss allocation of scarce medical resources.

D.   LEGISLATION IN THE UNITED STATES DEALING WITH THE USE OF THE BODY AND ITS PARTS FOR MEDICAL OR SCIENTIFIC PURPOSES

There is a wide range of American statutes dealing with use of the human body and its parts for various medical and scientific reasons. Most American states have statutes dealing with the use of unclaimed dead bodies by medicine and science for purposes of teaching anatomy and physiology, and for research.[73] It has been said that ideally, each pair of medical students should have a whole cadaver to study and dissect, but the supply is not adequate.

Most states also have enacted legislation dealing with ante-mortem gifts by the decedent of his body and its parts. These statutes differ considerably as to content and coverage; some of them do not grant the surviving spouse or next-of-kin a veto over the decedent's disposition.[74] Some are quite limited in their enumeration of permissible donees and purposes for donation of the organs, others are not. Normally the donor must be an adult. Certain formalities of execution are required.

One of the best of the existing pieces of legislation dealing with ante-mortem gifts is that of California, which specifies the persons with a right of control over the disposal of a dead body where the decedent left no contrary instructions.[75] The order of assumption of this right of control is specified: spouse, adult children, parents, persons in next degree of kindred in the order fixed by law as entitled to succeed to the decedent's estate.

Under the California law, the following persons are eligible to receive gifts of human bodies or parts thereof for the purposes stated:

'(a) the State Director of Public Health, any licensed hospital accredited by the Joint Commission on Accreditation of Hospitals, any licensed physician or surgeon, or any medical school, college, university, or teaching institution for use of medical education, research, advancement of medical science, therapy or transplantation to individuals;

(b) Any non-profit blood bank, artery bank, eye bank, or other therapeutic purpose operated by any agency approved by the Director of Public Health under rules and regulations established by the Director, for use of therapy or transplantation to individuals;

(c) Any specified individual for use in therapy or transplantation needed by him.'

The Ohio Act allows anyone of sound mind over twenty-one years old to give all or part of his body for research, educational or transplantation purposes, 'effective upon his death,' regardless of the wishes of his relatives to the contrary.[76] Specified donees include physicians, hospitals, schools and non-profit human parts banks. The donee is notified of the gift under the Act by a written card which can be revoked by the donor at any time up until death in the same manner as any gift.

In response to the growing demand for transplant tissue donors and because of the often piecemeal and inadequate legislative approach to this need before 1968 by the many American state statutes dealing with donation of cadaver tissues, the National Conference of Commissioners on Uniform State Laws drafted 'The Uniform Anatomical Gift Act' (hereafter 'Uniform Act') in 1968. The Uniform Act has received wide support throughout the country and been adopted by almost all the states.[77]

The Uniform Act deals with several problems that the piecemeal legislation enacted by most states did not solve: the individual who executes an ante-mortem gift of his body or any part prior to his death in one state, then moves to another state with different laws; the rights of surviving spouse or family to authorize anatomical gifts from the decedent in the absence of contrary instructions; the absence of a clear order of priority among survivors to a carry out the decedent's expressed intention; protection of physicians from civil or criminal liability for organ removal; the acceptable purposes for an anatomical gift and/or the permissible donees.

The Uniform Act regulates the following: by whom a gift may be made; to whom a gift may be made; for what purposes a gift may be made; in what manner may a gift be executed, delivered and revoked; what effect should a gift have on the rights of relatives; and the liability of the performing physician.

The Uniform Act allows removal to be authorized by persons in a stated order of priority where the decedent has executed no ante-mortem consent, unless the specified individual 'has knowledge that contrary directions have been given by the decedent.' By so providing, the Uniform Act avoids the problems of interpreting the 'person lawfully in possession' in the relevant section of the Human Tissue Act, 1961. The Uniform Act also appreciates the very limited time after death available for the removal of critical tissues like the kidney, liver and heart by setting out a specified list of survivors in order of priority, so as to facilitate expeditious execution of permission for removal and transplantation.

Any individual competent to execute a will is permitted by the Uniform Act to donate all or any part of his body, *ante mortem*, to any accredited physician, hospital, school, body-parts bank, or even for individual therapy, or transplantation. The Uniform Act allows execution of the gift by will or by any writing signed in the presence of and by two witnesses and duly delivered to the donee, if one is specified. Means for revocation of the gift are enumerated.

The Uniform Act ensures the donee or other person authorized (such as the performing physician) to utilize the gift, who acts in good faith, against civil liability (s.7(b)). Section 7(a) of the Uniform Act contains two wise provisions not commonly specified in prior legislation. First, time of death is left to be determined by the donor's attending physician alone. Second, the donor's physician in attendance at the terminal illness is not to be a member of the team of surgeons which transplants the donor's part or parts to another individual. This avoids any conflict of interest.

Since adoption of the Uniform Act irreversible cessation of all functions of the total brain, including the brain stem, has been judicially or legislatively accepted as an acceptable, alternative means of defining death in almost all states.[78] Transplantation needs such a definition because of many who are dead, but still hooked up to an artificial respirator.

Similarly to Britain, adoption of the Uniform Act in the United States has not produced the amount of organ donation hoped. In 1987, various amendments were proposed to the states for adoption, it being hoped they would facilitate more organ donations by the public. The proposed changes simplify the manner of making an organ donation and require that the wishes of the donor be followed. No witnesses to the gift document are required. The next of kin need not consent where the donor has executed a gift. There would be a duty of hospitals to ask patients on admission if they are organ donors and if so to obtain a copy of the gift document. With the consent of the doctor, the patient could be asked if he wished to be an organ donor.

Policemen, firemen and paramedics responding to an injury accident where death was possible would be required to search for a document of gift.

It remains to be seen whether these changes will become law in most states. While facilitating gifts on the one hand, they may well be seen as unduly pressuring the patient or raising fears of mortality where none are warranted or will be detrimental to the patient's treatment on the other hand. One of the more significant provisions proposed is one authorizing organ removal for transplant or other therapeutic purpose where neither the decedent nor next of kin are known to have any objection by the local health official authorizing the removal.[79] This is provided by Section 1(2) of the Human Tissue Act, after the making of such 'reasonable inquiry as may be practicable' to ascertain if there is any objection to donation.

The amendments to the Uniform Act prohibit the sale or purchase of an organ. Those who seek in good faith to follow its provisions are not liable in civil or criminal proceedings. Whether these changes will encourage more donors remains to be seen. Many states now provide a check-off on one's driver's license to indicate whether one is an organ donor, but these are not widely used by the public.

Transplants in the U.S. have become more common. They are still well below demand. In 1985 there were 28,926 cornea transplants (up from 20,209 in 1982); 719 heart transplants (up from 103 in 1982); 30 heart and lung transplants (up from 0 in 1982); 7,800 or more kidney transplants (up from 5,538 in 1982); 602 liver transplants (up from 62 in 1982); and 130 pancreas transplants (up from 35 in 1982). One reason more donors may not come forward is the lingering fear of many that the need for one's organs may encourage an overly-hasty pronouncement of death. The legislation seeks to eliminate this concern by requiring strict separation exist between the donor's medical treatment team and the transplant team. An added safeguard is the requirement of a second, corroborative medical opinion that death has occurred.[80]

E. THE DEFINITION OF DEATH

Death is intimately tied up with transplant surgery. Recent statutes, including the Human Tissue Act 1961, Ontario Human Tissue Act 1962–3, American Uniform Anatomical Gift Act 1968, and Danish Act 1967 merely refer to 'death' without attempting to offer any definition.

In the light of advancing scientific knowledge concerning simulation of life, traditional definitions of death are no longer accurate. *Dorlands' Illustrated Medical Dictionary*, twenty-fourth edition, defines death as 'The apparent extinction of life, as manifested by the absence of heartbeat and respiration. *Black's Law Dictionary*, third edition, defines death as 'total stoppage of the circulation of the blood and cessation of the animal and vital functions of the body such as respiration and pulsation.'[81] However, these standard definitions do not take adequate account of modern use of analeptic and tensive drugs, hypothermia, coronary perfusion, pacing and massage, and artificial respiration by pulmoflater, which can allow the body metabolism to function for hours, days and in some cases even months beyond traditional limits.[82]

Because of its extreme sensitivity to the absence of a normal oxygenated blood flow and its general inability to regenerate its tissue, the brain's 'death' is rapid and irreversible. The completely anoxic brain will generate no valid electro-encephalographic impulses.[83] Once such a condition has been determined, the flat electro-encephalographic rhythms suggest loss of brain function has become irreparable, which in turn implies an irreversible absence of life. However, further clinical tests are typically undertaken to assure the accuracy of the diagnosis.[84] In the UK existing protocols do not require electro-encephalograph testing to confirm brain death.[85]

Reliance is placed on such clinical findings as fixed pupils, unresponsivity to painful stimuli, no spontaneous respiration or movement and no gag or corneal responses.

The acceptance of brain death has done much to facilitate transplantation. Before its acceptance, legal uncertainty whether a person with no brain function, but with artificially maintained respiration and circulation was dead existed. An example is unreported case of *Re Potter*[86] Mr. Potter was admitted to the hospital with a severe head injury he had sustained in a fight with the named defendant. He stopped breathing after fourteen hours and was placed on an artificial respirator for twenty-four hours, at the end of which a kidney was removed for transplantation. After this nephrectomy the respirator was shut off and there was no spontaneous respiration or circulation.

Under traditional definitions of death, the victim in *Potter* was not dead until his breathing and circulation came to a persistent and complete halt when the respirator was finally turned off nearly two days after his admission to hospital. Yet if this were the case, the physician who removed the victim's kidney may well have been guilty of a crime (malicious wounding) and a civil wrong (battery), for the removal took place while the victim was still 'alive,' without his consent, and was not for his benefit. This seems rediculous. Nonetheless, the defendant also argued that the actions by the physician, in shutting off the respirator and allowing the patient-victim to die, served to break the chain of causation between the original wrongful act (the assault) and the death, which should release the original wrongdoer from legal liability for the homicide. It would seem that the judge agreed, for the defendant was committed for trial by the Coroner after a jury's finding of manslaughter, yet was convicted only of common assault by the court.

Brain death avoids these legal uncertainties. The physician cannot be tempted to prolong a life artificially in order to benefit some individual. Nor can the physician be accused of homicide for deciding to shut off the switch in a hopeless, brain dead case. There is no danger of the physician's acts breaking the causation chain of criminal liability connecting the wrongful act and the death, as appeared to happen in *Potter*, since the patient is already dead before the respirator is removed. Brain death is now well accepted both in Britain and in the United states. Many states have adopted statutes to clarify the definition. A Uniform Determination of Death Act has been adopted widely. It provides for both the traditional heart-lung and the brain definitions of death. It states,

'An individual who has sustained (1) irreversible cessation of circulatory and respiratory function, or (2) irreversible cessation of all function of the entire brain, including the brainstem, is dead. A determination of death must be made in accordance with accepted medical standards.

Diagnosis is left to the doctors to decide. This wisely allows for the application of improvements in the diagnosis of brain death.

In those states that have not adopted such a statute, the courts, when confronted with the issue, have uniformly accepted brain death as a proper means to determine death.[87] Accused criminal assailants have uniformly been rebuffed by the courts when attempting to argue that disconnecting their brain dead victim from the heart-lung machine was the true cause of death, not their initial assault.[88]

In Britain, similar rulings have come from both the Scottish[89] and, thereafter, the English[90] courts. The matter seems beyond dispute at this time. The *Potter* case would present no difficulties today; the original malefactor causing brain death would be guilty of homicide regardless of subsequent medical treatment decisions to connect or disconnect the victim to or from the respirator following diagnosis of brain death.

The public still seems somewhat suspicious of the brain death criteria at times.[91] Death should be clearly pronounced, entered in the medical record and the family, if available, advised before any transplantation goes forward. It may be necessary to continue the brain dead patient on the respirator for a period of time after diagnosis and confirmation of death. Although not legally required, in appropriate cases where the resources are available to do so, this allows the family a transition period to come to grips with the death. This may encourage a decision to support organ donation where the patient has not provided for it.

It is essential that physicians, the media and the public clearly understand that brain death does not mean merely unconsciousness, or a permanent vegetative state, but a complete death of the entire brain, which but for artificial, mechanical respiration provided in a hospital or other institution, would cause an immediate stoppage of the heart and the lungs. Sometimes even medical experts continue to be confused.[92] However, brain death need only be resorted to when the person is already dead by the traditional definition of no breathing and no heart beat, but has those functions artificially continued because he or she happens to have died where a respirator and other such high-tech equipment is readily at hand.

Where all but the lower brain stem has died – due to hemorrhage or absence of oxygen – the patient will be permanently comatose, but not brain dead. None of the brain death statutes, nor the decided cases equate brain death with anything less than death of the entire brain, including the brainstem, which controls circulation and respiration.

Of course with a living donor no problems of diagnosing death arise. However, other separate problems do exist, to which we now turn.

F.   THE 'CONSENTING' LIVING ORGAN DONOR

The use of living donors for organ or tissue transplants raises several distinct legal issues. One is the issue of consent: what must be disclosed to the donor before he can be said to have knowingly consented. Another is the issue of what can and cannot be legally donated: is there a limit to the right to consent? There is also the issue of competence: may children, the feeble-minded, conscripts, prisoners or paid donors give a valid and binding consent?

Several generalizations can be fairly safely ventured in regard to consent for medical purposes. If the treatment consented to has a recognized and accepted therapeutic purpose, the patient may consent to it. Consent also makes lawful certain non-therapeutic cosmetic operations on the individual, such as straightening of the teeth, removal of skin blemishes, perforation of the ears and tattooing.[93] However, consent will not justify homicide,[94] maiming or the infliction of serious harm for no therapeutic purpose, particularly where aspects of indecency, brutality, or the evasion of public duties are involved.[95]

An important distinction must be drawn between consent for tissue removal that will not, and that which will, be harmful to the living donor. The removal of naturally replaceable or repairable tissue – such as blood transfusions and skin grafts – does not create much, if any problem where proper consent is obtained.[96] Where no permanent or serious damage will result to the donor from the removal of tissue and where he and the donee are competent adults who knowingly and intelligently consent to the transplant, after a full explanation, no serious legal problem is likely to arise.[97] The important consideration here is not the 'extent' of the consent, but rather the 'capacity' for consent. The law is concerned only that the consent be given freely and knowledgeably and for that reason will be interested in the age, mental condition and capacity of the donor and the circumstances in which he consented.

The legal effect of consent by a living donor to the removal of tissue not naturally replaceable by his body is another matter.[98] Few legal problems have arisen from the use of live kidney donors, although the removals cannot be without some harm – at least potentially in weakening the donor's reserve should his remaining healthy kidney fail – to the donor. The high chances of satisfactory existence on one kidney probably explain why legal liability has not sought to be imposed for removal of one of the paired organs. If one competently decides to help another in this way, he should be able to do so. Even if the loss of one kidney does involve a slightly increased risk to the donor, most conclude it is clearly outweighed by the need of the prospective recipient.[99]

At the same time as the law will not allow consent to justify homicide, it is consistent that it will not allow the removal from living donors of unpaired vital organs such as the liver, lungs and heart. At least for the present, the law is not willing to justify a donor's death by the severity of the prospective recipient's need. Some suggest this is not necessarily the proper order of priorities, particularly where the donor is nearing death. Professor Sir Thomas Smith, for example, found it difficult to accept the legal state of affairs that allows a person to give his life to save another from drowning, or for his country, but does not allow a person to save another – probably a loved one – who is dying from a defective vital organ.[100] This position is hard to argue with, provided death is reasonably near, consent is free and knowing and external coercion is absent. However, the life saver intends to save himself as well as the one in peril, a critical difference.

Between these two extremes then – on the one hand that a living donor may consent to the removal of tissue that will involve little or no risk to his health, such as skin or blood, and on the other hand that a living donor may not give up his life in the form of a vital, unpaired organ for another's benefit – exists a difficult and unsettled legal terrain. The questions that arise will be resolved by balancing the harm to the donor against the benefit to the donee. It is likely that a free, knowing consent will be upheld, where the risk involved in the donation is in fair proportion to the benefit that is likely to be conferred upon the donee by the transplant.[101]

Several cases from Massachusetts serve to point out that situations may arise where both the capacity to consent and the extent of the consent are at issue. The cases involved the question of whether the consent given by the parents/guardian of twin children was sufficient to protect the hospital and involved staff from legal liability (assault and battery) for the performance of surgery beneficial to one twin (the recipient), but not to the other (donor).[102] All three cases involved kidney transplants of one organ from one healthy twin to the other. In all the cases the children consented as well as their parents or guardians.

Before proceeding with the kidney removal and transplants, the hospital in each case sought a declaratory judgment from the Massachusetts court as to the lawfulness of the procedure. The opinions handed down are very similar. The courts held that no civil or criminal liability would be incurred by the hospital where the operation was necessary to save the sick twin and where the healthy twin consented to and knew all the consequences of the operation. Basing their opinion on expert medical and psychiatric testimony, the courts held the operation to be also, in effect, for the benefit of the donor twin, for if the transplant were not allowed and the ailing twin died as a result the healthy twin would suffer 'grave emotional disturbance.' The donor twins in each case were in their teens.

These Massachusetts cases have drawn considerable comment. Lord Kilbrandon, the Scottish judge, referred to the cases as 'a courageous piece of sophisticated reasoning.'[103] Professor Daube of Oxford, contrariwise, felt that children on no account should be transplant donors, suggesting the Massachusetts cases were,

'cheating by maintaining . . . that the child would suffer trauma if he were not allowed to give his twin a kidney or whatever it might be.'[104]

Professor Freund of Harvard would agree with Daube that minors are, in fact, incapable of consenting to removal and transplantation, but only in those situations where the operation would not be of 'benefit' to them.[105] Such a suggestion unfortunately does not resolve the problem raised by the Massachusetts cases. The question of what in fact constitutes a 'benefit' to the donor must still be ascertained.

An older American case, *Bonner v. Moran*,[106] is instructive for the light it sheds on the issue we have been considering – namely, the ability of a child to consent to a tissue removal not strictly for his own benefit, but for transplantation to another. Aside from the unreported Massachusetts cases, it appears to be the most significant of only a very few other judicial pronouncements in point. The defendant physician in *Bonner* took a skin graft from a fifteen year old boy without getting his parents' consent. The graft was to aid the boy's cousin and he apparently consented. The Circuit court, in remanding the case for a new trial, held that (1) the parent's consent was necessary before operating on a child; (2) a surgical operation is a technical battery and excusable only by the patient's consent, express or implied; (3) where a child is close to maturity the surgeon may be justified in operating on the basis of his consent alone; and, (4) because the present operation was not for benefit of the child, it was a necessity to obtain the consent of the parents before preceding.

The case is significant in that it did not conclude because the operation was not for the benefit of the patient that a valid consent to proceed could not be given the physician. It should be borne in mind, however, that a skin graft – notwithstanding the unusual complications that developed in *Bonner*

– normally involves only a temporary and minor discomfort to the donor, no permanent or severe disablement.

While no hard and fast rule can be laid down,[107] American physicians are said to refuse to operate on children for their benefit if they are less than ten years old unless their parents' consent has first been obtained.[108] Obviously ability to give an informed consent will vary from child to child and depending on the complexity of the procedure. Professor Daube, while advocating that 'children should on no account be donors,' suggests that the age of consent for transplants be lowered to the general age of conscription, seventeen or eighteen years old.[104] Duff feels children can consent as early as seven and almost always to any procedure by age fourteen.

However, it is one thing for a child to consent to beneficial treatment, another to consent to donate tissue that brings no physical benefit and creates risk of harm. Australia, for example, normally prohibits any live child tissue donation.

Potential transplant donors other than children are considered to pose problems of capacity to consent. Among them are prisoners, soldiers, the feeble-minded or insane, wards, medical students and relatives of the prospective recipient. Perhaps relatives pose the most subtle difficulties. Their sometimes dubiously free and full capacity to consent is not caused by elements of external coercion or lack of understanding. It is caused rather by their affinity to the needy recipient, by internal coercion if you will. It has been suggested that psychological as well as physical testing should be utilized to screen potential donors, particularly relatives who may volunteer to donate under familial pressures, but are actually ambivalent or hostile to the operation.[110]

Finally, capacity to consent can be corrupted by the offering of payment in return for 'donation' of an organ for transplantation. While indemnification for organ donors is perhaps desirable, few think it wise by purchasing a patient's consent to encourage an unsavoury traffic in body parts, as in the days of Burke and Hare. Nonetheless, there are those who see no real difference between the voluntary and the paid donor, so long as both are well aware of the risk involved.[111] The two may be similar, but the complications arising from their use may be quite different.

Even if undue pressure is not brought to bear because of a monetary reward, the question is still raised as to what the patient must be told for his consent to donate an organ or tissue to be deemed legally adequate. In Britain, the answer will in almost all cases be what the doctors feel it is necessary to tell the donor.[112] In Britain a doctor need only disclose to his patient what other ordinarily skilled doctors would disclose under the circumstances.[113] This so-called 'reasonable doctor' test applies, whether the physician is diagnosing, treating or seeking the consent of the patient to treatment. It apparently matters not whether the consent is being sought to therapeutic or to non-therapeutic treatment.[114]

Normally it is for the doctors to set the standard of disclosure. However, the court may in unusual circumstances find that 'disclosure of a particular risk is so obviously necessary to an informed choice on the part of the patient that no reasonably prudent medical man would fail to make it.'[115] What this means is that even though ordinarily skilled doctors would not disclose a risk, the court may say it is negligent not to disclose it if it concludes it is unreasonable not to do so. This provides some protection to the donor, but basically he or she will have to decide on donation after hearing the risks that most doctors would disclose. These risks, of course, may or may not be what most reasonable people contemplating an organ donation would want to know before making up their minds. The reason for this is that consent involves not only an evaluation of medical risks, but it also is dependent on non-medical components of basic communication such as the patient's emotional state, intelligence and desire to be informed.[116]

Many American jurisdictions follow the same rule of disclosure. However, as discussed in Chapter 5, in more recent times a 'patient-oriented' standard of risk disclosure has been espoused by a number of state and federal courts.[117] This standard, known as the material risks standard of disclosure requires that the patient be informed of all information that a reasonable patient would deem material or significant under the circumstances. The idea is that this standard seeks to protect the patient's right to self-determination by requiring disclosure of that risk information a reasonable patient would want to know, not what a reasonable physician would elect to disclose. As one court has put it,

'The duty of a physician to inform the patient of the consequences of a proposed treatment stems from the right of every competent adult human being to determine what shall be done with his own body.'[118]

When a living donor is being asked to donate tissue or an organ, it is not for his physical benefit. It may be for his emotional benefit and to give him peace of mind he has done the right thing for a loved one, but this is a subjective thing difficult to evaluate. It seems proper that the donor be given all relevant information of risks and complications, for he is much like an experimental subject: both are being asked to assume a risk primarily to benefit another or others, which only incidentally will benefit the patient, if at all.

The donee should not be forgotten. He too must consent to the procedure, although it is for his benefit. Norrie has pointed out that whether the 'reasonable physician' standard or the 'material risks' standard is applicable,

'the recipient of the donation must be given information concerning the risks of the operation itself and its consequences (e.g. the possibility of tissue rejection), the chances of its success, possible alternative modes of treatment, the consequences of failure, and, indeed, the consequences of success (e.g. the need, particularly with heart transplants, to receive various anti-rejection drugs for the rest of the patient's life.)[119]

There are limits to the right to consent as we have discussed. Children only under the most compelling circumstances of family need will be allowed to consent to donation of non-regenerative tissue. Non-paired vital organ donations have not as yet been permitted by anyone.

While kidneys can be given to aid a family member, or perhaps a friend, if the donor is adult and competent, sale of a kidney for profit not compassion is almost certainly against the law, exposing both donor and surgeon to criminal liability. Where the removal will clearly and irrevocably harm the donor, it will likely be considered unlawful and immoral. The use of children born without a brain (anencephalics) as donors poses this issue clearly.

G. THE ANENCEPHALIC (MISSING BRAIN) BABY AS DONOR

About every 2,000 births, or even less frequently,[120] a baby is born without all or most of its forebrain. The presence of a malformed brain stem may allow circulation and respiration to continue for a brief few days, but all such babies die. Their condition is hopeless. No treatment can help them, except comfort care until they die.

Anencephalic babies may have perfectly healthy other vital organs – heart, lungs, kidneys, liver – as well as transplantable tissue – thymus, marrow, cornea, pituitary, intestine.

Of the approximately 2,500 anencephalic babies born each year in the U.S., 95 percent live for less than a week.[121] The need for small organs to treat acutely ill newborn with kidney, liver, heart and other dysfunction could be met to considerable degree by using the anencephalic newborn as donors.

Newborn organs require less immuno-suppression than more mature organs. Because of size and function limitations they can only be used for neonatal recipients.[122]

The anencephalic newborn is a live-born person under the law. He is not brain dead. The forebrain is missing, but the brain stem provides transient heartbeat and respiration. Thus, before organs may be removed either brain death or cessation of circulation and respiration must occur. A few hospitals that consider tissue transplantation appropriate in such cases follow the protocol of placing anencephalic infants on a respirator. Periodically the respirator is turned off. If the child fails to breathe on its own for several minutes then the child is considered dead and arrangements are made for organ removal.[121] To some this is artificial, for such neonates would not be candidates for respirator support unless they were candidates for organ donation.

Others have suggested that the definition of brain death should be expanded to include the absence of a forebrain.[122] Such a definition would allow surgeons to consider the anencephalic as brain dead and eligible for organ removal. This would allow greater time for removal of organs and a greater chance they would be perfused and healthy at the time of removal. The transplant team would not be involved in diagnosis of death, counselling the family and perinatal or neonatal management of the anencephalic. The diagnosis of brain absence, rather than subject to the normal two doctor corroboration required for brain death, might include confirmation by neurologist, neonatologist and bioethicist.

Others feel such a change is inappropriate, because it would expand our traditional definition of death to include the absence of a functioning forebrain.[123] How then could the patient with a brain, but in a persistent vegetative state without a functioning forebrain, be distinguished?[124] To consider such persons dead would be a radical departure from established notions of death and raises the spectre of considering severe neurological deficit as a justification for vital organ removal. This is unwise.

It seems clear that organ donors – whether anencephalic, in persistent vegetative state, or otherwise – must first be allowed to die before physicians should consider organ donation. Although this will prevent the usefulness of organs at times, it is the necessary price to pay to ensure that our reverence for all life is preserved, that all efforts are directed to what is best for the patient, whether prospective donor or not, and that public acceptance of transplantation is not prejudiced by what are seen as premature arrangements for organ removal. At the same time, the subject of organ donation should be discussed with the parents of an anencephalic following diagnosis, which may often be done during pregnancy, and after they have dealt with their grief. It may be, as experience to date seems to show, that 'the family should be allowed to salvage from their tragedy the consolation that their loss can provide life to another child.'[122]

Most oppose anencephalic babies as donors. Recently the only active U.S. medical protocol for their use was abandoned.[125]

However, in the UK the moratorium imposed in 1986 has recently been lifted and the issue appears to be one now left to ethical committees to decide based upon the particular circumstances presented.

H.   THE FETUS AS DONOR

Both British and U.S. law recognizes the fetus as a potential human being, but not a full person within the eyes of the law.[126] If a fetus is aborted, should its organs or tissue be available for transplant? Where the fetus is viable, is capable of independent existence, the answer must be no. However, what of fetuses that are aborted, either spontaneously or medically, and born dead, but with certain tissue or organs sufficiently mature so as to be usable to help another? Here a strong argument can be made that transplantation may be appropriate. Certain controls are, however, necessary.

The British Medical Association has drawn up interim guidelines.[127] They provide, similar to the recommendations of the Peel committed which considered the matter in 1972, that,

1. Tissue should be obtained only from dead fetuses following spontaneous or therapeutic abortion.

2. The mother must consent to use of fetal tissue for research and/or medical purposes.

3. The contemplated transplant may not interfere with or influence the abortion decision, its timing or method. The health of the mother should be foremost.

4. The abortion must be performed in accordance with the Abortion Act 1967.

5. The donor should remain anonymous.

6. There should be no connection between donor and recipient.

7. The generation or termination of a pregnancy solely to produce transplantable tissue is unethical.

8. There may not be any financial reward for the donation of a fetus or fetal tissue.

9. Fetal organs may be used as complete or partial organs for transplant, except for nervous tissue (including the brain).

10. Nervous tissue may only be used as isolated neurones or tissue fragments for transplantation.

11. Every project that involves transplantation of fetal tissue must be approved by the local ethical research committee.

These guidelines are sound. Abortions should not be induced for monetary reward. The question whether a woman should be able to donate a fetus following abortion in order to salvage an ill family member is a much more difficult one. If an unintentional pregnancy may be terminated and the resulting fetal tissue used, a strong case can be made for working a significant improvement in the health of the living by an intended pregnancy and abortion. As Brahams has described the position, 'A feckless woman who became pregnant by casual intercourse could then ethically provide fetal tissue, whereas a caring woman who planned the event could not.'[128]

The problem, of course, is not to encourage creation of life knowing that it will be sacrificed before live birth. Although it may yet be premature, as research on the use of fetal tissue develops more clearly the therapeutic benefits it offers for others, it may well be proper to allow pregnancy and abortion where no money is paid, but a condition of a loved one not otherwise curable may be significantly improved or cured by the use of fetal tissue. A bioethics committee could be constituted to pass on such requests. Limitations could be imposed, such as limiting to one induced abortion, limiting the age of the fetus and requiring a showing of clear and substantial medical benefit to the recipient.

Fetal tissue may be of marked importance in treating Parkinson's Disease, Alzheimer's Disease, stroke and diabetes. It may, however, become less important because of advances using connective tissue cells modified genetically to secrete nerve growth factor.[129] It may also be of assistance in treating immuno-deficient conditions by the transfer of bone marrow and liver tissue and metabolic-endocrine imbalance by the use of thymus and pituitary tissue. Fetal tissue has even been transplanted into another, *in utero* fetus to treat genetic immune deficiency disease.

In the U.S. no clear government policy or statute exists regulating the transplantation of fetal tissue. Some preliminary steps have been taken to prohibit government funding for the use of fetal tissue from an induced abortion, but they have not been formalized. An advisory committee of the National Institutes of Health has recently concluded fetuses from induced abortions may be used for medical or scientific research purposes. Its recommendations were similar to those of the British Medical Association.[130] More definitive recommendations will have to await more evidence on the effectiveness of such fetal tissue transplants, as well as the availability of donors and the means of preserving fetal tissue.

With proper controls, the benefits potential offered appear substantial. While we do not wish to encourage abortion, there is nothing unethical about using tissue from aborted fetuses to help others. The BMA and NIH guidelines are sensible and should allow research to continue while avoiding abuse.

I.   CONCLUSIONS

'Science has made us Gods before we are even worthy of being men.'[131]

This sums up many of the issues we have discussed in this book. Science has enabled man to conquer many of the technical problems that once barred the interchange of human body parts. However, many ethical and moral issues remain.

One of the most difficult ethical problems is posed by the fact that demand for vital organs greatly exceeds supply. Public acceptance of transplantation seems clear, yet the supply of donors remains low. For example, of the 100,000 or so people who die each year from accidents or stroke and are diagnosed brain dead, only approximately 20,000 are suitable vital organ donors because of age, condition of organs and general health.[132] Of those, only about 3,000 actually donate organs. The scarcity of organs makes selection very difficult.

We will have more to say on the subject of fairly allocating scarce medical resources in Chapter 12. However, organs must be allocated on the basis of where they will do the most medical good. This involves the likelihood of a successful transplant (age, tissue type, general health, blood type, psychosocial stability, etc.), the degree of improvement it should afford (lifesaving) and the duration of benefit it will provide (age, general health, etc.)

Most agree that political, social or financial criteria should not control donee selection. On the other hand, if medical indications are similar, it is likely transplant surgeons will opt for the patient who offers the greatest social worth. Given two equally suitable recipients, the concert pianist, university professor or professional baseball player will undoubtedly be chosen over the unemployed or undistinguished person. Recognizing this reality, several transplant centers have in the past relied on a broad-based citizens panel to advise them on suitable organ recipients after taking into account medical suitability and social worth.[133] Social worth is intended to mean contributions made to society, not social standing, wealth or eminence.

Society may decide that certain patient selection limitations are proper and to be applied to all who are similarly situated. The National Health Service, for example, does not routinely make hemodialysis available to those over 55 where demand for continuous dialysis machines by younger persons has absorbed fully the supply. This age can be increased if resources are available. Legislative and social policy making bodies are the proper ones to make such decisions, not doctors treating individual patients.[134]

The physician should not have to choose between patients on any but the principles of a humanitarian healer. If society is unwilling to pay the price necessary to provide maximum medical resources, then the physician can only pick and choose as best he can in an effort to bring the most relief and comfort and to do the most medical good. Society can spend money on hot school lunches, a battleship, or a new transplant unit, as it wishes; if it decides on either the former objects, the physician cannot save everyone, but can only select patients for treatment on the basis of where he feels the 'most good can be done.'[135] Nothing more can be asked of him.

The sale of vital organs should be outlawed. Access to life-saving medical treatment or organs should not depend on the ability to pay. This is particularly true where kidney transplants can cost $30,000 or more, heart transplants $125,000 and liver transplants $260,000. Guidelines should continue to prohibit the commercialization of organ donation, so the poor and disadvantaged are not economically coerced to act against their free will. The threat is real given the recent report of impoverished Turks flown into Britain to donate a kidney for the wealthy in return for a stipend of £2,000–£3,000.[136] It is one thing to pay to encourage a non-harmful blood donation: it is quite another when what is sought is not naturally replaceable tissue. Even at that, problems have developed from the economically-deprived, suffering from AIDS or otherwise unhealthy, donating blood for money.

Living donors, particularly children, present ethical problems as donors. The use of living donors should generally be limited and even avoided wherever possible if the donation would permanently deprive the donor of a part or a function of his physiology, or, if temporary, it would be of substantial detriment to his functioning integrity as a human being and personality.[137]

Adults of full capacity who have been thoroughly and expressly advised of all medical risks involved in the proposed surgery by a physician not a member of the transplant team, should be allowed to consent to donate tissue in such circumstances, but only when the benefit to be derived by the recipient from the donation of such tissue clearly outweighs the detriment agreed to be suffered or risked by the donor. Such a limitation would make the giving of a vital organ, resulting in the donor's death, unacceptable in any situation. However, it would clearly warrant the donation of a kidney, for instance, where the donee would otherwise die, where the chances of success of the operation were high due to the familial relationship of the parties, and where there was likelihood that the donor could exist satisfactorily, barring complications, with one kidney. This type of legislation, rather than prohibiting consent by an individual to medical treatment, not for his benefit but for the benefit of another individual, would allow such consent to be given where a balancing of the risk involved against the hoped-for benefit to be derived warranted the surgery. Difficult borderline cases of application could be referred to the courts for declaratory judgment prior to surgery.

Under such a legislative formulation, children and incompetents could be excluded and, apart from court approval of specified application on behalf of the minor, only naturally replaceable tissue (for example, skin or blood) could be transplanted from a child and even then, only when the child was of an age to understand the general nature of his consent, when his parents or guardians had also consented and when the donation had been authorized by a second physician in no way involved in the transplant procedure, or approved by a court.

When the first edition of this book was written in 1970 'brain death' was new and controversial. The Harvard ad hoc committee had just released its criteria for brain death. In the 20 years since then brain death has been almost universally accepted. The medical profession, the courts, and the public has become comfortable with the concept that death has occurred when the entire brain has stopped functioning. Without a functioning brain, neither respiration nor circulation, the traditional hallmarks of life, can continue. Still, to ensure public confidence, when organs are to be taken for transplantation, death should be confirmed by not one, but two, physicians and neither should have any involvement with the transplant team. The fact a patient is a prospective organ donor should not and cannot be justification for relaxation of good medical practice standards that would be applied in any other case.

Cadaver donors could be increased if a legal presumption was enacted that provided organs would be available after death *unless* the decedent had expressly opted out or refused consent while alive. It has been suggested that the public interest in obtaining cadaver tissues for living recipients should be capable of subordination only by the wish of the deceased himself, expressed before death. To this end the law could, it is argued, presume consent to donate organs in all cases where the deceased had not objected formally by registration before his demise.[138] The burden of registering a written refusal to donate his tissues after death might not be an unduly heavy one to impose on the individual, particularly in today's increasingly computerized world. The refusal to donate could be a simple form, publicized and provided by the state, to be signed, verified and notarized, if desired, by the individual and returned to a central records registration office. Only hospitals authorized to perform transplants could be granted immediate access to these records upon the person's admission to the hospital in a terminal state. The carrying of such a refusal card on the person, as recommended by the American Uniform Act, or the wearing of a pendant or identification bracelet authorizing tissue removal upon death, are more uncertain and less desirable ways of accomplishing the same end. The could, however, be made supplemental to a central registration scheme.

Such legislative presumption of consent would cut off the discussed rights in the relatives at common law to acquire the dead body intact for burial. If desired, the transplanting surgeons could be disallowed from using any bodily parts that would 'disfigure' the cadaver prior to burial. While such a proviso might be an invitation to 'pointless litigation'[139] by bereaved relatives, it would wisely place some value on the emotional feelings of loved ones and next-of-kin, and would probably be more readily accepted by the public.

However, the enactment of such a legislative presumption of consent (to donate one's organs at death) can only be justified if it is clearly supported by a consensus among the lay public at large. It has the effect of requiring the individual to 'contract out' of his presumed donor status if he does not wish to so serve. While the burden on the individual may be light, it is nonetheless a restriction on his freedom of action that perhaps should not exist if there appear to be any substantial ethical objections to it.

The concept of 'required request' is now well established in the United States as a possible alternative. Federal law[140] requires hospitals to establish written protocols for the indentification of potential organ and tissue donors which make families aware of their right to donate cadaver body parts. Hospitals are excluded from Federal Medicare and Medicaid participation, which can produce 50 percent of their revenues and is essential, unless such protocols are in place and there is proper compliance with required request legislation in their state.

California's required consent law,[141] for example, mandates that all hospital deaths be considered promptly for organ and tissue donation suitability and that families of the decedent be offered the option to donate. This impetus is significant. A 1986 Gallup poll found that 75 percent of families offered the opportunity will consent to donation.

While medical staff are often uncomfortable raising these issues, they are expected to result in substantial donor increases. In addition, not raising the issue with the family deprives them of the right to be informed of the available donation option and to make the decision themselves. This may actually help ease the grieving process.[142]

Transplantation can bring great benefit to the hopelessly ill with organ failure, or to those in need of blood, bone marrow, corneas and other essential tissue. As we have seen, it offers the promise to cure congenital disease, as well as end-stage organ disease that may occur at different stages in life. The challenge of medicine and of society as a whole is to assure the public that death will not be pronounced or organs taken prematurely, that they will be used to help those in greatest need on a fair and impartial basis, and that the dedication of medical and financial resources to such procedures will not be disproportionate to the benefits derived.

When the American health care system has much to improve in its delivery of basic services to all, regardless of wealth or social station, the expense of transplants and the limited number they benefit can be questioned. It may be that only those recognized as cost effective – blood, cornea, and kidney transplants for example – will be socially and politically readily supported. Other, more esoteric, more expensive procedure – heart, lung, liver and fetal tissue transplants – may only be supported if predominantly successful, of substantial benefit, and not unduly demanding of finite resources and personnel.

The challenge is to promote the many medical advances and patient benefits offered by continuing advances in transplantation techniques without unfairly detracting from more basic care such as prenatal care for the poor, long term, humane custodial care for the elderly. This will be no easy task. It is one that will increasingly face our society. Open discussion and thoughtful analysis of these issues must be promoted as a necessary concomitant to technological advance. There are no simple answers. As in many of the challenges of life, a reasonable balance will have to be struck by society as in other areas of modern medical care, between what we would like and what we can afford. Just as transplant recipients must be selected based on who will be likely to benefit the most, so too must society choose to support that medical technology that offers the greatest good for the greatest number. A selection process will have to occur in the transplant arena not just among donees, but also between what we would like and what we can afford.

NOTES

1 Wasmuth and Stewart, 'Medical and legal aspects of human organ transplantation,' 14 *Clev-Mar. L.R.* (3) 442,443 (1965), (one of the classic articles on the subject.)
2 Louisell, 'Transplantation: existing legal constraints,' *Ethics in Medical Progress* (A Ciba Foundation Symposium). London: Churchill (1966) pp.78, 87.
3 'Supply of Donor Organs for Transplantation,' 1988 *The Lancet* 70.
4 'Cardiac Transplantation,' 4 *Brit. Med. J.* 757 (1967).
5 *Time*, 15 January 1968, p.42; *The Scotsman* 18 August 1969, p.1.
6 *The Observer*, 26 November 1967, p.1.
7 *The Scotsman*, 17 May 1968, p.1 (The 14 year old recipient died two weeks later.)
8 Patel, Mickey and Terraski, 279 *New Eng. J. Med.* 501 (1968).
9 *San Fran. Chronicle*, Oct. 8, 1989, 'Image' p.12.
10 *St. Joseph 2000*. Orange, Cal.: St. Joseph Health System, 1989, p.35.
11 *Los Angeles Times*, 13 April 1969, p.1.
12 Berman, 'The legal problems of organ transplantation,' 13 Vill.L.R. 751,754 (1968); 'Legal problems in donations of human tissues to medical science,' 21 Vand. L.R. 352,357 (1968).
13 Vestal, Taber and Shoemaker, 'Medico-legal aspects of tissue homotransplantation,' 18 *U. Detroit L.J.* 271, 273 (1955).
14 Vestal, Taber and Shoemaker, 18 *U. Detroit L.J.* 275.
15 *Foster v. Dodd* (1867) 3 Q.B. 67,77.
16 Wasmuth and Stewart, note 1 above, p. 452, citing *Pierce v. Swant Point Cemetery*, 10 R.I. 227, 14 *Am. Rep.* 667 (1872) at p.453 to the following effect: 'That there is no property right in a dead body, using the word in the ordinary sense, may well be admitted. Yet, the burial of the dead is a subject which interests the feelings of mankind to a much greater degree than many matters of actual property. There is a duty imposed by the universal feelings of mankind to be discharged by someone towards the dead; a duty, and we may also say a right, to protect from violation; and a duty on the parts of others to abstain from violation; it may therefore be considered as a sort of quasi-property.'
17 Alison, *Criminal Law of Scotland*, vol. i, Edinburgh: Blackwood (1832) p.461.
18 *Dewar v. H.M. Adv.*, 1945 J.C.5; Gordon, *The Criminal Law of Scotland*, pp.430–1.
19 Vestal, Taber and Shoemaker, 18 *U. Detroit L.J.* p.277.
20 *Larson v. Chase*, 47 Minn. 307, 50 N.W. 238 (1891), in overruling a demurrer to a complaint for damages due to unlawful mutilation of the

complainant's deceased husband, concluded 'That mental suffering and injury to the feelings would be ordinarily the natural and proximate result of knowledge that the remains of a deceased husband had been mutilated, is too obvious a complaint to admit of argument.' (The wife's mental suffering and nervous shock were the only damages alleged); Accord, *Pollick v. Workman*, (1900) 2 F.354.

21 *In re Cornitius's Estate*, 154 Cal. App. 2d 422 (1957).

22 *Cohen v. Groman Mortuary, Inc.*, 231 Cal. App. 2d 1, 5–6 (1965) (surviving spouse); *Smith v. Vidovich*, 242 Cal. App. 2d 206, 207 (1966) (majority of surviving children where no surviving spouse); the foregoing cases were decided under California Health and Safety Code sec.7100, which codifies the common law order of responsibility for burial of a dead body.

23 'Indecent treatment of a corpse as a common law crime,' 4 Ark. L.R. 480 (1950).

24 Perkins, *Criminal Law*. Brooklyn: Foundation Press (1957) p.339, citing *State v. Bradley*, 136 Me. 347, 351, 9 A.2d 659 (1939).

25 1945 J.C.5.

26 This bizarre charge apparently was drawn from Hume, who cites it in relation to an Edinburgh man hanged for throwing the unclad body of his dead wife out of a third-story window on to the High Street.

27 105 Tenn. 177, 58 S.W. 213 (1900).

28 215 Ark. 851, 223 S.W. 2d. 809 (1949).

29 See Mason, *Forensic medicine for Lawyers*. London: Butterworths, 1988 (2d.3d.), p.32

30 Ibid, p. 28.

31 Chayet, 'Consent for autopsy,' 274 *New Eng. J. Med.* 268 (1966).

32 Couch, Curran and Moore, 'The use of cadaver tissues in transplantation,' 271 *New Eng. J. Med.* 691 (1964).

33 213 N.E. 2d.870 (1966).

34 Chayet, 'Further notes on consent for autopsy,' 274 *New Eng. J. Med.* 1019, 1020 (1966).

35 *Time*, 25 April 1969, p.61. The well-known authoress of *Payton Place*, Grace Metalious, was frustrated from giving her cadaver to a medical school due to repudiation of such a gift by her next-of-kin after death, acting under the prior Massachusetts law; see, *Holland v. Metalious* 198 A.2d 654 (N.H. 1964).

36 1913 S.C. 394.

37 (1901) 3 F. 918.

38 154 Tenn. 295, 294 S.W. 1097 (1929).

39 128 Wisc. 453, 102 N.W. 40.

40 128 N.Y.S. 161 (1911).

41 267 N.Y. Supp. 2d 374 (1966), discussed in Sanders and Dukeminier, 'Medical advance and legal lag: hemodialysis and kidney transplantation,' 15 UCLA L.R. 357, 403 (1968).

42 *Rex v. Lynn* (1788) 2 T.R. 734, 100 Eng.Rep. 394.

43 Alison, *Criminal Law of Scotland* p.463, discussing the case of John Campbell, the medical student from Aberdeen, who was only imprisoned for fourteen days and ordered to pay £100 to the Aberdeen Imfirmary.

44 Hume, *Commentaries* i, 85.

45 Gordon, *Criminal Law of Scotland* (citing *Soutar* (1882) 5 Couper 65 and *H.M. Adv. v. Coutts* (1899) 3 Adam 50).

46 Price, 'legal rights and duties in regard to dead bodies, Post mortems and dissections' (1951) 68 *S.A.L.J.* 403, 405,423.

47 *Ibid.*, p.407.

48 Gordon, Turner and Price, *Medical Jurisprudence*. Edinburgh: Livingstone (1953) p.239.

49 Vestal, Taber and Shoemaker, 18 *U. Detroit L.J.* 283,287.

50 Technically, a donor can only 'give' or make a 'gift' of his cadaver or its organs if he owns it in a 'property' sense. It is not clear whether an individual 'owns' his body after death, or even during his life. As a result, it may well be that a person can only make a direction of how he wishes his cadaver to be used, but cannot make a gift of what he technically does not and cannot own, of what is *res extra comercio*. It is submitted that a person, by virtue of a limited or quasi-property right in his body, may make a gift of it for post-mortem use, as long as such use is not contrary to public policy or good morals, thus the use of the terms 'gift' and donate' in this context.

51 Reemtsma, 'Legal aspects of organ grafting,' 13 *W. Med. J.* 141, 142 (1966).

52 *R. v. Ensor* (1887) 3 T.L.R. 366, 367.

53 *Pollok v. Workman* (1900) 2 F. 354, 355; see also, *Conway v. Dalziel* (1901) 3 F. 918, *Hughes v. Robertson* 1913 S.C. 394, discussed in Norrie, 'Human Tissue Transplants: Legal Liability in Different Jurisdictions' 34 *Internat'l. and Comparative Law Quart.* 442, 463 (1985); *Bonilla v. Reeves* (1966, N.Y. App.) 267 N.Y.S. 2d 374.

54 Meyers, 'Organ Transplantation and the Law,' *Impact of Science on Society*, Vol. xxi, No. 3 (Paris: UNESCO, 1971), p.225.

55 *San Francisco Chronicle* 14 July 1989, p. A26.

56 *Strachan v. J.F.K. Mem. Hosp.* (1988) 538 A.2d 346.

57 2 and 3 Will. 4, c.75.

58 9 and 10 Eliz. 2, c.54, s.i.

59 (1958) Dears and B. 590.

60 See Caplan, 'Ethical and Policy Issues in the Procurement of Cadavar Organs for Transplantation,' 311 *N. Eng. J. Med.* 981 (1984); Bruce, 'Open discussion on surgical ethics, with special reference to the problems arising from transplantation,' 7 *International Federation of Surgical Colleges News Bulletin*, May 1967, p.17.

61 Nabarro, 'Renal Transplantation,' House of Commons, 13 March 1968.

62 15 and 16 Geo. 6 and 1 Eliz. 2,c.28, s. 2s.

63 Report of the working party on the supply of donor organs for transplantation: Conference of Medical Royal Colleges and their Faculties in the U.K. (London, DHSS, 1987).

64 1988 *The Lancet* 70.

65 Perhaps due to subconscious fear of mutilation, even if post-mortem, or fear of premature cessation of efforts to sustain life.

66 Brahams, 'Kidney for Sale by Live Donor,' 1989 *The Lancet* 285.

67 Discussed in Chapter 3, *supra*; the Act, however, does not prohibit payment for surrogate pregnancy services between private individuals where no third party is involved.

68 *A. v. C.* (1985) F.L.R. 445, 449 (surrogacy contract); see also, *R. v. Coney* (1882) 8 Q.B.D. 534 (prize fight.)

69 *R. v. Donovan* (1934) 2 K.B. 498; *Bravery v. Bravery* (1954) 3 All E.R. 59.

70 *H.M. Advocate v. Rutherford*, 1947 J.C.I.; *People v. Conley* (1966) 64 Cal. 2d 310.

71 Norrie, *supra*, 34 *Internat'l. and Comp. L. Quart.* 442, 461 (1985)

72 Caplan, 311 *N.Eng.J.Med.* 981, 983 (1984).

73 Chayet, 274 *New Eng. J. Med.* 268, 269 (1966).

74 As La. Rev. Stats (1962) 17 Sec.2351–5, which states in Sec.2351 that 'Every inhabitant of this state of the age of 21 years or older, of sound mind, may, by an instrument in writing and constituting a donation, arrange or provide for the disposition to be made of his body or any part or organ thereof, after death; provided that the disposition mentioned is made for the purpose of advancing medical science, or for the replacement or rehabilitation of diseased or injured parts or organs of the bodies of living persons. Any body or part or organ thereof . . . may be used in accordance with the terms of the donation immediately upon the death of the donor and without order of court or authorisation by next of kin, or any other person . . .'

75 Health & Safety ss.7151–7158.

76 Ohio Rev. Code s.2108.01–06 (May, 1967).

77 A comprehensive review of the Uniform Act can be found in Sadler and Sadler, 'Transplantation and the law: the need for organized sensitivity,' 57 Geo. L.J. 5, 18–31 (1968); see also, Stason, 'The uniform anatomical gift act,' 23 Bus.Law. 919 (1968) (Professor Stason was chairman of the Uniform Act's Drafting Committee).

78 Meyers, *Medico-Legal Implications of Death and Dying* (Dec., 1988, Cum. Supp.), ss.4:7–4:8, pp. 18–20; Calif. Health & Safety s. 7180(a).

79 The organ request must come from a physician, hospital, appropriate organ procurement organization, medical or dental school or university, the removal must not interfere with autopsy, be in accord with accepted medical standards, be followed by cosmetic restoration where appropriate, and a permanent record of all relevant information be maintained. s.4(a), Uniform Anatomical Gift Act, as amended (1987).

80 See, for example, Calif. Health & Safety Code s. 7181.

81 For a judicial use of this definition, altough one indicating that inability to resuscitate might be a preferable definition of death in a given case, see, *Estate of Schmidt*, 261 Cal. App. 2d 262, 273 (1968).

82 See Keith Simpson, 'Moment of death,' 3 *Abbottempo* 22,23 (1967); Elliott, 'When is the moment of death?', 4 *Med. Sci. Law* 77 (1964).

83 Hamlin, 'Life or death by EEG,' 190 *J. Am. Med. Ass.* 112 (1964).

84 205 *J. Am. Med. Assn.* 337 (1968), (the 'Harvard Ad Hoc Committee' criteria).

85 Black, 'Diagnosis of Brain Death,' 1976 *Brit. Med. J.* 2, 1187; Black, 'Brain Death,' 299 *N. Eng. J. Med.* 338 (1978).

86 *The Times*, 26 July 1963; the case is noted extensively in 'When do we die?' 4 *Med. Sci. Law* 59 (1964); Elliott, loc. cit.; Louisell, op. cit., pp.92–3 (citing from (1963) 31 Med.-Leg. J. 195).

87 See, for example, *Swafford v. State* (1981, Ind.) 421 N.E. 2d 596;

People v. Bonilla (1983, N.Y. App.) 467 N.Y.S. 2d 599; *People v. Mitchell* (1982) 132 Cal. App. 3d 389.

88 *State v. Meints* (1982, Neb.) 322 N.W. 2d 809; *State v. Johnson* (1977, Ohio App.) 395 N.E. 2d 368; *State v. Ferro* (1979, Ariz.) 603 Pac.2d 74; In *People v. Lai* (1987 NY Supreme Court) 516 NYS 2d 300, the court held that it was not reversible error for the trial court to refuse to define death only as failure to or cessation of circulatory and respiratory systems and it was proper for the court to include brain death in the definition of death. Defendant had shot the victim which caused severe injury to his brain, but respiration and circulation continued as a result of the respirator and blood pressure medication. He was diagnosed as brain dead. Thereafter pursuant to the anatomical gift act (Public Health Law Section 4300 et sec.) he underwent surgery and some of his vital organs were removed for transplant purposes, after which the respirator was turned off. The defendant argued the shooting did not cause his death, but rather the transplant surgery did. The court rejected this theory as virtually all other cases have.

In *People v. Eulo* (1984, NY) 482 NYS 2d 436, the Court of Appeals held that the term death used in state statutes encompassed cessation of cardiorespiratory functions or cessation of functioning of the entire brain even though the victim's heartbeat and breathing are being maintained by artificial means. Once a victim is diagnosed as dead, no subsequent medical procedures such as a vital organ removal can be deemed a cause of death. In this case the victim of a gunshot wound suffered brain death and while still being maintained on the respirator her kidneys, spleen, and lymph nodes were removed for transplant purposes after which the respirator was disconnected. The court had the following to say on brain death at page 445.

'Considering death to have occurred when there is an irreversible and complete cessation of the functioning of the entire brain, including the brain stem, is consistent with the common-law conception of death (citation). Ordinarily, death will be determined according to the traditional criteria of irreversible cardiorespiratory repose. When, however, the respiratory and circulatory functions are maintained by mechanical means, their significance, as signs of life, is at best ambiguous. Under such circumstances, death may nevertheless be deemed to occur when, according to accepted medical practice, it is determined that the entire brain's function has irreversibly ceased.

Death remains the single phenomenon identified at common law; the supplemental criteria are merely adapted to account for the 'changed conditions' that a dead body may be attached to a machine so as to exhibit demonstrably false indicia of life. It reflects an improved understanding that in the complete and irreversible absence of a functioning brain, the traditional loci of life – the heart and the lungs – function only as a result of stimuli originating from outside of the body and will never again function as part of an integrated organism.'

89 *Finlayson v. H.M. Advocate* 1978 S.L.T. (Notes) 60.
90 *R. v. Malcherek, R. v. Steel* (1981) 2 All E.R. 422.
91 *Dority v. Superior Court* (1983) 145 Cal. App. 3d 273; *Re Haymer* (1983, Ill. App.) 450 N.E. 2d 940.

92 See *Rasmussen v. Fleming* (1987, Ariz.) 741 Pac.2d 674, 680, (phys-
    ician gave evidence erroneously equating brain death with permanent
    loss of consciousness.); see also, 261 *J.Am. Med. Assn.* 2205 (1989).

93 See Strauss, 'Bodily injury and the defence of consent' (1964) 81
    S.A.L.J. 344.

94 *H.M.Adv. v. Rutherford*, 1947 J.C.1, S.L.T.3; *People v. Roberts*, 211
    Mich. 187, 178 N.W. 690 (1920).

95 See generally *F.v. Berkshire Health Authority*, (1989) 2 W.L.R. 1025
    (H.L.); see also, *Rex v. Donovan* (1934) K.B. 498 (sexual indecency);
    Wright's Case, Co. Litt. 127a (1604) (begging); generally, Hughes,
    'Two views on consent in the criminal law' (1963) 26 M.J.L.R. 233.

96 Forbes, 'Legal aspects of blood transfusion and of therapy in general,'
    4 *Med Sci.Law* 26 (1964).

97 *Schloendorff v. N.Y. Hospital*, 211 N.Y. 125, 105 N.E. 92 (1914),
    ('Every human being of adult years and sound mind has a right to
    determine what shall be done with his own body.' per Cardozo, J.)

98 Harvey, (1967) 30 *Mod. L. R.* 591, 593.

99 Daube, *Ethics in Medical Progress*, London: Churchill, 1966, p.195.

100 T.B. Smith, 'Law and the human body: the relevance of consent,'
    Address to the Royal College of Surgeons, Edinburgh, 17 November
    1967;

101 See Von Bubnoff, 'Rechtsfragen zur homologen Organtransplanta-
    tion aus der Sicht des Strafrechts,' *Goltdammer's Archiv fur Strafrecht*
    65–81 (1968).

102 The cases are reported and discussed in Curran, 'A problem of
    consent: kidney transplantation in minors,' 34 *New York Univ. L.R.*
    891 (1959).

103 Lord Kilbrandon, 'The human body and the law,' paper presented to
    Univ.of Aberdeen Law Society, 26 Feb. 1968, p.12.

104 Daube, *Ethics in Medical Progress*, p.198.

105 Freund, 'Ethical problems in human experimentation,' 273 *New
    Eng.J. Med.* 687, 691 (1965).

106 126 F.2d 121 (D.C.Cir. 1941).

107 See discussion on treatment of children and consent in Chapter 6,
    supra.

108 Curran, *op. cit.*, p.893.; see Note, 'Cumpulsory medical treatment
    and the free exercise of religion,' *Ind. L.J.* 386 (1967).

109 Duff, 'Guidlines for Deciding Care of Critically Ill or Dying Patients,'
    in Shannon (ed.), *Bioethics* (3d ed), p.141.

110 Olser, 'In two minds about the same kidney,' *The Times*, 28 April
    1968, p.10.; In the case of *Lawse v. University of Iowa Hospitals* (1988,
    Iowa App.) 434 NW 2d 895, a living kidney donor brought an action
    against the hospital and physician for wrongful removal, claiming he
    was not properly advised of the risks of removal and was in fact
    coerced into consenting to the removal to save the life of his brother.
    The matter was ruled barred by the statute of limitations. Plaintiff
    donated a kidney to his brother which was not successful. His remain-
    ing kidney failed and he required a cadaver donor kidney.
        The court pointed out there was some concern whether or not a
    donor can give informed consent to the removal of a kidney for a

relative because of the pressures involved and that perhaps a higher standard of voluntaryness for organ donation then for therapeutic medical procedures because of this potential for duress should be applied. Page 897. No ruling was made on this issue.

111 Nielubowicz (Warsaw), in 7 *International Federation of Surgical Colleges News Bulletin* 20 (May 1967).
112 See discussion on Consent to Medical Treatment in Chapter 5, *supra*.
113 *Sidaway v. Bethlem Royal Hospital* (1985) 2 W.L.R. 480 (H.L.).
114 *Gold v. Haringey Health Authority* (1987) 3 W.L.R. 649 (C.A.).
115 (1985) 2 W.L.R. 480, at 505 (Lord Bridge).
116 *Cobbs v. Grant* (1972) 8 Cal. 3d 229.
117 *Canterbury v. Spence* (1972, D.C. Cir.) 464 Fed. 2d 772; *Cobbs v. Grant, supra*; *Harnish v. Children's Hosp. Med.Ctr.* (1982, Mass.) 439 N.E. 2d 240.
118 *Crain v. Allison* (1982, D.C. App.) 443 A. 2d 558, 561.
119 Norrie, 34 *The Internat'l. & Comp. L. Quart.* 442,451 (1985).
120 The number may be as low as 1 in 25,000 in the U.K.
121 *The Christian Science Monitor*, 29 March 1988, p.32.
122 Harrison, 'Organ Procurement for Children: The Anencephalic Fetus As Donor,' 1976 *The Lancet* 1383–85.
123 *Ethical Currents*, No. 14, Spring, 1988, 'Searching for Organs,' pp.1, 2.
124 Capron, 'anencephalic donors: separate the dead from the dying' *Hastings Ctr. Rpt.* 17(1), 1987, pp.5–8.
125 261 *J.Am. Med. Assn.* 1773 (1989).
126 See discussion in Chapters 1 & 2, *supra*.
127 1988 *The Lancet* 1119.
128 Brahams, 'Fetal Spare Parts' 1988 *The Lancet* 424; But see 1988 *The Lancet* i, 1005 ('we should not try to dress up the abortion by hiding it in a cloak of respectability and saying it will do some good.')
129 *Santa Barbara News-Press*, 30 March 1989, p.A7.
130 *Wall St. Journal*, 7 November 1988, p.1.
131 J. Rostand, 'Pensees d'un biologiste' (1939), quoted by Hamburger, *Ethics in Medical Progress*, p.134.
132 'Transplantation: The Ethical Delemmas' *Transplant*, Vol.5, No.4 (fall, 1987), p.1.
133 Sanders and Dukeminier, 'Medical advance and legal lag: hemodialysis and kidney transplantion,' 15 *U.C.L.A. L.Rev.* 357, 371 (1968).
134 Schneiderman and Spragg, 318 *N. Eng. J. Med.* 988 (1988)
135 Schreiner, *Ethics in Medical Progress*, pp.127, 130.
136 Brahams, 1989 *The Lancet* 285.
137 Lord Kilbrandon has suggested similar legislation along these lines; his rough draft is as follows:
    'Any person of full age and capacity may consent, in writing, to any medical or surgical treatment which is to be carried out in a designated hospital, provided that the risks attendant thereon are not excessive and notwithstanding that the treatment is not being carried out for the benefit of the person himself.'
    (*Ethics in Medical Progress*, pp. 213–14.)
138 Lord Kilbrandon, the Scottish jurist and chairman of the Scottish

Law Commission, has, once again, provided us with the rough statutory framework:

'In any designated hospital it shall be lawful to remove from a dead
person any organ required for medical or scientific purposes unless
the hospital authorities have reason to believe that the deceased in his
lifetime had forbidden this to be done, provided that such removal
shall not disfigure the dead body.'

Ethics in Medical Progress, p.158.

139 Daube, *Ethics in Medical Progress*, p. 192. Would the removal of an
eye, for example, be considered to 'disfigure' the corpse?

140 Public Law 99–509.

141 AB 631, 'Required Consent Law.'

142 'Giving Families the Option', Queen of the Valley Hosp., *Physician*,
Summer, 1989. p.8.

8

Transsexualism

A. INTRODUCTION

Transsexualism,[1] is a little understood term. Medical comment is sparse, and there is little legal comment on transsexualism. A handful of judicial decisions have dealt with transsexuals over the past 30 years.

What does this infrequently heard term mean? Transsexualism has been called a 'split between the psychological and the morphological sex,'[2] 'a female personality in a male body.'[3] The individual concerned, in most cases a male,[4] has an intense, usually obsessive desire for a complete sexual transformation: physically, mentally, legally and socially.[5] Contrary to the transvestite, who merely desires to, and is gratified by, 'enacting' the woman's role by dressing himself in woman's clothes, the transsexual wants to 'be' a woman, to function like a woman and to be accepted as a woman; dressing as a woman is only one means to this end.[6] Some feel that the urge of the transsexual male to be 'all woman' may in fact be the result of a rather shallow and distorted view of what a woman is really like socially, sexually, anatomically and emotionally,[7] but in severe cases there is no doubt it presents medicine a very complex challenge to effectively treat.

The male transsexual has the feeling of 'being in reality a woman,'[8] whom nature by some cruel mistake has burdened and embarrassed with male genitalia. His visible sex organs are objects of disgust and deformity. Consequently, he 'only lives for the day when his hated sex organs can be removed.'[9] So long as they live with these male organs, transsexuals are miserable, morbidly longing for the 'conversion' surgery which they think will make them look as they really should. If such conversion surgery is not readily available, which is common, owing to the controversial nature and legal uncertainty that surrounds the operation(s),[10] the transsexual may well attempt self-castration, other mutilations and even suicide, or fall into a reactive psychosis.[11] Such self-abuse is apparently not at all rare.[12]

The so-called 'conversion' surgery sought so obsessively by true transsexuals actually consists of several operative procedures. Normally, however, these are advised in severe cases and then only after other less drastic measures, including psychiatric and hormonal treatment of the patient, has failed.[13] The patient is required to dress and live as if a woman for an extended period, often a year or more, before surgery. Although the problem is not physiological, but psychological-psychosexual, for severe cases there appear to be no satisfactory curative methods currently at the disposal of psychiatry;[14] it is felt that the transsexual's mind 'cannot be adjusted to [accept] the body.'[15]

If psychiatric and hormonal treatment is ruled out as ineffectual, or prescribed along with surgery, the operation may – barring legal complications – be carried out. It involves castration, peotomy, perhaps formation of the scrotum into female, labia-like folds by plastic surgery, and even may include[16] formation of an artificial vagina by inlay grafting.

Once the surgery has been performed, it is far from a foregone conclusion that the patient's problems and anxieties will be solved. That conversion surgery will bring relief to the patient is true; that it will bring lasting relief is quite another matter. The subject's feminization cravings may continue and meet tragic frustration in the realization that he or 'she' cannot acquire child-bearing ability, but has accomplished only a change in the secondary sex characteristics.[17] Some patients demand the implantation of ovaries or a uterus, thinking they can thus become capable of pregnancy.

The incidence of transsexualism, while difficult to estimate, is clearly low.[18] Nonetheless, an estimated 2,000 patients have received surgical treatment under the National Health Service in Britain and perhaps 3,000 to 6,000 in the United States.

The most publicized transsexual case was probably that of Christine Jorgensen, a young man who went to Denmark shortly after 1950 and eventually succeeded in undergoing conversion surgery for 'change-of-sex.' A thorough report of her case was published by her attending physician,[19] who operated only after insuring freedom from legal liability. This brought attention to a very unfortunate disorder, fortunately suffered by only a few.

With a transsexual the influence of psychologic sex on normally evident biologic sex must be evaluated. The intent is to determine what sex predominates. This is often complicated by the existence of no less than eight recognized criteria of sex: chromosomal sex, gonadal sex, sex hormone pattern, internal sex organs, genital sex, *habitus*, assigned sex and sex role.[20] The first two of these criteria are normally thought to be critical in determining ultimate gender identity.[21] The law has generally considered these indicia of biologic sex to control.

Chromosomal sex results from conception, when the female egg or ovum (X) is fertilized by the male sperm (X or Y). The Y chromosome exists only in the male. However, many consider chromosomal sex not dispositive due to the effects of other factors: genetic, endocrinal, body configurational, psychologic and environmental.

Gonadal sex refers to the evident reproductive sex glands. It is consistent with chromosomal sex (ovaries in XX; testes in XY). Where both ovaries and testes develop in the individual, he or she is a hermaphrodite.

Sex hormone pattern refers to the hormones produced by testes or ovaries which produce male or female gender characteristics. They can be produced in abnormal amounts.

The internal sex organs are not determined until after three months gestation *in utero*. They can develop in a manner inconsistent with external sex characteristics.

Genital sex refers to the external sex organs or genitalia. The *habitus*, or secondary sex characteristics, refers to bodily form and appearance (phenotype).

Sex role is the intangible, psychological aspect of sexual identity. It is always inconsistent with genital sex and normally with chromosomal sex in the transsexual. This is the cause of the transsexual's mental torment and longing for sex reassignment or conversion surgery.

Transsexuals have raised issues not previously established in the law. The precedents are relatively few on both sides of the Atlantic. First we look at the United States.

B.   UNITED STATES

Transsexual surgery is more common today than it once was. In the 1950s Christine Jorgenson, now deceased, but still probably the most publicized case, had to travel to Denmark for surgery. It has been estimated that some 3,000 to 6,000 adults have undergone hormonal and surgical sex changes in the United States. Another 30,000 to 60,000 consider themselves candidates but medical and psychological selection criteria disqualify all but a few. There may be 10,000 transsexuals in the United States today.[22]

In the United States of the 1950s, the traditional legal climate towards transsexualism and attendant conversion surgery could be summarized by saying that,

'in the strict sense of the word, there are no laws concerning either transvestism or the various medical aspects concerned with sex transformation. But this fact in no way prevents or nullifies the popular conception that everything connected with this subject is illegal in this country.[23]

This 'popular conception' of illegality no longer obtains. While transsexualism has had a short legal history, a number of states – by legislative or judicial action – have dealt with it in recent years. The social and legal system seems to tolerate it as unfortunate, but perhaps necessary in rare cases. Absent harm to others, it is unlikely to be held criminal or proscribed by the law. A number of transsexual surgeries have occurred and, as in Britain, no criminal prosecutions of doctors or patients have been reported. The law has not been anxious to intervene in this intensely personal and compelling matter.

The first American judicial authority[2] dealing with transsexualism involved the issue of sex registration, not the legality of the surgical procedures themselves. Petitioner had apparently been able to undergo conversion surgery and assume the name and role of a woman in society without legal restriction. The New York City Board of Health had referred the question of whether it should grant such a change of sex registration to the New York Academy of Medicine. The Academy report decided not to follow the lead of the ten states which had permitted similar registration changes. It stated that 'male-to-female transsexuals are still chromosomally males while ostensibly females,' apparently considering the chromosomal criterion of sex dispositive. The Academy questioned whether it was the wisest course to cater to the transsexual's needs by granting him a legal female's status. It stated:

> 'it is questionable whether laws and records such as the birth certificate should be changed and thereby used as a means to help psychologically ill persons in their social adaptation.
>
> ... The desire of concealment of a change of sex by the transsexual is out-weighed by the public interest for protection against fraud.
>
> ... Sex can be changed where there is an error of course, but not when there is a later attempt to change psychological orientation of the patient and including such surgery as goes with it.

The New York Board of Health accepted and incorporated the Academy of Medicine's reported conclusions in denying petitioner's request. The Court upheld the Board's action as being within its administrative discretion.

The difficult question, which was not considered by the Board of Health or by the Court in the *Weiner* case, is by what criteria it is determined that 'an error' has been made in sex classification. Before it can be determined whether an individual has been assigned improperly to one sex or the other at birth, a greater consensus on what constitutes the determinative criteria of sexual status must be reached, if in fact such a consensus is possible in light of the numerous and varied factors that are recognized to be influential in determining an individual's sex.

The decisions in the United States since this early case can be broken down into several categories. These generally include: legality of surgery, testing for and determination of sexual status, revising birth certificates, ability to marry, divorce and annulment, child custody and visitation, and discrimination.

1. *Legality of sex-reassignment surgery*

The legality of 'transsexual' or 'conversion' or 'sex-reassignment' surgery is well-established, although no appellate courts appear to have expressly addressed the issue. Those courts that have considered other implications of the surgery have not questioned its legality.[24] This, along with no statutes prohibiting the surgery, is strongly persuasive of its legality, provided it is performed for therapeutic purposes by a licensed physician. As in Britain, abortion stands out as the only surgical procedure proscribed by the criminal law.

While at one time it was common for American transsexuals to travel abroad for surgery, that is no longer true. One noted surgeon in Casablanca, for example, had alone performed some 700 procedures by 1974.[25] This is no longer true and physicians in a number of centers may perform the procedure on appropriate therapeutic indications. Times have clearly changed from 1954 when one commentator observed that,

'there is hardly a district attorney in the country who would not inform a doctor that it would be illegal for the doctor to perform such an operation.'[23]

No doctors have been charged with criminal wrongdoing or prosecuted for performing sex reassignment surgery for therapeutic purposes. Nor have any patients been prosecuted for doing so.

The risk of civil liability of the physician is likely greater. There is legal risk in performing this surgery because it is severely mutilating and irreversible. Probably the most significant legal risk, presuming performance by a licensed surgeon based on clinically established grounds and after other, less severe treatment options have proved unsuccessful, is failure to obtain the patient's informed consent to the surgery, or failure to fully and properly evaluate the suitability of this drastic treatment for the particular patient involved.[26] While more pronounced, these are risks that are not uncommon to other invasive or complicated surgery. However, as with other operations we have considered involving the human reproductive system or capacity, feelings for regulation, or even prohibition are not uncommon.

Conversion surgery, because of its irreversible and severe consequences, is treatment of last resort. Psychotherapy is attempted, but is ineffectual in severe cases.[27] Hormonal-endocrinal therapy is utilized. Commonly, the transsexual is required to dress, act and live as if a woman for an extended period of time prior to surgery.[28] A year is not unusual.[29]

Where the patient is not competent to give an informed consent to medical treatment, conversion surgery could not be legally performed without prior court approval. It is likely a court would require clear and convincing proof the surgery was necessary to protect the best interests (physical, mental or emotional health) of the patient and that other, less invasive forms of treatment were ineffectual. Cases dealing with sterilization of an incompetent patient offer the best analogy to the legal requirements that would likely be imposed.[30]

2. *Determination of sexual status*

As discussed earlier, there are no less than eight recognized criteria for determining sex. Normally sex is determined by physical examination immediately following birth. Normally it appears evident from external genitalia and primary sex characteristics. The transsexual will have the genitalia of his or her biological gender. Normally chromosomal makeup will be consistent with genital sex. The transsexual born a female will have the XX female sex chromosome, not the XY male sex chromosome. The Y chromosome controls the development of the male testes and the production of male androgen hormones.

As pointed out by one physician with substantial experience in performing conversion surgery,

> 'I don't change men into women. I transform male genitals into genitals that have a female aspect. All the rest is in the patient's mind.'[26]

The New York City Health Department, in adopting rules allowing transsexuals to make certain changes in their birth certificates (changing name, but leaving sex blank), concluded that conversion surgery is really a form of psychotherapy, a means of setting the patient's mind at ease without changing the body cells that govern sexuality.[31]

The English decision in *Corbett*[32] concluded sex must be determined by what it termed biological criteria: chromosomal, gonadal and genital. However, several American decisions have departed from this approach. In a New Jersey case, the court found that sex reassignment surgery had 'harmonized' the gender and genitalia of a male transsexual born with male physical characteristics.[33] The court concluded that since the person was 'physically and psychologically unified and fully capable of sexual activity as a woman,' she was legally a female for marriage and spousal support obligations. The judge in *Corbett* had found that sex reassignment surgery was not capable of producing a female 'naturally capable of performing the essential role of a woman in marriage.'[34]

In a similar decision to that of the New Jersey court involving the well-known tennis player Dr. Renee Richards, a New York court found the requirement of a chromosomal test unnecessary to determine sexual status.[22] The U.S. Tennis Association sought to prevent Dr. Richards from competing as a female without passing a newly-adopted Barr body or sex-chromatin test to ascertain the existence of the XX female sex chromosome. Historically the Association had relied upon a phenotype test (observation of primary and secondary sexual characteristics) to determine sex.

The court found the imposition of the newly-adopted test discriminatory, unfair and legally improper. Dr. Richards had 'her' male sex organs removed, an artificial vagina fashioned by plastic surgery and endocrine therapy. The court concluded,

> 'When an individual such as Plaintiff, a successful physician, a husband and father, finds it necessary for his own mental sanity to undergo a sex reassignment, the unfounded fears and misconceptions of Defendants must give way to the overwhelming medical evidence that this person is now female.'[35]

Despite these rulings, most courts continue to hold sex as a biological phenomenon and to limit or deny female rights of birth certificate registration and marriage to male transsexuals.[36] Most feel that if changes in the criteria for determination of sex, or in the sexual rights of transsexuals are to occur, they should most appropriately come as a matter of social policy from the legislatures, not the courts.

3. *Revision of birth certificates*

Several state laws, including Arizona, Louisiana and Illinois, permit the birth record of a transsexual to be changed following sex reassignment surgery. Another twelve states have permitted by administrative or judicial action the same result. New York City, following study of the problem by the Academy of Medicine, permitted the transsexual to file a new birth certificate with a changed name, but with the sexual identity left blank, rather than changed, after proof of convertive surgery.[37] In upholding this policy, a New York court concluded that, 'the desire of concealment of a change of sex by the transsexual is outweighed by the public interest for protection against fraud.'[38]

Other courts addressing the issue have denied changes to the birth certificate on the basis that only errors made at the time of entry at birth may be corrected. The transsexual is normally classified correctly at birth, unless issues of true hermaphroditism are involved. Thus, sex reassignment surgery later in life does not change the accuracy of the original birth certificate entry.[39] This is not to say that the legislature cannot change this by statute if desired as a matter of social policy.

4. *Ability to marry*

Marriage is regulated by statute. For example, a typical provision is,

> 'Male persons of the age of eighteen, and female persons of the age of sixteen years, not nearer of kin than second cousins, and not having a husband or wife living, may be joined in marriage.'[40]

Thus, to be married, the couple must be of opposite sex. The majority U.S. view is that the male to female transsexual remains a male for marriage purposes and cannot marry another male.[41] However, a minority recognizes the right to marry where conversion surgery creates the ability for sexual relations (from male to female) and the physical appearance and psychological orientation are one.[33]

5. *Divorce and annulment*

At common law consummation of the marriage was recognized as necessary to create a legally binding relationship. Where, because a male transsexual has undergone female sex reassignment surgery, there is no ability to consummate a marriage, it may be annulled as a nullity. Some courts have gone so far as to say that public policy recognizes a marriage for the purpose of begetting children.[42] The concept here is survival of the species, with marriage as the vehicle to ensure it. However, procreation can obviously occur without marriage and many may see the interpersonal bonds of love and support as the basis for marriage, from which procreation may result, but need not for the validity of the legal relationship.

Marriage being recognized as a contract between a man and a woman, two of the same sex may not form a legal union unless legislation permits it as in Denmark and Sweden.[43] Thus, in the U.S., if one is not considered of the opposite sex of the spouse, even after convertive surgery, annulment will be granted.[42,44]

However, in those cases where the court has accepted sex reassignment surgery as effecting a valid change of sex, marriage will be permitted, as well as the divorce and support rights which flow from it.[33] Until a consensus on the criteria of sexual identity and how to apply them is reached, courts can be expected to *continue* to reach different results on these issues. This will depend on the strength of the evidence offered in some cases,[45] on the court's assessment of the purpose and function of marriage in other cases.[32,42]

6. *Child custody and visitation*

Child custody and visitation is legally established at or after divorce based on the best interests of the child, not on the wishes of the parents.[46] If it is concluded that the parent's behavior will be harmful to the child, custody and even visitation can be denied by the court acting for the welfare of the child. In the case of *Daly v. Daly*,[47] the Nevada Supreme Court upheld the decision of a trial judge to terminate the parental rights of a transsexual father to have any further visitation rights with his 10 year old daughter from a former marriage. The child had developed serious emotional problems and behavioral abnormalities after being told by her father that he was a transsexual and intended to undergo sex reassignment surgery to become a woman. The dissent in the case pointed out that it was not appropriate to sever the father's parental tie to his daughter, even though visitation at least at the time, was not advised. The dissenting opinion concluded,[48]

'In psychological distress, the father has consulted legitimate and respected medical authorities. The advice given by those medical authorities may offend the religious precepts of many. In the ultimate judgment of history, such advice may well yet be condemned as quackery. Still, I respectfully submit that a court of law should not stigmatize an emotionally distressed person for following the advice of highly trained and licensed physicians, who are practicing medicine under government authority, and who possess the most exalted credential their profession can bestow. Nor should any parent be stigmatized for attempting to forewarn a child concerning medical procedures the parent is about to undergo pursuant to such advice.

... As I assess the record, the fact that the appellant father has suffered emotional problems which are foreign to the experience of this court's members, and has followed the possibly poor advice of eminent medical authorities in his attempt to relieve them, does not justify a total and irrevocable severance of appellant's formal legal tie to a child he obviously cares about and desires to help nurture. By holding that such a severance is justified in these facts, it seems to me, we are being unnecessarily and impermissibly punitive to the exercise of a medical option we personally find offensive, thereby depriving a child of a legal relationship which might well be to the child's advantage in the future.'

The case points out the strong emotional element present in many of the legal decisions dealing with transsexuals. The fact that many find this very unfortunate malady abhorrent undoubtedly has influenced a good number of the relatively few cases to deal with the rights of the transsexual. The risk of unequal treatment remains great.

7. *Transsexualism and discrimination*

As mentioned, the transsexual may be at risk of prosecution merely for dressing and acting as a woman. Many statutes prohibit this. For example,

'No person shall appear upon a public street . . . in a dress not belonging to his or her sex, or in an indecent or lewd dress.'[49]

While rarely enforced, they remain a source of potential liability or, more likely perhaps, harassment and discrimination in the case of transsexuals. For example, in one case a transvestite or transsexual was arrested and charged with prostitution and criminal impersonation for dressing as a woman.[50] The impersonation charge was dismissed, the court finding that mere cross-dressing was not sufficient to support such a criminal charge. Rather, it had to be accompanied by a criminal intent, an intent to deceive, to be a crime.

In the case of Dr. Renee Richards,[45] the evidence made it clear that the U.S. Tennis Association had created a new sex identification test, the sex-chromatin test, for tournament play qualification, which was specifically aimed at preventing her from competing as a woman. The court found it to be arbitrary and discriminatory where the medical evidence was that Dr. Richards was anatomically like a woman after hysterectomy and ovariectomy and should be classified as female. However, it has not been uncommon to use sex chromosome tests in athletics for years, which makes the result in the case at least arguably less compelling. One can recall, for example, certain Eastern Bloc female shotputters having to pass such tests as pre-Olympic Games qualification more than two decades ago.

It can be argued that no discrimination exists in such cases if one accepts conversion surgery does not change sexual identity, but rather only changes primary and external sexual characteristics to match psychosexual orientation of the individual. As stated by Committee on Public Health of the New York Academy of Medicine in its report entitled, 'Change of Sex on Birth Certificates for Transsexuals,' 'male-to-female transsexuals are still chromosomally males while ostensibly females.'[51] This of course brings us back to where we started: what is it that should determine the sexual identity of a person. Medicine and the courts seem no farther forward on this in 1990 from what they were in 1970 when *The Human Body and the Law* was first published.

Despite the somewhat harsh results in some of these cases, it is probably fair to say that a considerable amount of tolerance exists in these unfortunate cases if no harm to another is threatened by fraud or otherwise. Dr. Harry Benjamin, reporting some years ago on the performance of forty-four conversion operations, noted that twelve of the subjects had since been married, some had divorced, and one had been granted a legal child adoption.[1] Whether full disclosure of assigned sex at birth was made to marriage partner or to judge in all these cases seems doubtful in light of the later cases discussed above.

Two other practitioners have reported on several interesting, but unreported and unappealed cases involving transsexuals.[23] In one, a man underwent conversion surgery in Mexico and subsequently filed a petition for change of his name and civil status in a California court. The court denied the petition. In another California case, a similar petition was granted. However, the facts were unusual in that petitioner therein had a birth certificate made out in the name of 'Baby S...' and bore no given name. Furthermore, the county recorder was willing to register the new name and stated sex, so resort to the court was made unnecessary. In still another case, the individual was apparently able to obtain a change in name, though no action was taken by the court with reference to change of the person's sex registration. Another individual is reported to have been granted a United

States passport in his female role and characterization, once his physician had written to the proper government authorities recommending such action.

In a Baltimore, Maryland, case,[52] the judge issued a court order to have a sex change operation performed on a seventeen-year-old transsexual boy. He also relieved the surgeon of any criminal liability. This action followed repeated delinquency by the boy (such as stealing wigs for personal use). The surgical application for the operation was strongly supported by his parents, the probation officer concerned, and a noted Johns Hopkins University psychologist. As discussed in Chapter 6, only a clear finding of best interests could support such a decision.

The U.S. is now a society much more accepting of unorthodox dress, appearance, and lifestyles. Patient autonomy has few restrictions unless harm to another can be shown.[53] If the surgery is deemed necessary to treat the patient, after other less invasive procedures have failed, it is consistent with prevailing medical practice, and the patient has given an informed consent,[26,54] the court is unlikely to intervene. Prohibition would have to come from the legislatures, which have not seen fit to meddle in this area. While little used mayhem statutes might be stretched to apply, this has not occurred and should not under the circumstances mentioned.

While the threat of prosecution is restrictive, it is clearly not prohibitive of either physician or patient involvement where the surgeon feels sufficient medical indication exists. Nonetheless, it is probably true that most surgeons would not perform or approve of the conversion operation for fear of professional or social criticism or legal liability. While other doctors may be willing, they may not get permission from their hospital boards for what remains a controversial surgery.[51,55] There are other inhibiting factors from the patients perspective, including fear of adverse publicity or social stigma, the cost involved, and the complicated nature of the surgery, which often involves considerable pain, lengthy hospitalization and convalescence.

C. ENGLAND

There are no statutes which regulate the legality of conversion surgery for transsexuals in England. The matter is one, like most medicine,[56] left to the discretion of physician and patient. No judicial decisions have sought to outlaw the practice. In fact, it is known that such surgery does occur. As mentioned, this includes some 2,000 cases performed by the National Health Service.[57] Professor Williams does not believe transsexual surgery raises problems of legality, despite the fact it may involve removal of the sex organs.[58]

English courts have only recognized a biological definition of sex, not a psychological one. Thus, in the *Corbett* case[59] a converted transsexual was held not to be a woman for purposes of validating a marriage, the court noting that the marriage could not be consummated with an artificial vagina. The judge concluded,

> 'Having regard to the essentially heterosexual character of the relationship which is called marriage, the criteria must, in my judgment, be biological, for even the most extreme degree of transsexualism in a male or the most severe hormonal imbalance which can exist in a person with male chromosomes, male gonads and male genitalia, cannot reproduce a person who is naturally capable of performing the essential role of a woman in marriage. In other words, the law should adopt in the first place, the first three of the doctors' criteria, i.e. the chromosomal, gonadal and genital tests, and if all three are congruent, determine the sex for the purpose of marriage accordingly, and ignore any operative intervention.'

Similarly, in the *Rees*[57] case, decided more recently by the European Court of Human Rights, concluded that a transsexual registered at birth as a female based on female biological characteristics could not marry another female under U.K. laws. The court held that the right to marry granted to men and women under Article 12 of the European Convention for the Protection of Human Rights and Fundamental Freedoms referred to the traditional marriage between persons of opposite biological sex.

There are those who feel biological sex should not be the criterion used to prohibit transsexual marriage, if the essential, non-procreative function of marriage to love and support each other exists.[60] For example, in May, 1989, the Danish Parliament, following the Swedish example in 1988, passed legislation allowing homosexual couples to marry and to acquire all marital rights except for adoption of children and recognition by the state Lutheran Church.[43] Opponents called the law 'contrary to nature.'

In another English case the husband was granted a divorce based on his wife's refusal to have sex and dressing as a man.[61] The wife was apparently a transvestite. Another husband was granted annulment where his wife's hermaphroditism had prevented formation of a normal vagina and consummation was evidently not possible.[62] The uncertainly of the law in this area is illustrated by a case where a transsexual woman was treated as a 'man' for national insurance registration, but as a woman for sex discrimination claims.[63]

The main concern of the law in this area should be to avoid concealment or other confusion. If a transsexual is allowed, for example, to change his sex on his birth certificate, third parties could be misled. As the European Court of Human Rights pointed out in the *Rees* case, if such a change was allowed third parties 'would be deprived of information which they had a legitimate interest to receive.[57] At the same time, sensitivity to accommodating the severe medical and psychological needs of those few transsexuals is necessary and proper to the greatest extent possible, so long as no harm is done to others as a result.

What of the legality of the procedure itself? While a matter of informed consent and sound clinical judgment in the case of a competent patient, prior court approval would undoubtedly be required where there exists an inability to give a knowing consent.

In a recent decision, the House of Lords upheld the right of physicians to provide treatment to adult incompetents without their consent if it is deemed to be in their best interests.[64] Lord Griffiths in his concurring opinion pointed out that there was a limit to the physical harm to which a person could lawfully consent. He cited the examples of outlawed bare-knuckle prize fighting[65] and suicide.[66] He believed sterilization of an incompetent could only be performed with the consent of a high court judge. The majority in the case did not feel such judicial approval was legally compelled, but did feel it was 'highly desirable from a 'good practice' point of view. The effect is the same. It is clear from this case that it would be bad practice and unwise for a practitioner to perform sterilisation, and even more so conversion surgery, on an incompetent without prior court approval, even if felt to be clearly in his best interests.

If supported by informed consent and sound medical advice, conversion surgery can undoubtedly be lawfully performed. The Crown has not chosen to challenge the 2,000 or more surgeries reported to have occurred. The legislature has not sought to intervene. Thus, while controversial, with strong moral overtones, the procedure of conversion surgery appears to be lawful if its advisability for the welfare of the patient is supported by reasonable clinical judgment exercising prevailing standards of good medical care.[67]

D. SCOTLAND

In Scotland, as in England, there is little relevant material on transsexualism. Stair,[68] in his classic coverage of Scots law mentions hermaphroditism only incidentally while discussing the validity of marriage, characterizing it as a condition, 'where the one sex doth not eminently predominate.' The only early commentator on Scots Law who mentions the problem of sex classification is Forbes, who in his 'little known and not very authoritative'[69] text states:

> 'The Sex is Male, or Female, or Hermaphrodite, i.e. both Male and Female, which is esteemed to be of that Sex which is most Prevailing in the Person.'[70]

The hermaphrodite has conflicting biologic sex characteristics and is often not a transsexual. Forbes apparently relied on Justinian's Digest for his statement of Scots Law, which ascribed the more beneficial sex of male to those of doubtful sexual identity at birth.[71]

The issue of 'true hermaphroditism' has been considered in modern times in Scotland. It arose in an unreported case decided by a single judge which involved an individual originally (at birth) registered as female, but whose sexual identity had been subsequently ordered changed to male in 'The Register of Corrected Entries.'[72] Later it became necessary because of third party interests to seek judicial determination of this individual's sex. The judge was referred to a number of old authorities, none of which were in point on the question of how to determine sex. One, Sanchez,[73] had suggested that in cases of true hermaphroditism, where male and female characteristics were equally existent in the person, 'he' should be able to make a final and irrevocable choice as to preferred sexual status. Rejecting such a suggestion and following civilian thought in this area, the Scots judge concluded that public policy and the law required him to hold that all persons born are either male or female,[74] but recognized that a true hermaphrodite might at least arguably be considered of both sexes and therefore legally of neither, necessitating a third sexual category for these rare cases, if and when they could be determined.

The judge called upon medical evidence, which suggested four fundamental criteria of sex: chromosomal, gonadal, apparent or phenotypal and psychological. The individual concerned allegedly possessed the normal female chromosome constitution (46XX), testicular as well as ovarian tissue, predominantly female-appearing (though predominantly male-functioning) genitalia and generally male psychosexual attitudes. After weighing these medical considerations, the judge concluded that though the party involved was a so-called true hermaphrodite, male characteristics prevailed. Thus, he should be allocated to the male sex.

There is one reported Scottish case dealing with an alleged transsexual, *X Petitioner*.[75] It involved a petition brought under s.63 of the Registration of Births, Deaths and Marriages (Scotland) Act of 1954, requesting alteration of petitioner's name and sex as it appeared on the Register from male to female. X was the father of two, but was separated from his wife, his feminine characteristics having caused a breakdown of the marriage. While raised as a male, he had long since been a transvestite, had developed feminine breasts and had atrophied male genitalia. At the time the petition was brought he was quite happy to act like a woman. The petition was denied, s.63 being interpreted to allow only changes of entries originally entered incorrectly, not incorrect because of alleged changes in sex subsequent to registry at birth.

If for no other reason than the infrequency of judicial pronouncement in this area, the Sheriff's words are worth quoting. He concluded:[75]

> 'The doctors are careful to stress that this is not a case of hermaphrodism, but is a genuine case of the very rare condition of transsexualism and that the changes which have taken place are quite irreversible.

For the present purpose, I, of course, accept that diagnosis. It is, however, stated that skin and blood tests still show X's basic sex to be a male and that the changes have not yet reached the deepest level of sex determination. It seems to be accordingly that while X could be described as an abnormal male, it would not be possible to describe him as a female.

X Petitioner had registered a change of name to a female form in the Books of Council and Session. He was apparently permitted by the British Medical Association to appear by this name on this register of qualified medical practitioners. Judicial sanction was, however, not needed or sought for this action.

In discussing the case, Professor Smith has expressed the thought that if expert medical opinion of sufficient repute supported a petitioner's claim that sexual identity really should be changed, the Court of Session might by its power of declarator recognize such a change of sexual status.[76] At present, this appears unlikely to happen, particularly as to any National Health Service operation. Such a change in sex might be supported by expert medical opinion, either because sex had been originally misappraised or because an individual without clear-cut gender identity (hermaphroditic gender identity) had made the relatively easier 'shift' from one side of the sexual identity line to the other.[74] None of the eight earlier mentioned criteria of sex are absolutely dispositive of the issue, and due to their predominantly physiological nature, it is difficult to imagine a change of sex so convincing as to gain 'unquestionable' medical support. However, medical science may yet discover a single criterion, dispositive of true sexual identity.

While the Scottish supreme court in civil matters, the Court of Session, might sanction a change of sexual status, to the satisfaction and relief of a petitioning transsexual, it is also possible that the Scottish supreme court in criminal matters, the High Court of Justiciary, could use its declaratory power to define new crimes to hold the performance of conversion surgery criminal. The fact that both these courts are composed of the same judges obviously lessens the likelihood of this occurring. Still, the arguably indecent or criminal aspects of the severe demembration involved in such demasculinizing surgery might be considered to contravene prevailing standards of decency, the patient's consent and psychosexual craving for the operation notwithstanding.[77]

At common law only abortion has been held criminal among surgical operations. It, however, involves taking the potential life of another. Scots and English law have never held any other surgery performed on an individual for therapeutic purposes criminal.

Severe symptoms may call for severe remedies and on occasion conversion surgery is medically indicated and has been carried out in Scotland without legal challenge. This is not likely to change. Of course, patient consent and surgeon's care are always issues as in any other surgeries. It should be borne in mind that the physician, operating under bona fide standards and credentials in Scotland, is given very wide discretion by the law. As Dr. Gordon has put it,

> 'In practice, however, there is a very wide umbrella which covers all surgical operations performed by recognized doctors in accordance with accepted medical procedures. . . .
>
> The only exception in practice to the protection afforded to surgical operations is where the operation itself is illegal and the only example of such an operation which has so far been considered by the common law is abortion.'[78]

And so, as in England, the legal right of the transsexual in Scotland to therapeutic treatment by conversion surgery, when supported by reputable medical opinion, seems clear. What is far from likely is the right to change sexual status in the eyes of the law for birth or marriage. This appears most unlikely. The right to change sexual status is limited by traditional legal and social notions of sex as a biologically-defined phenomenon. Traditional morality and avoidance of fraud or deceit underpin the generally unsympathetic attitude of the courts.

E.   CONCLUSIONS

Given the strong moral overtones and the rare incidence of transsexualism, any change in existing law seems unlikely. Sexual status will in all likelihood continue to be defined in most instances biologically. New genetic research may uncover a more conclusive means of ascertaining 'true' sexual status. However, given the many facets that combine to create sexual identity, this seems unlikely. The psychological element cannot be overlooked.

When all other treatment fails, conversion surgery may be deemed necessary and it should be viewed as other serious surgery. When medically indicated and undertaken with the informed consent of the competent patient, or for the best interests of the incompetent patient following judicial review and approval,[25] it should not be unlawful. The patient should be supported to the greatest extent legally possible, without causing harm or any material deception to others.

The interest of the law in England, Scotland and the U.S. has been principally to recognize only male or female sexual identity, not to permit change of sex registration on birth certificates or other important records that could deceive others relying upon them and to deny same sex marriage even if sex reassignment surgery has occurred. However, we have seen the cases reach mixed and at times conflicting results, depending on the evidence presented and perhaps the personal views of the judge. Otherwise, the law has elected to largely stay out of the picture.

It seems that sexual identity at birth on birth certificates should not be altered, absent mistaken designation at birth. However, other entitlements and rights such as certain registration, insurance, employment status and other personal rights, including marriage, should be based on the sexual attributes that predominate in an individual. Marriage is probably the most difficult to resolve. As the *Corbett* case[59] in the UK and the *Ladrach* case[23] in the U.S. illustrate, courts are unlikely to permit other than hetrosexual marriage absent specific entitlement legislation.

Cases of true transsexualism are exceedingly rare. Conversion surgery should be treatment of last resort, only after other, less invasive therapies have failed, diagnosis is clear, psychological suitability has been confirmed, a substantial trial period of desired dress, social identity and role has been undertaken, and informed consent has been assured to the greatest extent possible. However, the law should not unduly intrude upon medical discretion in the treatment of this most unfortunate malady. In general it has managed to avoid doing so. This attitude of deference should continue while efforts continue to find better means of treatment and of accurate sexual identification.

NOTES

1 The term seems to have been coined by Dr. Harry Benjamin of the United States. His works on the subject include 'Transsexualism and tranvestism as psychosomatic and somato-psychic syndromes,' 8 *Am. J. Psychother.* 219 (1954), 'Clinical aspects of transsexualism in the male and female,' 18 *Am. J. Psychother.* 485 (1964), and *The Transsexual Phenomenon*. New York: The Julian Press (1966).

2 *Anonymous v. Weiner*, 270 N.Y.S. 2d 319, (1966), quoting from Dr. Benjamin.

3 Hamburger and Sturup, 'Transvestism: hormonal, psychiatric and surgical treatment,' 152 *J. Am. Med. Ass.* 391 (1953).

4 Barr and Hobbs, 'Chromosomal sex in transvestites,' 1954 *The Lancet* 1109. One commentator indicated that the male to female ration is about 3.7 to 1 (603 male to 162 female cases): Pauly, 'Male psychosexual inversion: transsexualism,' 13 *Arch. Gen. Psychiat.* 172, 179 (1965).

5 Bowman and Engle, 'Sex offences: the medical and legal implications of sex variations,' 25 Law and Contemporary Problems 292, 306 (1960).

6 Benjamin 8 *Am. J. Psychother.* 219, 220 (1954).

7 Worden and Marsh, 'Psychological factors in men seeking sex transformation,' 157 *J. Am. Med. Ass.* 1292, 1293 (1955).

8 Hamburger and Sturup, *op. cit.*, pp.391–2.

9 Benjamin, *loc. cit.*

10 Of 100 cases reviewed by Pauly, 48 were successful in obtaining some

alteration of sexual anatomy; 42 were surgically castrated, 30 obtained penectomy and 20 an artificial vagina. Pauly, *op. cit.*, p.176.

11 Hamburger and Sturup, *loc. cit.*; Benjamin, *op. cit.*, p.229.

12 *Ibid.*; in discussing a selection of 100 reported cases involving transsexuals, Pauly reports that 6 performed autocastration, 3 amputated their penis and 9 attempted self)mutilation. Pauly *op. cit.*, p.167. See, for example, the discussion of a Swiss case in 1963 *Excerpta Criminologica* s.1066.

13 Hamburger and Sturup, *loc. cit.*

14 *Ibid*; *Doe v. Dept. Public Health* (1977, Minn.) 257 N.W. 2d 816, 819.

15 Benjamin, 18 *Am. J. Psychother.* 458, 468 (1964).

16 Sometimes, in young transsexuals, the sexual motive for the operation to include creation of a vagina may be quite strong. The transsexual may well be attracted to normal heterosexual men and perhaps even to promiscuity. Benjamin, *The Transsexual Phenomenon*, pp. 113–14.

17 Benjamin, 8 *Am. J. Psychother.* 228 (1954), 18 *Am. J. Psychother.* 469 (1964).

18 Lukianowicz, 'Survey of various aspects of transvestism in the light of our present knowledge,' 128 *J. nerv. ment. Dis.* 36, 57 (1959); Hamburger and Sturup, *op. cit.*, p.393.

19 Hamburger and Sturup, *loc. cit.*

20 Moore, 'Recent developments concerning the criteria of sex and possible legal implications,' *31 Man.Bar News* 104 (1959).

21 Stoller, note 74.

22 See *Richards v. U.S. Tennis Ass'n.* (1977, N.Y. Supr. Ct.) 400 N.Y.S. 2d 267.

23 Sherwin, 'The legal problem in transvestism,' 8 *Am. J. Psychoter.* 243 (1954); see also, Bowman and Engle, 'Sex Offenses: the medical and legal implications of sex variations' 25 *Law and Contemp. Probs.* 292 (1960).

24 See, for example, *Reisner v. Vigilant Ins. Co.* (1988, N.Y. Supr. Ct.) 524 N.Y.S. 2d 602; *In Re Ladrach* (1987, Ohio Prob.) 513 N.E. 2d 828); *Daly v. Daly* (1986, Nev.) 715 Pac. 2d 56; *K. v. Health Division* (1977, Ore.) 560 Pac.2d 1070; *M.T. v. J.T.* (1976, N.J.App.) 355 A.2d 204; *Richards v. U.S. Tennis Ass'n.*, *supra*; *People v. Simmons*, (1974, N.Y. Crim. Ct.) 357 N.Y.S. 2d 362; *B. v.B.* (1974, N.Y. Supr. Ct.) 355 N.Y.S. 2d 712; *Hartin v. Director of Bureau of Records, Etc.* (1973, N.Y. Supr. Ct.) 347 N.Y.S. 2d 515.

25 See, Benjamin, 18 *Am. J. Psychoter.* 464 (1964); *Time*, 21 January 1974, p.63, discussed in *B. v. B.*, *supra*, 355 N.Y.S. 2d 712, 717.

26 See *Reisner v. Vigilant Ins. Co.* (1988, N.Y. Supr. Ct.) 524 N.Y.S. 2d 602.

27 See *Doe v. Dept. Public Welfare* (1977, Minn.) 257 N.W. 2d 816, 819.

28 *In Re Ladrach*, *supra*, 513 N.E. 2d 828, 829.

29 *Daly v. Daly*, *supra*, 715 Pac. 2d 56, 57.

30 Calif.Prob.Code §2356(d); *Conservatorship of Valerie N.* (1985) 40 Cal.3d 143; *Wentzel v. Montgomery General Hospital, Inc.* (1982,Md.) 447 A.2d 1244 (cert. den. 459 U.S. 1147); *Re Moe* (1982, Mass.) 432 N.E. 2d 712.

31 *Hartin v. Dir. of Bureau of Records, Etc.*, *supra*, 347 N.Y.S. 2d 515, 518.

32 *Corbett v. Corbett* (1970, P.D.A.) 2 W.L.R. 1306, 2 All E.R. 33.

33 *M.T. v. J.T.*, *supra*, 355 A. 2d 204.

34 Accord, *B. v. B.*, *supra*, 355 N.Y.S. 2d 712.

35 400 N.Y.S. 2d 267, 272.

36 *In Re Ladrach*, *supra*; *Daly v. Daly*, *supra*; *Hartin v. Dir. of Bureau of Records, Etc.*; *Anonymous v. Weiner* (1966, N.Y. App.) 270 N.Y.S. 2d 319; *B. v. B.*, *supra*, (note 51).

37 N.Y. City Health Code §207.05(a)(5).

38 *Hartin v. Dir. of Bureau of Records, Etc.*, *supra*, 347 N.Y.S. 2d 515, 518.

39 *In Re Ladrach*, *supra*, 513 N.E. 2d 828, 831; *K v. Health Division*, *supra*, 560 Pac. 2d 1070, 1072; *Anonymous v. Weiner*, *supra*.

40 Ohio R.C. §3101.01

41 *In Re Ladrach*, *supra*, 513 N.E. 2d 828; *B. v. B.*, *supra*, 355 N.Y.S. 2d 712; see also, *Corbett v. Corbett*, *supra*, note 59.

42 *B. v. B.*, 355 N.Y.S. 2d 712, 717.

43 See *San Fran.Chronicle*, 27 May 1989, p.A15.

44 *Anonymous v. Anonymous* (1972, N.Y. Super. Ct.) 352 N.Y.S. 2d 499; *Baker v. Nelson* (1971, Minn.) 191 N.W. 2d 185.

45 *Richards v. U.S. Tennis Ass'n.*, *supra*, 400 N.Y.S. 2d 267.

46 *In Re Baby Girl M* (1987) 191 Cal. App. 3d 786 (withdrawn); *In Re Eric B.* (1987) 189 Cal. App. 3d 996.

47 (1986) 715 Pac. 2d 56.

48 715 Pac. 2d 56, 64.

49 Columbus, Ohio, Munic. Code §23.43.04, discussed in *People v. Simmons* (1974, N.Y. Crim. Ct.) 357 N.Y.S. 2d 362, 365.

50 *People v. Simmons*, *supra*, 357 N.Y.S. 2d 362.

51 *Hartin v. Dir. of Bureau of Records, Etc.*, *supra*, 347 N.Y.S. 2d 515, 517.

52 Reported by Benjamin, *The Transsexual Phenomenon*, p.116, *et. seq.*

53 See discussion in Chapter 10.

54 See Discussion in Chapter 5.

55 See, Moore, 97 *Canad. Med. Ass. J.* 292 (1967).

56 See Chapter 2 on abortion for the most notable exception.

57 *Rees v. U.K.* (1986, Euro. Ct. of Human Rights) 1987 *Fam. Law* 157; Mason & McCall Smith, (2d ed., 1987) *Law & Med. Ethics*, p.35; 128 *J. New. Ment. Dis.* 36, 57 (1959); 25 *Law & Contemp. Probs.* 292, 306 (1960).

58 G. Williams, 'Consent and public policy,' 1962 *Crim. L.R.* 154, 159.

59 *Corbett v. Corbett* (1971) p.83, (1970) 3 W.L.R. 1306, 2 All E.R. 33.

60 1987 *Fam. Law* 157, 159; 24 *Med. Sci. Law* 163 (1984); 1980 *J. Med. Ethics* 92

61 *T. v. T.* (1961) 105 *Solicitor's J.* 933

62 *B. v. B.* (1955) p.42 (31 *Man. Bar News* 115, 116–7 (1959).)

63 *White v. British Sugar Corp.* (1977) I.R.L.R. 121.

64 *In Re F (Mental Patient) (Sterilisation)*, (1989) 2 W.L.R. 1025.

65 *Attorney General's Reference No. 6 of 1980* (1981) Q.B. 715.

66 The Suicide Act 1961 de-criminalized suicide, but provides up to 14 years for aiding or abetting suicide.

67 On the broad legal discretion given the medical profession in the exercise of its clinical judgment see, *Hunter v. Hanley* 1955 S.C. 200

(Scot. Ct. Sess.), *Bolam v. Friein Hosp. Mgt. Committee* (1957) 1 W.L.R. 582 (Engl. C.A.).

68 *Institutes*, 1,4,6.
69 Smith, T.B., 'Law, Professional Ethics and the Human Body' (1959) *S.L.T.* (News) 245, 247.
70 Forbes, *Institutes of the Law of Scotland* (Edinburgh 1722) pt. 1, bk.1, chap.1, p.18.
71 D.1.5.9.; T.B. Smith, *loc. cit.*
72 T.B. Smith, *A Short Commentary on the Law of Scotland.* Edinburgh: W. Green (1962) p.250.
73 *De Sancto Matrimonii Sacramenum Disputationum*, Disputatio CVI, p.380.
74 This conclusion would seem to be in conformity with prevailing medical opinion on this issue; namely, tha   ere are only two sexes (male-female) and only two genders (mascui. -feminine), but that there are many degrees of each. See Stoller, 'The hermaphroditic identity of hermaphrodites,' 139 *J. new. ment. Dis.* 453,456 (1964).
75 (1957) *S.L.T.* (Sh.Ct.) 61–62.
76 See Smith, T.B., *Short Commentary*, p.250.
77 Smith, T.B. (1959) *S.L.T.* (News) 247.
78 G.H. Gordon, *The Criminal Law of Scotland*, p.775.

9

Experimentation

A. INTRODUCTION

'Although it is the duty of the physician or surgeon to keep up with advancements, it is also his duty to refrain from experiments.'

This statement,[1] perhaps as well as any other, expresses the seeming dilemma in which the current state of the law dealing with medical experimentation places the practitioner-experimenter. Medical science relies on research and experimentation, as do all other sciences, to advance its knowledge in man's fight against sickness and disease. Inevitably, such experimentation must utilize human subjects if it is to have primary significance. For any new therapy, drug or treatment there must always be the first patient or subject. There must always be those who serve, in a sense, as the 'Guinea Pigs of Hippocrates.'[2]

The need for and the existence of human medical experimentation is illustrated by the awesome fact that today's typical physician relies on drugs developed since 1950 for more than 90 percent of his patient prescriptions.[3] Medical experimentation has been practiced through the centuries since the early days of Galen,[4] not infrequently on unwilling prison subjects. Despite that reality, it has only been relatively recently that legislative protections have been forthcoming and court decisions involving 'planned and directed medical research on human beings'[5] have been fully examined and tested in the courts. Some years ago, one legal authority noted,

'There has ... not yet crystallized a set of specific guidelines, commonly understood and applicable, to ensure that human research may go forward on the highest scientific and ethical planes with due legal protection for both the subject and the investigator.'

Historically, experimentation was carried out quietly, by a few physicians, normally for therapeutic purposes. Little legal attention was given to it. During World War II extensive experimentation was carried out in aid of the war-effort; often it was not therapeutic. U.S. prisoners, the feeble-minded and the insane were used to research bacterial infection, dysentery and malaria treatments.[7] Sometimes informed consent was obtained and

239

other times it was not. This basically utilitarian approach to research continued after the war until the 1960s and produced with it some clear ethical and legal excesses,[8] but few were heard to complain.

However, commencing in the 1960s the world medical community and the public in general became much more concerned with personal autonomy and avoiding further excesses in medical experimentation.[7] Since that time, considerable legal development has occurred. For example, in 1974 in the U.S. the National Research Act became law, creating a National Commission for the Protection of Human Subjects of Biomedical and Behavioral Research. From that has developed specific federal guidelines for the conduct of experimental medical treatment and the protection of the patient or subject's rights. Many states have passed legislation imposing explicit controls on experimentation. In Britain, the Medical Research Council published its Report, *Responsibility in Investigations on Human Subjects* in 1962.[9] The Declaration of Helsinki was drafted by the World Medical Association in 1964 to guide physicians in the proper respect and treatment of patients undergoing experimental or research therapy and later amended in 1975.[10]

All of these statutory enactments and professional guidelines have done a great deal to protect the patient and to assure that his or her participation in such treatment is voluntary and knowing. However, their application in specific cases is not always easy or clear.

In more recent years, the advent of atomic, genetic and other modern biomedical research and development brought home the awesome power and responsibility of researchers. The development of informed consent further strengthened this trend. There have been shocking disclosures of unethical and non-therapeutic research activities by organizations such as the Army and the CIA in the United States. In enacting the National Research Act, the U.S. Congress heard vivid testimony concerning experimental surgery, prison research, university-centered research abuses, such as the Tuskegee Syphilis Study, where live bacteria or virus was injected into patients, genetic manipulation and similar improprieties.[11]

The 1970s saw the common appearance of hospital ethics committees for research review mandated by law (Institutional Review Boards) in the U.S., as well as local ethics committees in the U.K.[12] That heightened awareness has continued to this date, though, as we shall see, legal developments have been sparse and not always clear.

1.   *What is experimentation*

Some authorities[13] equate medical experimentation and medical research, considering both to include all attempts at inducing or altering bodily or mental functions by clinical procedures for the general advance of health.

Others[14] see experimentation as involving a wide range of practices: deviation from accepted modes of treatment; therapy in areas where there is no accepted mode of treatment; use of drugs and the like on patients not for immediate therapy, but for the eventual improvement of sufferers who may or may not include the patient; and finally, use of non-patients as experimental subjects. A fairly concise, though incomplete, definition of medial experimentation has been offered by one student of its legal aspects. He fails to include experimentation carried out with no intention of helping the particular patient. He states[15] that it encompasses

'those situations where there is an application of a new, insufficiently proved drug, instrument or method of treatment, the validity of which has neither been accepted nor rejected by the medical profession and the purpose of which is to help the patient and to advance medical science.'

Medical experimentation, it is submitted, must be defined both in terms of means and purpose. Its purpose can be either to cure or heal a particular patient, to find a cure for patients similarly situated, to seek some broad, perhaps unrelated, prevention of disease, to advance the state of medical science's knowledge for application to future, unidentified patients, or to accomplish any combination of these objectives. Any given medical treatment becomes experimental when the means used are ones not generally accepted by the medical profession or its appropriate sector. The experimental means utilized may be either unique or deviational in light of accepted practice.

Aside from these definitions of medical experimentation, all of which type it as distinct from the general practice of medicine, there are those who feel that all medical practice involves experimentation, differing only in degree, not kind.[16] It is true, in one sense, that all medicine is experimental, by its very nature of dealing with the never identical symptoms, reactions and needs of individual patients.

Some say that experimentation is never absent from the physician's office, for he does no more than 'practice' medicine on patients who are in fact 'voluntary experimental subjects.'[17] However, in the general practice of medicine, the patient's cure or comfort must be considered as always paramount. In medical experimentation the outcome of treatment applied to the subject may not be intended to, nor actually, result in any personal benefit to him. And for that matter, the experimenter's 'subject' may not be a 'patient' at all, being in perfect health himself.

While the law has not as yet set out the permissible limits for experimentation to the degree that it has with general medical practice, this has seemingly not impeded the carrying out of wide ranging experiments or clinical tests on human beings in recent times. For instance, the following medical experimentation was undertaken in the United States during and after World War II: the use of healthy prisoners in malaria, hepatitis, common cold and intestinal protozoa testing; the use of servicemen for physiological stress and even hallucinogenic drug testing; school children for poliomyelitis (Salk-vaccine) and influenza vaccine testing; 'normal' mental patients for nutrition and even whole communities for water supply fluoridation to prevent dental cavities.[18] There are reports of prisoners being given untested, psychogenic or mind-altering drugs.[19] Just how widespread medical experimentation is today is difficult to gauge; but one must recognize that its existence is widespread.[20]

2. *The legal framework*

From a legal point of view, medical treatment which falls within the confines of accepted, standard practice causes few problems. Such treatment must be consented to – expressly or impliedly – by the patient, although undertaken for his benefit by the physician.[21] Under a broad definition, recognized medical treatment might be classified as experimental owing to the peculiarity presented by any given patient's case. However, it is not thought of as such in the public mind, barring some undesirable or unforseen results. The carrying out of standard medical practice is regulated by formulations of negligence, which determine the duty of care owed to the patient in circumstances when 'malpractice' is alleged.[22] In these circumstances,

> 'The law requires that the physician shall have the degree of learning and skill ordinarily possessed by physicians of good standing practicing in the same locality and that he shall use ordinary care and diligence in applying that learning and skill to the treatment of his patient. Whether he has done so in a particular case is generally a question for experts and can be established only by their testimony unless the matter at issue is within the common knowledge of laymen.[23]

When undertaking normal, accepted treatment, the physician will not be held responsible merely because the result is unsuccessful or untoward. The physician is not the guarantor of outcome. He or she will be held only to a standard of treatment that is proven to be customarily applied in the treatment of similarly afflicted individuals, in the same community and under similar circumstances.

If a physician's treatment is alleged to constitute malpractice or negligence, it will not be tested against the highest quality medical treatment that could have been obtained by the patient, but, rather, will be tested against the skill of practitioners in the same locality, be it rural or urban, and those belonging to the same school of medical thought, so long as a recognized portion of the medical profession ascribes to such a school of thought or method of treatment.[24] On rare occasion even if the doctor conforms to normal, accepted treatment, the courts may find him liable for any harm it causes if it is not considered legally reasonable.[25]

In determining whether or not conduct by a member of the medical profession has satisfied those standards of skill and learning to be expected in the circumstances, the law will make provision for human weakness and mere errors in judgment, so long as such errors do not render the skill and judgment actually exercised by the physician substandard, careless or unreasonable in light of prevailing practice or knowledge as applied to the particular treatments involved.[26]

It is, however, that medical treatment which does not fall within the above, rather flexible category of ordinary or accepted practice with which we are predominantly concerned here. It is this type of deviational, un-practiced or unaccepted treatment that the law has classed, often imperfectly, as experimentation.

Nearly all of the cases that either discuss the question of experimentation or are cited either in favor of, or in opposition to, the particular viewpoint on medical experimentation, are cases involving simple medical malpractice. With few exceptions, the cases all involve a therapeutic setting, where treatment is being carried out for the benefit of the particular patient, where carelessness is involved or an untested or deviational procedure is carried out, not intentionally for the propose of expanding scientific knowledge in a truly experimental context, but, rather, because of lack of skill, judgment or due care on the part of the physician in seeking to render beneficial treatment to the particular patient. Generally, the judicial pronouncements which are on record in this area indicate that the judges solved the problems confronting them as cases involving deviational, untested or unaccepted treatment as a result of professional carelessness or ignorance. They did not approach the cases as involving a preconceived intention on the part of the physician to carry out a new form of treatment, with the patient's knowing consent, in order to expand scientific knowledge, in addition to or exclusive of any intention to cure the patient of any malady that may or may not have even been involved.

There seems little reason to doubt that traditional formulations of medical malpractice and negligence could be equally well applied to the experimental context.[27] However, few cases have come before the courts and been tried and decided on the basis that here was a truly experimental situation, carried out with all proper care, and only after obtaining the subject's full and knowing consent for the primary purpose of determining the desirability of the new drug or form of treatment, and only secondarily for the purpose of benefitting the particular patient.

Few if any physicians have ever defended a lawsuit, be it for civil damages or criminal sanctions, on the basis that the method of treatment involved was experimental in nature, but was carried out with the patient's consent and with all due care, and therefore no liability should ensue. When such a case does arise, it could involve either therapeutic experimentation, for the benefit of the particular patient involved, or nontherapeutic experimentation, strictly or primarily for the benefit of other individuals or the advancement of medical science in general. Depending on the nature of the experimentation in issue, very different results might well be expected. Certainly it would seem that a much more complete risk disclosure to obtain consent for non-therapeutic experimentation should be necessary to negate any liability than would be the case for therapeutic experimentation.[28]

3.   *Statutes concerned with consent to experimentation*

Some statutory law has developed over the past 25 years in the area of medical experimentation. Apparently, none exists in England or Scotland, although the Medicines Act 1968 closely monitors the introduction of new drugs. One of the few American enactments to explicitly recognize experimentation is the 'New Drug' section of the Food, Drug and Cosmetic Act.[29] The Act prohibits introduction of a drug into interstate commerce prior to a full investigation into its safety for use. However, the legislation recognizes an experimental exception to this prohibition in the case of,

> 'drugs intended solely for investigational use by experts qualified by scientific training and experience to investigate the safety and effectiveness of drugs.'[30]

An amendment to the Act[31] exhorts physicians to obtain advance, informed consent of all those to whom the experimental drugs are prescribed, but permits the physician to decide within his own discretion whether and when it is 'not feasible or in their professional judgement, contrary to the best interests of such human beings' to inform them that their use of the drugs is experimental and to seek their prior, voluntary consent. This is a statutory acknowledgement of the physician's so-called 'therapeutic privilege' not to disclose information deemed harmful for the patient, if this conclusion is the result of reasonable medical judgment.[32]

The Commissioner of Food and Drugs has promulgated strict regulations to implement this law.[33] The regulations require that consent of the individual be obtained *in all cases* where the investigational drugs are administered 'primarily for the accumulation of scientific knowledge,' thus recognizing the different nature of primarily non-therapeutic versus primarily therapeutic experimental use of drugs, and requiring consent in all of the former cases. In those therapeutic instances, where the investigational drugs are being used for the treatment of the particular patient, the regulations still require that consent be obtained in 'all but exceptional cases.' For purposes of imposing the consent requirement, the regulations define 'exceptional cases' as being those in which

'. . . it is not feasible to obtain the patient's consent or the consent of his representative, or in which as a matter of professional judgment exercised in the best interests of a particular patient under the investigator's care, it would be contrary to that patient's welfare to obtain his consent.'

'Not feasible' is defined as those situations in which the investigator is not capable of obtaining consent because of his inability to communicate with the patient or his representative, as, for example, when the patient is in a coma and his representative cannot be reached and it is imperative that the drug be administered without delay. The regulations define 'contrary to the best interest of such human beings' as being those situations where the physician in the exercise of his professional judgment determines that under the particular circumstances of this patient's case, the patient's best interest would suffer if consent were sought prior to treatment. This is the so-called 'therapeutic exception' to informed consent which we discussed in Chapter 5.[32]

Finally, the U.S. regulations concerning the use of experimental or investigational drugs attempt the very difficult task of defining what it means by the term 'consent.' The regulations state:

'Consent means that the person involved has the legal capacity to give consent, is so situated as to be able to exercise free power of choice, and is provided with a fair explanation of pertinent information concerning the investigational drug, and/or his possible use as a control, so as to enable him to make a decision on his willingness to receive said investigational drug. This latter element means that before the acceptance of an affirmative decision by such person the investigator should carefully consider and make known to him (taking into consideration such person's well-being and his ability to understand) the nature, expected duration, and propose of the administration of said investigational drug; the method and means by which it is to be administered; the hazards involved; the existence of alternative forms of therapy, if any; and the beneficial effects upon his health or person that may possibly come from the administration of the investigational drug.'

The regulations detail the specific information which must be disclosed to the patient to obtain his or her informed consent to experimental treatment. Treatment is deemed experimental if it is for research or investigational purposes. As discussed in Chapter Five, the following must be explained to the patient before his consent to experimental treatment may be validly obtained:

1) A fair explanation of the medical procedures proposed and their purposes;
2) An identification of any experimental procedures;

3) A description of attendant discomfort and any reasonably expected risks;

4) A description of any benefits reasonably expected;

5) An offer to answer any questions;

6) A disclosure of any appropriate alternative treatments or procedures that could benefit the patient.

7) A statement the patient may withdraw his consent at any time without suffering prejudice in treatment.[34]

The effectiveness and desirability of these regulations has yet to be tested in any particular judicial decision. However, the regulations are admirable in their attempt to tackle the very difficult problem of defining the requirements necessary to obtain the patient's consent in an experimental or investigational context.

The question of consent by the patient or subject is perhaps the fundamental legal and ethical consideration in the area of medical experimentation. The law's paramount concern in this area, as in all other areas involving bodily intrusion, is that of preserving the individual's bodily integrity and autonomy. Therefore, it can be argued that if truly knowing and voluntary consent of the patient or subject has been obtained prior to any medical experimentation, the primary concern of the law in this area has been satisfied.

Generally, the patient's informed consent to an innovative and experimental procedure may be solicited by the physician who plans to undertake the procedure or use the drug or device for therapeutic purposes, provided the innovative nature of the procedure is explained, as well as the available options and the dangers involved.[35] The consent given is limited to the scope of the request. For example, consent to established treatment or surgery does not carry with it, nor imply, consent to medical research on the patient or human tissue derived during surgery which is unrelated to the treatment.[36] It is also true that commercial use or exploitation of any of those tissues, as for genetic or pharmacological purposes, may not be undertaken without express, prior patient consent, or liability for conversion will lie.[36]

There are limits to consent. Not any procedure should be possible if consent is given. For example, the English courts have held that consent cannot be given to engage in bare knuckle prize fighting,[37] or indecent assault[38] and this could be extended to certain controversial and mutilating surgery if its benefit to the patient were unproven or harm to reproductive capacity was involved.[39]

Reasonable efforts must be made to minimize the risks of experimental treatment. Animal subjects should be used first to ascertain, preliminarily, risks. Human trials are normally justified only after adequate animal trials. Animal testing is generally subject to licensing requirements, as in Britain under the Medicines Act 1968, Part II. Thorough research into and review of other efforts and experimental studies should be required. The law should also be concerned with the method by which the experimentation is carried out, the preparations for it, its stated purpose, and proper documentation of it, including clear and complete written informed consent forms.

Aside from the Pure Food, Drug and Cosmetic legislation on the federal level, there are a number of state statutes on the books in the U.S. which regulate medical experimentation. For example, California law provides that if experimental treatment is proposed, or the use of an investigational or research drug or device which has not received FDA approval for general use is involved, the patient or subject must first be given and sign the 'Experimental Subject's Bill of Rights.'[40] That document requires that the individual concerned,

a) Be informed of the nature and purpose of the experiment.
b) Be given an explanation of the procedures to be followed in the medical experiment, and any drug or device to be utilized.
c) Be given a description of any attendant discomforts and risks reasonably to be expected from the experiment.
d) Be given an explanation of any benefits to the subject reasonably to be expected from the experiment, if applicable.
e) Be given a disclosure of any appropriate alternative procedures, drugs or devices that might be advantageous to the subject, and their relative risks and benefits.
f) Be informed of the avenues of medical treatment, if any, available to the subject after the experiment if complications should arise.
g) Be given an opportunity to ask any questions concerning the experiment or the procedures involved.
h) Be instructed that consent to participate in the medical experiment may be withdrawn at any time and the subject may discontinue participation in the medical experiment without prejudice.

In addition, the patient or subject must also be given a signed and dated copy of his consent form, after the procedure has been explained to him and he has given written consent to it. The consent form must include the following information to be valid,[41] which disclosure closely mirrors what the federal FDA consent standards require,

1) An explanation of the procedures to be followed in the medical experiment and any drug or device to be utilized, including the purposes of such procedures, drugs, or device. If a placebo is to be administered or dispensed to a portion of the subjects involved in a medical experiment, all subjects of such experiment shall be informed of such fact, however, they need not be informed as to whether they will actually be administered or dispensed a placebo.
2) A description of any attendant discomfort and risks to the subject reasonably to be expected.

3) An explanation of any benefits to the subject reasonably to be expected, if applicable.

4) A disclosure of any appropriate alternative procedures, drugs or devices that might be advantageous to the subject, and their relative risks and benefits.

5) An estimate of the expected recovery time of the subject after the experiment.

6) An offer to answer any inquiries concerning the experiment or the procedures involved.

7) An instruction to the subject that he or she is free to withdraw his prior consent to the medical experiment and discontinue participation in the medical experiment at any time, without prejudice to the subject.

8) The name, institutional affiliation, if any, and address of the person or persons actually performing and primarily responsible for the conduct of the experiment.

9) The name of the sponsor or funding source, if any, or manufacturer if the experiment involves a drug or device, and the organization, if any under whose general aegis the experiment is being conducted.

10) The name, address, and phone number of an impartial third party, not associated with the experiment, to whom the subject may address complaints about the experiment.

Most United States medical licensing statutes confine the practice of medicine to the four fundamentals of (1) diagnosis, (2) treatment, (3) operation, and (4) prescription, with respect to disease, pain, injury, and the like. Research or experimentation, while perhaps implicitly part and parcel of all the above fundamentals, is nonetheless not expressly included in any of the statutes. The California provision[42] is fairly typical and states:

'The physician's and surgeon's certificate authorizes the holder to use drugs or what are known as medical preparations in or upon human beings and to sever or penetrate the tissues of human beings and to use any and all other methods in the treatment of diseases, injuries, deformities, or other physical or mental conditions.'

It can be seen that the provision does not expressly make reference to experimentation, nor is it of sufficient latitude to include medical experimentation that does not have as its immediate purpose treatment of the human being involved but rather is aimed at the advancement of science. Without experimentation many of the miracles of modern science would be unavailable. It is a recognized and important part of medicine, if properly regulated. The statutes and professional standards we have referred to seek to do this. Now we will look at how the courts have dealt with experimental treatment.

B. LEGAL DECISION-MAKING

1. *The Slater case (1767)*

The first judicial pronouncement in the Common Law world involving liability for an alleged medical experiment appears to be *Slater v. Baker and Stapleton*.[43] The facts involved an action on the case against a surgeon and an apothecary for unskillfully disuniting the callous of plaintiff's leg in an attempt to reset a prior break. This novel procedure, carried out by a well-known physician of the times, was done without the patient's consent and, according to expert medical testimony, was contrary to existing, satisfactory methods of mending broken legs by compression and consequently was not indicated. Plaintiff was awarded damages.

The *Slater* case came to be cited as authority for the bald proposition that a physician experiments at his peril and is liable for any ill results from such treatment. Such a result would unfairly burden legitimate experimentation, making the physician in effect the guarantor of the result in a procedure inherently involving an uncertain outcome. There was experimentation in *Slater*, the defendants using a 'heavy steel thing that had teeth' vainly to extend (rather than, in the accepted practice, to compress) the complainant's leg into straightness. The Court mentioned that '[i]t seems as if Mr. Baker wanted to try and experiment with this new instrument.' The Court, however, was apparently satisfied to ground liability simply in negligence, 'ignorance and unskillfulness,' for defendant did, 'what no surgeon ought to have done.'[44]

Slater did not recognize the defendant's actions as being true medical research or experimentation, carried out under proper conditions to expand the knowledge of medical science. The facts did not commend such an approach. Rather, the Court saw defendants' treatment as nothing more than an unskilled and unjustified departure from recognized, satisfactory practice concerning a relatively simple medical problem.[45] Nonetheless, cases that followed relied on *Slater* as precedent.

2. *The American Cases*

a. *Civil cases. Slater v. Baker* was followed by the leading American case of *Carpenter v. Blake*.[46] *Carpenter*, as *Slater* had some one hundred years before, involved a physician's deviation in treating his patient from an 'established mode of practice.' The New York Court, attempting to establish an objective standard for this type of case, stated that such departures would constitute negligence unless it could be shown by practical tests to be just as likely as prevailing treatment to work a cure or otherwise benefit the patient. The Court, again implying a very narrow standard, went on to state:

'[W]hen the case is one as to which a system of treatment has been followed for a long time, there should be no departure from it, unless the surgeon who does it is prepared to take the risk of establishing, by his success, the propriety and safety of his experiment.

The rule protects the community against reckless experiments, while it admits the adoption of new remedies and modes of treatment only when their benefits have been demonstrated, or when, from the necessity of the case, the surgeon or physician must be left to the exercise of his own skill and experience.'

The rule pronounced in *Carpenter* only covered those situations where some departure was made from a recognized method of treatment. The rule was too narrow to cover those cases of experimentation where no approved medical practice existed. Even so, *Carpenter* did not provide much leeway for cases where there was an accepted practice, but a new and improved method presented itself, although still in experimental form. *Carpenter* appeared to largely squelch experimental incentive in such cases, since liability would follow any harm in their use, no matter what care and skill was exercised.

A more liberal approach to these types of experimental cases was propounded in *Jackson v. Burnham*.[47] The Court said that a physician utilizing a method contrary to one already established must 'justify his experiment by some reasonable theory.' This test, instead of holding the experimenting physician liable or not depending on the success of his departure in treatment, rather shifted the burden of proof to him by requiring him to show, in effect, that a qualified physician exercising ordinary care and skill in the circumstances would have acted (experimented) similarly. This is a fair standard to impose; one based on reasonableness. In so holding, the Colorado Court came very close to what appears to be the preferred modern outlook in this area.

Perfection is not asked of physicians. The social good they provide mandates that they be held to standards of reasonable care, but not beyond. If the case presents a new problem or condition, for which no routine therapy exists, the patient, once having been properly informed of risks and alternatives and having consented, must trust to the skill and experience of the physician selected and can recover damages only by showing ignorance or unskillfulness in treatment, not the failure of the treatment per se. Even in situations where a particular injury or untoward result suffered by a patient as a result of a particular treatment is something that rarely occurs, no inference of negligence or lack of due care on the part of those conducting the treatment will ordinarily arise, it being recognized at least by the more modern decisions that such an inference would place an unreasonable limitation on the use of operations or new procedures involving an inherent risk of injury even when due care is used.[48]

The unfortunate result of the *Carpenter* holding is that a physician will be held liable for the untoward results of his chosen treatment, merely because he happens to feel a departure from long-followed practice within the profession is indicated, regardless of whether or not the particular atypical procedure he follows is a very promising one and one warranted by the peculiarities of the patient he confronts. In a sense, the *Carpenter* holding imposes a species of strict liability without fault on the performing physician, should he determine that treatment deviational from the norm is indicated. It is highly unlikely that the *Carpenter* ruling would be followed by a court today, unless it were shown that no physician exercising due care would have undertaken such a form of treatment in the prevailing circumstances. In that case, it would be unreasonable to do so.

The better reasoned cases indicate that the circumstances may well condone, if not require, a departure from recognized practice, even though its results are unsuccessful. An early example is the case of *Miller v. Tober*.[49] Therein, the physician used a leg treatment not generally accepted, but which had been known on rare occasions to succeed. The treatment failed and defendant surgeon was held not liable. His actions were not actionable, the only alternative being immediate amputation of the patient's limb.

In *Langford v. Kosterlitz*,[50] a California court upheld an action in negligence against a surgeon who, without advising his patient, had 'experimented' in the treatment of his asthmatic condition by injecting alcohol and then novocaine into the nasal ganglion, rather than the normal, reverse process. The error damaged the patient's optic nerve, resulting in blindness. While the court talked of experimentation, the case went off on a theory of negligent departure from accepted practice, owing to ignorance and/or lack of skill (malpractice) on the physician's part. Courts have often confused the two. This is yet another example.

In *Fortner v. Koch*,[51] where a doctor was sued for allegedly using improper, harmful drugs in treatment, the court remarked:

'We recognize the fact that, if the general practice of medicine and surgery is to progress, there must be a certain amount of experimentation carried on, but such experiments must be done with the knowledge and consent of the patient or those responsible for him, and must not vary too radically from the accepted method of procedure.'

This indicates the modern rule. The patient's consent must be obtained only after full and proper disclosure of the risks, and benefits of and alternatives to the procedure. The decision to experiment – to deviate from standard practice – must be a medically reasonable one justified by a comparison of those risks and benefits, considering both their likelihood and their magnitude. As stated by Basic Principle 4 of the Declaration of Helsinski, adopted by the World Medical Association in 1975, research on a human subject is only justified if 'the importance of the objective [the benefit] is in proportion to the inherent risk to the subject.'[10]

The more modern U.S. cases decided on the issue of experimentation commonly raise the question either of whether the doctor failed to properly inform the patient of the risks and alternatives available so as to ensure an informed consent,[52] or whether the manufacturer of a particular product failed to properly warn of the risks inherent in the particular product.[53] The court in the *Gaston* case[52] recognized that often the risks and benefits of new or experimental drugs are imperfectly known. Even if they turn out to be less valuable or more dangerous than thought, that does not mean that liability should follow, provided that pre-clinical research of the drug justifies studying the drugs in human beings. The court found that the distribution of the drug was justified in the light of facts which were known or should have been know to a reasonably prudent manufacturer. However, the manner of distribution must also be non-negligent, which means a proper warning of the risks must be given by the manufacturer and should include clear advice that the drug is experimental and should provide any warning of risks that could be known through the exercise of reasonable care.

b. *Criminal cases*. It was also recognized early that a physician should not be held criminally liable where he had embarked on an experimental course of treatment in good faith, although abortively, to effect a cure, even if his medical credentials were not satisfactory. In *State v. Schulz*,[54] a conviction of criminal manslaughter against a quack doctor, who had given his patient-victim a substance without even knowing its contents in an effort to attain cure, was reversed. The Court stated:

> 'The interests of society will be subserved by holding a physician civilly liable in damages for the consequences of his ignorance, without imposing upon him criminal liability when he acts with good motives and honest intentions.'[55]

Thus, the basis for experimental treatment on a patient, as well as the manner in which it is conducted, should be reasonable and in good faith to avoid liability. For criminal liability to be imposed the negligence must be gross or aggravated. The general American rule as to whether or not criminal liability will follow from death of a patient resulting from negligent medical treatment was stated rather fully a good number of years ago in the case of *Hampton v. State*,[56] as follows:

> 'The law seems to be fairly well settled, both in England and America, that where the death of a person results from the criminal negligence of the medical practitioner in the treatment of the case, the latter is guilty of manslaughter, and that this criminal liability is not dependent on whether or not the party undertaking the treatment of the case is a duly licensed practitioner, or merely assumes to act as such, acted with good intent in administering the treatment, and did so with the expectation that the result would prove beneficial. The real question on which

criminal liability depends in such cases is whether there was criminal negligence. That *criminal negligence is rather a matter of degree, incapable of precise definition and whether or not it exists to such a degree as to involve criminal liability is to be determined by the jury.* *That criminal negligence exists where the physician or surgeon, or person assuming to act as such, exhibits gross lack of competency, or gross inattention, or criminal indifference to the patient's safety,* and that this may arise from his gross ignorance of the science of medicine or surgery, and of the effect of the remedies employed, through his gross negligence in the application and selection of remedies, his lack of proper skill in the use of instruments, or through his failure to give proper instructions to the patient as to the use of the medicines; that where the person treating the case does nothing that a skilled person might not do and death results merely from an error of judgment on his part, or an inadvertent mistake, he is not criminally liable.' (emphasis supplied.)

While the cases in point indicate it is unlikely that more than civil liability will be imposed on a doctor who acts with due care and good motive, the reasonableness of the chosen treatment is obviously relevant. For instance, in *State v. Lester*,[57] a charge of second degree manslaughter was upheld against the defendant physician for causing his patient's death by x-ray burns. The patient had consented to the well-intentioned treatment, but her physician's unreasonable means of performing it was considered sufficiently careless to be classed as 'culpable negligence' and a public offense. While use of experimental treatment may well be indicated in difficult or terminal cases not amenable to conventional treatment, there must be a reasonable basis for its selection by the physician, consent by the patient, and it must be administered in a reasonable fashion without reckless disregard of its risks or gross negligence.

In a more recent case, *Hyman v. Jewish Chronic Disease Hospital*,[58] an inquiry into the hospital records of twenty-two patients arose out of an experiment carried out on these patients without their consent, for which both prominent physicians were censured. The physicians injected live cancer cells into the patients in an experiment to test their immunity and reactions. The patients were not told the injections contained cancer cells and were led to believe the injections were a part of their normal therapy.

The physicians claimed their action was justified, there being no increased medical risk to the patients of contracting cancer from the injections. This was disputed. A Medical Association Review Board found the two doctors guilty of fraudulent and deceitful conduct and recommended suspension of their licenses. Eventually, the two physicians, one particularly well known and regarded in cancer research, were put on probation for a year, but no judicial proceedings were undertaken.

There was repugnance felt regarding the physicians' non-disclosure to the patients at the Jewish Chronic Disease Hospital, particularly because the experimentation was not carried out with the intention of aiding their maladies, but rather was solely for the good of science and the general advance of cancer research.

Patients need not be told the nature of the experiment in all cases. An ignorant consent may be quite proper if the patient explicitly and knowingly waives his right to be informed.[59] However, even then the risks cannot be life-threatening and must be reasonably proportionate to the benefits sought to be obtained.

The fact that a patient is adult and competent to decide on treatment does not mean that he or she will be permitted to undertake experimental treatment. There may be other policies involved that conflict with the patient's right to free choice. Despite recognition in the United States that the right to individual privacy encompasses medical treatment decisions,[60] it is not an absolute right. The public policy interests of the Food and Drug Administration in ensuring against prescription and use of drugs that are dangerous or of unproven efficacy has been held strong enough to prevent terminal cancer patients from obtaining and using laetrile to treat their illness.[61]

Quite apart from federal regulation, parents have no right to rely on laetrile or other unproven, experimental medical treatments for their seriously ill, dependent children when other, recognized treatments exist.[62] While parents may choose between reasonable medical treatments for their children,[63] their obligation to act in the best interests of their children requires that they not expose them to quackery, unsafe, or unreasonable treatment.[64]

The reported American cases touching on medical experimentation do not seem to represent either a clear or consistent picture. One commentator noted, some time ago, which is still largely true, that,

> 'Reported cases have not yet considered modern controlled medical research as such, and have not yet established limits within which human research may be pursued. Cases which have involved conduct labeled "experimentation" have been decided basically on issues of disclosures or consent, negligence, lack of qualification, improper activity (quack procedures, medicines or devices) or unlicensed practice of medicine usually arising in cases of departure from accepted diagnosis, therapy or other practice. These fact situations, sometimes erroneously called experimentation, have tended to confuse or have failed to recognise the distinction between research and practice.'[65]

The emergence since the 1970s of FDA mandated Institutional Review Boards (IRBs) in most American hospitals has significantly changed the legal picture and shifted the emphasis on legitimization of medical experimentation from a retrospective one of judicial review to a prospective one of administrative authorization. This charge has significantly reduced judicial involvement in experimental treatment reviews. These boards are mandated by FDA regulations to review the protocols, specifically including the adequacy of informed consent forms of disclosure, of experimental procedures, drugs or devices, involving federal funding. Since virtually all hospitals and other research institutions receive federal funding, proposed use of experimental drugs or devices must first obtain the approval of the IRB that, (1) the benefits of the procedure outweigh the risks to the patient, and (2) the patient will be fully informed of the nature and purpose of the procedure, its anticipated risks and benefits, available alternatives and the right to withdraw at any time without prejudice to receiving the best care otherwise available.[34] The composition of the IRB is mandated to make it as broad-based as reasonably possible. The typical IRB contains approximately 10 to 15 members, including several physicians, a hospital representative, a social worker, a community representative or two, a lawyer, a bioethicist and a member of the clergy. All untoward results of any approved experimental procedure must be promptly reported to the IRB and the FDA for review.

This institutional framework has, over the past decade, transferred authority to approve and monitor the majority of experimental procedures from the individual physician to such committees. It has also reduced the influence of the courts and put at risk those treatments undertaken without IRB approval if any untoward result occurs. The result is a substantial improvement in control of experimental treatment and protection of patient autonomy in U.S. hospitals and clinics. The proliferation of hospital-based ethics committees has also undoubtedly raised the consciousness of practitioners and provided an educational vehicle for informing on ethical and respectful treatment of the patient. The apparent consequence of these developments is a paucity of cases reaching the courts suggesting improper experimental method or ethics. This is not to say there are none.[19,48] There are not many.

3. The British Cases

There are few British cases in point dealing with experimentation. Death, of course, may be a risk in human experimentation and good motive or inadvertence will not inevitably protect the physician from criminal liability. In *Rex v. Burdee*,[66] *not* involving experimentation by a qualified, licensed practitioner, a manslaughter conviction was upheld against a quack physician who had prescribed cold water foot baths and a three day fast for the acutely ailing patient. Death soon followed. Expert medical testimony stated that such treatment had 'accelerated' death, which actually resulted from an undoubted heart condition. The holding of the case was summed up in the following terms:

'Any person, whether licensed or unlicensed, who deals with the life or health of another person is bound to use competent skill and sufficient attention; if the patient dies for the want of either, the person is guilty of manslaughter.'

Like most cases in this area, this case simply presented poor practice not experimentation. It does not equate experimental treatment with bad practice. Thus, it is of very little value. It does, however, point out the importance of not confusing experimentation, a legitimate and essential part of medical practice, with quackery or ignorant treatment.

In Scotland, a charge of culpable homicide could conceivably be brought against a physician for a death caused negligently during experimental treatment. However, in the absence of malice or wickedness no such prosecution would be likely.[67]

Perhaps the case most aware of the balance to be struck between the advance of medical science and the reliability of treatment in individual cases is the Scottish decision, *Hunter v. Hanley*.[68] The opinion by Lord President Clyde is one of the very few pronouncements in Scottish law on medical negligence, which may be attributed as 'a tribute to the high standard in general of the medical profession in Scotland.'[69]

It should be noted that, *Hunter v. Hanley* also did not involve allegedly experimental treatment. Nonetheless, its reasoning could be applied to such a situation. As it was, *Hunter* involved allegedly negligent treatment. However, it contained suggestions of experimental treatment. The pursuer (plaintiff) was receiving intramuscular injections of penicillin in the hip for treatment of chest troubles. On the twelfth injection of the series, the hypodermic needle broke off inside the patient, between hip and pelvis. The patient alleged negligence both in selection of the type of needle used and also in its actual use by the physician. Suit was unsuccessful, it being held that the mere fact that defendant had deviated from standard practice did not, of itself, constitute proof of negligence.

The lucid reasoning of Lord President Clyde in the case is worth quoting for the light it sheds on the whole area of medical negligence in general, but more particularly on the standards under concern by which to judge medical experimentation:

'In the realm of diagnosis and treatment there is ample scope for genuine difference of opinion and one man clearly is not negligent merely because his conclusion differs from that of other professional men, nor because he has displayed less skill or knowledge than others would have shown. The true test for establishing negligence in diagnosis or treatment on the part of the doctor is whether he has been proved to be guilty of such failure as no doctor of ordinary skill would be guilty if acting with ordinary care. . . . The standard seems to be the same in England. . . .'

The following remarks by the Lord President could be applied by analogy beyond the limited factual situation raised in *Hunter* to cover instances of pure or generalized medical experimentation:

'It follows from what I have said that in regard to allegations of deviation from ordinary professional practice ... such a deviation is not necessarily evidence of negligence. Indeed it would be disastrous if this were so, for all inducements to progress in medical science would then be destroyed. Even a substantial deviation from normal practice may be warranted by the particular circumstances. *To establish liability by a doctor where deviation from normal practice is alleged, three facts require to be established.* First of all it must be proved *that there is a usual and normal practice;* secondly it must be proved *that the defender has not adopted that practice*; and thirdly (and this is of crucial importance) it must be established *that the course the doctor adopted is one which no professional man of ordinary skill would have taken if he had been acting with ordinary care.* There is clearly a heavy onus on the pursuer to establish these three facts, and without all three his case will fail. If this is the test, then it matters nothing how far or how little he deviates from the ordinary practice. For *the extent of the deviation is not the test. The deviation must be of a kind which satisfies the third of the requirements just stated.*' [70] [Emphasis added]

Hunter is significant, for these guidelines laid down by the Lord President Clyde could govern cases of disputed medical treatment involving experimentation, both where a recognized practice exists and a departure therefrom is made, and also where no recognized practice does exist. In either instance, the physician's conduct is only actionable if in fact no doctor of ordinary skill would have so acted in the exercise of ordinary care. The test is a flexible and liberal one for physicians, but clear, coherent, and arguably adequate for dealing with all types of experimentation cases, attributes notably lacking from most of the decisions to confront the issue.

Of course, there may still exist those presumably rare instances where the court might have to say the treatment was not reasonable and the doctor is liable if harm follows from it, even if other reasonable doctors would have done the same thing. Good medical practice normally makes good law, but the question of what is good medical treatment, whether or not it is experimental, cannot be left *entirely* to the doctors to decide.[71] If the courts do not reserve the right to overrule an accepted medical practice on occasion, then patients' rights could be sacrificed to physician accepted, but unreasonable, treatment standards based on self-interest, carelessness or lack of wisdom.[72] As stated by Justice Learned Hand,[73]

'... in most cases reasonable prudence is in fact common prudence: but strictly it is never its measure; a whole calling may have unduly lagged in the adoption of new and available devices. It never may set its own tests, however persuasive be its usages. Courts must in the end say what is required; there are precautions so imperative that even their universal disregard will not excuse their omission.'

In *McHardy v. Dundee General Hospitals' Board of Management*[74] the issue of a physician's duty of care to his patient was again raised in light of allegations of negligence. Lord Cameron indicated that the onus of proving negligence was a heavy one for the pursuer and that mere error of judgment or even of diagnosis would not, by itself, be presumptive proof of negligence.[75] Lord Cameron's direction in the case is worth quoting, for, as with Lord President Clyde's reasoning in *Hunter*, it represents what, it is submitted, is an enlightened and realistic Scottish judicial attitude towards medical practice in general and one which could be brought to bear equally in cases of pure medical experimentation even where therapeutic benefit to the particular patient may not be the object of the treatment imposed. In relevant part, Lord Cameron stated:

> ... I think it is well that the search for further knowledge and experience should not be inhibited by undue apprehension or charges of negligence for the consequences to a patient of treatment or diagnosis where such may diverge from the normal. ... Medicine is not an exact science and the solutions of its problems are not susceptible of mathematical calculation, while the frontiers of medical knowledge are always moving and advance may often be achieved only at the cost of what in retrospect appear to be errors and divergences from the correct path as that is ultimately mapped out.'

Hunter was followed by several English cases, most notable among them *Bolam v. Friern Hospital Management Committee*,[76] where the defendant was absolved from liability for injury to plaintiff resulting from electro-convulsive therapy. The court found no negligence in the application of a treatment supported by a responsible body of medical opinion skilled in the area, notwithstanding the existence of another school of thought on the proper mode of treatment required in the circumstances.

In the English case of *Holland v. Devitt and Moore Nautical College*,[77] the judge held that a physician did not evidence negligence merely because he had made a slight departure from the textbook solution. He was entitled to rely on his common sense, experience and judgment in the treatment of each particular case. In *Roe v. Ministry of Health*,[78] which alleged negligence in the administration of a spinal anaesthetic, Lord Justice Denning summed up the competing interests by stating:[79]

> 'Medical science has conferred great benefits on mankind, but these benefits are attended by considerable risks. Every surgical operation is attended by risks. We cannot take the benefits without taking the risks. Every advance in technique is also attended by risks. Doctors, like the rest of us, have to learn by experience, and experience often teaches in a hard way.'

Risks cannot be eliminated, but they can be explained to the patient. In this way the doctrine of informed consent both legitimates and facilitates experimental treatment, even if risky, if otherwise medically indicated due to the patient's condition.

In one of the very few modern British judicial pronouncements on experimentation, a 27 year old paedophile was held able to consent to an experimental drug treatment to reduce testosterone to castration levels. He was willing to consent to this because of fears he would reoffend because of his uncontrollable sexual urges. Because of the controversial and experimental nature of the procedure, the Mental Health Commission refused to certify the proposed treatment. The subject's competence to consent was obviously also a concern. The high court granted judicial review to quash the M.H.C. decision and found the man to be competent to consent to this treatment.[80] He was aware that the procedure was experimental and had previously only been used on animals and older men. He was not required to understand every detail of the procedure before he would be found to have capacity to consent. The Judge concluded,[81]

'I cannot accept that a patient must understand the precise physiological process involved before he can be said to be capable of understanding the nature and likely effects of the treatment or can consent to it.'

The treating doctor should ensure the knowing consent of his or her patient. However, an over-zealous interest in research or the development of a new therapy may cloud his or her objectivity and judgment. There are still reports of reluctant or perhaps not fully informed patients undergoing experimental treatment or clinical trials in Britain, sometimes with tragic results.[82] One woman died due to the injection of intravenous cytotoxic drugs to which neither she nor her family had consented. Even the intern was uninformed of the experimentation.[83]

If the patient is incompetent – because of minority or infirmity – and a serious experimental treatment is proposed, even though therapeutic in purpose, it is probable that court approval from a high court judge must first be obtained. At least this appears to be true from a reading of the recent English decision in the case of *In re F (Mental Patient) (Sterilisation)*.[84] Lord Donaldson, M.R., in delivering the opinion of the Court of Appeal upholding the inherent power of the courts to authorize sterilization for an adult incompetent when in her best interests to do so, suggested that the public interest required the independent opinion of a judge before undertaking irreversible or controversial treatment of a non-emergency nature upon an incompetent patient.[85] The treatments falling into these categories included abortion, sterilization, organ donation or experimentation. No definition of experimentation was offered by the Court of Appeal. The decision has been affirmed by the House of Lords, although the remarks of Lord Donaldson pertaining to experimentation were not expressly approved. The House of

Lords agreed that it was a matter of good practice, if not legally compelled, that court approval be first obtained at least in cases of sterilization. The same reasoning would seem to apply to experimentation where any risk of patient incompetence exists and is not clearly resolved.

Although these judicial pronouncements are helpful in understanding the duty of care a physician must exercise, they are of limited value in helping to shed light on the legal attitude towards experimentation. The reported cases nearly all involve alleged negligence arising from therapeutically-motivated treatment of a particular patient; they do not involve planned clinical research and experimentation carried out professionally with appropriate safeguards to increase medical science's knowledge.[86] This is not to say, however, that the same standards of negligence could not be applied in a purely experimental or investigational context, the only different being the necessity of reference to the requirements of due care in the selection, preparation for, and execution of a particular experimental treatment rather than a recognized and accepted form of non-experimental treatment.

There is no reason why traditional notions of negligence and due care could not apply in instances of both experimental and non-experimental treatment of the patient. Cases involving true experimental situations, when they arise in the courts, will have to be judged by standards of care and duty appropriate to the experimental situation, not by those applied in cases involving negligence in standard, accepted practice. Nonetheless, as *Hunter*[68] and *Bolam*[76] and *In re F*[84] indicate, the test of the 'reasonable man (physician) in the circumstances' could well be applied in evaluating experimental treatment as negligent or non-negligent. The courts want and encourage doctors to do what they think is 'appropriate' to foster the best interests of their patients.[87] They prefer not to intervene, unless there has been wrongdoing,[68,76] or the patient is unable to give consent and questions are raised as to whether the treatment is in his best interests.[84]

The important thing for the courts to realize is that the circumstances under which the 'reasonable experimenter' acts are distinct and not subject to the same tests of treatment risks and benefits as those circumstances in which the 'reasonable general practitioner' acts. The standard of what is reasonable care can only be properly judged once this distinction in circumstances is recognized. One of the most difficult tasks is to define experimental: what makes treatment experimental and what makes treatment conventional. It seems the difference is often one of degree and is not so much delineated by the degree of risk involved as it is by the number of licensed practitioners who are convinced the potential benefits of the treatment justify its use in appropriate cases. Of course, the treatment must have been shown to work, or its acceptance is not justified. We shall have occasion to consider what standards of due care in the experimental setting should be practiced subsequently.

C.   EXPERIMENTATION AND CHILDREN

Research and experimentation is required to advance the knowledge and success of medical treatment on children as well as adults and on childhood diseases and other abnormalities. Children, however, are particularly vulnerable and present special legal and ethical issues to resolve. Some of those issues we have considered in Chapter 6, where we learned the basic rule that the goal of all medical treatment of children should be to accomplish a purpose consistent with their welfare and best interests.

Parents, until such time as children acquire the capacity to decide for themselves, have decision-making responsibility for their children. Although the Family Law Reform Act 1969 gives children over 16 the right to consent to treatment in England and various American statutes confer the right at 14 and sometimes younger, the fact remains that age is not the test, but rather capacity to decide is. Obviously this will vary depending on the wisdom, perception and sophistication of the child and the complexity, risks and benefits of the treatment.

This being said, it is one thing to ask a child or his guardian to consent to therapeutic experimentation, intended to benefit the child, quite another where the procedure is non-therapeutic. The latter requires a much heavier justification. If the treatment is only for the benefit of other children, then no serious risk to the child exposed to it can be countenanced, even with the consent of the parent. The parent or guardian has no legal or moral authority to authorize treatment harmful to the child. One exception may be where the child is hopelessly and terminally ill. In such instances if the parent can authorize withholding life-sustaining treatment (see discussion in Chapter 4) then certain non-therapeutic experimental treatment may be allowed, but only if it will *not* increase the pain or suffering of the child and it is fully consistent with his or her dignity as a person. It is also sensible that court authorization at least presumptively be required in such unusual instances.[84]

Several general principles can be set out. First, if the child is capable of deciding, neither his or her parents, nor anyone else should decide for him or her. If unable to decide, the surrogate decision-maker must keep the child's best interests paramount in his thinking.[84,87] Second, the risk-benefit ratio is the essential criterion. The expected benefits must justify (outweigh) the reasonably probable risks. Where the research is therapeutic and the child is very ill, the risks can be high and still be justified. Where the research is non-therapeutic, risk must be non-substantial, although it would seem a real hope of substantial benefit to others can be used to justify some, non-lethal, non-disabling, non-disfiguring risk, such as minimal pain or inconvenience.[88]

Thirdly, children should only be used for research if no other suitable subjects are available. As the British Paediatric Association has concluded, research should never be done on children if it can be done on adults.[89]

Finally, there should be no coercion or undue influence applied, but rather a fully informed consent, in writing, should be elicited from the child, or his surrogate, after full explanation of the risks and benefits and alternatives, including the no-experimental treatment alternative. As stated by a Canadian court, the patient being asked to consent to experimental treatment is entitled to a 'full and frank disclosure of all the facts, probabilities and options which a reasonable man might be expected to consider before giving his consent.'[90] Research Ethical Committees exist in the U.K. Ethical Committees and Institutional Review Boards[30] exist in the U.S. Research or experimental treatment protocols are to be submitted to them for review.[88] All child research or experimentation should be required to first obtain the approbation of such ethics committees.[84,88,89] A written protocol and consent form should be submitted for approval. Physician, child and parents should be available, if needed, to ensure the above principles have been honored.

D.   CODES AND ETHICS

While there are few cases or statutes dealing with medical experimentation there have been a sizable number of codes drafted by various bodies in an attempt to set out the proper framework and safeguards for the conducting of medical experimentation and research. The most famous code is undoubtedly the Nuremberg Code of 1948, which grew out of the Allied War Criminals trials against the experimental excesses of Hitler's Nazi physicians. The Code's ten points are headed by the first provision requiring the subject's full, knowing and voluntary consent.

The Code of Ethics of the Word Medical Association[10] is significant for the distinction it outlines between experimentation whose aim is essentially therapeutic for the 'patient' and experimentation whose essential object is purely scientific without direct therapeutic value to the 'subject' involved. In the former situation, the Nuremberg Code stresses the physician's informed belief that the new measure will be of therapeutic value and that the risk of its use is justified by the patient's need. In the latter situation, the World Medical Association Code stresses the acquisition of a fully informed, knowing and free consent.

Professor Paul Freund of Harvard has emphasized the distinction between clinical research or experimentation with a directly therapeutic aim for the 'patient' and that involving a 'subject' not likely to benefit directly form the treatment. He states:[91]

'The appropriate safeguards I would suggest may well vary as we move from the doctor-patient relation at one end to the normal or so-called normal subject at the other. In dealing with the patient, the doctor is guided by his dominant therapeutic aim and responsibility.... The patient is considered as an end and not a means.'

If the law is to deal satisfactorily with experimentation, it will need to recognize this distinction between therapeutic and non-therapeutic purpose more clearly than it has to date. If no commonly accepted therapy exists and a patient is severely ill, experimental treatment reasonably undertaken in his behalf is likely to be well regarded by the courts, regardless of its success of failure.[51] The same cannot be said of experimentation undertaken on a healthy subject or one suffering from an ill irrelevant to the purpose of an experiment which is not for the person's benefit. In this situation, the courts are much more likely to find the experimenter liable unless a clear and concise informed consent has been obtained with full disclosure.[46]

Many experiments, however, may be considered for the benefit of a person who is not sick or in need of therapeutic treatment. This was the case, for instance, with those women who tested – and continue to test – oral contraceptives, although the socio-economic need for contraception could well be considered therapeutic.

Even in situations where no benefit accrues to the experimental subject or is hoped to accrue, the law should make it possible for altruistic individuals to so volunteer. The root question – one common throughout this book and one which will be reiterated even in this chapter – is, to what degree of bodily intrusion or risk thereof, both physiological and psychological, can the individual expose himself by means of consent, consistent with public policy and general social notions of proper conduct regarding the inviolability of the human body? This issue, though a difficult one, can be resolved in general terms and the major elements necessary to its resolution will be submitted in the concluding remarks of this chapter in so far as the context of experimentation is concerned.

The American Medical Association has long had a simple code of ethics for human experimentation.[92] It demands the adherence to three basic requirements: the voluntary consent of the subject; the prior use of animal experimentation to investigate the dangers of each experiment; and the performance of the experiment under proper medical protections and management.

Many other organizations have promulgated codes to govern clinical research and experimentation, but none have the force and effect of law, although they might well be used as a guide by which to assess the propriety of a given experimenter's conduct, were it challenged in a court of law.

The Declaration of Helsinki is probably the most persuasive professional code of ethics on experimentation.[10] It was adopted by the World Medical

Association in 1975. It stresses the fundamental difference between therapeutic and non-therapeutic experimentation. It emphasizes that human research should be based on adequate prior laboratory and animal experimentation.

The Declaration mandates a formal protocol and its approval by an appropriate ethics committee before commencement of a biomedical research procedure. Benefit expected must be in proportion to foreseeable risk. Concern for the subject must always prevail over the interests of science or society. Hazards should be known. Informed consent must be obtained, preferably in writing.

In therapeutic research, the new procedure should promise greater benefit than existing treatment. In non-therapeutic research, the research should be discontinued if it may, if continued, be harmful to the subject.

The ethical and moral limits of human experimentation were commented upon in a speech to physicians by Pope Pius XII.[93] Stressing the incomplete right man has over the disposition of his own body and life according to Catholic theology, the Pope said that a patient,

'. . . has no right to involve his physical or psychic integrity in medical experiments or research when they entail serious destruction, mutilation, wounds or perils.'

His Holiness stated further that new scientific knowledge was not the greatest good and must be subordinated to the rights of humans and any 'moral rule of absolute value.' Science, in other words, must be prepared to take its place in the order of values below human dignity and bodily integrity.

Catholic theologians concerned with medical morals do, however, recognize that risks to life may be undertaken and that even life may be taken 'indirectly' when 'proportionate reasons' exist.

Few of the codes of ethics on experimentation comment on the type of subjects that should or should not be used in any given procedure. In experiments not for the immediate therapeutic value of the subject, all would require a full, knowing, freely given consent. To avoid subtle forces of coercion, some commentators suggest that no 'volunteers' should be accepted from among medical students or laboratory personnel, prisoners, children, or the institutionalized. Some feel the only exception to the rule that experimentation should be for the direct benefit of the subject should be when an adult of unimpaired judgment and under no possible duress freely and knowingly consents to the treatment.

Prisoners and inmates constitute perhaps the most difficult class of individuals in terms of obtaining a truly voluntary consent to non-therapeutic experimentation. There are those who would argue that consent by a prisoner to such a procedure must necessarily be inherently involuntary, because of the pressures to establish a good record and obtain early release or parole. Others believe prisoners do not volunteer expecting any reduction in sentence or for financial reward, but for more immediate reasons, such as to break the monotony of prison life, to boost the ego and feeling of social importance and to relate to the 'outside' and its people in a positive way.[94]

Prisoners have long been used in both American federal and state prisons for non-therapeutic, experimental subjects.[7,8,19] During World War II many prisoners and the feeble-minded in the U.S. were used as experimental subjects for malaria and other treatment felt to be of help in the war effort. The reasoning seemed to be that since soldiers were risking their lives for their country, these 'volunteers' could risk some pain, discomfort or other harm to support that effort.[95] In some states, prisoners must now consent in writing and have the privilege to withdraw at any time from any experiment.[96] Commenting on the practice of using prisoners for experiments in this particular state, a well-known professor has concluded:

'If no pressures are exerted, if no special parole favours are held out as bait (although serving as a subject can constitute favorable evidence on the parole record), and if freedom to withdraw at any time is preserved, there would seem to be good justification for use of adult prisoners who consent after being reasonably informed.[97]

While many would agree with this suggestion, it seems somewhat factious to argue that no special parole favours should be held out as a carrot to induce 'consent' to experimentation, but at the same time allow the subjects' volunteering to constitute favorable evidence on the parole record. The practical effect and therefore the coercive element would appear to be present in either situation. However, perhaps society is less likely to be concerned about the full protection of prison inmates from such coercion than it is in regard to members of the public in general, particularly where the beneficial effects of the particular experiment to the latter group are at least reasonably probable.

Others believe the use of experimental subjects should not be so restricted. How are we to solve children's diseases, they ask, if children cannot be used in experimentation? Medical opinion is clearly divided concerning the use of normal healthy children or children suffering from some irrelevant disease as subjects in medical research. There are those who advocate that,

'No medical procedure involving the slightest physical or mental pain may be inflicted on a child for experimental purposes unless there is a reasonable chance, or at least a hope, that the child may benefit thereby.'[98]

At the same time, other practitioners advocate that,

'... no procedure should be carried out involving risk or discomfort without a reasonable chance of benefit to that child *or other children*.' [Emphasis added][98]

Perhaps the latter observation is the more realistic one. However, to expose a child under sixteen to anything more than a very slight risk of harm or injury resulting from an experiment not for his benefit seems unjustified. Experimentation, in these circumstances, must give way. In situations where the children are approaching majority or are of such an age that they are considered to be capable of full understanding of the experimental procedure involved, most advocate that the child's consent alone is sufficient in those cases where the experimental treatment is clearly therapeutic in nature.[99]

The majority of comment would exclude large classes of individuals as acceptable subjects for medical experimentation on grounds of the danger of express or implied coercion. Others assert all experiments are permissible, given only the limitations of 'informed consent' and that they be 'carefully conceived and thought to be of potential benefit.'[100] One suggested procedure outlined to insure 'informed consent' requires it to be in writing, notarized, countersigned by the experimenter and another colleague not involved in the experiment and witnessed by two other individuals – such as relatives, friends or a court-appointed attorney for the subject – all in the presence of the subject.[101]

Even those strongly favoring non-therapeutic research with informed consent acknowledge that the experiment must be potentially directly beneficial to the subject where the possibility of death or serious harm exists, or the subject is less than sixteen years old, and that a local administrative or ethics board with a mixed panel of medical experts and laymen would have to approve any such planned experiment.

One other ethical difficulty posed by much of medical experimentation is its inevitable reliance on a 'control group': those who take sugar pills, for example, instead of a penicillin derivative and are used as a measure to determine the effects of the experimental substance or treatment. These people must consent to undergo the full rigors of the experimental therapy and cannot be told they will serve only as decoys. This, of course, involves a subtle but patent series of misrepresentations and may be ethically unpalatable to some. However, it is submitted, such a practice is generally recognized as inherent in many experiments involving more than one individual. People, in offering themselves as subjects for (non-therapeutic) experimentation, must be presumed to have understood and accepted this fact, provided they have expressly consented to it. Also, it involves no harm to the subject.

E. CONCLUSIONS

Experimentation should be legally defined and treated so that the issue becomes not one of research and experimentation as opposed to accepted medical practice, but rather one of whether the experimentation was justified in the circumstances, carried out with consent and proper skill and care and with due regard for the interests of the subject concerned.

A reasonable and much-needed legal approach to experimentation could be worked out with tools that are already available. An enacted legislative program could take advantage of some of the well-regarded codes that have been worked out in this area, such as those of Nuremberg and the World Medical Association. The basic concepts of these Codes could be incorporated into a broad and flexible statutory framework to guide and govern medical experimentation as could the oft-expressed thoughts and practices of leading practitioners and students in the field. Once the basic safeguards and procedures of these codes and writings were incorporated in legislation, the standards by which to determine whether or not a particular experimental treatment was undertaken with due care would be established and the question would merely be one, as in all cases of medical negligence, of determining whether or not the facts of the case constituted due care in light of these established standards of conduct. Additional procedural safeguards from those set out in the above-mentioned codes have been suggested. Hospitals or medical associations should convene ethics committees of qualified experts and laymen to serve as a review board prior to the undertaking of any non-therapeutic experimentation.

As has been suggested a number of times in other contexts of controversial surgery, the use of a second doctor could be utilized most effectively in the experimental context, by requiring the appointment of such a second, disinterested physician to ensure the patient's consent, to act as a monitor-investigator and to work along with the experimenting physician and his team to ensure that the approved procedures of the experimentation were carried out properly, that no other unauthorized procedures were carried out, and that the integrity of the patient or subject was observed, consistent with his consent, and at all times held paramount. The physician involved in the patient's therapy should be separate from any physician involved in research at the same time.[102]

If the subject's full consent has been obtained, and if the standards as generally set out by legislative enactment derived from the codes and comments that have been discussed above were complied with, then a presumption of due care should arise by operation of law. It would then be for the prosecuting or suing party to show that because of the peculiar nature or risk of the experimental conduct at issue or the nature of the subject or patient, due care necessitated certain additional, specified safeguards to be observed, before any liability, be it civil or criminal, could properly be imposed on the physician.

Once the general standards of consent and due care in the experimental context have been set out, there still remains the very difficult task of applying those standards to situations involving experimental treatment that differ widely as to the likelihood of success to be derived from said treatment, the degree of the socio-medical importance of any such success to be derived from the experimental treatment and, most important of all, the risk to the patient-subject involved. In the final analysis, the guiding principle to determine liability, due care and consent issues aside, must be whether the value of the experiment undertaken is greater than the risk to the subject involved. The greater the personal risk posed by an experiment, the greater also must be the therapeutic value of the experiment to the subject or to others and the social benefits to be gained or interests to be advanced. The criticism of such a guiding principle – namely, that it rests on a value judgment and as such is always subject to discriminatory application by those in a position to assert such a judgment – would seem to be irrefutable. But, for whatever solace or justification it may offer, the great bulk of our laws are based on value judgments that involve a weight or balancing process between conflicting goals or values. Several elements must be appointed weights in this balancing process between acceptance of the need for experimentation to go on – with at least some encouragement and protection – and security of the individual from undesirable and unnecessary harm.

First, the risk of harm to the individual must be considered. Second, the degree of the harm risked should be evaluated; here psychological as well as physical harm must be recognized. Third, the mental capacity of the individual concerned is relevant, as it effects his ability to consent.

Against these considerations must be weighed the physical condition of the person and the benefit he stands to gain from exposure to the experimentation. The extent of the benefit potentially to be gained is important, as is its existence. If a high degree of risk is involved in an attempt to benefit an individual by experimental removal of a mere wart or mole, then it is unlikely to be justifiable experimentation. The same will, however, not be true if an individual's very life is at stake, for the degree of benefit possibly to be derived is much greater.

Randomization is inevitable in experimentation. Some will be selected for promising new drugs or procedures, others will not, or will receive only a placebo. The drugs may help, or they may not. However, such limitations are unfortunate, but not unfair, so long as no invidious discrimination occurs. Until proven, experimental treatment will be given where it has the potential to do the most medical good and where other therapy is unavailable or ineffective. Until established, its availability will necessarily be restricted by cost, protocol restraints and availability of resources and qualified medical personnel. Questions of fair allocation will inevitably arise, which we will discuss in Chapter 12. However, within the control group those who receive the drug and those who do not must necessarily be chosen at random.

The advent of local ethical committees in both the U.S. and U.K. has and will do much to resolve these issues without legal entanglements. This is desirable, to be encouraged. Only in cases of dispute, disagreement, questioned motive, or negligence should resort to the courts be necessary.

NOTES

1 From Regan, L.J., *Doctor and Patient and the Law*, Mosby (3rd ed. 1956) p.30, quoted by Ladimer, 'Human experimentation: medicolegal aspects,' 257 *New Eng. J. Med.* 18 (1957)
2 Lansdown, 'Guinea Pigs of Hippocrates and the criminal law,' (1960) 77 *S.A.L.J.* 117.
3 Haggins, 'Due care by physicians in use of new drugs,' 14 *Clev.-Mar. L.R.* 506, 508 (1964).
4 Beecher, 'Experimentation in man,' 169 *J. Am. Med. Ass.* 461)2 (1959).
5 *Ibid.*
6 Ladimer, 'Ethical and legal aspects of research on human beings,' 3 *J. Pub. Law* 467 (1954).
7 Rothman, 'Ethics & Human Experimentation' 317 *New Eng. J. Med.* 1354 (1966)
8 Beecher, 'Ethics & Clinical Research' 274 *New Eng. J. Med.* 1354 (1966)
9 Cmnd 2382.
10 The Declaration, as revised in 1975, is reproduced in full in Mason & McCall Smith, *Law & Medical Ethics* (1987, 2d. ed.), p.326.
11 *U.S. Code Cong. & Admin. News*, 93d Cong., 2d Sess., Pamph. No. 7, p.2168 (note 6), (Sen. Rep. No. 93–381), discussed in *Clay v. Martin* (1975, 2d Cir.) 509 Fed. 2d 109, 113.
12 See 'Guidelines to Aid Ethical Committees Considering Research Involving Children' 1980 *Brit. Med. J.* 229, 231
13 Ladimer, *op. cit.*, p.482.
14 Freund, 'Ethical problems in human experimentation,' 273 *New Eng. J. med.* 687, 689 (1965).
15 Keaton, 'Liability for medical experimentation,' 40 *Cal. L.R.* 159, 162 (1952).
16 Shimkin, 'The research worker's point of view' (in a Symposium entitled, 'The Problem of Experimentation on Human Beings'), 117 *Science* 205 (1953).
17 Ivy, 'The history and ethics of the use of human subjects in medical experiments,' 108 *Science* 1 (1948).
18 Ladimer, 3 *J. Pub. Law* 467, 474 (1954).

19 *Clay v. Martin*, (1975, 2d Cir.) 509 Fed. 2d 109, (Naltrexone anti-narcotic dependency drug); *Mackey v. Procunier* (1973, 9th Cir.) 477 Fed. 2d 877 (succinylcholine 'fright drug').

20 See Lansdown, loc. cit.; *Hyman v. Jewish Chronic Disease Hospital*, 251 N.Y.S. 2d 818 (1964) discussed *infra*; Lear, 'Do we need new rules for experiments on people? 1966 *Saturday Review* (5 February 1961). One example: in New York City, after exposure of research being carried out without being reported to the authorities, it was felt necess-ary to issue a General Order in 1949 to all City hospitals requiring formal review and approval of research proposals and limitation of medical investigation to that specifically designed to the benefit of the involved patient. Ladimer, 257 *New Eng. J. Med.* 18, 23 (1957).

21 See discussion in Chapters 5 and 6.

22 Any of the standard texts in delict or tort may be consulted for the standard of care expected of a physician in the undertaking of accepted or ordinary medical treatment. See especially, the note in 29 Col. L. R., 985 (1929).

23 *Trindle v. Weaver* (1943) 23 Cal. 2d 330, 333; *Hunter v. Hanley* (1955) S.C. 200.

24 *Bryant v. Biggs*, (1951) 331 Mich, 64, 49 N.W. 2d 63.

25 *Sidaway v. Bethlem Royal Hosp. Governors* (1985) 1 All E.R. 643 (H.L.); *Texas & P.R. Co. v. Behymer* (1903) 189 U.S. 468, 470.

26 Prosser, *Torts*, 3rd ed., §32.

27 Mulford, 'Experimentation on human beings,' 20 *Stanford L.R.* 99 (1967).

28 The English decision of *Gold v. Haringey* (1987) 2 All E.R. 888, holds there should be no difference in the standard of disclosure required for therapeutic or non-therapeutic treatment. However, there birth con-trol was the intended result of the surgery. This can be viewed as therapeutic treatment. It does not need to cure the patient or prevent injury to be therapeutic if it benefits his or her mental and emotional health. In addition, it was for the benefit of the patient, a purpose and intent that may be entirely lacking in non-therapeutic research to increase knowledge or benefit others.

29 52 Stat. 1040, 1052 (1938), as amended 21 U.S.C. §355 (1952) (Supp. 1954, 1964). It should, in passing, be noted that a 1900 bill proposed for the District of Columbia would explicitly have controlled medical experimentation as no other American statute does. The bill, which failed passage, would have prohibited research on children, incom-petents and pregnant women and any investigations not intended for the amelioration of the patient's condition. The bill contained all the major safeguards that would eventually be written into the 1948 Nu-remberg Code (discussed *infra*); written description of the proposal, review by an authoritative body, performance only by qualified doctors, voluntary and fully competent consent by the individual concerned, termination on request of the subject and reporting of the results obtained. Ladimer, 257 *New Eng. J. Med.* 18, 23 (1957).

30 *Ibid.*; Haggins, *op. cit.* p.515.

31 21 U.S.C. 355 (i) (1968).

32 *Canterbury v. Spence* (1972, D.C.App.) 464 Fed.2d 772, 789 (cert. den. 409 U.S. 1064).

33 21 C.F.R. §130.37 (1968).

34 40 Fed. Reg. 11, 854, §46.3(c), (1975).

35 *Trantafello v. Medical Center of Tarzana* (1986) 182 C.A.3d 315, 320 (acrylic implanted to maintain cervical vertebral space following removal of disc.)

36 *Moore v. Regents of University of California* (1988) 202 C.A.3d 1230, 1254.

37 *Regina v. Coney* (1882) 8 Q.B.D. 534

38 *Rex v. Donovan* (1934) 2 K.B. 498.

39 See discussion in Chapters 2 and 8; *Bravery v. Bravery* (1954) 3 All E.R. 59 (Denning, L. J., dissent); *Rex v. Donovan* (1934) 2 K.B. 498.

40 Calif. Health & Safety Code §24172 (1978).

41 Calif. Health & Safety Code §24173(c), (1978).

42 California Business and Professions Code §2137 (1937)

43 (1767) 2 Wils. K.B. 359, 95 Eng. Rep. 860; See Devlin, *Samples of Law-making*, pp.97–9.

44 2 Wils. K.B. at 362, 95 Eng. Rep. at 862.

45 Ladimer, 3 *J. Pub. Law* 467, 481 (1954).

46 60 Barb. 488 (N.Y. 1871), rev'd on other grounds, 50 N.Y. 696 (1872).

47 (1895) 20 Colo. 532; 39 P. 577.

48 *Siverson v. Weber*, (1962) 57 Cal. 2d 834, 839.

49 (1914) 183 Mich. 252, 150 N.W. 118.

50 (1930) 107 Cal.App. 175.

51 (1935) 272 Mich. 273, 261 N.W. 762, at 765.

52 *Pound v. Medney* (1985, Ga. App.) 337 S.E.2d 772 (synthetic fiber hair implants).

53 *Gaston v. Hunter* (1978 Az.App.) 588 Pac. 2d 326 (Use of chymopapayn, an investigational drug, for the procedure of chemonucleolysis to treat low)back disc herniation.)

54 (1881) 55 Iowa 628, 8 N.W. 469.

55 8 N.W. 469, at 471; to the same effect are *Rice v. State*, 8 Mo. 561 and *Commonwealth v. Thomson*, 6 Mass. 134.

56 (1905) 50 Fla. 55, 39 So. 421.

57 (1914) 127 Minn. 282, 149 N.W. 297; Accord, *Peo. v. Hunt* (1915) 26 C.A. 514.

58 *Hyman v. Jewish Chronic Disease Hospital* (1964) 251 N.Y.S. 2d 818.

59 *Reibl v. Hughes* (1980, S.Ct.Can.) 114 D.L.R. (3d) 1; *Canterbury v. Spence, supra.*

60 *Roe v. Wade* (1973) 410 U.S. 113 (abortion); *Matter of Quinlan* (1976, N.J.) 355 A.2d 647 (withdrawing life-sustaining treatment when comatose).

61 *People v. Privitera* (1979) 23 Cal.3d 697, (cert.den., 1979) 444 U.S. 949.

62 *Custody of a Minor* (1978, Mass.) 379 N.E. 2d 1053 (laetrile and 'metabolic' therapy proposed by parents for three year old boy with leukemia).

63 *Matter of Hofbauer* (1979, N.Y.) 393 N.E.2d 1009; *Weber v. Stony Brook Hospital* (1983, N.Y.) 456 N.E.2d 1186.

64 *Hall v. State* (1986, Ind.) 493 N.E.2d 433; *J.V. v. State* (1987, Fla.) 516 So.2d 1133.

65 Ladimer, 3 *J.Pub. Law* 467, 510 (1954).

66 25 Cox 598 (1916); commented on but not commended in Williams, *Criminal Law* (2nd ed. 1961) p.108.

67 Gordon, *The Criminal Law of Scotland*, pp.361, 738, 755.

68 (1955) *S.L.T.* 213, 1955 S.C. 200.

69 Lord President Clyde, at 1955 S.C. 205; *Farquhar v. Murray* (1910) 3F.869, deciding the test of negligence for a physician to be the ordinary one of a reasonable man in the circumstances, was the only prior reported medical negligence case found.

70 (1955) S.C. at 204)6.

71 *Sidaway v. Bethlem Royal Hosp.* (1985) 2 W.L.R. 480 (H.L.)

72 See discussion in Chapter 5 on Consent; see, in particular, *Helling v. Carey* (1974, Wash) 519 Pac. 2d 981 (superseded by statute)

73 The *T. J. Hooper* (1932, 2d Cir.) 60 Fed. 2d 737, 740 (cert. den. 287 U.S. 662)

74 (1960) *S.L.T.* (News) 19.

75 Accord, *Crivon v. Barnet, etc.* (1958) C.L.Y. 2283 (wrong diagnosis of cancer and consequent wrong treatment not necessarily the same as negligent or unskillful diagnosis).

76 (1957) 1 W.L.R. 582.

77 (1960) C.L.Y. 2184.

78 (1954) 2 Q.B. 66.

79 At p.83; see also Addison, 'The medico-legal aspects of accepted practice and recognized hazards in medical treatment,' 2 *Med. Sci. Law* 284 (1961).

80 *R. v. Mental Health Commission ex parte W* (High Court, Stuart-Smith, LJ), May 26, 1988, *The Times* 27 May 1988.

81 The case is discussed in Brahams, 'Voluntary Chemical Castration of a Mental Patient' 1988 *The Lancet* 2, 1291; Dyer, 'Mental Health Commission defeated over paedophile,' 1988 *Brit. Med. J.* 296, 1660.

82 Brahams, 'Death of Patient Participating in Trial of Oral Morphine for Relief of Postoperative Pain,' 1984 *The Lancet* 1, 1083.

83 'Secret randomised clinical trials' 1982 *The Lancet* 2, 78; Brahams, 1982 *The Lancet* 1, 1028.

84 (1989) 2 W.L.R. 1025 (H.L.).

85 Also known as *Berkshire Health Authority and another* (Feb. 13, 1989, Court of Appeal), (May 4, 1989, House of Lords), *The Times*, 25 May 1989, reported in Brahams, 1989 *The Lancet* 340, 1089.

86 *Hyman Jewish Chronic Disease Hosp.* (1964) 251 N.Y.S. 2d 818 (note 20 *supra*) is a possible exception, but the case involved only a procedural point of evidence on appeal.

87 *In re C (A Minor) (Wardship: medical treatment)*, (1989) 2 W.L.R. 240 (C.A.).

88 Tindall, 'What Research of Children May Be Permitted?' 80 *J. Roy. Soc. Med.* 321 (1987)

89 1980 *Brit. Med. J.* 229

90 *Halushka v. Univ. of Saskatchewan* (1965, Sask.) 52 W.W.R. 608, 53 D.L.R.(2d) 436; see Freedman, 'The Validity of Ignorant Consent to Medical Research,' in Shannon (ed.), *Bioethics* (1987, 3d ed.), p.356.

91 Freund, *op cit.*, p.689; a very similar article is found by Freund in *Trial* (Oct.–Nov. 1966) p.46.

92 132 *J. Am. Med. Ass.* 1090 (1946).

93 Kelly, 'Ethical and religious directives for Catholic Hospitals,' *Morals and Medicine*, p.314.

94 McDonald, 'Why prisoners volunteer to be experimental subjects,' 202 *J. Am. Med. Ass.* 511, 512 (1967).

95 Rothman, 'Ethics & Human Reproduction,' 317 *N. Eng. J. Med* 1195, 1197 (1987).

96 Iowa Code Ann. §246.47 (Supp. 1966) provides: 'The board of control may send to the hospital of the medical college of the state university inmates of the Iowa state penitentiary and the men's reformatory for medical research at the hospital. Before any inmate is sent to the medical college, he must volunteer his services in writing. An inmate may withdraw his consent at any time.' Before the passage of this statute, the state attorney general was of the opinion that it was illegal to accept prisoner volunteers for medical research. Hodges and Bean, 'The use of prisoners for medical research,' 202 *J.Am Med. Ass.* 513, 514 (1967).

97 Stason, 'Role of law in medical progress,' 32 *Law and Cont. Probs.* 563, 594 (1967).

98 1953 *The Lancet* 2, 993 (Letters).

99 Stason, *op. cit.* p.593 (referring to *Restatement of Torts* §59, comment a (1939).

100 Kaplan, 'Experimentation: an articulation of a new myth,' 46 *Neb. L.R.* 87 (1967).

101 Strauss, 'Bodily injury and the defense of consent,' (1964) 81 *S.A.L.J.* 179, 193.

102 See *Moore v. Regents of University of California* (1988) 202 Cal. App. 3d 1230, 1254.

THE END OF LIFE

10

Terminating Life-sustaining Treatment for the Competent Patienta

A. INTRODUCTION

1. *Technological advances have complicated care*

Until recent times death was, by and large, a fairly simple and uncomplicated matter medically. Most people died at home, or if in hospital there was limited technology available to postpone the dying process. Analgesic drugs were available to make pain more tolerable, but resuscitative and artificial life-prolongation devices and procedures – vital organ transplants, renal dialysis, chemotherapy, artificial respiration and circulation, and various chemical stimulants to restart and maintain heart or other vital functions – were normally not available.

Technological advances over the past 40 years are vast. At the same time, due to improvements in both preventative and clinical medicine, diet and lifestyle changes, life expectancy has increased. Approximately 15 per cent of the British population, for example, is estimated to be aged 65 or older.

These technological advances have allowed many disease processes to be overcome and life extended, but at times the result has been unfortunate prolongation of the dying process. This is particularly so because six of ten Britons and eight of ten Americans die in hospitals, with all this technology readily at hand to be used.

Several factors have encouraged doctors to at times utilize nearly every conceivable procedure or technology available in treating patients. First, the traditional fee-for-service method of compensating health care providers in America, both by private and government insurance payors, has financially rewarded doctors, hospitals and laboratories in direct proportion to the number and scope of procedures and services undertaken. This system of compensation has undoubtedly encouraged abuses and over-utilization of medical resources, often to the detriment of humane individual care. This fee for service method of compensation is now fast becoming a thing of the past in the United States. It has been a much less significant factor in Britain due to the National Health Service. This distinction may in large part explain why Britain spends about 6 per cent of its GNP on health care and America nearly twice that amount.

In addition, the natural tendency of many doctors has been to use any available technology, in the hope it may improve the patient's condition or extend his life, even if the patient is suffering from a terminal and incurable malady. This has been seen as a logical extension of the doctor's ethical mission to save life wherever possible. The practice has extended many lives. It has also increased medical knowledge concerning such new devices and procedures, presumably for the benefit of many patients. However, for others it has increased the cost and prolonged the anguish of dying. As Vaux has stated,

'If biomedical acts of life extension become acts of death prolongation, we may force some patients to outlive their deaths, and we may ultimately repudiate the primary life-saving and merciful ethic itself.'[1]

Much of the mystery surrounding medicine has been removed by the modern media, which has found the unmasking of various, often sophisticated, medical procedures to be readily saleable to the public. As knowledge and the availability of new, life-prolonging medical procedures has increased, so has public familiarity with them. Particularly in the United States, a greater consumer's attitude toward the delivery of that health care has resulted, with many patients seeing even the most sophisticated medical technology as their right. This has also been caused by an increasing emphasis on individual rights of autonomy and self-determination concerning medical treatment choices. The emergence of 'informed consent' over the past three decades has made doctors and patients alike more aware of the importance of frank and honest communication between them and of the patient's paramount right to decide.[2]

Finally, fear of legal liability has, at times, undoubtedly encouraged the practice of 'defensive medicine;' that is, doing more than felt necessary to be sure that neither patient nor family later claims injury or death resulted from not doing what was necessary. In all three jurisdictions under consideration – Scotland, England and America – it is essentially true that 'good medicine makes good law' and that the 'law is content to follow good medical practice.' However, where the medical consensus is undeveloped, uncertain, or in evolution because of rapid technological changes and research advances in medicine, typical of the past 25 years, then greater risk exists that a court may see fit to decide the proper standard of care, perhaps adversely to the doctor.

2. *The role of informed consent*

The emergence of the doctrine of informed consent – more so in America than in Britain – has weakened the traditionally highly paternalistic approach of medicine to the patient. Since most people are aware – at least by

publicized stories, if not by actual experience – of cases of undue prolongation of the dying process by over-zealous reliance on 'hi-tech' medical
procedures, many want to avoid this in their care and treatment. Consent
provides the vehicle for the competent patient to limit life-prolonging
treatment. If the competent patient must consent before treatment can be
undertaken, then the ethical and legal corollary must be that he or she can
refuse consent to either continuation or commencement of treatment.[3] This
principle is of particular significance where the treatment commenced or
proposed is life-prolonging in nature, since the consequence of refusing
consent will be the demise of the patient.

Emphasis has changed from the ethical principle of beneficence in medical care, which supported a more paternalistic approach: the physician did
what was 'best' for his patient.[4] More recently the principle of autonomy has
emerged: the physician does what his patient consents to after being properly informed of his or her choices.

3. *Competing state interests*

Interests of the state or of society may intervene at times to restrict the
individual's right to exercise self-determination in medical care. These
instances are likely to be rare. However, if strongly enough rooted, the
state's interest may be represented in statutory enactment. The Abortion
Act 1967 is a clear example, representing the interest of the state in granting
a degree of legal protection to the fetus by restricting the instances where
abortion may be undertaken without criminal liability.

The state interests that might be asserted to limit the patient's right to
consent to or refuse medical treatment have been identified in the American
cases as: (1) the preservation of life; (2) the prevention of suicide; (3) the
protection of dependent third parties; and, (4) the promotion of medical
ethics and professional standards.[5] Where the patient is terminally and
incurably ill, these interests have little weight. However, where the patient
is not so afflicted, they gain added influence.

In the face of competent, informed refusal to consent, the American
courts have paid little more than lip service to these potentially counter-
vailing interests, finding them foreshadowed by the individual's right of
free choice. It is only in the instance where the validity of the patient's
consent is in question,[6] the patient is demanding not simply nontreatment,
but active mistreatment,[7] or the patient is clearly curable and children –
whether in being, or in utero – will be disadvantaged,[8] that the courts seem
willing to seriously consider overriding the express wishes of the patient.

The first instance, finding the patient incompetent, is obviously the
easiest route for doctors to rely upon in refusing to honor patient wishes or
in seeking affirmative treatment authorizations from the courts. It presents
the potential for paternalistic abuse by health care providers if the patient's

decision is deemed contrary to prevailing medical practice or there are fears of liability for abandonment or negligent nontreatment. However, the issue of competence is frequently present in treatment of the elderly and dying. Many patients will become borderline or variable in terms of capacity to give or refuse a knowing consent during and as the result of a terminal illness or because of the treatment for it.

4. *Patient autonomy is foremost*

Where the patient is clearly able to express himself or herself competently, there are few circumstances where the patient's decision should not be honored. Family or physicians are free to try to dissuade the patient, but the latter must be careful their viewpoint does not create undue or unfair pressure upon the patient, given the fiduciary relationship of trust, confidence and dependence presumed existent between patient and physician. If such competent refusals are presented to the courts in a petition seeking treatment authorization, which has not apparently occurred in Britain to date and seems unlikely to, the courts can be expected to honor the patient's competently-expressed treatment refusal, as they have in almost all such cases in the United States.

A refusal does not require any mistreatment by the doctor; it simply requires him to abstain from treating out of respect for patient autonomy. So long as the patient had been properly informed of the consequences,[9] this is a perfectly ethical course for the doctor to take. If the evidence is that the decision was reached competently, that is, based on an understanding of the treatment proposed and the likely material consequences of refusing it,[10] then there is no case for seeking to exercise jurisdiction based on any residual prerogative powers of *parens patriae*. This doctrine is resorted to only if it is necessary to protect the best interests of one judged incapable of doing so himself.[11] For example, an English court has recognized that a competent adult may refuse a life-saving blood transfusion, as mandated by her religious beliefs as a Jehovah's Witness. While not necessary to a decision in the case, there was nonetheless no suggestion by the judge that the doctor could or should overrule the refusal of the patient.[12] Similarly, the Florida Supreme Court recently upheld the right of a competent adult to refuse a blood transfusion or other medical treatment on religious grounds, even if it meant imminent death.[13] Doctors overruled the wishes of a Jehovah's Witness and gave her a life-saving transfusion. The court held that the individual's rights to personal privacy and to religious freedom outweighed the doctors' interest in saving lives where possible to do so, even though two minor children would be left with only one parent if she died.[13]

That leaves only the interests of dependent third parties – presumably minor children – to justify court intervention in the face of a competent patient's refusal of treatment. While courts are likely to order curable treatment for a single parent, the extreme reluctance of the courts to interfere is shown by American decisions which have declined to compel curable treatment, competently refused, on the basis that the surviving children can be cared for by a surviving spouse alone, or by other family members.[13]

5. *Suicide may be implicated*

Some physicians or family members may be concerned that honoring a patient's treatment refusal may amount to aiding and abetting a suicide, prohibited in England by the Suicide Act 1961, Section 2(1) and in the United States. Unless affirmative steps are taken by the individual, recognizing they will aid the patient to commit suicide, there normally would not be any liability. Suicide connotes an affirmative act (an overdose of pills), or a deliberate omission (starvation by fasting) with the intent to bring about one's death.[14] Suicide is, after all, an act of 'self-destruction.' It presumes that the individual himself or herself is the causative agent for death.

Where the patient is suffering a terminal and incurable illness, the illness, not any act or conduct of the individual, is the underlying cause of death. If the illness is allowed to run its natural course, without active medical intervention, it causes death. Intent is a critical factor. If the individual does not want to die, but does not want to live with the treatment burdens that his or her illness entails, there is seemingly no intent to bring about one's death by refusing further life-prolonging treatment.[15] This may be a matter of degree. Refusing dialysis in end-stage kidney disease is one thing; refusing food and water capable of normal ingestion in such a case is quite another thing.

Since suicide and attempted suicide are not criminal, the real issue is the risk of a physician or family member being considered to have aided and abetted a suicide. No such prosecution has been reported in Britain. Where the physician honors the competent refusal of treatment by his patient, he ethically and legally simply allows the patient to exercise his or her right to refuse treatment. This is proper, since '[t]here can be no doubt as to the rights of the competent adult to refuse treatment,' including 'opposition to forced feeding.'[16]

Where, however, the physician or family member actively provides the means for the patient to take his or her life, such as placing the barbiturates by the bedstand, then there is a specific act intended to aid suicide which, if proven, would clearly support criminal liability, with imprisonment of up to 14 years.[17] However, there are no reported prosecutions of physicians for prescribing pills in order to help a patient commit suicide. Absent proof of an act and of specific intent, criminal liability for assisting a suicide will not obtain.[18] While the motive of the doctor, humanitarian though it may be, will provide no defense to the crime,[19] intent is a prerequisite to liability.

That is a strong impediment that undoubtedly in large part explains the lack of successful prosecutions of physicians on either side of the Atlantic. In addition, professional opinion in this area is changing and there is emerging support for assisting the competent patient in *extremis* to end his life where his pain is not controlled by treatment.[20] Experience shows there is very little chance in Britain of a physician being found guilty of serious criminal liability by a British jury.

Given these conflicting interests, the law has developed fairly clearly. Individual autonomy holds a strong place in the law. First we look to English Law.

<h3 style="text-align:center">B. ENGLAND</h3>

1. *Life-prolonging treatment may be withdrawn*

Where a competent patient refuses further life-prolonging treatment, the consequence will be his death. If he has been properly informed of that consequence, the choice is his in English law. As Brahams has stated,[21]

> 'In Britain, fortunately, medical decision making where the patient is competent is still a matter for the individuals concerned and nobody else.'

Decisions to withdraw life-prolonging treatment are made in the United Kingdom, since not all patients elect to continue with active, interventionist medical treatment until the moment of death. In addition, physicians are not obligated of offer, to institute, or to continue futile treatment that is of no use in improving a hopeless prognosis.[22] No physician has been prosecuted in Britian for honoring the decision of a competent patient to forego further treatment. As Twycross has aptly stated,

> 'a doctor has no legal, moral or ethical obligation to use drugs or apply treatments if their use can be described as prolonging the process or distress of dying.'[23]

Eventually all patients must die. When treatment offers no positive benefits, it need not be continued and may harm the patient if it is.

The legal position is unambiguous. As reflected by the words of Lord Bridge in the well-known *Sidaway* case,

> 'It is clearly right to recognize that a conscious adult patient of sound mind is entitled to decide for himself whether or not he will submit to a particular course of treatment proposed by the doctor, most significantly surgical treatment under general anaesthesia.'

This principle logically follows from the fact that medical treatment may only be undertaken on a competent adult with his or her consent. Where the patient is not competent to refuse treatment, or treatment is intended to shorten life, a different situation exists both legally and morally.

2. *Deliberately shortening life is murder*

Murder is the killing of a person with malice aforethought (premeditation and deliberation). Three murder prosecutions have been reported undertaken in England in recent times against physicians for allegedly deliberately causing death by the giving of drugs.

a. *The case against Dr. Carr.* In the most recent, Dr. Carr was accused of attempting murder by the injection of a massive barbiturate (phenobarbitone) into his patient who was suffering from inoperable lung cancer.[24] The doctor was acquitted. The case confirms two earlier cases of physician acquittal, not in small part apparently resulting from at least the following three factors: (1) British juries, like their American counterparts, are not the least prone to convict doctors of murder, absent proof of the most compelling persuasiveness; (2) where a terminal or life-threatening malady is suffered by the patient, it is most likely to be found the cause of death; and, (3) the British public may well favor medically-provided assistance for a peaceful passing in hopeless cases of intolerable pain.[25]

b. *The case against Dr. Arthur.* In 1981, Dr. Leonard Arthur, a pediatrician, was called to examine a Down's Syndrome baby whose distressed parents had rejected the infant. The Doctor entered a note in the record, 'Parents do not wish it to survive. Nursing care only.' He prescribed a morphine-type drug, dihydrocodeine, to be given as needed to alleviate the infant's distress. The baby was not fed, and died after 69 hours, allegedly due to lung stasis caused by the drug's toxicity. He was accused of murder.[26] While involving neither an adult, nor a competent patient, the case is significant for being one of the very few prosecutions against a physician presented to an English jury. For this reason its facts are repeated here.[27] The doctor contended death from natural causes – broncho-pneumonia brought on by the Down's Syndrome. When evidence during the trial showed evidence of substantial other congenital abnormalities as shown by post-mortem histological analysis, the murder charge was reduced to attempted murder.

A number of respected medical experts called for the defense testified that the treatment prescribed by Dr. Arthur was within accepted norms of prevailing neonatal medical care. The Judge, in summing up, instructed the jury that the medical profession could not rely upon established codes of practice as a defense to a criminal charge if such practice conflicted with the law and that no one had power of life or death over another. However, in what must have influenced the jury not to convict, the Judge concluded, 'I imagine you will think long and hard before concluding that doctors of the eminence we have heard here have evolved standards that amount to committing a crime.'[28]

After a lengthy trial it took the jury only two hours to return a unanimous verdict of acquittal. To what extent the attitude that parents and the doctor should be allowed to let a severely handicapped baby die influenced the jury not to convict is not clear. It surely played a role. Still, the case points out the reluctance of English judges and juries to meddle with the physician-patient relationship, even where the patient was a newborn and decisions were made for him by his parents which were determined to be reasonable by hindsight and the later discovery of handicaps other than merely Down's syndrome. It stands as yet another example that an English jury has yet to convict a physician of criminal conduct for terminating or withholding life-sustaining treatment from a patient.

c. *The case against Dr. Adams.* In the earliest of the three modern cases of homicide brought against a physician in England, that of Dr. John Bodkin Adams,[29] after a 17-day trial the jury took only 45 minutes to return a verdict of not guilty. Dr. Adams was accused of prescribing and administering large doses of heroin and morphine with the intent of causing the death of his 84 year old patient, in whose estate he also was listed as a modest beneficiary.

In what has become a classic summing up to the jury, Mr. Justice Devlin advised the jury that if the act was intended to kill and did in fact kill it was murder. It did not matter if the victim was close to death anyway and that her life was only cut short by weeks or days, it was murder just the same.

The Judge further advised that no special defense was available to the doctor because he acted to shorten life mercifully to avoid the severe pain or helpless misery of the patient. Motive was irrelevant.

However, Lord Devlin then went on to state that,

> 'If the first purpose of medicine, the restoration of health, can no longer be achieved there is still much for a doctor to do, and he is entitled to do all that is proper and necessary to relieve pain and suffering, even if the measures he takes may incidentally shorten human life.'[30]

The remarks of Lord Devlin in the trial of Dr. Adams that life may not be *deliberately* shortened, even briefly in a terminal illness, were reiterated in the recent trial of Dr. Carr. There, Mars-Jones, J. stated,

> 'However gravely ill a man may be ... he is entitled in our law to every hour ... that God has granted him. That hour or hours may be the most precious and most important hours of a man's life. There may be business to transact, gifts to be given, forgiveness to be made ...'[30]

d. *The principles from these cases.* What emerges form these three cases seems to include the following:

1. No matter how merciful the motive, any deliberate act to bring about the death of another which does so is murder. Motive is irrelevant. The fact it is a physician makes no difference.

2. The criminal law offers no excuse or justification to a doctor, or to any

other, who intentionally brings about death, even if it is to relieve 'severe pain' or 'helpless misery.'

3. The fact that the victim is terminally ill, with only days or weeks to live, does not change murder into any lesser offense.

4. While drugs may not be prescribed or administered to deliberately bring about, or to purposely accelerate the time of death, they may be given when and as medically appropriate to relieve pain and make the patient as comfortable as possible, even though the indirect, unintended, and inevitable (although known) consequence is to hasten somewhat the patient's death.

5. The criminal law recognizes that if medicine cannot accomplish its primary goal, to save the patient, then it has a legitimate secondary goal, that of reliving pain and suffering, even though this can at times adversely affect remaining longevity.

6. The mere fact that certain treatment (or nontreatment) standards are acceptable to a responsible body of medical opinion will not ensure that such standards are lawful. While it is unlikely that reasonable medical practitioners will evolve standards of practice that run afoul of the criminal law, that is a matter for the courts to decide, not the doctors. This is a rule as equally applicable to civil as to criminal liability. Normally conformance of conduct with prevailing medical practice will insulate the doctor from civil liability for negligence in treatment[32] or in advising[33] his or her patient. However, in both civil and criminal cases the court remains the final arbiter of whether that prevailing practice is lawful.[34]

3. *All patients must eventually die*

Although neither an English nor a Scottish court has yet been called upon to rule upon the legality of the decision of a physician to abide by the wishes of his or her patient to be allowed to die, there seems little doubt the practice is not uncommon in the United Kingdom. It must be, for, as Twycross has said, 'A doctor practices medicine in the knowledge that eventually all his patients will die.'[35] Decisions are taken by patient, family and physicians, as they have been for years, in a very private, personal context. If no complaint is filed by anyone, the criminal law machinery never becomes involved. Even in the rare case when a complaint is voiced, it is clear that it will very rarely result in prosecution.

The English prosecutorial apparatus, while less reluctant than its Scottish counterpart, has nonetheless traditionally considered that except in rare instances of abuse, matters of medical ethics, of decisions whether to treat and if so, how actively to treat, as well as decisions over terminating treatment, are difficult decisions best resolved in the clinical setting between patient, family and physicians. Consequently, save and except for the case against Dr. Arthur,[26] no criminal actions have been pursued over a physician's termination of life-sustaining medical treatment in England. Even in Dr. Arthur's case the 'treatment' at issue was feeding, although questions were raised concerning excessive administration of the drug dihydrocodeine. In the cases against Dr. Carr and Dr. Adams the issue was not terminating treatment, but rather administering excessive dosages of narcotic drugs to induce death. Such actions are conceived by most as more active and more culpable, yet the juries had little difficulty returning acquittels in both cases.

That is not to say that individuals not exercising clinical judgment, as physicians must, will not be prosecuted in Britain for accelerating the death of the terminally ill. For example, in an unreported Scottish case, a nurse was successfully prosecuted for injecting patients with insulin in an effort to ease their expected deaths. In the English case of Beecham, the defendant was given a 12 months suspended prison sentence for assisting his hopelessly ill adult daughter to commit suicide. She suffered from cancer, multiple sclerosis, and persistent, severe pain. She had made two prior suicide attempts. He was found guilty of aiding and abetting a suicide in contravention of the Suicide Act 1961, s.2. The Judge asserted, in sentencing Mr. Beecham, that 'offenses of this nature must in all circumstances be met with a term of imprisonment' so as to reflect the gravity of the offense.[36]

4. GUIDELINES NEEDED

While guidelines and treatment withdrawal standards for the hopelessly ill must be socially and legally acceptable, they must also be broad enough to allow discretion in making treatment decisions. The clinical picture is likely often to vary greatly, as will the views and attitude of the patient and his family. While the spouse or other family members may not overrule the competent decision of the patient, they will be involved and influential in most decisions. These decisions need to be made openly, with proper documentation in the patient's medical record. This is a protection against abuse, encourages candor, promotes the development of consensus on appropriate standards of treatment, and helps to remove the uncertainty that may discourage others from making clear treatment choices, or respecting those that are made by patients and family.

Open discussion and recommended guidelines or general policies for treatment aired in the literature of the most affected professions – medicine, law, religion, ethics, and realistically so, economics and politics[37] – will be helpful. Campbell has stated the case well,

> 'We must adhere to 'due process' in arriving at life and death decisions through the development of general policies or broad guidelines that can be agreed within the kind of framework that most colleagues and the majority of the public would find acceptable.'[38]

Such guidelines and policies will of course need to be flexible, subject to regular review, and involve input from the social scientists and ethicists as well as the technicians. This will encourage widespread acceptance. It should discourage the need to resort to legislative or judicial guidance. The latter has occurred in America, not always with desirable solutions offered, although most deal with the rights and remedies of the incompetent, not the competent patient. As to the competent patient, we will consider the position as developed legally through a number of judicial decisions in recent years in America, after looking at Scotland.

C. SCOTLAND

No criminal prosecution against a Scottish doctor for terminating medical treatment at the patient's request has been reported. Perhaps the most likely explanation, aside from good medical practice, is that these matters are normally private, rarely involve other than patient, doctor and immediate family, and even if reported to the prosecuting authorities, would not be pursued unless presenting the clearest or most egregious evidence of malfeasance. This will rarely be present in the care of the incurably and terminally ill.

In Scotland, responsibility for prosecuting crimes in vested with the Lord Advocate representing the Crown and with the Procurator Fiscals who operate under him. The Lord Advocate has wide discretion as to the crimes he elects to charge and prosecute. In difficult or controversial cases the Fiscals normally seek guidance from the Crown Office in Edinburgh before proceeding. If it is not believed a jury will convict, normally a case is not brought. Because of the historically high standing accorded the medical profession in Scotland and the general deference paid it by the courts,[39] the disincentives to prosecuting a doctor in Scotland are very, very substantial.

The lack of prosecutions in Scotland should not be taken to suggest the law of homicide is any more lenient to that in England. While even deliberate assistance in ending the pain-filled life of a terminally ill patient might well not be prosecuted or, if prosecuted, punished with the 'full pains of the law,'[40] it is still clearly murder[41] and punishable as such. The consent of the victim provides no excuse or justification for homicide.[42] Nor does the humanitarian motive of the doctor or relative absolve in any way of criminal responsibility. Hume[43] long ago stated this rule:

> 'It is not material to the notion of guilt, that the offender have himself been fully conscious of the wickedness of what he did. Though he were persuaded that it was innocent, or even meritorious, yet still this cannot save him from the judgment of the law.'

Although strict as written, the criminal law is applied and interpreted by people – Crown prosecutors, judges and juries. Juries are most disinclined to convict doctors, trying to help their patients, of serious crimes. The same is true of those seeking to end the hopeless suffering of loved-ones. In the unreported case of *Dryden Alexander Brown*[44] a husband who had killed his mentally-ill wife, fearing her return to a mental hospital, confessed. He was charged with culpable homicide due to his diminished responsibility (mental anguish) and sentenced to only 15 months.[45] This result is indicative of considerable flexibility in the criminal law as applied.

If the patient is competent and has been properly informed of his or her treatment options, it is without question unlawful for a physician to impose medical treatment of any kind upon a competent adult patient without his or her consent both in Scotland,[46] as well as in England.[47] The consequence of treating without consent, no matter how well intentioned, is civil liability for trespass to the person or assault, and criminal liability for assault and battery.

The patient's consent must be voluntary and knowing.[48] If consent must be given, then it follows that it can be refused. It is only the right to refuse which gives meaning to the right to consent. There is nothing in the law to suggest that either physician or family may overrule the competently expressed refusal or revocation of consent to treatment by an adult patient. As Mason & McCall Smith put it, 'the principle of self-ownership is now firmly established and is reflected legally in the concept of battery; justification for interference with the patient's right to accept or decline treatment would now be very difficult – if not impossible – in the face of expressed wishes to the contrary.'[49]

Honoring the wishes of a competent patient not to undergo further treatment also does not create criminal liability for suicide or attempted suicide in Scots law. During the 17th Century suicide and attempted suicide were crimes in Scotland.[50] However, as in England, neither is now recognized as a crime.[51] Since there is no principal crime, it seems unlikely there would be 'art and part' liability imposed on a doctor in Scotland for aiding and abetting a suicide. However, if the quantum of assistance given was particularly clear and substantial, then the crime of culpable homicide might well be changed.[52] For instance, where the physician withholds treatment at the request of the patient, to honor his or her request to be allowed to die, criminal liability may flow if a clear breach of duty is proven; that is, if no reasonable physician under the circumstances would have withheld such treatment.[53] However, this seems most unlikely if the patient is competent since, as we have seen, he or she may rightly elect to refuse consent to further treatment. Honoring the decision of a competent patient to refuse further treatment is respecting the patient's autonomy, not encouraging his or her suicide, so long as the consequences have been explained with due care to the patient and the refusal is knowing and informed.

D.   UNITED STATES

1.   *The right of bodily integrity*

The right of the competent adult patient to refuse life-sustaining treatment rests on several bases in American law. First and foremost is the common law right of the individual to bodily integrity. This basic right to 'inviolability of the person' was first clearly enunciated by the Supreme Court in 1891.[54] However, it is the statement of Judge Cardozo in a New York case[55] which is most often quoted to summarize the principle,

'Every human being of adult years and sound mind has a right to determine what shall be done with his own body; and a surgeon who performs an operation without his patient's consent commits an assault for which he is liable in damages.'

This case did not involve the termination of life-sustaining treatment. No cases raised this issue until after post-war technology allowing artificial or mechanical prolongation of vital functions was developed starting in the 1950s. This technology grew out of the 'iron lungs' used to treat polio victims. The first clear reiteration of Justice Cardozo's remarks came in a 1960 case.[56] The court concluded,

'Anglo-American law starts with the premise of thoroughgoing self-determination. It follows that each man is considered to be master of his own body, and he may, if he be of sound mind, expressly prohibit the performance of life-saving surgery or other medical treatment.'

Since 1960, a large number of cases have acknowledged that a competent adult patient has the clear right to refuse life-sustaining medical treatment.[57] However, as we shall see, this rule is subject to some qualifications.

2.   *The right of privacy*

The second basis for the right to refuse life-sustaining treatment is the patient's right to privacy. This is a recently articulated right, it is constitutional in dimension, but it is found nowhere in the U.S. Constitution or the Bill of Rights. Rather, it is an implied right, one 'emanating' from the express individual freedoms enumerated in the Constitution. It was not expressly recognized until 1965,[58] although earlier cases had decided there was a constitutionally protected right of individuals to procreate,[59] and to rear and educate their children as they deemed fit,[60] which are hard to justify under any of the express guarantees of the Bill of Rights, other than an individual's right to 'liberty and the pursuit of happiness.'

In the 1965 case, the right of privacy was held broad enough to protect the choice of married couples to use contraceptives. Since then it has been applied by the U.S. Supreme Court to certain 'fundamental' personal rights, many of which are clustered around the concept of reproductive and sexual freedom. The right of privacy has been held to protect the right to marry,[61] to receive contraceptives,[62] to procreate,[63] to have an abortion,[64] and even to possess pornographic materials in the privacy of one's own home.[65] The Supreme Court has yet to extend the privacy right to refusing life-sustaining medical treatment, but few believe it would not be so extended. The court has elected not to review cases where decisions to withhold[66] or withdraw[67] life-sustaining medical treatment have been endorsed by state courts. Mr. Justice Douglas, who authored the majority opinion in the *Griswold* case first recognizing the constitutional right to privacy, has for one concluded that it applies to medical treatment decisions.[68] Few doubt this conclusion.

A number of state courts have held the constitutional right of privacy applies to treatment termination decisions.[69] As the New Jersey Supreme Court stated in its seminal *Quinlan* case,[70]

> 'Presumably this right [of privacy] is broad enough to encompass a patient's decision to decline medical treatment under certain circumstances, in much the same way it is broad enough to encompass a woman's decision to terminate pregnancy under certain conditions.'

In the American federal system, powers not expressly given the federal government by the Constitution, or necessary to carry them out, are reserved to the states. Many states have adopted the right of privacy as an express provision of their respective state constitutions.[71] This, of course, has made explicit that the right exists, although it has still been for the courts to apply it to medical treatment decisionmaking.[72]

As with the common law right of bodily integrity, the constitutional right of privacy is also not absolute. It is subject to counterbalancing considerations.

3. *Statutory rights*

Approximately 40 states have adopted so-called 'living will' or 'natural death' statutes. While differing to varying degree in their scope and procedural requirements, most provide that an individual may refuse further life-sustaining treatment which serves only to briefly and artificially prolong the natural dying process resulting from a terminal illness. Typically, the patient's 'Directive' must be executed with the formalities of a will, it often is not binding on the physician if executed prior to diagnosis of terminal condition, and applies only where death is 'imminent' or expected within a short time.[73] The result is that these statutory provisions have been relied on infrequently in practice by dying patients. Of more significance is the durable power of attorney for health care. It allows a competent patient to authorize another person to make all treatment decisions for her if and when she later becomes incompetent to do so. The document is being increasingly used in the United States. It is not uncommon now for individuals to execute such a durable power of attorney, appointing his or her spouse, adult child, other family member or friend to make treatment choices if incompetence later occurs. It is often done at the same time as a will.[74]

4. *Competing considerations to autonomy*

The individual's right to decline life-sustaining treatment is not absolute. Certain state or societal interests have been identified as providing counter-weight to the rights of the individual. Four are commonly articulated: (1) preservation of life; (2) prevention of suicide; (3) protection of dependent third parties; (4) promotion of medical ethics and good practice standards. While these interests are frequently referenced in treatment termination cases, they are only rarely found of sufficient weight to overrule the competently expressed wishes of the individual.

a. *Preservation of life.* Preservation of life is probably the strongest of these interests. It is implicated to a greater or lesser extent in all treatment termination cases. However, the more grim the prognosis, the less weight it is accorded. Since most treatment termination decisions are made in the context of incurable and terminal illness or injury, the deference due this state interest of preserving life is limited. The same is true where life can be preserved, but only at great burden to the patient. The well-known Karen Ann Quinlan decision by the New Jersey Supreme Court put it this way,

> 'We think that the State's interest contra [treatment termination] weakens and the individual's right to privacy grows as the degree of bodily invasion increases and the prognosis dims. Ultimately there comes a point at which the individual's rights overcome the State interest.'[75]

Very few cases have overruled a patient's choice to forego treatment on the basis of preserving his or her life. Such cases have typically involved blood transfusions refused on religious grounds by patients clearly curable, not terminally ill. The two cases most often cited for this proposition both involved dependent third parties, in one a seven month old child, in the other an apparently viable fetus of 32 weeks gestation.[76] Competence was also in doubt in at least the case involving the young, dependent child. Thus, substantial reasons, other than preservation of the patient's life, existed to justify treatment.

No cases have overruled the competent decision of an adult patient without dependents to refuse further life-sustaining treatment when faced with a serious and incurable illness. As stated bluntly in one recent decision,

> 'The right of a competent adult patient to refuse medical treatment is a constitutionally guaranteed right which must not be abridged.'[77]

b. *Prevention of suicide.* Suicide and attempted suicide are not criminal acts any longer in the United States.[78] Aiding and abetting suicide is commonly a separate crime.[79] The American courts have had little difficulty in concluding that electing to forego life-sustaining treatment in the face of a terminal and incurable condition is not suicide, nor are those honoring the patient's election guilty of any malfeasance.[80]

It has been held, for example, that a spouse has no obligation to summon medical help or take other action where the other spouse competently elects to allow death to occur by ceasing life-sustaining medication.[81] A spouse or other family member may not overrule the health care decisions of a competent adult.

Even if an affliction is curable, it has been held that exercise of the right to refuse life-sustaining treatment (blood transfusion) because of religious convictions is not suicide.[82] The same is true where an illness, though not terminal, is incurable and causes substantial pain or physical intrusiveness to treat.[83] In neither case is suicide involved. In neither case has the person intentionally brought about his or her death by affirmative act. Rather, if death comes it is not self-induced. It is the consequence of an unintended mortal illness or injury which requires treatment to forestall death but which treatment is considered unacceptable to the person. Autonomy is considered the greater value and controls. An often-quoted statement of the Massachusetts Supreme Court summarizes it this way,

'The interest in protecting against suicide seems to require little if any discussion. In the case of the competent adult's refusing medical treatment such an act does not necessarily constitute suicide since (1) in refusing treatment the patient may not have the specific intent to die, and (2) even if he did, to the extent that the cause of death was from natural causes the patient did not set the death producing agent in motion with the intent of causing his own death. . . . Furthermore, the underlying State interest in this area lies in the prevention of irrational self-destruction. What we consider here is a competent, rational decision to refuse treatment when death is inevitable and the treatment offers no hope of cure or preservation of life. There is no connection between the conduct here in issue and any State concern to prevent suicide.'[84]

c. *Protection of dependent third parties.* The state has an interest in preserving the family unit and in avoiding parentless children who may be dependent on the state for support and maintenance.[85] Thus, where a parent's decision to decline treatment is considered as not given competently, the courts are more likely to take that as a basis for compelling life-saving treatment, particularly where the patient is curable.[86]

Where the patient is pregnant with a viable fetus, she may be compelled to accept treatment at least long enough to result in a live birth.[87] Here the mother's privacy rights to refuse treatment (and, in effect, to abort as a result) run head on into the rights of a viable fetus to a live birth. The question has arisen whether such a fetus may be taken by caesarean[88] before the mother dies, or whether the mother may have treatment (and feeding) imposed to await a natural birth. Two cases have decided that such treatment can be compelled,[88] but none have yet raised the issue of a mother electing to forego life-sustaining treatment. If her refusal of lifesaving care will not harm the fetus, it presumably would be upheld.[82,89]

If abortion after viability can be prohibited by the state, except where necessary to protect the mother's health,[89] it would seem to follow that her health cannot be seriously risked to save the fetus.[90] Compelling life-sustaining treatment may not harm health, but may seriously impinge upon individual liberty and bodily integrity rights.

No case has presented a competent, single parent with minor children who is curable, but wishes to refuse life-saving treatment.[91] Treatment would likely be ordered.[88] However, if a spouse would remain to care for the children probably no treatment would be ordered.[92] The same is true where cure is offered but only for a short or very burdensome life expectancy.[93]

d. *Promotion of medical ethics.* Where patients are terminally or incurably ill, the ethical dictates of medicine call for the patient to be made comfortable if cure cannot be effected.[94] Futile treatment, which does not improve the patient's prognosis for recovery, need not be given or continued. The patient should be offered treatment which offers reasonable benefit to him or her; treatment that has a reasonable chance of providing benefits to the patient which outweigh the attendant burdens of the treatment.[95] Thus, if the treatment is not beneficial, there is no ethical impediment to withholding or withdrawing it.

An important ethical precept is to honor individual choice and autonomy. The physician is legally compelled to do so by the doctrine of consent to medical treatment. Accordingly, honoring the competent patient's treatment refusal is ethically proper. This is true even where the doctor feels treatment would be proper and beneficial. So long as the physician has fulfilled his or her duty to properly inform the patient of treatment (and nontreatment) risks, benefits and alternatives,[96] the ethical obligation to the patient has been accomplished.[97] The patient has the right to make the treatment choice. Once he or she does, the physician must respect it. If the right of the patient to self-determination is to have meaning, it must be given precedence over the views of others, including family, physicians or other caregivers.[77]

While the patient can refuse or consent to treatment, he or she may not compel mistreatment.[98] The physician generally retains the option to transfer the patient to another physician when a disagreement over treatment arises. However, such a transfer is only appropriate if it can be accomplished without harm to the patient.[99] The welfare of the patient comes before the particular sensibilities of the doctor or nursing staff, particularly where the patient is simply exercising his or her right to decline further treatment.[100]

e. *Other competing interests.* There may be other public policies implicated by a competent patient's decision to refuse life-sustaining treatment. In rare instances, public policy may require that the treatment refusal be disregarded. The only reported instance where this has occurred involved prisoners. In one such case[101] the court compelled treatment (chronic dialysis) for a prisoner given evidence that to do otherwise would give in to the patient's use of the refusal as a vehicle to effect transfer to another facility and would be inimical to the state's need for orderly prison administration. Other cases have reached the opposite result in the prisoner hunger strike context.[102]

What one must conclude is that while American courts give lip service to various considerations in opposition to individual autonomy, only very rarely will the competent patient's decision to refuse treatment be overridden. One can find very few instances indeed where a court has said any public policy outweighs the individual's right to refuse further medical care. Certainly this is true where competence is clear and the patient suffers a terminal[103] or serious and incurable[104] malady, regardless of age.

5. *Nontreatment*

If the physician has not commenced treatment of the patient, no duty to treat has arisen between doctor and patient and the doctor need not be concerned over accepting a patient's refusal to authorize treatment, even life-sustaining treatment. However, the doctor is not excused from making the likely consequences of the patient's decision clear to him or her, so that the refusal is a knowing one. While the doctor has no duty to treat when faced with a refusal by a competent patient, the doctor must nonetheless exercise reasonable care to see that the patient makes a competent refusal.[105] This must include in the case of life-sustaining treatment an explanation of the nature and purpose of the treatment proposed, so that it is clear to the patient that death is expected to follow from nontreatment. If this raises further questions from the patient, then the doctor would be duty-bound to answer them truthfully.[106] Having done so, the treatment decision is then up to the patient.

6. *Futile treatment*

More common will be the situation where the patient has undertaken a course of treatment which has not proved successful. The doctor-patient relationship will clearly be established and the question is more likely to be withdrawing life-sustaining treatment which has proved too great a burden, or provided too little benefit to the patient. Here the doctor may be sensitive to issues of patient abandonment or malpractice if treatment sustaining life is to be withdrawn. Again, however, if the decision to refuse further treatment is a knowing, informed one by the patient, if the doctor has fulfilled his or her duty to disclose sufficient information concerning the consequences of treatment withdrawal, then the doctor has fulfilled his or her duties to the patient. The decision is then up to the patient.

7.   *Withholding and withdrawing treatment no different*

The law should not treat withdrawal of treatment different than withholding it in the first instance. Commencement of any reasonably promising treatment should be encouraged where a life may hang in the balance. Decisions on withdrawal are likely to be more informed than those on withholding treatment, since the former permits a reasonable clinical trial, a chance for patient and family to come to terms with what presumably is a hopeless prognosis, and an opportunity for the doctor to be more certain of diagnosis and prognosis, which puts the doctor in a better position to fully inform the patient of the treatment alternatives, if any, which remain. If the law requires no further showing to withdraw treatment than to withhold it, it encourages commencement of treatment without fear it may be more difficult to stop it once started. The traditionally different treatment of 'wrongful' omissions (non-criminal in the absence of an established duty to act) and commissions (criminal) by the criminal law undoubtedly explains the concern that seems to exit in this area. However, the law should strive to encourage treatment that offers hope of benefit to the patient. It should not discourage such treatment by making withdrawal of hopeless or fruitless treatment more difficult than withholding it in the first instance.

8.   *The 'omission'-'commission' distinction artificial*

In the doctor-patient relationship, whether criminal or civil liability should be imposed on the doctor is properly determined by duty, not by characterizing particular conduct as being a commission (malfeasance) rather than omission (nonfeasance). Most would agree it is proper for a doctor to allow a patient to die, where the patient has competently refused further treatment, further treatment is futile, or is no longer medically indicated. But it is never proper for a doctor to take deliberate and active steps to end a patient's life.[107] This fits nicely within the traditional rubric of omission-commission. However, on closer analysis, commission is arguably always involved when further treatment is withdrawn to allow a patient to die. It is only where no treatment regime has been undertaken, where hospitalization has not occurred, that it can be logically asserted that only omission is involved in not treating. While this may occur where the patient knows, perhaps from earlier courses of treatment, that a new treatment effort is futile, in most instances the realization will only occur after at least a reasonable clinical treatment effort.

For example, in the aftermath of an acute myocardial infarction, it is proper to institute cardiopulmonary resuscitation and, if necessary, to place the patient on an artificial respirator to support breathing. If, however, after a reasonable clinical trial the patient fails to regain consciousness and it is reliably concluded that cerebral anoxia has resulted in a 'persistent vegetative state,' with no reasonable hope of regaining consciousness, then most would agree that legally and ethically the artificial, mechanical respiration may be withdrawn.[108] Is the act of turning off the respirator, 'pulling the plug,' in such a case commission, an affirmative act to end a particular life-sustaining treatment, or omission, a decision not to provide further artificial respiration and to allow nature to take its course? There seems to be no right answer to this question.[109] It points out that one can decide what result one wishes the law to reach, then characterize the conduct or lack thereof as an act or omission, so as to legally conform to the desired result.

9. *Duty should control*

What needs to be determined is whether a duty exists between doctor and patient, if so, the scope of that duty, and whether it requires a particular course of conduct from the doctor in the circumstances.[110] A duty clearly exists from doctor to patient where treatment has been commenced and the doctor-patient relationship created. The duty is to treat the patient in a non-negligent manner, that is, in a manner consistent with ordinary treatment standards recognized as proper by a responsible body of medical opinion.[111] If a responsible body of medical opinion would conclude, in the circumstances, that artificial respiration should be withdrawn, then the doctor's duty has been fulfilled if he elects to do so.[112] As a result, no civil liability attaches unless, in the rare instance, the court exercises its independent review and concludes that legally no reasonable and responsible doctors should have reached such a treatment decision.[113] The law does not require the unreasonable or the extraordinary from the physician.[114] The physician legally need only provide reasonable care.

If treatment offers more anticipated benefits than burdens, there is a duty to undertake it unless competently refused by the patient. That is the key issue, not whether an act is an omission or a commission. Where the treatment is futile, or imposes burdens of pain and suffering substantially greater than the benefits it offers the patient, the act of the physician in withholding or withdrawing the treatment is not a deliberate act to end life; rather, it is ceasing treatment which there is a legal duty to continue. Robertson[114] has stated it well,

> '. . . a physician's *duty* to undertake a medical procedure is determined by what can reasonably be expected in light of customary medical practice, the likelihood of success, and the available alternatives.'

Similarly, in the criminal law context, proof the doctor has taken a treatment decision supported as proper by a responsible body of medical opinion would normally absolve the doctor of any criminal liability.[115]

However, just as in the civil law context, doing what other responsible doctors do does not ensure freedom from criminal liability.[116] It is still possible that a standard of practice accepted as proper by a responsible body of medical opinion violates the prohibitions of the criminal law. The accepted practice standards of any profession will have normally been adopted with awareness of and an intent to comply with the criminal law. However, since medical practice standards evolve and are likely to develop in areas not yet dealt with explicitly by the criminal law (or the civil law), medicine may find on occasion it is in conflict with the law as written, if not as applied.[117]

The distinction between omission and commission is further attenuated in the doctor-patient relationship because that relationship, as we have seen, creates a duty of due care to the patient. When such a duty exists, then omission, a failure to act, will be treated similarly to commission by the criminal law. If 'but for' the doctor's failure to act (i.e., failure to treat), the patient would have survived, then a charge of murder or culpable homicide will lie under English[118] and Scottish[119] law just as if death resulted from a deliberate, affirmative act designed to cause death.

D. CONCLUSIONS

1. *Court involvement only if disagreement*

Unless there is some dispute or disagreement between patient, family and/or physicians, the legal machinery need not be involved in decisions to withdraw life-sustaining treatment made by competent patients. However, in cases where death is the anticipated consequence, examination and written corroboration of diagnosis, prognosis and informed patient refusal by a second physician is a wise safeguard. He or she can corroborate the diagnosis and prognosis, verify that the patient has been adequately informed of available treatment options and the likely consequences of treatment withdrawal, and verify that the patient's refusal is a knowing and voluntary one.[120]

2. *Personal autonomy foremost*

Absent the situation where a young, otherwise healthy parent, who is needed to provide care for dependent children who are without another parent is curable, but refuses treatment, it is hard to contemplate treatment being forced upon any competent adult. There may, on occasion, be situations where a strong public policy supports compelled treatment. Prison administration is one instance. The avoidance of harm to the public health, as by vaccinating or otherwise treating a communicable disease, is another.[121]

Where incompetence is clear or suspected, the result may well be different and the subject is much more complex. It is to the incompetent patient that we now turn our attention.

NOTES

1 Vaux, 'Debbie's Dying: Mercy Killing and the Good Death,' 259 *J. Am. Med. Assn.* 2140, 2141 (1988).
2 The earliest of the informed consent cases is probably *Salgo v. Leland Stanford Jr. Univ. Bd. of Trustees* (1957) 154 Cal. App. 2d 560
3 *Barber v. Superior Court* (1983) 147 Cal. App. 3d 1006; *Rasmussen v. Fleming* (1987, Ariz.) 741 Pac. 2d 674.
4 Campbell, AGM, 'The right to be allowed to die.' 9 *J. Med. Ethics* 136, 137 (1983)
5 See, for example, *Matter of Conroy* (1985, N.J.) 486 A. 2d 1209.
6 *State Dept. Human Services v. Northern* (1978, Tenn. App.) 563 S.W. 2d 197.
7 *U.S. v. George* (1965, D.C. Conn.) 239 Fed. Supp. 752; *Bouvia v. County of Riverside* (1983) Riverside Co (Cal) No. 159780.
8 *Application of Pres. and Directors of Georgetown College, Inc.* (1964, D.C. Cir.) 331 Fed. 2d 100; *Re Osborne* (1972, D.C.App.) 294 A.2d 372; *Jefferson v. Griffin Spalding Co. Hosp.* (1981, Ga.) 274 S.E. 2d 457.
9 Mason and McCall Smith *Law and Medical Ethics*, London: Butterworths, 1987 (2d ed.) p. 157, cite *Truman v. Thomas* (1980) 27 Cal 3d 285 as representing an absurd result 'encouraging malpractice litigation unduly.' In *Truman*, the California Supreme Court held that if a patient declined a recommended diagnostic procedure, the physician should be sure that she understood the risk she was accepting (undetected cancer) by doing so. This does not seem an unsensible result, since it seeks to ensure that if a refusal to treatment is given, it will be a knowing and information-based refusal, just as any consent to treatment should be.
10 See Skegg, *Law, Ethics and Medicine*, Oxford: Clarendon Press, 1985, p.56; Lord Justice Lawton, 76 *J. Roy. Soc. Med.* 289 (1983).
11 *T. v. T.* (1988) 2 W.L.R. 189; Dyer, 1987 *Brit. Med. J.* 257
12 *R. v. Blaue* (1975) 1 W.L.R. 1411.
13 *Public Health Tr. of Dade County v. Wons* (1989, Fla.) 541 So. 2d 96; *Re Osborne, supra.*
14 Suicide may be defined as the intentional taking of one's own life. Funk and Wagnells, *College Dictionary* (1939) p. 1126. See also, Kennedy, 'The Legal Effect of Requests By the Terminally Ill and Aged not to Receive Further Treatment from Doctors,' 1976 *Crim. L.R.* 217, 226
15 *Bouvia v. Superior Court* (1986) 179 Cal. App. 3d 1127.
16 Mason and McCall Smith, *Law and Med. Ethics, supra*, p.205; accord, *Smith v. Auckland Hosp. Bd.* (1965) N.Z.L.R. 191, 219 (Grasson, J.); *Schloendorff v. Society of New York Hospital* (1941, N.Y.) 105 N.E. 92, (Cardozo, J.).
17 See Lord Edmund-Davies, 'On Dying and Dying Well' 70 *Proc Roy. Soc. Med.* 71 (1977).

18 *A-G v. Alble* (1984) 1 All E.R. 277, (1984) Q.B. 795. Some would argue helping a patient to die who has elected to refuse further life-prolonging treatment is suicide assistance. Joseph Fletcher, 'The Right to Choose When to Die,' *Hemlock Quarterly*, Jan., 1989, p.3.

19 *R. v. Court* (1988) 2 All E.R. 221 (H.L.); In the U.S., criminal charges are known to have been filed against eight doctors since 1950 alleging homicide guilt for allegedly taking steps to terminate the life of a suffering, terminally ill patient. Four came to trial, with three being acquitted and one being found guilty. Two had the charges dismissed by the court (*People v. Barber* (1983) 147 Cal. App. 3d 1006). One committed suicide before trial and one is awaiting trial. *Hemlock Quarterly*, Jan. 1989, p.6.

20 Wanzer, et. al. 'The Physician's Responsibility Toward Hopelessly Ill Patients, A Second Look' 320 *N. Eng. J. Med.* 844, 848 (March 30, 1989), ('it is not immoral, for a physician to assist in the rational suicide of a terminally ill person).

21 Brahams, 1988 *The Lancet* 1006.

22 Kennedy, 1976 *Crim. L. R.* 217, 228; Campbell, 9 *J. Med. Ethics* 136, 138–39 (1983).

23 Twycross, 'Debate: Euthanasia – a Physician's Viewpoint,' 8 *J. Med. Ethics* 86, 87 (1982).

24 *The Times*, 30 Nov. 1986, p.1, discussed in Mason and McCall Smith, *Law and Med. Ethics*, pp.231–2.

25 Dawson, 'Easeful Death' 1986 *Brit. Med. J.* 1187. Some American opinion polls suggest a similar view.

26 *The Times* 6 Nov. 1981, pp.1, 12; see reports of the case found in Gunn & Smith, 1985 *Crim. L.R.* 705, Brahams, 1986 *Crim L.R.* 387, and Brahams, 9 *J. Med. Ethics* 12 (1983).

27 See discussion in chapter 4, *supra*.

28 Brahams, 9 *J. Med. Ethics* 12, 13 (1983).

29 Palmer, 'Dr. Adams' Trial for Murder,' 1957 *Crim. L.R.* 365

30 Palmer, 1957 *Crim. L.R.* 365, at 375

31 Mason and McCall Smith, *Law and Medical Ethics*, pp.231–2.

32 *Hunter v. Hanley* 1955 S.C. 200

33 *Sidaway v. Bethlem, etc.* (1985) 1 All E.R. 643, at 661 (H.L.)

34 *Sidaway v. Bethlem, etc.*, (1985) 1 All E.R. 643 at 663; *James McAlpine Fatal Acc. Inquiry* (Glasgow Sheriff Ct. Jan. 17, 1986, Unrept.).

35 Twycross, 'Debate: Euthanasia – A Physicians Viewpoint,' 8 *J. Med. Ethics* 86, 87 (1982); see also, Campbell, AGM, 'The Right to be Allowed to Die,' 9 *J. Med. Ethics* 136, 138–9 (1983).

36 Horder, 'Mercy Killings – Some Reflections on Beecham's Case' 52 *J. Crim. Law* 309 (1988).

37 See discussion in Chap 12, Allocation of Medical Resources.

38 Campbell, AGM, 9 *J. Med. Ethics* 136, 138 (1983).

39 See Lord President Clyde's remarks in *Hunter v. Hanley* 1955 S.C. 200, at 205, quoted in Chapter 5, Consent.

40 Smith, (1959) *S.L.T.* (*News*) 245, at 246.

41 See Gordon, *The Criminal Law of Scotland*, p. 128.

42 *H.M. Advocate v. Rutherford* 1947 J.C.I.

43 Hume, *Commentaries*, vol. 1, ch. 1, p.25.

44 Meyers, *The Human Body and the Law* Edinburgh: The University Press, 1970 (1st ed.), p.145.

45 For a similar result in a recent English case, see Holder, 'Mercy Killings – Some Reflections on Beecham's Case,' 52 *J. Crim. Law* 309 (1988), discussed *infra*

46 See discussion in Chap 5, Consent; Walker, *The Law of Delict in Scotland*, p.493; Gordon, *Criminal Law of Scotland*. Edinburgh: W. Green & Son Ltd., 1978 (2d ed.), p. 828; *Adamson v. Martin* 1916 S.C. 319

47 *Sidaway v. Bethlem, etc.* (1985) 1 All E.R. 643 (H.L.)

48 *Chatterton v. Gerson* (1981) 1 All E.R. 257.

49 Mason & McCall Smith, *Law and Medical Ethics*, pp. 235–6.

50 Sir George Mackenzie, *Laws and Customs of Scotland in Matters Criminal* (1699)

51 T.B. Smith, *A Short Commentary on the Law of Scotland*. Edinburgh: W. Green and Son Ltd., 1959, p. 183; 'Legal aspects of suicide,' (1958) *S.L.T.* (News) 141, 143.

52 T.B. Smith, *Short Commentary*, p. 182; T.B. Smith, 'Law, Professional Ethics and the Human Body,' (1959) *S.L.T.* News 245; see Gordon, 'Suicide Pacts' (1958) *S.L.T.* (News) 209.

53 *R. v. Arthur* (1981), discussed in 1985 *Crim. L.R.* 705, 1986, *Crim. L.R.* 387, and 9 *J. Med. Ethics* 12 (1983).

54 *Union Pacific Railway Co. v. Botsford* (1891) 141 U.S. 250, at 252.

55 *Schloendorff v. Society of New York Hospital* (1914, NY) 105 N.E. 92 (overruled, on other grounds, *Bing v. Thunig* (1957, N.Y.) 143 N.E. 2d 3.

56 *Natanson v. Kline* (1960, Kan) 350 P. 2d 1093, at 1104.

57 See, for example, *Re Farrell* (1987, N.J.) 529 A. 2d 404; *Re Lydia Hall Hosp.* (1982, N.Y. App.) 455 N.Y.S. 2d 706; *Bartling v. Superior Court* (1984) 163 Cal. App. 3d 186; *Bouvia v. Superior Court* (1986) 179 Cal. App. 3d 1127.

58 *Griswold v. Connecticut* (1965) 381 U.S. 479.

59 *Skinner v. Oklahoma* (1942) 316 U.S. 535.

60 *Pierce v. Society of Sisters* (1925) 268 U.S. 510; *Prince v. Massachusetts* (1944) 321 U.S. 158.

61 *Loving v. Virginia* (1967) 388 U.S. 1.

62 *Eisenstadt v. Baird* (1972) 405 U.S. 438.

63 *Carey v. Population Services International* (1977) 431 U.S. 678.

64 *Roe v. Wade* (1973) 410 U.S. 113

65 *Stanley v. Georgia* (1969) 394 U.S. 557; but held it does not extend to protection of sodomy practiced in private between consenting adults. *Doe v. Commonwealth's Attorney for Richmond* (1967) 425 U.S. 901.

66 *Re Phillip B* (1979) 92 Cal App 3d 796 (cert. den. 445 U.S. 949).

67 *Conservatorship of Drabick* (1988) 200 Cal. App. 3d 185, cert. den. (1988) 109 S.Ct. 399; *Matter of Quinlan* (1976, N.J.) 355 A. 2d 647, (cert.den. (1976) 429 U.S. 922).

68 *Doe v. Bolton* (1973) 410 U.S. 179, at 213.

69 *Bouvia v. Superior Court* (1986) 179 Cal. App. 3d 1127; *Bartling v. Superior Court* (1984) 163 Cal. App. 3d 186; *JFK Mem. Hospital v. Bludworth* (1984, Fla.) 452 So 2d 921; *Guardianship of Hamlin* (1984,

Wash) 689 Pac 2d 1372; *Conservatorship of Torres* (1984, Minn) 357
N.W. 2d 332; *Rasmussen v. Fleming* (1987, Ariz) 741 Pac 2d 674.
70 (1976) 355 A. 2d 647, at 663
71 See, for example, Calif. Const., Art.1, Sec.1; Ariz. Const., Art. 2,
Sec.8.
72 See cases cited in footnote 69 above.
73 See, for example, Calif.Health and Safety Code §§7185–7195; see
generally, Meyers, *Medico-Legal Implications of Death and Dying*, Chap
16.
74 Meyers, 'The Durable power of Attorney for Health Care: A New
Element of the Estate Planning Package' 1985 *Estate Planning and
Calif. Prob. Rptr* 73.
75 *Matter of Quinlan* (1976, N.J.) 355 A. 2d 647, 664.
76 *Application of Pres. and Directors of Georgetown College, Inc.* (1964,
D.C. Cir) 331 Fed. 2d 1000, (cert. den. (1964) 377 U.S. 978.), 7 mos.
old child dependent on mother); *Raleigh Fitkin – Paul Morgan Mem-
.Hospital v. Anderson* (1964, N.J.) 201 A.2d 537 (cert. den. (1964) 377
U.S. 985), (viable fetus.)
77 *Bartling v. Superior Court* (1984) 163 Cal.App. 3d 186 (competent 70
year old man with serious, probably incurable ailments, but not diagnosed as terminally ill.)
78 *Joseph G.* (1983) 34 Cal. 3d 429, 433; Matthews, 'Suicidal Competence
and the Patient's Right to Refuse Lifesaving Treatment,' 75 *Calif.
L.R.* 707 (1987).
79 (See, for example, Calif. Penal Code §401, which provides,
'Every person who deliberately aids, or advises, or encourages
another to commit suicide, is guilty of a felony.
80 *Matter of Quinlan, supra*, 355 A 2d at 665; *Welfare of Colyer* (1983,
Wash) 660 Pac. 2d 738; *Bartling v. Superior Court* (1984) 163 Cal. App.
3d 186, at 196; *Bouvia v. Superior Court* (1986) 179 Cal. App. 3d 1127;
Re Farrell (1987, N.J.) 529 A. 2d 504; *Brophy v. New England Sinai
Hospital, Inc.* (1986, Mass.) 497 N.E. 2d 626, at 638.
81 *People v. Robbins* (1981, N.Y. App.) 443 N.Y.S. 2d 1016, at 1019; Cf,
People v. Roberts (1920, Mich) 178 N.W. 690 (murder conviction for
mixing poison and placing next to wife's bed at her request).
82 *Wons v. Public Health Trust* (1987, Fla. App.) 500 So. 2d 679. *Mercy
Hosp. Inc. v. Jackson* (1985, Md. App.) 489 A. 2d 1130 (vacated as
moot, 510 A 2d 562).
83 *Bouvia v. Superior Court, supra*; *Matter of Quinlan, supra*.
84 *Supt. of Belchertown v. Saikewicz* (1977, Mass.) 370 N.E. 2d 417, 426.
85 *Re Osborne* (1972, D.C.App.) 294 A.2d 372.
86 See *JFK Mem. Hosp. v. Heston* (1971, NJ) 279 A 2d 670; *Application of
Pres. and Dir. of Georgetown College, Inc., supra*.
87 *Raleigh Fitkin – Paul Morgan Mem. Hosp. v. Anderson, supra*.
88 *In re A.C.* (1988, D.C. App.) 533 A 2d 611; *Griffin Spalding County
Hospital* (1981; Ga.) 274 S.E. 2d 457.
89 See *Roe v. Wade* (1973) 410 U.S. 113; but cf. *Webster v. Reproductive
Health Services* (1989) 109 S.Ct. 3040 (Chapter 2, *supra*).
90 See discussion in Chap. 2, *supra*.
91 In the *Jackson* case (note 82) the mother, 26 weeks pregnant, was
competent and married. She consented to caesarian delivery, but no

blood. The evidence was this would not put the fetus at risk. The trial court and appeals court upheld her right to refuse. She delivered without blood being needed and the case was then dismissed as moot. See generally, Bamberger, 'Mercy Hospital, Inc. v. Jackson: A Recurring Dilemma for Health Care Providers in the Treatment of Jehovah's Witnesses' 46 *Md. L. Rev.* 514 (1987).

92 *Public Health Tr. of Dade County v. Wons* (1989, Fla.App.) 541 So. 2d 96; *Re Osborne* (1972, D.C. App.) 294 A. 2d 372.

93 *Re Farrell* (1987, N.J.) 529 A. 2d 404; *Matter of Rodas* (1987, Colo Dist Ct.) No. 86 P.R. 139, (aff'd. *Ross v. Holltop Rehab. Hosp.* (1987, D.C. Colo.) 676 Fed. Supp. 1528).

94 Twycross, *supra*, 8 *J.Med. Ethics* 86 (1982); Campbell, *supra* 9 *J. Med. Ethics* 136 (1983); Ruark, et. al, 'Initiating and Withdrawing Life Support,' 318 *N. Eng.J. Med.* 25 (1988); Tomlinson and Brody, 'Ethics and Communication in Do-Not-Resuscitate Orders,' 318 *N. Eng. J. Med.* 43 (1988); Wanzer, et. al., *supra*, 320 *N. Eng. J. Med.* 844 (1989).

95 *Barber v. Superior Court* (1983) 147 Cal. App. 3d 1006, 1018

96 See discussion in Chap. 5, *supra.*

97 The 'Patient's Bill of Rights,' promulgated by the American Hospital Association in 1972, has been enacted into law in some states and adopted by many hospitals and medical associations. It povides, among its 12 ethical guidelines, that,
    '1.) The patient has the right to considerate and respectful care . . . 4.) The patient has the right to refuse treatment to the extent permitted by law, and to be informed of the medical consequences of his action.'

98 *U.S. v. George* (1965, D.C. Conn.) 239 Fed. Supp. 752.

99 *Grimsby v. Samson* (1975, Wash.) 530 Pac. 2d 291; *Morrison v. Washington County* (1983, Ala.) 700 Fed. 2d 678

100 *Bouvia v. Superior Court* (1986) 179 Cal. App. 3d 1127; *Re Requena* (1986, N.J. App.) 517 A 2d 886.

101 *Commissioner v. Myers* (1979, Mass.) 399 N.E. 2d 452; accord, *State ex rel White v. Narick* (1982, W.Va.) 292 S.E. 2d 54

102 *Zant v. Prevatee* (1982, Ga) 286 S.E. 2d 715

103 *Re Farrell* (1987, N.J.) 529 A 2d 404; *Satz v. Perlmutter* (1978, Fla. App.) 362 So. 2d 160, app'd (1979, Fla) 379 So 2d 359.

104 *Bouvia v. Superior Court, supra; Bartling v. Superior Court* (1984) 163 Cal. App. 3d 186; *Lane v. Candura* (1978, Mass. App.) 376 N.E. 2d 1232.

105 *Truman v. Thomas* (1980) 27 Cal. 3d 285.

106 *Sidaway v. Bethlem, etc.* (1985) 1 All E.R. 643, at 661)663 (H.L.)

107 After the verdict in the case of Dr. Arthur, *supra*, the Director of Public Prosecutions (London) stated that, 'Doctors who *deliberately* speed death should face the prospect of life imprisonment.' (emphasis added). See Havard, 'The Legal Threat to Medicine,' 1982 *Brit. Med. J.* 612.

108 No British cases have specifically addressed this issue. All American cases to address it have held the withdrawal proper. See, for example, *Matter of Quinlan* (1976) 355 A 2d 647; *Barber v. Superior Court* (1983)

147 Cal. App. 3d 1006; discussed further in following Chapter Terminating Treatment for the Incompetent Patient.

109 See Fletcher, 'Legal Aspects of the Decision Not to Prolong Life,' 203 *J. Am. Med. Assn.* 65 (1968).

110 *Barber v. Superior Court* (1983) 147 Cal. App. 3d 1006.

111 *Hunter v. Hanley* (1955) S.C. 200;

112 *Hunter v. Hanley, supra; Bolam v. Friern Hosp. Management Committee* (1957) 1 W.L.R. 583

113 Or, if the evidence is they all would, then the court may feel compelled on rare occasion to conclude that no reasonable and responsible doctors *should* have reached such a treatment decision. See *Texas and P.R. Co. v. Behymer* (1903) 189 U.S. 468 (Holmes, J.); *Helling v. Carey* (1974, Wash) 519 p.2d 981; see also, *Sidaway, supra* (1985) 1 All E.R. 643, 663.

114 Robertson, 27 *Stan. L.R.* 213, 236 (1975).

115 *R. v. Arthur, supra*, note 53; *Barber v. Superior Court* (1983) 147 Cal. App. 3d 1006.

116 *R. v. Arthur, supra*, note 53.

117 Witness the selective practice of active medical euthanasia in the Netherlands which runs counter to the criminal law, but where the policy of the government is not to prosecute if strict professional guidelines for the practice have been satisfied (ie. terminal and incurable illness, extreme pain or discomfort, earnest, knowing and repeated patient requests for assistance in dying, competent patient, two physicians concur not other way to ease the suffering). See Wanzer, et. al., note 20, *supra*.

118 *R. v. Instan* (1893) 1 Q.B. 450; *R. v. Gibbons and Proctor* (1918) 13 *Crim. App. R.* 134.

119 *Isabella Martin* (1877) 3 Couper 379 (Scot.); *R. v. Instan, supra*, probably also reflects the position of the law in Scotland, Gordon, (1958) *S.L.T.* (News) 209.

120 *Re Farrell, supra*, 529 A.2d 404.

121 *Jacobson v. Massachusetts* (1905) 197 U.S. 11.

11

Terminating Life-sustaining Treatment for the Incompetent Adult Patient

A. INTRODUCTION

1. *What is incompetence?*

When we are dealing with medical treatment it is important to understand the use of the terms competent and incompetent. To some these have a particular meaning. For example, a person who is unable to manage his or her own affairs and to avoid the adverse influence of artful or designing persons is legally incompetent and may have a guardian or conservator appointed to manage his or her affairs. This is commonly known as a guardian or conservator of the *estate,* for it does not necessarily connote the person is unable to care for himself. If the individual is unable to care for himself – to feed, wash, clothe and protect himself – then a different kind of legal incompetence is involved. It requires the appointment of a guardian or conservator of the *person* in the U.S. and in England, or the appointment of a tutor-dative in Scotland.[1] This person becomes legal surrogate for the person, substitute decision maker.

The fact that a patient has been adjudged legally incompetent does not automatically mean he or she cannot decide upon medical treatment.[2] Whether a person has the power to decide upon his or her medical treatment depends upon whether or not that person has the capacity to consent (or refuse consent) to that treatment.[3]

Thus, it is important to recognize that an incompetent patient is simply one lacking the capacity to make an informed choice on treatment. If the patient can give an informed consent, then he is competent to decide. It matters not that he is legally incompetent to manage his own affairs, to care for himself, or that he is institutionalized. So long as the patient is able to reach a rational decision based on relevant information concerning his medical condition, then he is competent to decide.[3,4] It is also true the fact a patient is incompetent one day does not mean he may not be competent to decide the next.[3]

While the terms competent and incompetent are commonly used, it

303

would probably be less confusing to simply classify patients as those with the mental capacity to decide their treatment and those lacking it. The courts and commentators have not, by and large, done this, but it is important to understand the meaning of the terms. This will avoid confusing the person with certain legal disabilities, but perfectly capable of deciding upon his treatment, from one, whether or not under such a legal disability, not capable of doing so.

To be competent to decide then, a patient should be capable of understanding the general nature and purpose of the proposed treatment, its significant risks and the feasible alternatives to it.[5] He should then be able to reach a rational decision whether to consent or refuse consent. Rational means only that the decision is one based on intelligent reasoning or understanding. It need not be reasonable, common, accepted or wise to be rational. If the patient comprehends the nature and consequences of his decision, it matters not that others may consider it to be 'unwise, foolish or ridiculous.'[6]

2.   *Why incompetence?*

Incompetence, or an inability to make treatment choices rationally, may be caused by many things. The lack of maturity and understanding in children creates a presumption of incompetence to decide which is greatest in the tender years of childhood, becomes less with growing older and most feel largely disappears by about age 14.[7] Children are given the statutory right to decide treatment at age 16 in England and Wales, often earlier in the United States. These statutes, while granting express legal entitlement to decide at a certain age, do not prevent younger children with the requisite understanding from consenting to treatment at an earlier age. Children are presumed able to decide at puberty in Scotland, girls at 12, boys at 14. Because of congenital anomaly or handicap, some children will never develop the capacity to decide for themselves. They also will never have the opportunity to express their views or wishes regarding treatment in a competent or rational way. For these patients, no one can say how they would decide if capable of doing so.

At the other end of the age scale are the elderly. As they approach death in their declining years progressive degenerative changes in the brain, minor strokes, or illnesses like Alzheimer's disease may rob them of the capacity to decide. In an increasingly aging population, senility and loss of competence are an inevitable by-product of increasing proportions.

At any age illness or accident may cause traumatic or disease-induced interference with normal mental capacity. Sudden loss of oxygen to the brain from heart stoppage, stroke, surgical complication, drowning or suffocation may cause loss of partial or all cognitive brain function. The result may be a patient in permanent coma with all cognitive brain functions destroyed – the persistent vegetative state – from which there is no hope of recovery.[8] Certain drugs given to relieve pain or to reduce mental agitation in seriously or terminally ill patients may remove competence. Analgesics such as morphine-based drugs often used by physicians for cancer patients are an example of this.

Finally, the anxiety, fear, stress, strain, or other emotional overlay of a life-threatening illness may cause an otherwise rational patient to be incapable of deciding treatment choices. It may be true that many patients suffering an incurable and terminal disease are '*ex hypothesi*, not in a condition to make a rational choice.'[9]

For all these reasons it is important that a legal and moral framework exist for deciding upon treatment for a person when they are incapable of doing so themselves. We have already seen that in an emergency, typically resulting because of an acute, unexpected and incapacitating illness or injury, the law relies on several doctrines to permit beneficial treatment to be undertaken without the patient's consent.[10] Consent may be 'implied,' or it may be felt that 'necessity' requires that treatment be undertaken, or that it may be pursued as clearly in the 'best interests' of the unconscious or otherwise incapable patient.'

However, where incompetence is a chronic or recurrent situation and the treatment issue does not present an emergency requiring immediate, unexpected action, these doctrines may well not apply.[12] The questions remain of who is to decide for the patient and on what basis?

B.   WHO DECIDES FOR THE INCOMPETENT PATIENT?

1.   *Scotland*

Traditionally, the attending physician in consultation with the family, have made treatment choices for the incompetent patient in Scotland.[13] This includes decisions to withhold or withdraw treatment in cases of hopelessly and terminally-ill patients.

If there is uncertainty how to proceed, or disagreement between physicians and family over treatment it may be appropriate to petition the court for appointment of a tutor-dative to make medical treatment decisions for the incapacitated patient.[14] However, these procedures are exceedingly rare, with only two reported in modern times.[15] This indicates several things. First, as a practical matter, the advice of the physician is almost invariably followed in Scotland and disagreements are rare.[16] Second, those disagreements that do exist are resolved privately between physician(s) and family. Other physicians, nurses and social workers may be involved in reaching consensus,[17] but the almost total absence of court petitions on these issues reflects the fact they are invariably resolved in private.

Guardians do not play any role in deciding treatment for others in Scotland, save for limited situations involving treatment of the mentally ill in relation to their particular mental handicap.[18] Beyond that there is no general guardianship law in Scotland or in England. There is, however, the right of parents or local authority in Scotland to seek a court order relating to normal parental rights.[19] This may include decisions to authorize, or in appropriate circumstances, to refuse further life-sustaining medical treatment for children,[20] but the law has not been so tested and applied as yet.

Aside from these limited exceptions the attending physician and available family will continue to make decisions as to when treatment should no longer be actively pursued for the dying or hopelessly ill patient. This private and traditional system of decisionmaking seems to have worked well, is practical and leaves the decision among those the patient would presumably want to decide when to say 'enough.'

2. *England*

The situation in England is very similar to that in Scotland. Family and physician decide on treatment and when to terminate it as futile or needlessly prolonging life for a loved one no longer competent to decide. Where the patient is a minor, the parents normally decide, but the courts retain wardship powers to authorize or reject treatment to protect the welfare and best interests of the child.[21]

As in Scotland, guardianship proceedings in England are narrowly authorized only to accomplish treatment of the mentally incompetent that is related to that condition.[22] No statutory powers of wardship, guardianship or *parens patriae* are vested in the courts to control treatment decisions for adult incompetents. However, the House of Lords has filled this gap in the law by finding an inherent jurisdiction in the courts to declare a proposed treatment for an incompetent of any age lawful where found to be in the best interests of the incompetent.[23]

From these few precedents it has been reasoned that physicians, parents or other available family should decide treatment for the incompetent patient, having in mind his or her previous, oral or written, competently-expressed wishes and best interests.[24] It is recognized that doctors turn off respirators and discontinue other artificial life-prolonging medical treatment in hopeless or terminal cases when patients are incompetent, but no prosecutions have resulted.[25]

3. *United States*

The right of the spouse or other family to decide on treatment for a patient incapable of doing so was not well established at common law. As in

England and Scotland, the long-recognized practice has been for physicians, in consultation with the family, to decide upon treatment, including
life-sustaining treatment, for the patient no longer or never competent to
decide.[26] The reality, of course, is that we all must die, that age, infirmity
and analgesic or other medications will often combine to cause incompetence and, in every cause, at some point, all treatment fails and the patient
must either be pronounced dead or allowed to die.[27] It is senseless to involve
others than those most concerned with the patient's welfare in such cases:
family and physicians.

More recently the courts have acknowledged that where the patient is
incompetent the authority to consent to treatment, and thereby the power
to refuse consent, is transferred to the patient's guardian or conservator if
one has been appointed, and if not to the closest available relative or
family.[28] Some state legislatures have expressly set out legal priorities
among family or other surrogate decision-makers. The typical order is
guardian or conservator, spouse, adult child or children and parents.[29] Of
most significance has been the recent adoption of durable power of attorney
legislation in all states, which permits a competent person to appoint while
competent an agent or attorney-in-fact with power to decide *all* treatment
issues for the patient in the event of his or her later incompetence.[30]

Permitting a patient to designate in advance who will decide for him when
he is no longer able to do so accomplishes several important purposes. First,
it maximizes the patient's right of self-determination in medical care, a
fundamental personal right. Second, it maximizes the likelihood that the
surrogate decision-maker will know what the patient would want done.
This should minimize the likelihood of unwanted or inappropriate treatment for the patient. Third, it eliminates uncertainty for health care providers concerning what to do or who to ask.

Where no formal surrogate appointment has been made by a durable
power of attorney, the available family is the presumed choice to consult
with the physicians and decide upon treatment for the incompetent patient.
They presumably know the patient and his or her values and wishes best.
They presumably care most for the patient and are most genuinely
interested in his or her welfare and best interests. They are normally
available. Finally, while never pleasant, supporting the dying process is one
of the social responsibilities the family is expected to shoulder, as it should
with the birth of children and the care and feeding of loved ones of any age.
Where no family is available or is estranged, a good friend of the patient may
well be the most appropriate surrogate. This may often be true, for
example, with a homosexual afflicted with AIDS. The idea is that the
surrogate should be in the best position to know the patient's wishes
concerning treatment and is most concerned with the welfare and comfort
of the patient.[31]

C. WHAT CRITERIA SHOULD GUIDE THOSE DECIDING TREATMENT
    FOR THE PATIENT INCAPABLE OF DOING SO

1. *Traditional physician paternalism*

Traditionally there is little question that physicians having the interests of
their patients uppermost in their minds, did what they felt was best for their
patients. Fewer treatment options were available. The limits to extending
life were far greater before the advent of modern medical technology:
artificial respiration and circulation, radiation and chemotherapy, transplantation, dialysis, heart bypass surgery and the myriad of modern drugs
to stimulate and sustain vital bodily functions.

Patient expectations were lower, the trust inherent in the doctor-patient
relationship had not been eroded by much publicized malpractice claims
and the perception of overcharging due to defensive medicine, high insurance rates and high salary expectations of U.S. doctors, and the modern
emphasis on informed consent and self-determination in medical care had
not yet occurred. In contrasting British and American medical practice,
Professor Campbell has stated that in Britain,

> 'Much is still left to the doctor's discretion, to trust in his knowledge
> and to his judgment of what seems best for the patient. This quaint,
> old-fashioned and much maligned paternalism which in so many ways
> is still a feature of British medicine has largely disappeared from
> hospital practice in the United States.'[32]

While this paternalistic approach is, as we have discussed, most secure in
Scotland and less so in England, there are those that feel it is not always in
the patient's best interests.[33] This is not to say that the patient reigns
supreme and decides on treatment without regard to the views and thoughts
of the physician. Both physician and patient should form an integral part of
the decisionmaking process.[34] The physician must inform and educate,
evaluate and predict, ask questions and answer them. Only then can the
patient make an informed choice.

The same process should occur when the patient is incapable of informed
choice. Only this time the agent, family member, or other surrogate must
make the informed choice called for, with the help of the doctor. The
patient should not lose rights or privileges merely by virtue of his mental
incapacity.[35] He or she is entitled to the same respect and thoughtful care.
However, incompetence requires that these rights and privileges to exercised for the patient rather than by him.

2. *Trying to do what the patient would want*

The first goal of any treatment decision for the incompetent patient should
be to do what the patient would decide if able to do so.[36] This is known in the

U.S. as the so-called 'substituted judgment' rule. It requires that the substitute decision-maker 'attempt to reach the decision that the incapacitated person would make if he or she were able to choose.'[37] It is a subjective decision, one that seeks to replicate what the patient would want, whether or not reasonable, or what most others would want done.[38] To be effective, however, it requires that the patient expressed himself in a relevant way on the subject while competent.

If the patient has not competently told others what he would want done in the event of stroke or coma or terminal cancer, others cannot presume to accomplish what has not been expressed. Thus, while favored, the 'substituted judgment' rule may often not apply. People as a rule do not like to talk of their own illness or death. If they do not, their wishes may be unknown when such illness occurs and they are unable to decide for themselves.

3. *Wishes expressed while incompetent*

If the patient is incompetent, his views may still represent good evidence of what he would want done if competent.[39] There are no clear answers to this supposition. However, if such views are consistent with good medical practice, they are likely to be supported by the doctors. Also, following these wishes does honor the individual and respect his individuality despite the onset of incompetency. The danger, of course, is whether there exists a correlation between wishes expressed while incompetent and results desired if one is competent.

4. *How clear must patient preferences be?*

The articulation of preferences for or against life-sustaining treatment will vary greatly, from non-existent, to vague and general, to precise and specific. Some will be written, others oral only, still others implied from conduct, attitude, religious views and general philosophy of life. This raises the issue of how explicit the patient's wishes must be in order to be binding once the patient loses capacity to decide.

Some American courts have concluded that when the decision is whether to withdraw life-sustaining treatment, the evidence of the patient's wishes must be 'clear and convincing.'[40] This is a higher standard of proof than that normally required by preponderance of the evidence, which means simply that something is more probable than not. Clear and convincing evidence is that which creates a clear conviction, without hesitancy, as to the truth of the particular facts involved.[41] The idea here is that life-sustaining treatment should only be withdrawn from a patient without capacity to decide upon evidence that leaves virtually no doubt about what the patient would want. Absent such clear and compelling proof, it is felt that life should be maintained unless it is unquestionably not in the patient's best interests to do so.

Other courts have, however, said that to honor the competently-expressed wishes of a now incompetent patient only when they can be proved by clear and convincing evidence rather than fulfilling the wishes of the patient may actually frustrate them.[42] If too stringent a standard of proof is imposed, many people who have given reliable evidence of their preferences would not necessarily be treated in accordance with those views because of their perceived lack of adequate certainty.

5. *The 'best interests' standard*

Some courts have concluded that a best interests standard is the one best suited to deciding upon treatment for the incompetent patient. It is the standard *all* courts have applied to decide upon treatment or nontreatment where the competent wishes of the patient were unknown, unexpressed or unclear. A Californian court in recently upholding the removal of a respirator keeping a hopelessly comatose 44 year old accident victim alive, concluded that the patient's surrogate (a court-appointed conservator) was duty bound to *consider* any relevant expressed preferences of the incapacitated patient.[42] However, the conservator was not bound to follow them. Rather, he was to act in the patient's best interests, by deciding, in good faith, based upon medical advice, whether or not treatment was necessary.[43] The preferences of the patient were deemed to assist in reaching such a decision, but not to supplant it.

a. *F. v. West Berkshire Health Authority* (1989). In the recent decision of the House of Lords upholding sterilization of an incompetent adult incapable of dealing with pregnancy, childbirth and child rearing,[23] it was held that adult incompetent patients could lawfully only receive treatment in their best interests. Treatment was held to be in a patient's best interests only if it was life-saving, or carried out to improve or to avoid deterioration of physical or mental health.[44] It was held up to doctors, acting reasonably in accordance with accepted standards of practice to determine this.[45] The corollary of this would logically seem to be that if life-sustaining treatment will not improve a patient's health and not prevent deterioration in physical or mental health, it is not in the patient's best interests and should not be provided or continued in the absence of a contrary declaration by the court.

However, what of treatment that does not improve health, but does prevent deterioration? The use of an artificial respirator to sustain a vegetative state patient may well fit this definition, since the permanently unconscious can and have survived for many years in such a state.[46] The House of Lords apparently did not have this in mind in reaching their recent decision. English legal precedent strongly supports the view it is not legally required and it is not in an incompetent patient's best interests to be actively medically treated to be kept alive where he or she is permanently un-conscious and unable to communicate with and relate to those around him because of severe, irreversible brain damage[47] particularly where terminally ill.[48]

b. *Preventing health deterioration.* The House of Lords decision to define treatment in a patient's best interests, while well-intentioned, seems too simplistic. One cannot say that treatment is in someone's best interests merely because it will prevent deterioration of health. As we have seen, a respirator, tube feeding and a catheter for elimination provided for the permanently comatose patient may prevent further deterioration of health, but very few indeed would say such invasive and non-productive treatment is in that patient's 'best interests.' Most would say, after a reasonable clinical trial has confirmed the diagnosis, that such treatment is futile, non-productive, undesirable and may well be a positive violation of the dignity of the patient and an invasion of his remaining bodily integrity.[49] Nearly all courts to face this question have found it in such a patient's best interests to allow other than comfort care to cease.[50] The American Medical Association has likewise concluded,

> 'Even if death is not imminent but a patient's coma is beyond doubt irreversible and there are adequate safeguards to confirm the accuracy of the diagnosis and with the concurrence of those who have responsi-bility for the care of the patient it is not unethical to discontinue all means of life-prolonging medical treatment.'[51]

c. *'Proportionate' treatment.* A better standard for determining patient best interests is whether or not the treatment is 'proportionate.' It involves a weighing of the benefits and burdens of treatment from the patient's perspective. A proposed treatment is proportionate if it offers a reasonable chance of providing benefits to the patient which outweigh the burdens attendant to it.[52] If that is not the case, then the treatment is disproportion-ate. In weighing the benefits offered by and the burdens attendant upon treatment, it has been suggested the following are particularly relevant factors:

1) The length of time that the treatment proposed is likely to extend life;
2) The quality of the life extended – not to others, or to society, but to the particular patient;
3) Whether the treatment proposed is reasonably likely to improve the prognosis for recovery, or to restore or preserve function;
4) The degree of discomfort or pain which may reasonably be expected to result from, or be alleviated by, the proposed treatment.[52,53]

d. *'Ordinary-extraordinary' treatment disfavored.* The proportionate treat-ment approach is preferable to the commonly expressed 'ordinary-extra-ordinary' treatment dichotomy; the latter derives from Catholic moral theology.[54] Under it, only ordinary medical care is morally compelled.

'Ordinary' care includes all medicines and treatments which offer a reasonable hope of benefit without 'excessive' pain or other inconvenience. 'Extraordinary' care includes all medicines and treatments which do not offer a reasonable hope of benefit, or which do so only with excessive pain, expense or other inconvenience. The American Medical Association, for example, in 1976 concluded that,

> 'The cessation of the employment of *extraordinary* means to prolong the life of the body when there is irrefutable evidence that biological death is imminent is the decision of the patient and/or his immediate family and/or his lawful representative, acting in the patient's best interest.'[55]

The use of these terms has become disfavored, for they may mask rather than clarify whether a particular treatment is of benefit to the patient.[56] The same treatment may be ordinary for one patient – the conscious polio victim unable to breathe on his own – but extraordinary for another – the unconscious patient in a persistent vegetative state. The same treatment may be ordinary in one instance – a respirator in the immediate aftermath of a cardiopulmonary arrest – and extraordinary in another – the same respirator after a reasonable clinical trial has not caused spontaneous heartbeat or respiration to return.

e. *'Productive' treatment standard inadequate.* Referring to treatment as beneficial or productive may alone be inadequate. It should be understood in a holistic sense for the patient. A treatment may medically be productive in treating an illness, but may exact an unacceptable price from the patient in terms of pain and suffering, humiliation, or expense. While tube feeding and pain medication may be beneficial for a patient with cerebral palsy in terms of permitting continued, conscious existence, it may be considered an intolerable physical and emotional burden by the patient.[57] The same may be true for a blind patient with end-stage renal failure in need of chronic blood dialysis.[58] The same may be true for a totally paralyzed patient in pain being fed by gastrostomy tube inserted surgically through the stomach wall.[59] And, finally, the same may be true for a patient suffering from a severe, incurable neurological disorder making the patient insentient, but in need of either mechanical respiration or tube feeding.[60]

6. *Conclusion*

Patient welfare and best interests are synonymous.[44] Patient autonomy and the democratic goal of individual self-determination requires that incompetence not rob the patient of the right to decide. There are only two ways to clearly do this. One is for the patient while competent to either designate another to make all treatment choices for him in the event of incompetence,[33] or to express himself clearly in writing on what treatment he would want or not want if later incompetent. Another is for someone else who is aware of the patient's wishes and desires concerning treatment to decide for him based on that knowledge. In that case the patient's wishes may have been expressed orally, or even by conduct.

Where the patient has not competently expressed is views on treatment, another standard must be applied. That standard is the best interests or welfare of the patient. While there is no assurance it will dictate what the patient would have wanted, it is what most people in the circumstances would want done or not done. What this means in practice is that 'proportionate'[35,52] treatment will be found in the patients' best interests because it offers health benefits that are greater than the burdens – risks, pain, side effects, expense, invasiveness – of the treatment. It is better to apply an imperfect standard, but one based on reason and predominant social attitudes, then to abdicate any decision for fear of being wrong to the mindless prolongation of what may be highly invasive, dehumanizing, expensive, and/or unproductive medical treatment.

As one court has recently put it,[61]

'While William's coma precludes his participation, it is still possible for others to make a decision that reflects his interests more closely than would a purely technological decision to do whatever is possible. Lacking the ability to decide, he has a right to a decision that takes his interests into account.'

The decision of whether treatment, including life-sustaining treatment, is in a patient's best interests will be a mixed medical and lay decision. What reasonable practitioners think is medically indicated will carry great weight, but should not be conclusive. The House of Lords recently concluded in *F. v. Berkshire Health Authority*[44] that whether treatment is in a patient's best interests should be decided in accordance with prevailing standards of reasonable medical practice.[45] However, the better practice, it seems,is for the patient's viewpoint and the impacts upon the patients quality of life to play a significant part in this decision.[53,56] Doctors have no corner on this information. Family, close friends or loved ones will normally know best the role quality as well as merely prolongation of life played in the patient's thoughts and attitudes and feelings. At times physicians may perceive ethical or legal pressures to treat which run contrary to the patient's best interests or expressed preferences. In the landmark Karen Quinlan case[56] the evidence was that prevailing medical practice standards and ethics required continuation of the artificial respirator, despite the diagnosis of persistent vegetative state.[63] The New Jersey Supreme Court, in overruling this practice and allowing removal of the respirator, suggested that, at times, physician self-interest and fear of civil liability or even criminal liability, or an over-zealous desire to apply technology in the quest to reverse illness or injury, might run counter to what was best for the patient.

Quality of life does not connote a social evaluation of the patient's worth. It simply means that the degree of physical and mental functioning and the degree of pain, discomfort or personal humiliation – from the patient's perspective – may properly be considered in deciding upon treatment withdrawal or withholding. Quality of life should be a physiological, not a social concept. It is patient oriented. It is not dependent on impact upon, benefit or burden to others.

D.   TERMINATING LIFE-SUSTAINING TREATMENT

1. *Brain death*

Neither Scottish,[64] English,[65] nor American[66] legal authorities have had any difficulty in upholding the cessation of further medical treatment for patients who are brain dead. This only occurs when a patient is in a hospital or other medical institution equipped with heart-lung mechanical ventilators to artificially maintain respiration and circulation. Such patients cannot maintain either of these vital functions spontaneously and, but for their connection to such a machine, would meet the traditional definition of death, cessation of circulation and respiration.[67] The brain controls circulation and respiration. When it is dead neither can function, except to the extent artificially induced by machine. Brain death is really just a modern means of verifying death in instances where machines keep blood pumping and lungs inflating and deflating. Because, however, it is not a long-established definition, nor one well-understood, prevailing medical practice is to have the diagnosis verified by a second, qualified physician.[68]

Brain death is only present where the entire brain, including the brain stem, has ceased irreversibly to function. The upper brain, which controls all thought, feeling and consciousness, can die when deprived of oxygen for 5 or 6 minutes, whereas the brain stem can survive for several times longer without an oxygenated blood flow. When the upper brain dies – due to stroke, trauma, shock, or other cause – the brain stem may live on. If so, the patient is not brain dead but rather in a persistent vegetative state (PVS).

2. *Persistent vegetative state*

When the patient is in PVS there is no hope for his return to a conscious, cognitive state. A large number of appellate courts have considered the advisability of removing either the respirator or the feeding tube keeping such patients alive.[50,69] With only two exceptions,[70] treatment withdrawal has been authorized. This has been done either because the evidence presented to the court made it clear the patient would not want his life prolonged under such circumstances, or it was concluded that such treatment was futile, offered no hope of improving the health of the patient or returning him to a conscious state, or such treatment was not considered necessary to continue. The courts generally have equated best interests with conscious existence without intolerable pain. Where treatment offered no reasonable possibility of achieving that condition, its continuance was not in the best interests of the patient and not legally or ethically compelled.[61]

The recent decision refusing to authorize discontinuance of treatment for patients in PVS was a 4–3 split decision. In the case, *Cruzan*, a young woman ran off the road in her car, suffered cardiac and respiratory arrest and her brian was without oxygen for approximately 14 minutes. She was placed on a respirator and remained in a coma for the ensuing five years. She was fed by a gastrostomy tube surgically implanted in the immediate aftermath of her coma with the consent of her husband. The court was asked to authorize removal of the feeding tube. The physicians testified she could be maintained by mechanical ventilator and tube feeding for perhaps 30 years. Thus, she was not considered terminally ill.

The trial judge in *Cruzan* authorized the thirty year old woman's guardians to remove her gastrostomy tube, concluding she would want that done. The Missouri Supreme Court reversed, holding the order was tantamount to starving the patient, not letting her die. The burdens of treatment were not considered great, her own desires were vague and uncertain and the court concluded that only 'clear and convincing' evidence of her opposition to continued treatment would justify its removal. *Cruzan* has now been upheld by the U.S. Supreme Court, holding states may require clear and convincing evidence before finding life-support should be withdrawn from an incompetent patient.[71] The remaining cases and scholarly comment support allowing these patients to die where the prognosis for recovery of sentient existence is hopeless, a reasonable clinical trial has proved futile, and there is no evidence the patient would want treatment to be continued under the circumstances.

Physicians in some cases may have ethical or other philosophical objections to removing a respirator or, more particularly, a feeding tube providing nutrition and hydration to a patient. Physicians should not be compelled to act against their conscience and should be entitled to transfer care of the patient in such cases to someone not so troubled, if it can be done without harm to the patient.[72] However, the patient's welfare comes first, not the physician's sensibilities.[73] The same is true where no one else will accept the transfer.[73]

Where the patient is reliably diagnosed as being in PVS, then rarely will continued treatment be recommended. Physicians generally see treatment as futile and providing no benefit in such cases to the patient.[74] Thus, unless there is evidence the patient would want continued treatment, in almost all settings it will be discontinued, privately, after consultation between physicians and family or other loved ones. Whether the *Cruzan* decision will upset this established practice remains to be seen.

3. *Severe and permanent mental impairment and limited life expectancy: the terminal but conscious patient*

As a result of illness, diseases such as Alzheimer's, stroke, or trauma, the patient may be severely and permanently mentally incapacitated and face a distinctly limited life expectancy. As in most cases of incurable and terminal illness, there comes a time when efforts to sustain or prolong life must and do recede and efforts to ease the dying process take priority. This is clearly the practice on both sides of the Atlantic, since all treatment must eventually fail and all patients eventually die.[75]

On occasion these cases have reached the American courts, primarily due to physician or hospital fear of legal repercussions from withdrawing treatment. The *Conroy* case[71] articulated a rather complicated three-pronged test, saying in such circumstances treatment (including artificial feeding) could be withdrawn if: (1) clear and convincing evidence showed the patient would refuse consent if competent; (2) some trustworthy evidence showed the patient would refuse consent and the burdens of continued treatment clearly outweigh the benefits; or, (3) no evidence of patient intent exists, but continued treatment would be inhumane because of severe, unremitting pain. These tests could be applied where the patient was terminally ill – that is, with a life expectancy of less than one year.[76]

There is no accepted definition of 'terminally' ill. An incurable illness which shortens the patient's normal life expectancy would seem to be terminal. However, few physicians are disposed to impose a death sentence on their patient unless the outlook is clearly grim and death expected in the near future. Any time is arbitrary, but a life expectancy of less than one year seems a reasonable parameter to place on terminal illness.[77]

In the *Grant* case,[60] decided by the Washington Supreme Court, the patient was not comatose but was severely mentally and physically incapacitated and in the advanced stages of a terminal and incurable neurological disorder known as Batten's disease. Her death in the near future was inevitable and she had almost no awareness of her environment. The court held the 22 year old unmarried woman's mother could, in consultation with the attending physicians, conclude further treatment was not in her best interests and refuse to authorize any 'life sustaining procedures utilizing mechanical or other artificial means including cardiopulmonary resuscitation, defibrillation, the use of a respirator, intubation and insertion of a nasogastric tube [for feeding], and intravenous nutrition and hydration.'[78] Judicial review was not required.

In the *Saikewicz* case[38] decided by the Massachusetts Supreme Judicial Court, judicial review was held appropriate before the surrogate for a congenitally incompetent 67 year old patient terminally ill with leukemia could refuse life-prolonging chemotherapy. The treatment had many serious side effects and if successful would only extend life for a few months. Given the substantial burdens and the limited benefits of treatment, it was concluded not to be in the patient's best interests.

In the recent *O'Connor* case[79] from New York, the Court of Appeals[80] held that a nasogastric tube should be maintained in a 77 year old patient severely mentally and physically handicapped as a result of several strokes. Her daughters contended she would not want her life artificially extended under the circumstances, but the court held the patient's wishes in this regard were not proved by clear and convincing evidence and, therefore, life-sustaining treatment must be provided. The court held further that such treatment could not be withheld based on a 'best interests' analysis, but only on the basis of clear evidence from prior statements that the patient would want that result; in the words of the court, 'that the patient held a firm and settled commitment to the termination of life supports under the circumstances like those presented.'[81]

Where physicians and family or other surrogate concur that the decision to withdraw treatment is probably what the patient would have wanted, they will normally also conclude that withdrawal is in the patient's best interests, and vice versa. Rarely will severely terminally ill patients want treatment whose burdens clearly outweigh its benefits. Factors of importance will include the prognosis with treatment, the risks, side effects, invasiveness, humiliation and expense of the treatment, the impact of treatment on the family, the expressed preferences, religious views, attitudes, and/or philosophy of life of the incompetent patient and the consequences (i.e., pain and prognosis) of non-treatment.

Where some dispute or disagreement exists between family and physicians as to indicated treatment, prognosis, or patient preferences, the courts will need to become involved to appoint guardian, conservator, or other patient representative and to authorize treatment or its withdrawal.[82] However, this should not be the norm. Courts are generally ill suited to handle these cases. As stated by the New Jersey Supreme Court, 'Courts are not the proper place to resolve the agonizing personal problems that underlie these cases. Our legal system cannot replace the more intimate struggle that must be borne by the patient, those caring for the patient, and those who care about the patient.'[83] Courts are, however, able to resolve disputes where the parties cannot do so. This is rare and should continue to be. These decisions are best made in private as they always have been by those most concerned with the welfare of the patient.

In addition, as recently pointed out by the House of Lords, in rejecting routine court approval for treatment of incompetents, 'if every operation to be performed or other treatment to be given, required the approval or sanction of the Court, the whole process of medical care for such patients would grind to a halt.'[44] Nonetheless, the Lords went on to conclude that court approval of incompetent sterilization as a 'matter of good practice' was highly desirable because of its irreversible nature and its moral implications. From this reasoning it could be inferred that life-sustaining treatment withdrawal from an incompetent patient in Britain may well require prior judicial approval as a matter not of law, but of 'good practice' because of its irreversible nature. The legal picture remains unclear until a case presents the issue for resolution. In the interim doctors, at least in England where the limited judicial activity in this area seems to have occurred, may be prompted to seek High Court approval as a precaution before withdrawing life-sustaining treatment from an incompetent where death is not imminent.

There is certainly no good reason to do that in cases where the patient is incurably and terminally ill with death expected immediately and all agree treatment is not beneficial to the patient. Other situations may be less clear, particularly given an evolving medical consensus on indicated treatment in other hopeless cases such as PVS, severe and progressive dementia, end-stage renal and liver disease, or other cases where medical resources may be felt contraindicated because of invasiveness, cost and availability, side effects or other burdens, and of limited if any benefit to health. As treatment withdrawal guidelines and standards of practice become more clearly articulated, the less likely will be the temptation to seek judicial sanction in such cases.[74,75]

4.   *English judicial observations on the limits to treatment*

In two cases where treatment had been aggressively pursued, despite the likelihood of severe disability, judicial *obiter dictum* (discussion unnecessary to the decision reached in the case) has suggested it need not have been under the circumstances. In both cases the patients were not competent. The judicial comments were by the Master of the Rolls, Lord Denning. In the first, the patient had suffered a cardiac arrest and irreversible brain damage following a normally minor surgical procedure (D & C).[84] A malpractice action resulted and at trial five years later the patient was only 'intermittently sentient' and required constant care for feeding, grooming, and sanitation. Lord Denning commented, 'Many might say: "T'were better she had died."'[85]

In the second case, complications during a high-risk delivery caused an extended period of efforts to resuscitate the newborn with consequent brain damage.[86] At trial the boy was 10 years old, but was 'no better than a baby nine months.' He was unable to speak, sit up, stand or walk, had no bowel or bladder control and needed constant care. He was however, able to breathe on his own and swallow soft foods. Again, Lord Denning commented, 'Seeing this boy's present condition, most would say: "What a pity they did not let him die."'[87]

While representative of the views of only one Judge, these remarks undoubtedly reflect the view of a good part of the judiciary, as they do of the public at large, that overly-zealous continuation of medical treatment can produce undesirable consequences for the patient and his family. They also imply a judicial recognition that continued medical treatment in such cases is not legally mandated. There is a limit to all treatment. The productivity of treatment must be considered, not merely its availability, before it is commenced, or continued.

Lord Scarman, who has figured prominently in probably the two most significant English legal decisions concerning medical treatment over at least the past decade,[88] has expressed the view this way,

'It is of great social importance that technological advance should not be allowed to extend indefinitely the existence of the irretrievable human wreck.

... There is no medical or legal difference in the view that the withdrawal of [medical] support from 'Homo' who is no longer 'sapiens' is not a killing.'[89]

Lord Justice Devlin, another distinguished jurist, has gone so far as to state that 'proper medical treatment consequent upon illness or injury plays no part in legal causation.'[90] In other words, if proper medical care is given, it plays no role in the legal liability – be it civil or criminal – for death. The catch here is who decides if it is 'proper' treatment. And, as we have seen, it is not solely the medical profession, but rather judges and juries at the end of the day. For this reason, some 'defensive medicine' undoubtedly operates to extend treatment beyond the limits set by responsible medical practice. It is likely to do so until a clear consensus exists as to when life-sustaining treatment should be withdrawn or withheld. Openly discussed and formulated general medical treatment guidelines for the care of the terminally and incurably ill are desirable to foster such a consensus.

5. *Is feeding medical treatment?*

Some feel that while 'medical' treatment in hopeless cases can be withheld or withdrawn, that feeding should not be.[91] It is distinguished from other treatment on several grounds: it is basic, humane, comfort care that should be extended to all, like touching, warmth and personal hygiene; if it is not supplied, the patient dies from lack of nourishment, not from the underlying disease; removing (or withholding) nourishment is an express act intended to kill the patient.[92] Several courts have concurred with these views.[70,79,93] However, the vast majority of American courts have not agreed.[94] Rather, they see *artificial* feeding in the same light as artificial respiration: both are medically supplied means of supplanting a normal function to sustain life. The underlying illness has caused the inability to breathe spontaneously or to swallow. If the artificial life-support – be it respirator, nasogastric or gastrostomy tube – is removed, the cause of death is the underlying malady. The removal simply allows that natural process to occur without further, active medical intervention.

Courts have permitted feeding tubes to be removed in cases of patients in PVS,[94,61] or in a near comatose condition with severe and terminal mental and physical disabilities.[60,71] They have allowed a competent, seriously and incurably ill patient to do so, even though not terminally ill.[57]

Several state legislatures have expressly prohibited the removal of hydration and nutrition from an incompetent patient, although allowing other life-sustaining procedure to be removed which are serving only to artificially prolong the moment of death.[95] Other states severely restrict the circumstances where hydration or nutrition may be removed. However, courts have held that such statutes cannot restrict the individual's right to reject treatment, including feeding, which is protected by the common law right to self-determination and bodily integrity,[96] or the constitutional right to privacy,[97] or both.[57]

Most medical comment does not distinguish between artificially provided nutrition and other forms of life-sustaining treatment.[74,75,91] Where the patient is not terminally ill it is supplied unless there is explicit, competent rejection as in the case of an executed Durable Power of Attorney for Health Care. Where the patient can take nourishment orally, with or without assistance, it should be provided.[98]

In the last analysis the decision to provide or continue artificial feeding to the incompetent is one, as with other medical treatment, of proportionality. The benefits that continued nutrition provide must be compared to the burdens it imposes. Those burdens are essentially from the patient's personal perspective, but also may at times include the burden on the physical, mental or financial health of the remaining family. Where the patient is competent, his wishes should be honored. Where the patient is incompetent, relevant and competent expressions of desire should be honored. Proportionality need only be determined where patient wishes are unstated or inconclusive. Where it is relevant, the greater the physical and emotional invasiveness of the treatment sustaining life, including artificial feeding and the more hopeless the prognosis for improvement in health, the less will be the obligation to do other than keep the patient comfortable by the use of misting and to provide nourishment capable of being taken manually, not medically supplied.

E.   THE DISTINCTION BETWEEN TERMINATING INAPPROPRIATE TREATMENT AND EUTHANASIA

It is one thing not to prolong life by withholding or withdrawing treatment not wanted by a patient or not in his best interests. We have discussed in the foregoing pages many examples of this. It is quite another thing to actively intervene to bring about the patient's death. The latter is unethical[99] and unlawful.[100] The British Medical Association, in reaffirming its stand against euthanasia, recently stated its position in this way

'Doctors should regard patients as authorizing treatment, and should respect those authorizations and any decision to withdraw consent. But autonomy works both ways. Patients have the right to decline treatment but do not have the right to demand treatment which the doctor cannot, in conscience, provide. An active intervention by a doctor to terminate a patient's life is just such a "treatment." '[99]

Taking a somewhat contrary position, a group of U.S. physicians recently concluded it was permissible to provide medication to a competent, terminally ill patient who was ready to die, knowing the patient would use it to commit suicide in certain circumstances. They stated,[100]

'If care is administered properly at the end of life, only the rare patient should be so distressed that he or she desires to commit suicide. Occasionally, however, all fails. The doctor, the nurse, the family, and the patient may have done everything possible to relieve the distress occasioned by a terminal illness, and yet the patient perceives his or her situation as intolerable and seeks assistance in bringing about death. Is it ever justifiable for the physician to assist suicide in such a case?

Some physicians, believing it to be the last act in a continuum of care provided for the hopelessly ill patient, do assist patients who request it, either by prescribing sleeping pills with knowledge of their intended use or by discussing the required doses and methods of administration with the patient. The frequency with which such actions are undertaken is unknown, but they are certainly not rare. Suicide differs from euthanasia in that the act of bringing on death is performed by the patient, not the physician.

The physician who considers helping a patient who requests assistance with suicide must determine first that the patient is indeed beyond all help and not merely suffering from a treatable depression of the sort common in people with terminal illnesses. Such a depression requires therapeutic intervention. If there is no treatable component to the depression and the patient's pain or suffering is refractory to treatment, then the wish for suicide may be rational. If such a patient acts on the wish for death and actually commits suicide, it is ethical for a physician who knows the patient well to refrain from an attempt at resuscitation.'

While this practice was distinguished from taking an active step to deliberately cause the death of the suffering patient, it is rather close to it. It might be likened to the reported practice of some physicians in Holland preparing a lethal injection for their dying patients when all reasonable means of palliative care have proven unsuccessful, but asking the patient to administer the dose himself.[101]

In Holland, 'killing someone at his own request' is a separate class of homicide punishable by up to 12 years imprisonment. Doctors are not prosecuted where they follow the guidelines of the Dutch Medical Association. These include repeated and specific competent requests to die by the patient, the use of counseling, the inability of palliative care to make the patient comfortable in light of physical and mental pain and suffering considered to be unbearable, and the concurrence of a second physician.

Other European jurisdictions, contrary to England, Scotland and the United States, make special provision for euthanasia or mercy killing. A portion of the Norwegian Penal Code, dating from 1902, makes special provision for the mercy killing of those hopelessly ill, or where the victim knowingly requested his death.[102] The Swiss Federal Penal Code has provided a lesser penalty (three days to three years) for homicide upon the victim's 'serious and urgent request.'[103] The German Penal Code contains similar provision.[104] Other national penal codes, as diverse as Italy, Netherlands, Spain, Poland, Japan and Uruguay, have provided penalty mitigation where the homicide is from compassionate motive (due to illness) and/or earnest request of the victim.[105]

Despite no express provision for mitigation in the law, as interpreted by compassionate judges and juries the law in Scotland,[106] England[107] and the United States[108] appears flexible enough as currently written to preserve the sanction against homicide, but to allow for extenuating circumstances to be properly and humanely considered.[109] In all three jurisdictions results occur which clearly show the law will not unduly punish one who for compassionate reasons heeds the request of another to end their life.

It remains debatable whether the Civilian systems of continental Europe, by recognizing humanitarian motive and consent of the victim, allow more flexibility and fairness in the treatment of dying. The British and American solution is better, for the weight of the law should prohibit mercy-killing. The physician-patient privilege would be greatly undermined if there was fear that death might be taken into the hands of the physician or family member. Patients should know their destiny is their own while competent and even while not, mercy-killing remains illegal.

With rare exception, pain even in the most intractable cases can be fully controlled with sensitive and informed attention. In hospices where cancer is the predominant diagnosis, 95 per cent of all dying patients can have satisfactory pain control.[110] Thus, the real issue is proper medical care in these cases, not suicide or euthanasia.[111] There are no current proposals to authorize euthanasia. The emphasis of the law should remain on condoning treatment withdrawal in hopeless cases so as not to unduly prolong dying. It should not seek, nor does it need to seek to condone affirmative acts to bring about death.

Where treatment is withheld because not indicated by prevailing standards of good medical practice, it is lawful in both Britain and the United States even if death follows.[112] Neither futile nor medically disproportionate treatment, whether or not life-sustaining, need be given. Disproportionate treatment is not in the patients best interests and is not legally or morally required.[44,52]

F.   CONCLUSION

What needs to be remembered with incompetent patients, as with those fully competent, is that medical treatment is only worthwhile, moral and indicated if it will help the patient. Preservation of life is normally of help and value to the patient, but life is not an absolute value to be preserved at any cost and regardless of prognosis. Death is an integral and inevitable part of life.

> 'If biomedical acts of life extension become acts of death prolongation, we may force some patients to outlive their deaths and we may ultimately repudiate the primary life-saving and merciful ethic itself.'[113]

In a similar vein, 20 years earlier, Elkington stated,

> 'In his efforts to preserve life and restore health, the physician sometimes may fail to give enough consideration to his other obligation, namely, to relieve suffering and to allow the patient, if he is to die, to die with comfort and dignity.'[114]

What must be realized is that all life comes to an end, and we must distinguish that while life must be preserved in all cases, there is no use or morality in drawing out the inevitable process of dying by disproportionate means. The point at which *life* is no longer *being preserved* at an acceptable quality *for the patient*, but *death is being needlessly prolonged*, is a tenuous, often difficult, and individual one to pinpoint,[115] but it is a task for the humanity of the physician in consultation with the patient if able and his loved ones. Patient autonomy should be the guiding principle, but best interest is the next best criterion in the absence of clear patient preferences. While continuing to prohibit mercy-killing or aiding suicide, the law should leave treatment termination decisions to the private context of physician, patient (if able), and family or other loved ones (if not able), save and except for the rare case of unresolved dispute, disagreement, base motive or poor treatment.

What promises to impinge increasingly more on this decision-making matrix is the external factor of limited medical resources. It is to that subject that we turn the attention of our final chapter.

NOTES

1 Ward, 'Revival of Tutors-Dative (*Morris, Petitioner*),' 1987 *S.L.T.* (News) 69; Calif. Probate Code §§1500, 1800, 1880, 2351, 2355.
2 *Matter of Conroy* (1985, N.J.) 486 A.2d 1209.
3 *Conservatorship of Waltz* (1986) 180 Cal. App. 3d 722.
4 *State Dept. of Human Services v. Northern* (1978, Tenn. App.) 563 S.W.2d 197 (app. dism. as moot, 436 U.S. 923).
5 See discussion on Consent in Chapter 5; *Cobbs v. Grant* (1972) 8 Cal.3d 229.
6 *Re Maida Yetter* (1973) 62 Pa. D. & C. 2d 619; dissent of Burger, J. (as he then was) in *App. of Pres. and Dir. of Georgetown College, Inc.* (1964, D.C. cir.) 331 F.2d 1000, 1017.
7 See discussion on Treatment for Minors in Chapter 6; Duff, 'Guidelines for Deciding Care of Critically Ill or Dying Patients', in Shannon *Bioethics* (3d ed., 1987) pp. 135, 141.
8 See, for example, as to causes and the resulting medico-legal issues, *Brophy v. New England Sinai Hosp. Inc.* (1986; Mass.) 497 N.E. 2d 626; *Barber v. Superior Court* (1983) 147 Cal. App. 3d 1006.
9 Anglican Church, *On Dying Well*. London: Church Info. Office, 1975, p. 13.
10 See discussion in Chapter 6.
11 See Walker, *The Law of Delict in Scotland*, supra, p.345; *F v. Berkshire Health Authority and another* (House of Lords, May 4, 1989), *The Times*, 25 May, 1989, discussed in Brahams, 1989 *The Lancet* 1089, 340; *T v T* (1988) 2 W.L.R. 189.
12 *Estate of Leach v. Shapiro* (1984, Oh. App.) 469 N.E. 2d 1047.
13 Campbell, 'The right to be allowed to die,' 1983 *J. Med. Ethics* 136, 139.
14 *Morris, Petitioner* (Court of Session, 1986) 1987 *S.L.T.* (News) 69.
15 Ward, 'Revival of Tutors-Dative' 1987 *S.L.T.* (News) 69; *Dick v. Douglas* 1924 *S.L.T.* 578.
16 Campbell, 'The right to be allowed to die,' 1983 *J. Med. Ethics* 136, 137.
17 Campbell, 'Deciding the care of severely malformed or dying infants,' 1979 *J. Med. Ethics* 65, 66; Campbell, 1979 *J. Med. Ethics* 141.
18 Mental Health (Scotland) Act 1984, s. 41(2).
19 Law Reform (Parent and Child) (Scotland) Act 1986, s. 3(1).
20 Thomson, 'Sterilisation of Mentally Handicapped Children' 1988 *S.L.T.* (News) 1, 3).
21 *Re B. (A Minor)*, (1987) 2 W.L.R. 1213 (H.L.); *Re D. (A Minor)*, (1976) 1 All E.R. 326 (Heilbron, J.).
22 Mental Health Act 1983, s. 8.
23 *In re F (Mental Patient) (Sterilisation)* (1989) 2 W.L.R. 1025 (H.L.); *The Times* 25 May 1989, discussed in Brahams, 1989 *The Lancet* 1089, 340.
24 See, for example, Gillon (ed), 1988 *J. Med. Ethics* 60; 1988 *The Brit. Med. J.* 1376, 1377. The English Enduring Powers of Attorney Act 1985 does not include medical decisions.
25 *Finlayson v. H.M. Advocate* 1978 S.L.T. 60; *R. v. Malcherek* (1981) 1 W.L.R. 690; Skegg, *Law, Ethics and Medicine*. Oxford: Clarendon

Press, 1985, p. 163; see discussion of prosecution of Dr. Adams (alleged excessive heroin and morphine injections), Dr. Arthur (alleged improper dihydrocodeine injections and starvation) and Dr. Carr (alleged excessive barbiturate injections) discussed in preceding chapter, the only reported physician prosecutions (all found not guilty).

26 *Matter of Storar* (1981, N.Y.) 420 N.E. 2d 64 (Jones, J., dissenting).
27 See Twycross, 'Euthanasia – A Physician's Viewpoint,' 1982 *J. Med. Ethics* 86.
28 *Cobbs v. Grant* (1972) 8 Cal. 3d 229, 244; *Barber v. Superior Court* (1983) 147 Cal. App. 3d 1006. *Guardianship of Grant* (1987, Wash.) 747 Pac. 2d 445.
29 Wash. Rev. Code 7.70.065.
30 Meyers, 'The Durable Power of Attorney for Health Care: A New Element of the Estate Planning Package,' 1985 *Estate Planning and Calif. Probate Rptr*. No. 4, p. 73.
31 Joint Committee on Bioethics of the San Diego Co. Med. Soc. and San Diego Co. Bar Assn., 'Proposed Guidelines on Foregoing Life-Sustaining Treatment,' June 8, 1989, p.5.
32 Campbell, A.G.M., 1983 *J. Med. Ethics* 136.
33 See Kennedy, 'The Patient on the Clapham Omnibus,' 47 *Mod. L.R.* 454 (1984).
34 Pres. Comm'n., *Making Health Care Decisions*. Wash. D.C.: U.S. Gov't. Print. Office, 1982, pp. 36, 132.
35 *Morgan v. Olds* (1987, Iowa App.) 417 N.W. 2d 232, 236.
36 Pres. Comm'n., *Deciding to Forego Life)Sustaining Treatment*. Wash. D.C.: U.S. Gov't. Print. Office, 1983, p. 5; *Morgan v. Olds* (1987, Iowa App.) 417 N.W. 2d 232; *Rasmussen v. Fleming* (1987, Ariz.) 741 Pac.2d 674, 688; *Gray v. Romeo* (1988, D.C.R.I.) 697 Fed. Supp. 580.
37 *Deciding to Forego Life-Sustaining Treatment, supra*, p. 132.
38 *Sup't of Belchertown State School v. Saikewicz* (1977, Mass.) 370 N.E. 2d 417.
39 *In re Hier* (1984, Mass. App.) 464 N.E. 2d 959.
40 *Cruzan v. Harmon* (1988, Mo.) 760 S.W. 2d 408; *Matter of Westchester Co. Med. Ctr. (O'Connor)* (1988, N.Y.) 534 N.Y.S. 2d 886; *Conservatorship of Valerie N.* (1985) 40 Cal. 3d 143; *Re Conroy* (1985, N.J.) 486 A.2d 1209. Cruzan, U.S.S.C. No. 88–1503 (June 25, 1990).
41 *State v. Hodge* (1984, N.J.) 471 A.2d 389.
42 *Conservatorship of Drabick* (1988) 200 Cal. App. 3d 185 (cert. den., U.S.S.C.).
43 200 Cal.App.3d 185, 212, 216; Calif. Probate Code §2355(a) provides that the conservator for an incompetent has the obligation to consent to treatment deemed in good faith to be 'necessary'. This must mean treatment that is in the best interests of the conservatee.
44 (1989) 2 W.L.R. 1025, 1067.
45 See *Bolam v. Friern Hosp. Mgt. Committee* (1957) 1 W.L.R. 582 (cited with approval by Lord Brandon in *In re F, supra*.)
46 *Matter of Quinlan* (1976, N.J.) 355 A.2d 647 (10 years).
47 *Whitehouse v. Jordan* (1980) 1 All E. R. 650; *Lim v. Camden and Islington Area H.A.* (1974) 1 Q.B. 196 (Lord Denning, M.R.).
48 *In re C. (A Minor) (Wardship: Medical Treatment)*, (1989) 3 W.L.R. 240; *Re B. (A minor)*, (1981) 1 *W.L.R.* 1421 (C.A.), discussed in Chapter 4.

49 *United States v. Charters* (1987, 4th cir.) 829 Fed.2d 479 (no right to force antipsychotic drugs on patient); *Gray v. Romeo* (1988, D.C.R.I.) 697 Fed.Supp. 580 (no right to compel comatose patient to take nourishment by gastrostomy tube where patient if competent likely to refuse consent).

50 See, for example, *Matter of Quinlan* (1976, N.J.) 355 A.2d 647; *Satz v. Perlmutter* (1978, Fla. App.) 362 So.2d 160 (aff'd,, Fla., 1980, 379 So. 2d 359); *Severns v. Wilmington Med. Ctr. Inc.* (1980), Del.) 421 A.2d 1334; *Leach v. Akron Gen. Med. Ctr.* (1980, Ohio) 426 N.E. 2d 809; *Barber v. Superior Court* (1983) 147 Cal. App. 3d 1006; *Foody v. Manchester Mem. Hosp.* (1984, Conn. App.) 482 A.2d 713; *Guardianship of Barry* (1984, Fla. App.) 445 So.2d 365; *Matter of Colyer* (1983, Wash.) 660 Pac. 2d 738; *Rasmussen v. Fleming* (1987, Ariz.) 741 Pac. 2d 674; *Guardianship of Grant* (1988, Wash.) 747 Pac. 2d 445; *Re Gardner* (1987, Me.) 534 A. 2d 947; *Re Jobes* (1987, N.J.) 529 A.2d 434; *Brophy v. New England Sinai Hosp.* (1986, Mass.) 497 N.E. 2d 627; *Conservatorship of Drabick* (1988) 200 Cal. App. 3d 185. The appeals courts in only two instances have ruled otherwise, finding the wishes of the patient to be inconclusive and, accordingly, treatment continuance required. *Cruzan v. Harmon* (1988, Mo.) 760 S.W. 2d 408; *Matter of Westchester County Med. Ctr. (O'Connor)* (1988, N.Y.) 534 N.Y.S. 2d 886.

51 AMA Council on Ethical and Judicial Affairs, 'Withholding or Withdrawing Life-Prolonging Medical Treatment,' March 15, 1986.

52 *Barber v. Superior Court* (1983) 147 Cal. App. 3d 1006, 1019.

53 Joint Committee on Bioethics of the San Diego Co. Med. Soc. and San Diego Co. Bar Assn., 'Proposed Guidelines on Foregoing Life-Sustaining Treatment,' June 8, 1989, p.5.

54 Kelly, Gerald, S.J., 'The Duty to Preserve Life,' 12 *Theol. Studies* 550 (1951); Kelly, 'The Duty of Using Artificial Means of Preserving Life' 11 *Theol. Studies* 203 (1950).

55 AMA Judicial Council Resolution 74 (A-76), (emphasis supplied.)

56 *Matter of Quinlan* (1976, N.J.) 355 A.2d 647; *Barber v. Superior Court* (1983) 147 Cal. App. 3d 1006.

57 *Bouvia v. Superior Court* (1986) 179 Cal.App. 1127.

58 *Re Lydia E. Hall Hosp.* (1982, N.Y. App.) 455 N.Y.S. 2d 706.

59 *Re Rodas* (1987) Mesa Co. (Colo.) Dist. Ct. No. 86 PR 139; see related case, *Ross v. Hilltop Rehab. Hosp.* (1987, D.C. Colo.) 676 Fed.Supp. 1528.

60 *Guardianship of Grant* (1988, Wash.) 747 Pac.2d 445.

61 *Conservatorship of Drabick* (1988) 200 Cal.App.3d 185, 208.

62 Relying on the test laid down in *Bolam v. Friern Hosp. Mgt. Committee* (1957) 1 W.L.R. 582; see also, *Hunter v. Hanley* 1955 S.C. 200, discussed in Chapter 5 on Consent.

63 Permanent unconsciousness and loss of all cognition due to death of the higher brain, leaving only the metabolic functions – temperature, circulation, respiration – controlled by the brain stem to continue.

64 *Finlayson v. H.M. Advocate* 1978 *S.L.T.* (Notes) 60.

65 *R. v. Malcherek* (1981) 1 W.L.R. 690.

66 *Dority v. Superior Court* (1983) 145 Cal. App. 3d 273; *People v. Mitchell* (1982) 132 Cal. App. 3d 389; *Re Haymes* (1983, Ill. App.) 450 N.E.2d 940; *State v. Swafford* (1981, Ind.) 421 N.E. 2d 596.

67 *Black's Law Dictionary* (4th ed., 1968) p. 488; *Thomas v. Anderson* (1950) 96 Cal. App. 3d 371.
68 Meyers, *Medico-Legal Implications of Death and Dying*, Chap. 4, 'Brain Death.'
69 See cases collected in Meyers, *Medico-Legal Implications of Death and Dying*, Chap. 12 (1981 and Dec., 1988, Cum. Supp.)
70 *Cruzan v. Harmon* (1988, Mo.) 760 S.W. 2d 408, cert. granted (1989) U.S. O'Conner, note 79 infra.
71 U.S.S. Ct. No. 88–1503 (June 25, 1990, Rehnquist, C.J.)
72 *Conservatorship of Morrison* (1988) 206 Cal.App.3d 304; *In Re Requena* (1986, N.J. Super.) 517 A.2d 886.
73 *Gray v. Romeo* (1988, D.C.R.I.) 697 Fed. Supp. 580; *Bouvia v. Superior Court* (1986) 179 Cal. App. 3d 1127.
74 'Position of the American Academy of Neurology on certain aspects of the care and management of the persistent vegetative state,' 1989 *Neurology* 39(1): 125; see discussion in *Ethical Currents*, Spring, 1989, No. 18, p. 7.
75 Twycross, 'Euthanasia – a Physician's Viewpoint,' 8 *J. Med. Ethics* 86 (1982); Wanzer, et.al., 'The Physician's Responsibility Toward Hopelessly Ill Patients' I and II, 310 *New Eng. J. Med.* 955 (1984) and 320 *New Eng. J. Med.* 844 (1989); Ruark, et.al., 'Initiating and Withdrawing Life Support,' 318 *New Eng. J. Med.* 25 (1988).
76 486 A.2d 1209, 1231.
77 See also, *Matter of Dinnerstein* (1978, Mass. App.) 380 N.E.2d 134; Mason and Meyers, 12 *J. Med. Ethics* 67 (1986).
78 747 Pac.2d 445, 458.
79 *Matter of Westchester Co. Med. Ctr. (O'Connor)*, (1988, N.Y.) 534 N.Y.S. 2d 886.
80 New York's highest state court is its Court of Appeals. Most states have an intermediate Court of Appeals, and as their highest court, a state Supreme Court, usually composed of 7 Justices.
81 534 N.Y.S. 2d 886, 892.
82 See, for example, *Re Clark* (1986, N.J. Super) 510 A.2d 136 (aff'd. 524 A.2d 448); *Matter of Colyer* (1983, Wash.) 660 Pac. 2d 738.
83 *Matter of Peter* (1987, N.J.) 529 A.2d 419.
84 *Lim v. Camden Islington Area H.A.* (1974) 1 Q.B. 196.
85 (1974) 1 Q.B. 196, at 216.
86 *Whitehouse v. Jordan* (1980) 1 All E.R. 650
87 (1980) 1 All E.R. 650, at 654.
88 *Sidaway v. Bethlem, etc., supra*, 1 All E.R. 643 (dissenting opinion); *Gillick v. West Norfolk and Wisbeck Area Health Authority* (1985) 3 All E.R. 402 (HL), (majority opinion).
89 Lord Scarman 'Legal Liability and Medicine,' 74 *J.Roy.Soc.Med.* 11, 14 (1981).
90 Quoted by Skegg, in *Law, Ethics and Medicine, supra*, p.165.
91 See generally, Lynn (ed.) *By No Extraordinary Means: The Choice to Foregoing Life-Sustaining Food and Water*. Bloomington: Indiana Univ. Press, 1986; Steinbrook & Lo, 'Artificial Feeding – Solid Ground, Not a Slippery Slope,' 318 *New Eng. J. Med.* 286 (1988); Meilander, 'On removing food and water: against the stream,' 1984 *Hastings Ctr. Rpt.* 14(6):11–13.

92 May, et.al., 'Feeding and Hydrating the Permanently Unconscious and Other Vulnerable Persons,' *Issues in Law& Med.* (Winter, 1987).

93 *Matter of Storar* (1981, N.Y.) 420 N.E. 2d 64.

94 *Barber v. Superior Court* (1983) 147 Cal. App. 3d 1006; *Brophy v. New England Sinai Hosp.* (1986, Mass.) 497 N.E. 2d 627; *Rasmussen v. Fleming* (1987, Ariz.) 741 Pac.2d 674; *Corbett v. D'Alessandro* (1986, Fla. App.) 498 So.2d 368; *Matter of Jobes* (1987, N.J.) 529 A.2d 434.

95 See, for example, Okla. Public Health and Safety §3080.4 (1987).

96 *In Re Gardner* (1987, Me.) 534 A.2d 947.

97 *Corbett v. D'Alessandro* (1986, Fla. App.) 498 So.2d 368.

98 Mason & Meyers, 12 *J. Med. Ethics* 67, 70 (1986); Mason & McCall Smith, *Law and Medical Ethics*, p. 249.

99 British Med. Ass'n., *The Euthanasia Report.* London: Prof. Div. Pubs., BMA (Ethics), 1988; 1988 The *Brit. Med. J.* 1376; Gillon, 14 *J. Med. Ethics* 115 (1988). See also discussion in Chapter 10 and in particular the prosecutions against Doctors Adams, Arthur & Carr; Lord Scarman, 'Legal Liability and Medicine,' 74 *J. Roy. Soc. Med.* 11 (1981).

100 Wanzer, et.al., 'The Physician's Responsibility Toward Hopelessly Ill Patients' 320 *New Eng. J. Med.* 844, 847–8 (1989).

101 Brahams, 'The Euthanasia Debate,' 1988 *The Lancet*, i, 779, 780.

102 See St. John-Stevas, *Life, Death and the Law.* London: Eyre & Spottiswoode, 1961, p. 264; P. Devlin, *Samples of Lawmaking.* London: Oxford Univ. Press, 1962, p. 94; Williams, 1962 *Crim. L.R.* 154, 158.

103 Pestalozzi-Henggler, 'Euthanasia under the Swiss Penal Code' 15 *Souwest. L.J.* 393, 395 (1961).

104 Schonke-Schroder, *STGB Kommentar* (13th ed., 1967); Silving, 103 *U.Pa.L.R.* 350 (1954).

105 See discussion in Meyers, *The Human Body and the Law* (1st ed., 1970), pp. 152–155.

106 *Dryden Alexander Brown* (High Court, Dec., 1981), discussed in Gordon, *The Criminal Law of Scotland* (2d ed., 1978); Smith, T.B., 'Law, Professional Ethics and the Human Body,' 1959 *S.L.T.* (News) 245, 246.

107 See discussion in Chapter 10; Williams, *The Sanctity of Life and the Criminal Law.* London: Faber & Faber, Ltd., 1958, Chapter 8.

108 Kamisar, 'Some non-religious views against proposed 'Mercy-Killing Legislation,' 42 *Minn. L.R.* 969 (1958). *Repouille v. U.S.* (1947, 2d cir.) 165 Fed.2d 153; 34 *Note Dame Lawyer* 460 (1959). Williams, 38 *U. Colo. L.R.* 178 (1966).

109 Diminished responsibility as a defense in homicide cases is authorized by the Homicide Act 1957, s.2 in England and at common law in Scotland. However, the defense must prove the necessary abnormality of mind by medical evidence that is admitted by the court.

110 Calif. Ass'n. of Catholic Hospitals, *Networking* (Winter, 1988), Vol. 18, p.1.

111 See Wanzer, 'The Physician's Responsibility Toward Hopelessly Ill Patients II' 320 *New Eng. J. Med.* 844 (1989); Dr. Cicely Saunders, O.B.E., 'Pain and the care of the dying,' Edinburgh Med. Group, 27 Feb. 1968.

112 *Barber v. Superior Court* (1983) 147 Cal. App. 3d 1006; *In re C (A*

Minor) (Wardship: Medical Treatment), (1989) 3 W.L.R. 240 (C.A.); *Bolam v. Friern Hosp. Mgt. Committee* (1957) 1 W.L.R. 582; *Hunter v. Hanley*, 1955 S.C. 200.

113 Vaux, 'Mercy Killing and the Good Death', 259 *J. Amer. Med. Assn.* 2140, 2141 (1988).

114 Elkinton, 'The dying patient, the doctor and the law' 13 *Vill. L.R.* 740 (1968).

115 See the classic article by Fletcher, 'Legal Aspects of the Decision not to Prolong Life' 203 *J. Am. Med. Assn.* 65 (1968); see also, Hughes, 'Criminal Omissions,' 67 *Yale L.R.* 590, 158.

12

Distribution and Rationing of Scarce Medical Resources

A. INTRODUCTION

1. *The rapid growth of health care expenditures*

Most would agree that society has an obligation to its members to provide them with at least some minimal level of health care. Most societies recognize this obligation by subsidizing the cost of health care. In Britain the National Health Service (NHS) is intended to provide all with an adequate level of health care, funded by government taxes and other levies upon the populace.

In the United States, the federal government provides health insurance for the elderly and dependent through its Medicare and Medicaid programs. These government expenditures account for approximately 40 percent of health care expenditures. A similar amount is spent by private business to provide coverage for its employees. The remaining costs are paid for by state and local governments providing care for the indigent and by private individuals. These sources do not, however, provide coverage for all Americans. It is estimated that 35 million are without health insurance coverage[1] and up to 50 million have inadequate coverage. The U.S. annual health care bill amounts to $600 billion.

Both American and British health care systems, despite their different sources of funding and different approaches to distribution of health care services, are suffering the stresses and being forced to confront the difficult decisions of further resource allocation and rationing. Both governments are seeking ways to constrain and, if possible, reduce their financial underwriting of the health care system.

America spends approximately 11 percent of its gross national product on health care, twice what it spent 20 years ago, and twice the percentage spent by Britain. This expenditure by the United States is the most of any country in both real and proportional terms. Despite that increase in expenditure, the social measurements of the success of the health care system have not improved as might be expected. U.S. male life expectancy is 15th, female

7th and infant mortality 19th in the world.[2] The U.S. spends only 39 cents on care for children for each dollar it spends on adult care, whereas Britain spends $1.19 on children for each dollar spent on adult health care.

An essential conflict seems to exist between public desire and economic reality. While the public calls for more spending on health care, they also want no increase in taxes. While Americans want heart bypass and transplants funded by national health insurance, they also demand that the $150 billion budget deficit be reduced. More than 50 percent of Britons want more spent on health care to reduce hospital waiting lists for elective surgery, delays in seeing consultants and higher physician and nurse staffing levels,[3] but want no new taxes.

2. Causes for health care cost increases

What has caused this huge increase in health care spending over the past two decades without an attendant improvement in the quality of health care for all? There are many causes. One is natural inflation and increases in labor and materials. Another is increasingly intensive government regulation of both physical facilities, delivery of care and compensation. This has resulted in significant escalation of capital and administrative costs. The bureaucratic element of each health care dollar spent in the U.S. increased more than four-fold between 1960 and 1985.

Perhaps the most significant cost escalator has been the proliferation of high-technology procedures and treatment options, particularly for the terminally ill. American medicine has become 'procedure' rather than 'service' driven; while doctors may receive low reimbursement for non-invasive, preventive care, they receive high reimbursement for high-tech invasive treatment. The physician who advises his hypertensive and/or high blood-cholesterol patient to make dietary, lifestyle and exercise changes may receive $40 for this essential patient service, yet he who performs an angiogram blood vessel scan may receive $1,500 or more. The doctor who prescribes similar changes in habit for his patient with occluded coronary arteries and prescribes a blood thinner may receive $75, whereas the heart bypass surgeon who operates may receive $10,000 or more, and the hospital where he operates $25,000. One procedure may be no more effective in terms of life-expectancy than the other, but the financial incentives to the physician strongly promote the costly and invasive procedure. Hospitals also play a significant role in the formula. In 1984 the average hospital occupancy rate was only 67 percent.[4] Since hospital capital and equipment costs, depreciation and much of their labor costs remain fixed, their incentive to encourage use of available surgical, radiological, laboratory and other facilities is clear.

Some examples of this built-in preference for high-tech procedures will illustrate the powerful role it plays in American medicine. Bypass surgeries,

which typically cost in excess of $30,000 result in expenditures of more than
$2 billion per year, nearly 1 percent of public health care expenditures, yet
far less than that percentage of the population is served by the procedure.[5]
Renal dialysis and other treatment for end stage renal disease, which cannot
cure the patient, absorbs well over $2 billion to serve 100,000 patients,
while only about half that amount is spent on pre-natal care, which is
needed for at least 1,000,000 patients.

Biomedical research has created many modern, life-saving and life-sustaining technologies, not in small part because the 'fee-for-service' form of
compensation traditionally offered for their use has enabled providers to
pay the huge costs for their development. Linear accelerators, found in
many, even relatively small, suburban hospitals, used for radiation treatment of cancer, cost $1.5 million. The Magnetic Resonance Imaging (MRI)
radiographic scanner, a sophisticated extension of the X-ray, can cost from
$1 million to $2 million. The lithotriper, used to smash kidney stones
without surgery, can cost from $600,000 to $1.5 million. Where hospitals or
clinics are too small to afford such devices, it is common for them to contract
with mobile units, often owned by groups of physicians,[6] for such services.

In the U.S., physicians traditionally have been paid on the basis of 'fee for
service.' The more times they see and treat the patient, the more they are
paid. They are not paid a salary based on patient load as is common under
the NHS. Added to this inherent pressure on costs has been the 40 percent
increase in U.S. physicians over the past decade or so, increasing the
competition for patients and the inevitable upward spiral of health care
procedures.

Finally, media hype and other promotion of miracle cures, as well as
increased competition for patient population, has increased public awareness and demand for high-tech health care. Acute care intervention has
increased life expectancy, but not reduced health care expenditures, since
many elderly must now be medically supported because of an underlying
degenerative or chronic illness.

3. *Changes underway to contain costs*

Strong pressures are at work to contain health care costs. Large budget
deficits and health cost increases in the U.S. have prompted a fundamental
re-examination of the traditional fee for service method of health care
compensation. The federal government has adopted what is known as the
DRG ('Diagnostic-Related Group') system of payment for procedures.
While still procedure-driven, it sets a payment quota based on diagnosis. It
is not related to customary or even reasonable charges. It has largely shifted
costs to outpatient and nursing services and away from impatient hospital
services, but has not reduced overall expenditures as anticipated.

Private health insurers and employers are moving strongly away from so-called indemnity payment plans, which reimburse retrospectively for services provided. Prospective payment limitations are now being imposed by group insurance plans which pay a group of physicians or a hospital so much per person in the group per month for whatever care may prove necessary. It then becomes necessary for the health care providers to establish the level of medical care that will be provided in return for the pre-payment and how the monthly fee will be divided among the providers.

This system, whereby the physician acts as 'gatekeeper' to the health care delivery system, has long been a part of the National Health System. NHS physicians have, by and large, incorporated cost considerations into their medical treatment decisions.[8] For example, given the limits of available kidney dialysis machines in Britain, physicians rarely recommend dialysis for patients over 55 years old.[9] Age becomes a disqualifying factor in resource allocation. The same is true with cardiac bypass surgery. In the U.S. in 1972, before Congress funded renal dialysis, only 7 percent of recipients were over age 55.[7] After a little over five years of Medicare coverage nearly half the dialysis patients were over 55. Initial costs of the program, estimated to be $250,000, had by 1985 risen to $1.5 billion.

The question must be asked whether it is fair to impose on the caregiver the obligation to decide what care is economically justified and what is not? Most physicians feel it is not. They feel it is a public policy decision that should be made by the legislature, since budgetary, managerial and issues of social ethics are involved.[10] One combined group of physicians and attorneys who recently addressed the issue concluded,

'It is inevitable that the availability of resources will be considered in some decisions to provide or forego life-sustaining treatment. Questions concerning the rationing of available resources cannot be decided by individual physicians on a case by case basis, because there are no generally accepted standards for determining when the withholding of care from a single patient is justified to provide resources for other 'more deserving' patients. Rather, institutional policies should be developed to provide guidance to physicians in addressing this issue.'[11]

Society has asked medical care providers to decide how limited resources are to be allocated among patients, but traditionally this has been done only on the basis of medical management. The battlefield-inspired triage system operates in many emergency medical facilities to separate patients into hopeless cases, cases requiring immediate treatment and cases that will be treated only after those in immediate need. However, health care providers now are asked to consider economics as well as medical need and benefit in many instances of patient care. Both government and private payors are more and more inclined to pay fixed, prospective amounts of compensation to doctors and hospitals, which payments are based more on what payors can collect from taxpayers or customers' premiums than on what actual or desired medical care may cost at current rates.

A clear conflict of interest lurks in most of these payment schemes. Health Maintenance Organizations, the fastest growing segment of the U.S. private health care market, charge a flat monthly premium to their customers. The HMO then contracts with a group of local physicians and a hospital to provide full care for a per capita cost. The physicians group must then decide how to distribute its monthly receipts among its members. The less specialist consultations or diagnostic studies ordered for his patient by the originating physician, the more funds are normally left for him. Thus has created a clear tension between economic self-interest and patient best interests.

Similarly, since hospitals are now very largely paid a set fee per patient to whom care is offered or based on the diagnosis, not the treatment received, the financial incentive is to discharge the patient as soon as possible, with the least possible expenditure of costly resources, equipment or facilities use and personnel time.

While there may not be a constitutional right to any particular level of medical care in the U.S.,[12] or under the law in Britain,[13] it is also true that cost alone cannot dictate treatment decisions. As stated by a California court, 'it is essential that cost limitation programs not be permitted to corrupt medical judgment.'[14] Legally, if cost-cutting compromises care, or indicated care is withheld on economic grounds, legal liability for any untoward result may follow.[15] At the same time if a resource is unavailable to a physician, he cannot be held liable for the result caused from being unable to use it.[16]

This is not to say, however, that cost is not a legitimate factor in treatment decisions. Few would argue with the notion that the cost of a procedure or course of treatment is one burden imposed by that treatment on the patient, his family and society as a whole and it may, with other burdens of a physical or emotional nature be weighed against the benefits offered by treatment in deciding upon its advisability.[17] As has been expressed by both Sir John Donaldson, Master of the Rolls, and Lord Justice Brown in the English Court of Appeal, the courts are not the proper institution in society to pass upon the allocation of limited medical resources.[13] If unfairness or bad faith is involved, the courts undoubtedly have a role to play. Otherwise, cost containment decisions should be made by the most broadly based societal institution, the legislature and its elected representatives.[10]

Decisions on the availability of health care will need to be made. At present, costs are being contained solely to meet economic objectives, without consideration of their social and ethical implications. While physicians can be called upon to utilize the least costly of productive treatment alternatives and to carry out only beneficial, proportionate[18] treatment, restricting access to care because of cost requires a societal consensus. What then should the criteria for allocating or rationing health care be? This is a difficult issue to resolve as we shall see.

B. HOW CAN LIMITED MEDICAL RESOURCES BE FAIRLY ALLOCATED?

1. *Introduction*

Ration means to distribute in an equitable manner. Rationing is a reality of both British and American health care. Medical resources are scarce in both countries because they depend on funding for their existence and funding is always limited. Thus, although many particularly in the U.S., may feel whatever health care they will need is and should be available, the simple fact is that it is not.

Physicians in Britain tell their patients over 55 that they are not candidates for dialysis not because they would not benefit from it, but because adequate dialysis machines to service all the elderly suffering renal failure cannot be acquired with a limited NHS funding by Parliament. Physicians in California often refuse to see economically-deprived, pregnant women because they are uninsured and government reimbursement for pre-natal care and delivery care is not deemed adequate. Many other examples abound.

Given that access to health care must inevitably be limited, since the potential technology and its cost will always exceed the ability and/or willingness of society to fund it, the goal should be to find the fairest methods of allocation possible. This is no easy task. Economic reality, political pressure and personal value judgments play important roles in any allocation/rationing decision.

Before decisions on rationing are made, the full picture must be viewed. Approving the funding of one service will result in denial of support for another. 'Pro-life' advocates press for severe restrictions on a woman's right to abortion, but are they prepared to fund the additional social welfare and well-baby programs that the birth of unwanted children will spawn? Those confronted with the plight of a childhood leukemia victim may press for funding or insurance coverage for bone marrow transplantation for him, but what of the many birth complications that spending those funds on basic prenatal services could have avoided?[40]

There are obviously many factors to consider in each decision to ration medical care. Several key elements seem to emerge: patient age, patient prognosis, patient autonomy. We now consider those.

2. *Is age a proper factor?*

Twice as many people in Britain will be more than 80 years old in 2000 as were in 1970.[19] In the U.S. 2.5 million people were aged 85 or older in 1980 and the number could be as high as 10 times that by the year 2040.[20]

Eighty-five percent of American health care expenses are incurred in the last two years of life. While this may come at any time in one's life span, normally with life expectancies well into the 70s it is among the elderly. Those over 65 comprise 12 percent of the U.S. population, 15 percent in Britain.[21] By 2040 this percentage of elderly will be 20 percent, with yet greater demands on health care resources. At present those over 65 years old consume a disproportionate 35 or 40 percent, or more, of all health care costs.[21]

With longevity rising along with health care costs, something has to give. Either expenditures must rise significantly, which has severe limits with the competing demands of defense, debt retirement, education, transportation, old age and other welfare programs fiercely competing for each budget dollar, or the rate of per capita increase in health care expenditures must decrease.

With the acute care of the elderly consuming a large portion of the health care budget, some argue quite persuasively that age should become an explicit factor in restricting access to health care. Callahan argues[22] that after a 'natural life span' has occurred, say at age 80, Medicare should refuse to cover expensive life-extending technologies, but provide only palliative care necessary to relieve pain and suffering.[23] In his view, setting 'some ultimate limit is not to deprive and denigrate the elderly; it is only to recognize that we live in a finite world.'[24] In this way costs are controlled and medical resources remain available to provide care for the next generation.

Daniels comes to a similar conclusion,[25] but justifies it more on the basis that each person has a right to demand a reasonable quantum of health care in a lifetime, whether it proves necessary to use it early in life or late in life. The difficulty of course comes in denying care to a patient in need, particularly where it will be productive, based on past usage.

Callahan focuses the argument well when he points out he might like to live to be 100, but is it fair and reasonable to ask his neighbor to be taxed to pay for a transplant to accomplish it. His answer is no. He asserts, however, that, 'I can only ask of him that he help me to avoid a premature death, to live a reasonably long life, and to make my last years as comfortable as possible.'[24]

It may be restricting care based on age alone would not be particularly cost effective. A U.S. Congressional study[26] concluded most elderly people who die do not incur high Medicare costs in their final years. This in part may be true because the elderly by and large need long-term custodial, nursing and home care for chronic degenerative illness. It is precisely this need, large as it is, that is not covered by Medicare. Some feel that restricting future medical technology from the elderly may only slow future medical cost increases by 10 percent.[27]

Age should not be *the* factor in determining access to health care, but it should be *a* factor. Dr. Christine Cassel of the University of Chicago has put the reverse case, saying, 'We do not need an arbitrary age at which to define someone as socially dispensable . . . Instead we need a structure for an age-irrelevant society . . . where medical decisions are made on an individual basis.'[27] This seems to overstate the case. Medical decisions are not made in a vacuum. Age will often effect surgical or other treatment choices. It cannot be disregarded entirely.

Treatment should be proportionate.[18] Its benefits should outweigh its burdens. The preservation or restoration of functioning should be considered, as should the extent of life extension and the quality of the life extended. Age will, at times, play a significant role in the chance for a successful outcome because of the condition of organ systems in general. Even though cardiac bypass surgery is technically feasible at age 80, its risks, invasiveness, cost, and debated benefits over more conservative measures would seem to make it contraindicated given the length of remaining life expectancy and physical activity limitations already present at that age.

Society should openly acknowledge that age is a legitimate factor in treatment decisions. Where resources are limited, the desire of the physician is to do the greatest good for the patient. The heart transplant recipient over age 50 presents a more guarded prognoses because of likely cardiovascular disease and other age-induced changes in organ systems. He also has a lesser life expectancy than the similarly afflicted 30 year old recipient. For that reason, Medicare-Medicaid reimbursement criteria for heart transplants all but ensure those over 50 will not meet the required clinical criteria.[28]

Many medical treatment decisions of a routine or emergency life-saving nature are uncomplicated and treatment goes forward with little deliberation. However, many more decisions involve a complex matrix of factors to be weighed by physician, patient and family. These include: the intended benefits of the treatment, their permanence or duration and their likelihood; the degree of pain, inconvenience or humiliation involved in the treatment or recovery from it; the cost of the treatment; the nature of the risks of treatment, both in terms of likelihood and severity; the effect of the treatment on others – normally family or loved ones – physically, emotionally and financially; and, the improvement in quality of life for the patient from his or her own particular perspective. Age will play a role in the weight accorded to several of these factors, depending on the particular treatment involved. Clinical good judgment and common sense must be the guideposts here.

With certain highly invasive and costly procedures – most notably organ transplantation and cardiac bypass surgery – it is not unreasonable for government (and perhaps private) insurers to impose sound clinical eligibility criteria which will drastically reduce if not largely eliminate such procedures after certain advanced age. Hospitalization and antibiotic treatment for an otherwise healthy 85 year old with pneumonia is proportionate treatment, given cost, invasiveness and outcome evaluation. Surgery, transplantation, or chemotherapy in the hopes of some brief life extension for a 85 year old with metastatic cancer is not.

As we will discuss shortly, the use of age as a factor in treatment decisions should be combined with a health care delivery system that seeks to promote dignity, comfort and autonomy for those in their declining years, not unrealistic extensions of life at great physical and financial cost. This suggests other avenues for fair rationing of health care.

3.   *Concentrating on proportionate treatment is essential*

Rationing medical care is not something that we may have to face. It is here now. Britain and the U.S. ration health care, although in different ways.

British health care is intended to provide basic health care to all regardless of economic or social status. It does so at a politically acceptable level of expenditure by severely limiting access for elective procedures, by recognizing age as a legitimate factor in treatment decisions, particularly costly and resource-intensive ones such as dialysis and cardiac surgery,[29] and by providing treatment based on medically defined need, not on consumer demand.[8] Rationed out of the system are patient convenience (appointment and elective procedure waiting times, staffing levels, facilities), many elective procedures, costly, resource-intensive and scarce treatments for those over a certain age, and similar treatments for hopelessly ill patients.

Private health care remains an option in Britain for those who can afford it. The numbers of those who selected this option doubled in the past decade. Approximately 15 percent of all surgery, 20 percent of heart surgery and 25 percent of hip replacement surgery is done privately in the U.K. That is not an indictment of a system that only purports to provide an 'adequate' level of care for its constituents.

In the U.S., market and budget forces exert a strong and pervasive rationing influence on the availability of medical care. Large numbers of the population are without any insurance, or what coverage they have is inadequate. Those with some assets are not eligible for many government programs, yet are required to spend all they have in their declining years for long-term, unreimbursed custodial care. Without mandatory health insurance laws and with dramatically rising health insurance costs,[30] many private employers have either dropped or do not offer coverage for their employees.

Nonetheless, public and private medical insurance accounts for all but a handful of the health care dollars spent in the U.S. The spread of this insurance over the past 25 years has been a mixed blessing: more people are protected, but it has relieved the economic pressure to hold down costs that previously operated on both patients and physicians. Personal income has thus been greatly diminished as a rationing device. Surgery rates, once much higher for the elderly with above-average income than for those with below-average income, has with the advent of Medicare become essentially the same for both groups.

While Medicare has largely equated the opportunity for acute care among the elderly, most are in greater need of long-term institutional and home care which is not reimbursable. The result is the wealthy are well cared for with their own funds, or private insurance, the poor are not. The same is true with preventive care – such as prenatal well-baby care – compared to acute care. The latter is covered, the former is not.

Much of this relates to our discussion of 'proportionate' care, both earlier in this Chapter and in Chapter 11. Many feel medical care would be better allocated if it was distributed on the basis of outcome for the patient, rather than on a procedure or cost-oriented basis. Payors, public or private, should only pay for cost-effective treatment. Stated another way, payment should only be made when the benefit to the patient in terms of health and life enhancement is sufficiently great to justify the cost. If it is not, from a social point of view, the money is better spent elsewhere.

Many medical procedures are in common use because of media hype, manufacturer promotion, consumer demand, or because cost reimbursement is available, often without regard to outcome and benefit to the patient.[31] Example: Britain spends 70 percent less on cancer chemotherapeutic agents and performs coronary artery bypass surgery at about 10 percent of the rate in the U.S.,[8] yet life expectancy rates are equal in both countries. Example: About 250,000 bypass surgeries are performed in the U.S. each year, yet it is felt that perhaps one-third or more of these patients would have done just as well without it.[21] Example: More than 100,000 carotid artery cleanouts (endarterectomy) are performed in the U.S. each year, yet their benefit to patients remains unconfirmed.[32] Example: An 85 year old severely demented and unresponsive Medicare patient can receive a cataract operation or a kidney transplant, but not a new pair of glasses, a home health care aide or, even if healthy and independent, assistance in maintaining an apartment.[33]

So long as insurers pay for procedures with little concern for overall or long-term benefit to the patient, physicians and hospitals may be encouraged to promote and implement a high-tech, procedure-oriented approach to health care without sufficient regard for treatment proportionality and quality of life. Instead, the emphasis on reimbursement schemes both public and private must be away from short-term, critical-care, life-extension, invasive procedures, where long-term prognosis is poor due to age, disability or underlying illness, and towards long-term, supportive, custodial and home care, to maximize independence, quality of remaining life and feelings of self-worth.[32,33,34]

Whether the patient is elderly or not, health care should be imposed which will protect or improve the patient's health. Britain spends far less on chemotherapy because, as one commentator has noted,

'while British oncologists treat curable cancers just as readily as their American counterparts, they see no reason to treat incurable metastatic cancer by inflicting on patients a "treatment which brings them nothing but unpleasant side effects and is of no benefit." '[8]

The dedication of the individual physician to his or her patient is one of the most valuable attributes of the American health care system.[31] It is to be commended and encouraged. The relationship of trust and confidence between patient and physician is an important factor in treatment and cure. However, enthusiasm to cure must be tempered by reality that all patients eventually die and all treatment must eventually fail. Quality of life is undoubtedly more important for most than mere prolongation of life. For example, a recent Colorado poll showed 81 percent wanted their expected quality of life to be fully considered in any decision concerning critical care technology, 85 percent did not want artificial respiration or feeding if permanently comatose, 77 percent would decline resuscitation after cardiac arrest, if terminally ill, and 86 percent would decline active treatment for a newborn likely to survive with severe handicaps.[35]

It should not be necessary for the guardian of a terminally ill, lifelong incompetent suffering from leukemia to have to obtain a court order to forestall a nauseating course of chemotherapy recommended by doctors in the hopes of extending life for only six to twelve months.[36] It should not be necessary for the family of a permanently comatose young woman to obtain a court order to allow removal of continuing, costly mechanical respiration for the patient because the physicians refused to discontinue it at the parents' request.[37]

Substantial savings will be worked if payors require 'proportionality before payment.' Reasonable guidelines for many procedures could be drawn up by medical societies to serve as a guide for when invasive, expensive or scarce, resource-intensive procedures are indicated. These need to be flexible enough to allow for individual clinical judgment and patient peculiarities, but it can be done. Too many procedures are simply instituted without any kind of proportionality analysis. Granted that much of medical science is not precise, it does not need to embrace untested and unproven procedures simply because payment and the technology may be available. Dr. Relman, for example, has estimated that perhaps 25 percent of all procedures performed by well-meaning physicians, often in good hospitals, are either inappropriate, ineffective, or unnecessary.[32,21,38] Some of these procedures are undoubtedly harmful to patients.

Proportionality must be demanded by patients and payors and provided by physicians and hospitals. It will be a strong force in rationing without causing harm.

4. *The greatest good for the greatest number*

Given a finite budget and finite medical resources, should not allocation choices be based on the greatest good for the greatest number? Most would say yes.[39] If the same amount of money will provide proper prenatal care and enhance the odds of healthy delivery for ten times as many people as that money will support who are in end-stage renal failure, is not the choice made clear?

The Oregon legislature recently grappled with this precise issue. Being grossly underfunded for all medical programs, choices had to be made on what services to cut. The decision was made to eliminate funding for all transplants except kidney and cornea and instead to fund prenatal care services, including those for low-income and high-risk pregnant mothers. Great publicity occurred when a seven year old boy died for lack of insurance coverage for a needed bone-marrow transplant after the funding changes were implemented.

Media coverage of such unfortunate, but not necessarily unfair, situations, their immediacy and the natural supportive instincts of people, has probably encouraged an unrealistic public attitude that medicine can and should provide heroic, very costly care in all cases where cure is possible. This is unrealistic and detracts from the focus necessary to fairly apportion limited medical resources. Occasional examples of miracle cures or other 'heroic medicine' should not be used to create public expectations of the health care system.[40]

Oregon is in the process of setting permanent health care priorities. A series of citizens' forums showed organ transplants not to have a high priority in the public's mind. Of those polled, 15 percent supported funding them, 45 percent were opposed and 40 percent undecided.[41] A basic health package for all citizens received the strongest support. It was concluded that both efficiency and equity should play an important role in allocating health care services,

> 'Efficiency means the greatest amount of *appropriate* and *effective* health care benefits for the greatest number of persons is provided with a given amount of money. Equity means that all persons have an equal opportunity to receive *available* health services.'[41] (emphasis supplied.)

Other governmental health care providers are seeking to make similar decisions. Alameda County in Northern California, for example, has hired a bioethics consulting group to recommend to its legislative body what services are most important and what can most equitably be deleted. These decisions must be made on an institutional basis, as a matter of public policy, for physicians should not be asked to make them in individual cases. As two physicians have concluded,

> 'decisions about the allocation of such resources cannot be made at the doctor-patient interface. Rather, if the distribution is to be equitable, such decisions must be made in a closed system in which any limits the physician imposes on his or her patients are shared by all other physicians and patients in the same situation.'[42]

5. *Research remains an important element of rationing*

Medical research in the 20th century has been responsible for successfully conquering acute illnesses that previously had taken the lives of many. Many of the infectious diseases have been overcome with vaccines and other preventive care. Life expectancy has expanded as a result. Now more chronic, degenerative changes in the body and its tissues account for most deaths: heart disease, cancer and stroke.

As people live longer, debilitating illnesses of the joints – osteoarthritis and osteoporosis – and of the mind – Alzheimer's disease and Parkinson's disease – have become common. Research on these afflictions is in its infancy, but they impose significant requirements of long-term custodial care on our health-care system. Much of this care is unreimbursed. For example, while Medicare in the U.S. spends about 70 percent of its revenues for acute, hospital care, only about 6 percent is spent on custodial nursing and home health care.[43]

It is estimated that approximately half those over age 85 suffer from disabling dementia, the most common cause of which is Alzheimer's disease.[44] Approximately 20 percent of these elderly are in nursing homes, requiring expensive, long-term custodial care. In 1989 it was not unusual for monthly U.S. nursing home expenses to be $3,000. Since typically these expenses are not covered by health insurance, it is not hard to imagine the financially devastating impact of such expenses on patient or family savings.

If research results in effective treatment for these disabling, chronic illnesses, it could eliminate the need for long-term custodial care in many cases.[44] This could dramatically reduce expenditures and make unfair rationing or age-discriminatory health care decisions considerably less likely. Even strong advocates of age as a valid criterion for certain health care rationing acknowledge it should only be so where adequate emphasis is also placed on research to eliminate debilitating, chronic illnesses that now accompany old age in many cases.[45]

Research is also important to determine the effectiveness of new treatments once they become available.[46] New procedures should not become widespread until they are proven effective. The emphasis given to assessment of new treatments should be as great as that given to their creation.

Since medicine is not an exact science, the time to evaluate new treatments is when they are introduced since it will be much harder to differentiate between various applied treatments once commonly available and to eliminate access to some, but not others.[32] As one author has aptly put it, 'health care activity should not be confused with health care outcomes.'[8]

6.   *The role of patient autonomy in rationing*

The second half of the 20th century has clearly produced an increased awareness of and deference for the autonomy of the individual patient in health care decisionmaking.[47] The wishes of the patient if competent, or if expressed while competent, are normally to be honored. Since the consensus among the elderly seems to be not to undergo useless life-prolongation treatment,[35,45] greater acceptance of their wishes by physicians and hospitals should contribute to reduction of costly and unnecessary utilization of scarce and expensive technology in hopeless cases.[48] Most patients wish to die at home and until recent decades did so. Health insurers need to encourage a return to this ethic of dying by providing support for hospice and home health-care schemes.

No cost-driven pressures to decline treatment should be imposed on the patient by others. Patient competence should be clear. If it is, after full disclosure of alternatives to the patient, including the no treatment alternative, the wishes of the patient should be respected.[49] Health care providers must accept the wishes of the patent, even if they do not agree or feel technology is available to assist the patient. To do otherwise is to do violence to the dignity and self-determination of the individual.

C.   SOME THOUGHTS AND CONCLUSIONS ON MEDICAL CARE RATIONING

1.   *Ration based on outcome*

We have discussed some of the most important elements that should form the fabric of medical resource rationing: age, proportionality, research and patient autonomy. The first two – age and proportionality – are really inextricably woven together; the real issue they address is outcome, prognosis. Treatments, in other words, should be rationed based on their effectiveness, not on their availability. However, cost is also a major factor.

2.   *Cost effectiveness*

Unfortunately, an effective treatment may be very expensive or scarce. Heart transplants, once very expensive, but not very effective, are now very, very expensive, but they are also very effective.[50] Physicians cannot be asked to decide between treatments based only on cost-effectiveness. They must decide on clinical criteria, on the basis of proportionality. Proportionality may properly include the cost burden to the patient of the treatment alternatives available.

Physicians should be advocates for treatment that will help their patient. They should not decide whether a clearly beneficial treatment should be made available or not because of its cost. In close cases, where the clinical picture or the prognosis is unclear or guarded, the physician should consider cost or availability of resources. Most do. This is *in part* why U.S. surgeons infrequently accept heart transplant recipients over age 50 or 55 and British physicians infrequently accept dialysis patients over age 55. However, these decisions are also *in part* the result of physicians knowing that resources are limited and more good can be provided to another, probably younger patient. These external limits will always be imposed on the health care system. It is not the function of the system to impose those limits, but to work within those limits to do the most medical good.

Patients clearly have a right to consider cost in electing to forego treatment. The courts have begun to recognize this. In a recent decision upholding a mother's right to reject a life-saving blood transfusion, the Florida Supreme Court stated,[51]

> 'It does not necessarily follow that where there is a favorable medical prognosis the state's interest automatically overrides the patient's right to refuse treatment. In some circumstances the cost to the individual of the life-prolonging treatment, in economic, emotional, or as in this case, spiritual terms, may be too high. (citation.) That 'cost' must be looked at from the patient's point of view.'

Cost cannot be looked at alone. It must be looked at in terms of what it will buy. How effective will it be. The increasingly common decision for patient, physician, family and health care insurer will be whether the benefit to the patient from a particular treatment justifies its cost.

Faced with the fact of only 10 dialysis machines in the country, or only 100 transplantable hearts in a year's time, physicians can be asked to decide how best to apportion those resources on the basis of medical need and anticipated outcome. They should do so on these bases, which may at times include a medical evaluation of how long the patient will be able to live and with what quality of life from a physical or functioning point of view. Decisions should not be made on the basis of race, color, creed, ability to pay or social 'worth.' If social worth determinations are to be made, they are to be made by society through its elected representatives – if at all – not by doctors or courts.

Younger has stated the distinction well:

> 'Until we reach a public consensus about how to deal with these very difficult issues [rationing], individual clinicians and institutions should continue to separate concerns about patient welfare from broader social and economic policy issues. As professionals, we are there to serve our patients. As citizens, we can vote or lobby for policies that limit individual choice in the interests of a broader social good.'[52]

Cost-effectiveness in the sense of whether society obtains more benefit from £1 billion spent on cancer research and cure than on deficit reduction, a new missile system, environmental cleanup, or higher teacher wages is a political question for society. At this point in time both the American and British governments have answered the question. Neither is willing to fund all feasible medical care. Limits have been imposed because of other priorities. The consequence in both countries is, at times, an inequitable delivery of health care services that tends to favor the well-to-do and to prejudice the poor,[53] most notably outside the National Health Service. The better off get better medical care because they can pay for it, advocates for their position are stronger and they are likely to be more closely aligned socially with most physicians and, in practice, to have easier access to them. Still, some would argue that private medical care for those who can afford it is not an unreasonable, and certainly a very pragmatic, way of taking pressure off the public health system and thereby perhaps improving its quality and/or accessibility.

Given a finite allocation of funds to medical care, the issue then becomes which care will be funded. Will it be heart transplants or prenatal care? Who decides and how?

3. *Setting rationing standards*

Given the reality of limited resources, society has the obligation to set treatment priority criteria. Society has chosen to limit medical resources, but has largely ignored the concomitant responsibility to set policies for the equitable allocation of those resources. These decisions have been left, by default, largely to the doctors. Most decisions are reached implicitly, often unconsciously. This is neither fair nor proper. It has been said, 'to ration unconsciously is to ration unjustly.'[54] Explicit standards should be considered and adopted, for all to be aware of, debate, scrutinize, and if unwise or unfair, to change.

Society, through its elected representatives on a state and national level, and through ethics committees on a local level, must consider, debate and decide upon sound, non-discriminatory policies of medical resource allocation. If this is not done, these decisions are not made from the point of view of what is most fair or represents the best social policy. Rather, such allocations are controlled by the marketplace – he who can pay gets it – or by personal preferences of caregivers, or by chance – whoever is in need and on the doorstep when the resource is available gets it. While chance is the most democratic, none of these methods is particularly fair or socially responsible.

Representative legislative bodies can mandate the establishment of medical eligibility criteria for the various costly and scarce resources we have been discussing: dialysis, transplantation, coronary bypass, chemotherapy, radiation therapy, rare drug therapy, such as AZT for treatment of the HIV infection, and other chronic or resource-intensive procedures. Ethics committees, composed of physicians, nurses, social workers, lay representatives and the clergy, are best able to implement these mandates, since clinical developments, cost-saving, and research breakthroughs will continue to occur and will effect the eligibility criteria. Individual physicians can then rely on these criteria to selectively treat patients based on outcome and medical benefit, not economic or social status or on some other arbitrary basis. 'First come, first serve' will inevitably still play a role, for if there are empty beds they should be given to those in need, not withheld on the chance that others may appear more in need. The key starting point here is properly defining the medical need in advance for use of the resource in question.

Naturally, the eligibility criteria must take into account the availability of the resources in comparison to the need or demand for them. Little or no rationing criteria are necessary for commonly available, inexpensive and effective resources such as penicillin, basic emergency care, vaccinations, and the like, other than sound clinical judgment by the physician in their application. At the other extreme, where demand greatly exceeds supply and the resource is both scarce and expensive, such as cardiac or liver transplantation, strict eligibility criteria to bring patient expectations into rough balance with supply must be imposed.

The U.S. Health Care Financing Agency has, for example, imposed eligibility criteria for Medicare reimbursement of heart transplant expenses. These 'patient selection criteria' are intended to avoid 'unnecessary risk' to the patient (proportionately) and 'waste of scarce resources' (cost-benefit.)[28] The criteria limit age for eligibility to 50 unless the patient exhibits an 'adequately young physiological age.' There must be an absence of other disease and the patient must not suffer from behavior or psychiatric illness that would interfere with treatment or the disciplined medical regimen necessary to effect recovery. These criteria set clear priorities aimed at outcome, but allow reasonable room for the necessary exercise of clinical judgment in individual cases.

4. *Competing medical treatments*

Society's elected representatives also bear the responsibility to allocate funding between competing medical treatments. It is they who must decide how much they will allocate for dialysis, how much for home health care and how much for coronary artery bypass surgery. The U.S. Congress has already done this with abortion, for example, severely limiting public funding for it.[55] In a stunning departure from earlier rulings, the U.S. Supreme Court in its recent *Webster* ruling upheld the state of Missouri's prohibition on the performance of abortions in state facilities.[56] Aside from one's views on the state's right to intrude in a woman's abortion decision, such a ruling significantly impacts the rights of poor women, who cannot afford private abortions.

What must be done by Parliament in Britain and by the state legislatures and Congress in the U.S. is to evaluate medical treatments based on their benefit and their cost. If 1,000,000 patients can be provided with adequate prenatal care – to reduce infant mortality, birth defects and other complications of pregnancy – for the same cost as dialysis for 100,000 patients with end-stage renal disease, then a logical value judgment can be made to fund the former, not the latter, being the greatest good for the greatest number. If coronary bypass surgery absorbs 1 percent of all public health expenditures, yet benefits only 1/10 of 1 percent of the population in the U.S., is it justified? This kind of legislative analysis can result in ranking of medical services in order of social importance. From this can then come funding levels for various services, which will depend on their importance (cost benefit).

If the Oregon experience in attacking these rationing issues head on is representative, strongest support will be given to a basic health package for all citizens. This the NHS has accomplished probably better than the U.S. health care system. However, let there be no mistake that such a system can only strive to create an 'adequate' level of medical care, not an 'optimal' or 'desired' level of care. This has been easier to accomplish in Britain than in the U.S. in large part because the 'medical cultures' of the two countries are different.[8] We have seen this throughout this book.

Doctors have greater decision-making authority in Britain, because patients are less demanding consumers and more deferential and accepting recipients of care, and because the NHS imposes the burdens of cost-based rationing on its physicians to a much greater degree than has the U.S. health care delivery system. This is changing, but the differences remain. Practitioners in both systems want explicit rationing decisions made by society, not at the bedside.[42,57]

5. *Open debate is needed*

Setting difficult priorities between different medical treatments should be done openly and explicitly. A vigorous debate can be expected. Out of it should come compromise and consensus. These decisions should rest on value judgments that are acceptable to the general public. This process will inevitably shift some decision-making power from physician to 'society,' but this is necessary to relieve the physician of having to make what are largely social and political, not medical, decisions. As Dr. Grimes has stated, the issues 'are not medical but are managerial, financial, or ethical; in a government administered health service, they are political.'[57]

6. *Comprehensive, rational rationing is needed*

We must look at the big picture before making rationing choices. The effect of restricting care one place may well increase the need elsewhere. The U.S., for example, in recent years increased funding for neonatal heroic medicine, while at the same time exacerbating the demand for such intervention by reducing funding for prenatal care and education programs.[53] A comprehensive view of the health care system allows for a consideration of what patient populations or types of care will be affected by a decision to increase funding or levels of services elsewhere. Then social decisions on financial support of care that will provide the greatest medical good to the greatest number can be decided. The Oregon legislature decided funds for transplants other than kidneys and corneas should be reallocated to prenatal care using a comprehensive view of the health care delivery system in Oregon. While not all will or have agreed with it, it was a considered, public and explicit rationing decision made by the political instrumentality presumably most in touch with the social consensus and democratically responsive to it. Further such decisions are inevitable, but if they are considered, comprehensive, open, explicit and democratically arrived at, they seem all we can ask of the system. The results for some will be unfortunate – deprivation of certain kinds of care – but this does not make them unfair, unethical, or unwarranted.

7. *Reason and fairness the goal*

In an imperfect, finite world, with limited resources, society can only strive to distribute those resources as fairly and equitably as reasonably possible. If legislators act reasonably, without invidious discrimination, neither the law, individual patients, nor the medical establishment can expect more.[13,58]

As Lord Justice Oliver said in dismissing a legal challenge to inadequate NHS funding, 'it cannot be supposed that the Secretary of State has to provide all the kidney machines which are asked for, or for all the new developments, such as heart transplants, in every case where people would benefit from them.'[59] The funds are allocated by Parliament and the NHS can only be faulted if it acts unreasonably, in bad faith, or in breach of some duty imposed by law.

These issues will be discussed more commonly and more openly as time goes on and as rationing becomes more pervasive, given an aging population and seemingly no end to the development of new and expensive medical technology and treatment. Society cannot avoid the difficult choices that are and will continue to be even more necessary. Open discussion and debate will encourage reasonable, socially acceptable solutions, although unfortunate cases where no help can be given will remain, and may well become more common. The lack of a perfect solution, or one without unfortunate results in individual cases, should not dissuade us from striving for the fairest and most reasonable decisions of which we as democratic and charitable societies are capable of reaching.

NOTES

1 Rubin, Blehart, 261 *J. Am. Med. Assn.* 2849, 2851 (May 19, 1989).
2 Reinhardt, 'Hard choices in health care: a matter of ethics,' *Health Care: how to improve it: alternatives for the 1980s.* Ctr. for Nat. Policy, No.7, p.21. Some put the infant mortality figure at 19th worldwide.
3 'Most want more cash for NHS,' *The Times*, 3 November 1988, p.5.
4 Thurow, 'Medicine Versus Economics,' in Shannon (ed.), *Bioethics* (1987, 3d ed.), pp. 581, 586.
5 Mehlman, 'Rationing Expensive Lifesaving Medical Treatments,' 1985 *Wisc. L.R.* 239.
6 Some 10 per cent of U.S. physicians own health care facilities outside their own offices to which they often refer their patients. 261 *J. Am. Med. Assn.* 2850 (1989).
7 Besharov and Silver, 'Rationing Access to Advanced Medical Techniques' 8 *J. Leg. Med.* 507, 523.
8 Klein, 'Rationing Health Care' 289 *Brit. Med. J.* 143–4 (1984).
9 Macklin, *Mortal Choices.* Boston, Houghton Mifflin, 1988, pp.160–161.
10 See Grimes, 'Should Patients Who Smoke Be Referred for Coronary Artery Bypass Grafting?' 1988 *The Lancet* i, 1157; Schneiderman and Spragg, 'Ethical Decisions in Discontinuing Mechanical Ventilation,' 318 *N. Eng. J. Med.* 984 (1988).
11 Joint Committee on Bioethics of the San Diego County Medical Society and San Diego County Bar Ass'n., 'Proposed Guidelines on Foregoing Life-Sustaining Treatment,' June 8, 1989, p.7.
12 *Wideman v. Shallowford Comm. Hosp. Inc.* (1987) 826 Fed. 2d 1030.
13 *In re Walker's Application, The Times*, 26 Nov. 1987 (judicial review denied as failure to provide treatment not shown unreasonable); *R. v. Sec. of State for Soc. Services, ex parte Hicks* (1979) 123 *Sol. J.* 436; 'Rationing of Resources,' 1985 *Brit. Med. J.* 374; see also, *Collier v. West Midlands Health Authority*, (Jan. 6, 1988, Ct. of Appeal) 1988 *The Lancet* i, 133; Brahams, 1987 *The Lancet* ii, 1342 (Walker) and 1984 *The Lancet* ii, 1224 (*R. v. Secty. of State ex parte Hicks*).
14 *Wickline v. State of California* (1986) 192 Cal. App. 3d 1630 (review granted).
15 'Cost vs. Quality,' *Am. Bar. Ass'n. J.* June 1, 1988, p.26; Cal. Welfare and Inst. Code §14000.
16 *Whitford v. Hunter* (1954) 94 Sol. Jo. 758, discussed on 290 *Brit. Med. J.* 374, 375 (1985).
17 The accepted moral distinction in Catholic medical ethics between 'ordinary' (morally required) and 'extraordinary' (morally optional) treatment takes into account the pain, the *cost* and the other inconvenience attendant upon treatment in its category. See Kelly, Gerald, S.J., 12 *Theol. Studies* 550 (1951) and 11 *Theol. Studies* 203 (1950), discussed in Chapter 11.

18 See discussion in Chapter 11; *Barber v. Superior Court* (1983) 147 Cal. App. 3d 1006.

19 1984 *The Lancet* ii, 1226.

20 Schneider, 'Options to Control the Rising Health Care Costs of Older Americans,' 261 *J. Amer. Med. Assn.* 907 (1989).

21 *Business Week*, 6 February 1989, p 76.

22 *Setting Limits*. New York: Simon and Schuster, 1987; 'Old Age and New Policy,' 261 *J. Amer. Med. Assn.* 905 (1989).

23 Callahan, 'We Have the Right to Die of Old Age,' *Santa Barbara News Press*, 5 November 1987, p.A17.

24 261 *J. Amer. Med. Assn.* 905, 906 (1989).

25 *Am I My Parents' Keeper*. Oxford: Oxford Univ. Press, 1988; *Modern Maturity*, August–Sept. 1988, p.43.

26 U.S. Congress, *Life-Sustaining Technologies for the Elderly* (1987).

27 Schwartz and Aaron, *Modern Maturity*, August–Sept. 1988, p.42–3.

28 HCFA Ruling No. HCFAR 87–1, DRG (April 6, 1987), discussed in Besharov and Silver, 'Rationing Access to Advanced Medical Technologies' 8 *J. Legal Med.* 507 (1987).

29 Macklin, *Mortal Choices*. New York: Houghton Miffin, 1987 pp.160–161.

30 The average family premium for group health plan coverage in an HMO (Health Maintenance Organization) which contracts with a group of doctors and a hospital to provide care for so much per member per month regardless of care needed was about $250 per month in 1989. The cost for indemnity insurance paying whatever charges were imposed by the care providers for treatment was about $500 per month.

31 Fuchs, 'The "Rationing" of Medical Care,' 311 *New Eng. J. Med.* 1572–3 (1984).

32 Abram, 'The Future of Health Care in America,' 21 June 1988 (Testimony to Jt. Economic Committee, U.S. Congress).

33 Lynn, 'Legal and Ethical Issues in Contemporary Health Care,' 21 June 1988 (Testimony to Jt. Economic Committee, U.S. Congress).

34 Callahan, 'Old Age and New Policy,' 261 *J. Amer. Med. Assn.* 905, 906 (1989).

35 'Colorado Votes for Quality of Life' *Hemlock Quarterly*, April, 1989, p.4.

36 *Supt. Of Belchertown State School v. Saikewicz* (1977, Mass.) 370 N.E. 2d 417.

37 *Matter of Quinlan* (1976, N.J.) 355 A. 2d 647 (cert. den. 429 U.S. 922) The U.S. Supreme Court has, for the first time, granted hearing during its 1989–1990 term in a case from Missouri raising similar issues. *Cruzan*, No. 88–1503 (June 25, 1990).

38 *Wall Street J.*, 17 April 1989, p.B1.

39 See Gillon, 'Justice and allocation of medical resources,' 291 *Brit. Med. J.* 266 (1985).

40 Habgood, Rt. Rev., 'The ethics of resource allocation: a case study' 1983 *J. Med. Ethics* 21; Boyd, 'The ethics of resource allocation,' 1983 *J. Med. Ethics* 25.

41 Crawshaw, Garland and Hines, 'Organ Transplants – a search for health policy at the state level,' *West. J. Med.*, March, 1989, pp.361, 362.

42 Schneiderman and Spragg, 318 *New Eng. J. Med.* 984, 987 (1988).
43 *California Hospitals*, August, 1988, p.10.
44 Schneider, 'Options to Control the Rising Health Care Costs of Older Americans,' *J. Amer. Med. Assn.* 10 February 1989, p. 907–8.
45 See Otten, 'Ethicist Draws Fire With Proposal For Limiting Health Care to Aged,' *Wall St. J.*, 22 January 1988.
46 'Rationing: Divisive Questions, Deceptive Answers,' *Ethical Currents*, Fall, 1988, pp.1, 2.
47 See discussion in Chapters 5, 9, 10 & 11, *supra*.
48 Wray, et. al., 'Whithholding Medical Treatment From the Severely Demented Patient,' *Arch. Int. Med.*, Sept., 1988, pp.1980, 1984.
49 See discussion of informed consent in Chapter 5, *supra*.
50 See discussion in Chapter 7, *supra*.
51 *Public Health Trust of Dade County v. Wons* (1989, Fla.) 541 So. 2d 96, 100.
52 Younger, 'Who Defines Futility?' 260 *J. Amer. Med. Assn.* 2094–5 (1988).
53 See the discussions, for example, at 1988 *The Lancet* i, 1157; 1988 *The Lancet* i, 1350; 1984 *The Lancet* ii, 1224.
54 Glaser, 'Health Care rationing: Not if, but how' *Queen of the Valley Hosp. Physician*, Summer, 1989, pp.1, 4.
55 *Harris v. McRae* (1980) 448 U.S. 297.
56 *Webster vs. Reproductive Health Services, Inc.* (1989) U.S. 109 S. Ct. 3040.
57 Grimes, 'Should Patients Who Smoke Be Referred For Coronary Artery Bypass Grafting?' 1988 *The Lancet* i, 1157.
58 *Wideman v. Shallowford Comm. Hosp., Inc.* (1987) 826 Fed. 2d 1030.
59 *R. v. Sec. of State for Soc. Services, ex parte Hicks* (1979) 123 *Sol. J.* 436, March 18, 1980, Ct. of Appeal, 1984 *The Lancet* ii, 1224.

Subject Index

Note: Names are not repeated from the index of cases

abortion, 23–5, 335
  and use of fetuses for transplantation,
    205–6
  attempted, crime of, 35
  attempts to prevent by third parties, 4, 5,
    13
  cases concerning, 26, 28, 29, 30, 33, 41,
    43–5, 134, 135, 145 (*see also Roe v.*
    Wade in index of cases)
  fathers and, 4, 5, 33, 67
  late, 23–4, 28, 37, 41–2, 45
  law on, 2, 5, 6, 24, 26–8, 53 (*see also*
    under U.S.)
  public opinion on, 25, 39, 46
  saving fetuses after, 31–3, 37, 41–2, 45–6
  statistics, 23–4, 25, 28, 37nn, 38, 44, 53
  see also pregnancy, selective reduction of
abortion pill, 46
access
  to AID, 76
  to IVF, 60, 67
  see also resources
Acts of Parliament
  Abortion Act (1967), 2n, 5n, 14n, 15nn,
    17nn, 24, 26–8, 31–3, 34–5, 36–7, 53,
    61–2, 98, 278
  Anatomy Act (1832), 189, 190
  Children and Young Persons Act (1933),
    93n
  Children and Young Persons Act (1963),
    93n
  Congenital Disabilities (Civil Liability)
    Act (1976), 101n
  Corneal Grafting Act (1952), 191
  Family Law Reform Act (1969), 4n, 28,
    261
  Human Tissue Act (1961), 189–91, 194,
    195
  Infant Life (Preservation) Act (1929), 2n,
    5n, 14n, 15n, 17nn, 24n, 25n, 26, 27,
    31, 32, 34nn, 35+n, 37, 53
  Law Reform (Parent and Child)
    (Scotland) Act (1986), 8n (*cont.*)

Acts of Parliament (*cont.*)
  Medicines Act (1968), 244
  Mental Health Act (1959), 30, 134
  Mental Health Act (1983), 134, 163
  Mental Health (Scotland) Act (1984), 9n
  Offences Against the Person Act (1861),
    2nn, 5n, 25–6, 34n, 35n, 36–7
  Registration of Births, Deaths and
    Marriages (Scotland) Act (1954), 232
  Social Work (Scotland) Act (1968), 8n,
    157n
  Suicide Act (1961), 280, 285
  Surrogacy Arrangement Act (1985),
    62–4, 192
adoption, 46, 58; *see also* surrogacy
adultery, AID and, 57, 66
age
  and cost of medical treatment, 336
  and incompetence, 146
  and priorities for medical treatment,
    336–8, 342, 343, 344
age distribution of population, 276, 335,
  336
AID (artificial insemination by donor), 54,
  56, 57–8, 59, 66, 75–6
AIDS, 136, 307
AIH (artificial insemination by husband),
  54, 56–7, 66
Alzheimer's disease, 206, 304, 342
American Medical Association, 263, 312
amniocentesis, 69
anencephaly, 84, 86–7, 109, 203–4
animals, research using, 246
artificial insemination, *see* AID *and* AIH
assault, 35, 122, 136, 192, 196
Australia, 54, 59, 60, 68
autopsy, 184, 185, 186, 187–8
autotransplantation, 180, 182

balancing, 164, 261–2, 268
  of rights, 12, 16
Batten's disease, 316

Index of Cases